$15.95
MEG

Political Science in Africa

Edited by Yolamu Barongo

Political Science in Africa
A Critical Review

Edited by Yolamu Barongo

Zed Press, 57 Caledonian Road, London N1 9DN

Progressive and Socialist Books Depot, PO Box 4053,
U.I. Post Office, Ibadan, Nigeria.

Political Science in Africa: A Critical Review was first published worldwide by Zed Press Plc., 57 Caledonian Road, London N1 9DN, United Kingdom, and in Nigeria by Progressive and Socialist Books Depot, PO Box 4053, U.I. Post Office, Ibadan, Nigeria in 1983.

Copyright © Yolamu Barongo, 1983.

Copyedited by Beverley Brown
Proofread by Mark Gourlay
Cover design by Jacque Solomons
Typeset by Jenny Walters
Printed by The Pitman Press, Bath, U.K.

All rights reserved

British Library Cataloguing in Publication Data

Barongo, Yolamu
Political Science in Africa.
1. Political Science — Africa
I. Title
320'.0960   JA84.A/
ISBN 0 86232 033 X
ISBN 0 86232 034 8 Pbk

Contents

Acknowledgements	ix
Note on Contributors	x
Introduction — Yolamu R. Barongo	1

PART ONE   CONTENT AND RELEVANCE   5

1. **Teaching Political Science as a Vocation in Africa** — Omu Omoruyi   6
   - The American Heritage of Liberal Commitment   7
   - What Counts as 'Political'?   9
   - Revisiting Weber   11

2. **Science vs. Philosophy: The Need for A Relevant Political Science** — Henry I. Ejembi   17
   - Political Science: What Is It?   17
   - Political Science: What It Used To Be   18
   - The Responsibility of Philosophers   20
   - The Nigerian Example   23
   - The Need for Value-Orientation in National Life   25

3. **Teaching Political Science in African Universities: A Problem-Solving Approach** — Eme O. Awa   27
   - The Science-Value Problem   27
   - The Goals of Society and How to Achieve Them   30
   - How to Teach Political Science for the Here and Now   32
   - Requirements of Public Administration and Management   34

4. **The African Peasantry: Neglected by African Political Science** — Ebitini Chikwendu   37
   - Education for Underdevelopment   38
   - Taking the Peasantry Seriously   40
   - Education for Development   44

5. **Class Interests in the Teaching of Political Science in African Universities** — Wang Metuge 48
   Academics as Class Strugglers 48
   Bourgeois vs. Non-Bourgeois Methodologists 49
   Combat in the Theoretical Zone 50

6. **Towards a Development Oriented Political Science Curriculum** — Olatunde J. B. Ojo 56
   The New Orthodoxy 57
   Dangers of the New Orthodoxy 59
   Essentials and Dilemmas of 'Relevant' Curricula 62
   The University of Port Harcourt Experience 64

PART TWO   SCOPE AND APPROACHES   71

7. **Elections and Election Studies in Africa** — Denis L. Cohen 72
   Surveying the Field 73
   An Array of Approaches 76
   Theoretical Perspectives 80

8. **Public Administration in Africa: Separate Area or Sub-Discipline?** — J. B. Ojo 94
   Public Administration and Political Systems 95
   The Blinkers of Policy Implementation 96
   The Need for Practical Training 99

9. **Political Science and Political Economy** — Bjorn Beckman 101
   The Trap of Specialization 102
   The 'New Political Economy': Reformist Tendencies in Political Science 103
   Classical Political Economy and Marxism 105
   African Political Economy 108
   Political Economy and the State 108

10. **Primary Requirements for the Unity of Political Science and Economics** — Eskor Toyo 112
    Why Unity at All? 112
    Fighting Subjectivism 113
    Detotalizing the Fact-Value Distinction 115
    Possibility of Objective Laws 117
    Avoiding Dead Ends: Factors, Facts and Systems 119
    Economics and Politics: One Reality, One Science 123

11. **Imperialism and the Politics of Area Studies** — Okello
    Oculi — 129
    Divide and Travel — 129
    Predicting Socio-Political Events — 130
    Area Studies 'Gets Tough' — 131
    Anti-Imperialism and Area Studies — 134

12. **Alternative Approaches to African Politics** — Yolamu
    R. Barongo — 138
    Mapping the Continent: Previous Accounts of African Politics — 138
    The History of the Present: Political Foundations — 143
    The Politics of Poverty — 145
    Politics Past and Present — 150

PART THREE   THEORY AND METHODOLOGY — 155

13. **Non-Ethnocentric Flaws in Competing Non-Marxist Paradigms of Development** — Eskor Toyo — 156
    'Bombard the Headquarters', Attack Presuppositions — 157
    Going Astray With Positivism — 158
    Subjective or Objective? — 160
    Movement in Keynesiana — 164
    In the Rostovian Stagecoach — 165
    Systems That Cannot Systematize — 168
    Back to Psychologism — 169
    As Modernists See It — 171
    Marxist Method: The Stone the Builders Rejected — 172

14. **Dependency and Revolutionary Theory in the African Situation** — Franz J. T. Lee — 178
    Fundamental Hypothesis — 178
    Genesis of the 'Dependencia' Movement — 178
    Basic Theoretical Statements and Critiques — 181
    Relevance of 'Dependencia' Theories to Africa — 183
    Oil and Class Struggle — 185

15. **African Elite Theories and Nigerian Elite Consolidation: A Political Economy Analysis** — William D. Graf — 189
    Pre-Independence Elite Formation — 190
    Ethnicity and Class Struggle — 193
    Economic and Political Centralization — 197
    Recivilianization as a Holding Operation — 204

16. **Essence and Empiricism in African Politics** — Otwin Marenin … 211
    Consciousness and Class Consciousness … 213
    Problematizing a Marxist Methodology … 214
    Marxist Methodology in African Studies … 222
    The Concept of Interest … 230
    The Need for A Proper Marxist Methodology … 232

17. **The Tyranny of Borrowed Paradigms and the Responsibility of Political Science: The Nigerian Experience** — S. Egite Oyovbaire … 239
    The Tyranny of Received Ideas … 240
    The Neo-Liberal Paradigm … 242
    The Neo-Marxist/Structuralist Paradigm … 244
    The Environment of Political Science in Nigeria … 247
    Working Politics Plus Idealism … 249

Index … 255

Acknowledgements

The editor is grateful to the following for contributing effort to the preparation of this book:

The 1978-79 National Executive Committee of the Nigerian Political Science Association (N.P.S.A.) for its imagination in providing a conference theme that provided a forum for the initial critical evaluation of the state of political science teaching and research in African Universities; Dr. S. Egite Oyovbaire of the Department of Political Science, Ahmadu Bello University, Zaria, Nigeria with whom the original idea of publishing in book form a selection of the 1979 N.P.S.A. conference papers was discussed; Mr. Robert Molteno of Zed Press for the enormous administrative effort in clearing various hurdles through which the publication of the book had to go and for his valuable suggestions of the ways for improving the collection for this book; Bayero University, Kano for providing a Departmental research grant for editorial work and materials used in the preparation of the manuscript; Shehu S. Usman, Haruna M. Salihi, Ma'azu M. Yusuf and Kamilu F. Sani, Graduate Assistants in the Department of Political Science, Bayero University, Kano, Nigeria for their assistance in proofreading the manuscript; Professor C.S. Whitaker and Mr. Yacub M. Adam, colleagues in the same Department for reading through the draft of the Introduction and suggesting improvements. Finally, many thanks are due to Mr. Agah G. Akever, Chief Clerical Officer and Secretary in the Department of Political Science, Bayero University, Kano, Nigeria for his long hours spent typing the manuscript.

Note on Contributors

Professor Eme O. Awa is Professor of Political Science at the University of Nigeria, Nsukka. He has previously taught Political Science at the Universities of Ibadan and Lagos in Nigeria and worked as Chairman, Revenue Allocation Committee, East Central State of Nigeria, 1970-71 and Member of the Permanent Committee on Economic Organization of West African States (ECOWAS) since 1978, Professor Awa's publications include *Federal Government in Nigeria* (1964) and *Issues in Federalism* (1976).

Dr. Yolamu R. Barongo is Senior Lecturer and Head of Department of Political Science, Bayero University, Kano, Nigeria. He taught Political Science at Ahmadu Bello University, Zaria, Nigeria, 1974-78 and conducted a Graduate Seminar in African Politics at the University of Guyana, 1978-79. Dr. Barongo is the author of *Neocolonialism and African Politics: A Survey of the Impact of Neocolonialism on African Political Behaviour* (New York, Vantage Press, 1980).

Dr. Bjorn Beckman presently holds concurrent appointments as Associate Professor of Political Science, University of Stockholm, Sweden and Visiting Part-time Senior Lecturer at Ahmadu Bello University, Zaria, Nigeria. He has published many essays on West African Political Economy including a book, *Organizing the Farmers: Cocoa Politics and National Development in Ghana* (Uppsala, 1976).

Mrs. Ebitimi Chikwendu is Lecturer in Political Science at the University of Nigeria, Nsukka, Nigeria. Mrs. Chikwendu has special research interests in peasant politics in Africa.

Dr. Dennis L. Cohen is Senior Lecturer, Department of Political and Administrative Studies, University of Maiduguri, Nigeria. Previously, he taught Political Science at the University of Ghana, 1966-67; Universities of Birmingham and Aston, 1967-68; Makerere University, Kampala, Uganda, 1968-72 and the University of Botswana, Lesotho and Swaziland, 1972-78. Dr. Cohen's articles on African Politics have appeared in many journals and he is editor (with Dr. John Daniel) of *Political Economy of Africa* (London,

Longmans, 1981).

Mr. Henry I. Ejembi is Lecturer in Political Science at Ahmadu Bello University, Zaria, Nigeria from which he holds Bachelor's and Master's degrees in political science.

Dr. William D. Graf is presently Assistant Professor of Political Science, University of Guelph, Ontario, Canada. He has previously taught at the University of Maryland and the University of Benin, Benin City, Nigeria. Dr. Graf is the author of *Elections 1979* (Lagos; Daily Times, 1979) and editor of *Towards a Political Economy of Nigeria: Critical Essays* (Benin City, Koda Publishers, forthcoming).

Mr. Sam W.E. Ibodje is Lecturer in Political Science, School of Social Sciences, University of Port Harcourt, Nigeria. He has research interests in Local Government and is presently conducting a study of the Socio-political Environment of Local Government in Nigeria for the Ph.D. degree of the University of Birmingham.

Dr. Franz J.T. Lee is Professor of International Relations and Third World Studies at the University of the Andes, Merida, Venezuela. Professor Lee is a black South African. He has previously taught in West Germany and at the University of Guyana and has published extensively on African politics and problems in both German and English.

Dr. Otwin Marenin is Assistant Professor of Political Science, Department of Criminal Justice, Washington State University, Pullman, U.S.A. He has previously taught at California State University, Northridge, 1972-74 and Ahmadu Bello University, Zaria, Nigeria, 1974-78. Dr. Marenin has published a number of articles on African politics.

Comrade Wang Metuge is Senior Lecturer in Political Science at the University of Benin, Benin City, Nigeria and Vice-President (Central Africa) of the Association of African political Science. Comrade Metuge has previously taught at Ahmadu Bello University, Zaria, Nigeria, 1974-79.

Dr. Okello Oculi is Senior Lecturer in Political Science at Ahmadu Bello University, Zaria, Nigeria. He has previously taught political science at Makerere University, Kampala, Uganda and published a number of articles on African Politics.

Dr. Olatunde J.B. Ojo is Senior Lecturer in Political Science, School of Social Science, University of Port Harcourt, Nigeria. He has previously taught at a number of American Colleges and at the Institute of Administration, University of Ife, Nigeria. Dr. Ojo has published articles on African politics and contributed chapters in a number of books.

Dr. Omo Omoruyi is Associate Professor and Head of the Department of Political Science, University of Benin, Benin City, Nigeria. Professor Omoruyi served in the Constituent Assembly (1978) that scrutinized and approved the present Federal Constitution of Nigeria.

Dr. S. Egite Oyovbaire is Associate Professor in the Department of Political Science at Ahmadu Bello University, Zaria, Nigeria. He has published articles and contributed chapters in books on Nigerian politics. Dr. Oyovbaire is editor of a forthcoming book, *Democracy in Nigeria: Interpretative Essays* (Benin City, Koda Publishing Ltd).

Dr. Eskor Toyo lectures in Economics at the University of Calabar, Nigeria. Dr. Toyo has written extensively on Marxist political and economic theories and presented papers in this field in many conferences and student symposia in and outside Nigeria. His recent publications include: *Storms in the Nigerian Policy: The Process of Bourgeois Ascendancy and its Conflicts* (Kano, Triumph Publishing Co.)

Introduction by Yolamu Barongo

As a subject of academic and intellectual pursuit, political science has been studied and taught in African universities and other institutions of higher learning only since the early 1960s. Some aspects of the discipline, such as the rudiments of the institutions of government, were no doubt sometimes taught in schools and colleges before 1960 under the rubric of civics, public affairs or history. However, the inception of political science in concrete academic programmes in Black African universities coincides with the attainment of independence of particular countries.

There are two possible explanations for the lack of enthusiasm for the subject of political science during the colonial period and the sudden recognition accorded to it after independence. On the one hand, it is well known that colonial education policies limited opportunities for the education of the indigenous peoples to the mere acquisition of skills for occupations that supported the functioning of the colonial system: typists, administrative clerk, customs officials, low-ranking policemen, medical orderlies and elementary school teachers. Clearly, the training schemes for this level of workforce did not require political science syllabuses. Added to this was the overriding policy of minimizing the colonial subjects' level of political awareness in order to perpetuate colonial rule. Colonial governments were sensitive to the fact that the higher the level of education a person attained, in whatever branch of scholarship, the more likely such a person would be to question the legitimacy of the imperial regime. And as the study of political science was, more than any other subject, likely to impart skills of critical analysis of political life or to produce militant nationalists determined to end colonial domination, it was viewed by colonial education planners with suspicion and even open hostility. The attitude of colonial governments, therefore, was that higher education in general, and the teaching of political science in particular, were dangerous to colonial interests. Accordingly, education for the natives was to be kept narrow, superficial and virtually censored. Not until after independence was education liberalized and expanded. Following these changes university colleges that had existed during the colonial period, such as Legon in Ghana, Ibadan in Nigeria and Makerere in Uganda, were among the first institutions of higher learning in independent Africa to incorporate political science curricula in their degree programmes.

On the other hand, the rapid rate of social change that accompanied independence, and the attendant social, political and economic problems, brought into focus the importance of the social sciences in Africa. In an effort to comprehend these developments and to plan for orderly and controlled change, the new governments of independent Africa were compelled to rely increasingly on sociologists, economists and political scientists for the professional study of these problems and for expert advice. As the trained African social scientists were few or non-existent in the early years of independence, many of the social scientists who advised African governments were hired from Europe and North America or sent by official government agencies and international organizations as part of technical aid. Such official demands for social scientists in the newly independent countries increased the respectability of the social sciences. This in turn created favourable political commitment to the establishment of social science academic programmes in African universities with the objective of training nationals to replace expatriate advisers.

Moreover, the specific problems of modernization that tended to overwhelm the independent nations throughout the 1960s and, in particular, the problem of political instability, made Africa a fascinating research area for European and American political scientists. Consequently, the 1960s witnessed a period of intensive research and publication on African problems of development and modernization.

The work of these scholars had a three-pronged impact on the development of political science as an academic discipline in African universities. First, official attitudes towards the relevance of political science were favourably influenced by the important research findings of those Western political scientists. Secondly, the large volume of intriguing literature available on African politics and problems stirred the ambitions of a large number of university students who demanded training in political science. Then, with the increasing official recognition of the abilities and skills of political science graduates for civil service jobs, political science courses became very popular among university students who wished to take up careers in administration and foreign service. And, finally, as a result of the improved status of political science in relation to such traditionally prestigious disciplines as economics, law and medicine, more and more African political science graduates decided to undertake advanced studies of the discipline with the aim of becoming university teachers in political science.

By the end of the 1960s, therefore, political science was well established and respected in Africa as a subject worthy of academic pursuit. Its contribution to the understanding of the problems of society and to the overall national developmental effort were well recognized by governments. With the exception of the universities in many French-speaking African countries (which have persisted in the French tradition of subsuming political science under other disciplines such as history, public administration and law), most universities in Africa today have separate academic departments offering training in political science at undergraduate and graduate levels.

Introduction

The extent to which political science has taken root can also be gauged by the reasonably large number of African political scientists. Whereas, in the early period of its growth, political science was taught at universities largely by non-Africans, today most of the departments of political science are staffed mainly by Africans who first studied political science in the late 1960s and early 1970s. As a result of this growth in the political science profession in African universities, the new generation of African political scientists has become increasingly sensitive to the lack of a tradition of African political science scholarship. Since the time when political science found its place in African universities, its study, teaching and orientation of research programmes have been dominated by traditions of scholarship developed elsewhere, mainly in Europe and North America. Thus a decade of studying and teaching political science in Africa by African political scientists themselves has increasingly revealed the existence of deep-seated crises and problems that require careful examination. What has become evident in recent years has been the need for a critical review and assessment of the role and contribution of political science to the understanding and solution of the problems that face African societies.

The occasion for undertaking a preliminary review of the political science teaching and research in Africa was offered by the Nigerian Political Science Association conference that was held at the University of Benin, Nigeria in April 1979. Under the conference theme, 'The Teaching of Political Science in Nigerian Universities: Scope, Content, Philosophy and Methodology', a number of critical papers were presented and discussed in a serious and concerned atmosphere. It was shortly after this conference that the idea of preparing this book was conceived. Selected papers originally written for that conference constitute slightly over half the chapters in this volume; the rest were solicited and written by the authors to cover specific gaps not addressed by the conference papers.

Although the present collection does not pretend to be representative of the whole of Africa in terms of a geographical coverage of the experiences, topics and thinking in various countries and regions, it nevertheless deals with the major problems and crises that are facing the study and teaching of political science in Africa today. It should be noted, however, that these problems are not necessarily peculiar to the way political science is adapting itself to the African conditions. Many are, in fact, problems that have arisen in the course of the development of the field of political science elsewhere. For instance, similar problems were encountered during the evolution of American political science, some of which were resolved barely two decades ago. In other words, the issues raised here, the sentiments and mood in which they are expressed, bear on the political science discipline as a whole. Some are issues of a philosophical nature, concerning the discipline's purpose and objectives; such questions are raised in many of the articles in Part One. The responsibility of political science and its relevance to the problems actually confronting society are among the topics in political science to which many authors in this volume address themselves. Then there are the perennial problems of theory and method that have troubled political science for many years. All the authors whose articles appear in Parts Two and Three of the book have, in one way or another, attempted to grapple with these problems in the context of the practice of the political science profession in Africa. The current debate in Third World countries concerning the relative benefits of Marxist and non-Marxist theories and methodologies in the study and understanding of society also features very prominently in this collection.

Taken together, the work represented here reveals the fact that political science has taken firm roots in African universities and is developing very fast. By reading the book, either in part or in whole, political scientists will learn of the developments that have taken place in the course of the study and teaching of political science since the 1960s, as well as seeing the emerging trends and orientations that are being advocated by the younger generation of political scientists working in Africa.

Part One
Content and Relevance

1. Teaching Political Science as a Vocation in Africa

Omu Omoruyi

Since the late 1950s when the discipline of political science found its way into the programmes of African universities, political scientists in Africa have failed to concern themselves with the possible impact of their teaching and writing upon the larger society. There are two reasons for this shortcoming. One is the prejudice which the discipline of political science suffered and the other is the prolonged period of uncertainty as to the scope and content of the discipline. The first issue will form the focus of this paper.

The treatment of this problem cannot be dealt with without returning finally to the issues raised by Max Weber, and the context of liberal democracy his work presupposes. The luxury of Western scholarship, particularly in America, where issues of immediate relevance could be raised in almost all academic endeavours, has never permeated African scholarship and citadels of learning. Although isolated cases of incursion of academicians into the political realm can be cited, a concerted effort to examine their discipline has never assumed the proportion that it has for their counterparts in the Western world. Critics of Western scholarship centred around the university institution and the activities within the institution. The institution was designated as part of the system of oppression which they were fighting; hence activities within the institutions served to reinforce that system of oppression. Further, the claim of the social sciences (including political science) to being 'objective' was in fact a cover for reifying the present state of affairs, and ignoring even the possibility of 'liberation'. African political scientists, however, have never examined their universities either as extensions of the colonial system or as part of the undemocratic institutions in the wider society. Consequently there has never been a conscious effort on our part to examine the courses we offer to see whether these courses simply serve to reinforce the pre-existing colonial or neo-colonial system of 'objectivity'. We have, as a result, consistently laboured under the system of colonial or neo-colonial 'objectivity', sometimes masquerading as 'scientists', 'empiricists' or 'behaviouralists', and consequently shying away from the issue of liberation which, properly speaking, falls under the category of political act.

Western political thought has developed a consensus on the concept of society that different protagonists tended to postulate in different ways. African political scientists have not, disappointingly! Let us, for the purpose of comparison, take the system of political science in America from the time the discipline was institutionalized into an organization as the American Political Science Association. The practitioners have progressively shown concern with the possible effect of their teaching and writing on the wider society and gradually come to agree, consciously or unconsciously, on the nature of American society and of reality in general. Up to the 1950s this consensus accepted 1) liberalism; 2) democratic institutions of the American variety as natural and good for civilized society; and 3) dedication to reforming the institutions to make them more liberal. This consensus has continued up to the present, in spite of the attacks and resistance by a strong group of traditional American conservatives. This is the professional task now facing African political scientists

The American Heritage of Liberal Commitment

The tradition of American political science that has influenced the development and orientation of political science in Africa has primarily been reformist liberal. Ladd and Lipset's survey of the profession clearly shows that American political scientists in general stand politically to the right of sociologists but well to the left of the general population.[1] This liberal perspective permeates the writing and teaching of those committed to 'objectivity'. The philosophy of the teacher-student reinforcing mechanism is applicable to academics in general and to political science in particular: professors tend to recruit into the profession individuals who share the basic assumptions of their professors about the nature of the discipline. This brings into focus the question of what conception of African society political scientists in Africa have held over the years. What conception of society do they project through their teaching and writing? What ingredients can we identify that could constitute the mainstream of political science in Africa? It is difficult to answer these questions without dwelling on the orientations of the practitioners of the discipline. This in itself is a larger inquiry which the professional associations of political science in Africa should undertake.

The main question which one should ask is, to what extent have political scientists in Africa identified with those in the society whom they consider to be the 'wretched' and 'dehumanized'? To what extent have political scientists in Africa laboured to radically change the system? To these two questions the answers are in the negative. African political scientists have not considered their work as a means to raise the status of the wretched of African society nor have they laboured to radically change the system of values. On the contrary, they have laboured within the framework of a restrictive paradigm defined in terms of the known political cultures of Western Europe and North America. Advancing or advocating new possibilities tends to elude them. But, as Sheldon Wolin suggests, it is the political scientists who should be advancing or advocating new possibilities as the basis for more critical theory:

> The issue is not between theories which are normative and those which are not; nor is it between those political scientists who are theoretical and those who are not. Rather it is between those who would restrict the 'reach' of theory by dwelling on facts which are selected by what are assumed to be the functional requisites of the existing paradigm, and those who believe that it is . . . the task of the theoretical imagination to restate new possibilities.[2]

For Wolin, politics must and should be defined as a moral enterprise. Christian Bay would agree. Contrasting real as against pseudo-politics, Bay argues that real politics is concerned only

> with that activity aimed at improving conditions for the satisfaction of human needs and demands in a given society or community according to some universalistic scheme of priorities, implicit or explicit . . . Pseudo-politics, on the other hand, refers to activity that resembles political activity but is exclusively concerned with promoting public or private interest group advantage, deterred by no articulate or disinterested conception of what would be just or fair to other groups.[3]

For Bay, justice, as in the classics, is knowable. Unlike the classical formulation, however, he conceives of it as knowable to most if not all men, and his view of justice is based on the assumption that it is ultimately possible to create a society which will satisfy the real needs of all (relatively equal) persons as they perceive these needs. Bay would therefore emphasize the teaching of justice and other value imperatives and the reorganization of political science curricula, teaching and research to concentrate on methods of achieving these value imperatives. Can the teaching of political science in Africa be so oriented? I think so.

Christian Bay is not unique in this regard. Many, if not most, of those who subscribe to the 'New Left' critique of mainstream political science stress the moral dimension of the teaching of political science. To them the ends are given. They know the evils of the system. The goal of teaching and research is not to understand the system or to develop propositions about it which can be used by evil-minded bureaucrats but to devise ways of changing it fundamentally.[4] Thus Lewis Lipsitz makes his commitments quite explicit and urges that both research and teaching should concentrate on ways of promoting 'intellectual liberation'. Students would study 'the inequities and oppressiveness generated by many existing structures and processes . . ., political scientists should explore how to re-structure the society and assess the possibilities of developing institution for achieving such a restructure'.[5]

A similar view is urged by Marvin Surkin in terms of a 'phenomenological' approach to political science. What Surkin does not quite make clear is what he means by this. Somehow phenomenology justifies teaching *praxis*. All political science is by nature evaluative in his eyes, and values are realized through practice. To understand the world one must work to change it.[6]

From a rather different perspective, the same stance has been taken by a number of other social scientists. The argument is that objectivity in the social sciences is ontologically impossible; that one's work is necessarily embedded in a value frame and that the best one can do is to understand the source of one's values, and clarify them. However, since values permeate social research, empirical analysis will differ widely depending upon the value frame from which one starts.

Interestingly enough few, if any, political scientists have developed this position in systematic detail, although it has been much brooded upon. The main arguments have come from that eminent sociologist Alvin Gouldner in his seminal work *The Coming Crises in Western Sociology*.[7] Gouldner takes a position very much like the one all too briefly summarized above. Gouldner explicitly calls for a social science which orients itself to 'liberating' mankind, and at the same time he calls upon social scientists to examine and clarify the sources of their own value orientations. Like Surkin, he is convinced that new possibilities can only be realized through *praxis*, i.e. through using research and teaching to create new realities. Social science which limits itself to describing reality 'objectively' is *ipso facto* guilty of reifying the present and supporting its repressiveness.

Gouldner's position does find some support in the writing of political scientists like Henry Kariel whose emphasis, however, seems less focused upon direct attempts to restructure the social order than upon using the classroom experience itself to liberate both students and teachers. To Kariel, politics involves just those areas where limits can be challenged, and it is the function of the teacher to encourage his or her students to challenge limits wherever possible.[8] Teaching then takes on the practical characteristics (or so it seems to me) of group therapy in which students and teachers join in awakening new possibilities in themselves. Process becomes more important than content. Teaching or learning experience, classroom environment and students' exposure to democratic school organization may turn out to be more reinforcing of liberating ideas than the content of the courses. The foregoing therefore raises critical questions for the nature of the 'political'.

What Counts As Political?

Weber and others understood the political in the following formulation: 'politics' for us means striving to share power or striving to influence the distribution of power, either among states or among groups within a state.[9] In this tradition we have also Robert Dahl. 'A political system is any persistent pattern of human relationships that involves, to a significant extent, power, rule or authority.'[10] If the political is thus understood, then the teaching of political science should indeed be utterly remote from the political and it would be abominable and absurd to think otherwise. There should never be any 'striving' in the classroom 'to influence the distribution of power ... within the state'. In short, if the political is understood as thus narrowly confined to the question of power, then the teaching of political science is most emphatically not a 'political act'.

Obviously then, when I argue that the teaching of political science should partake of the political, I proceed from a different understanding of what the political is. Easton's well-known definition[11] moves in the direction of the understanding employed here. In contrast with the Weberian reduction to power considerations, which makes the question of values epiphenomenal, Easton's formulation of the 'authoritative value' tries to make a place closer to the centre for the 'values' which are what the 'authoritative allocation' is all about. But the emphasis in Easton is inevitably still on the process of allocation, which is power in a more sensible and genteel guise, but power still. This is because, like all fact/value-distinguishing political scientists, Easton has to treat values as subjective preferences deriving from objective underlying forces; and in the most important instances this is ultimately to treat values as merely reflecting prior power distributions or relations. Easton's effort to restore the importance of value considerations in the political process was thus foredoomed. He is unable to treat seriously the most important political consideration — namely, what moulds the values themselves? Where do these values come from? We know that this is what political struggles are all about but the substantive content of the 'values' is itself perhaps the most important single determinant of what the 'authoritative allocation' will be. This is simply to say that opinions about what is right and wrong are themselves the most important autonomous causal element in the political process. In short, we must understand politics as comprehending, at least equally with power as such, the *purposes* of power. And this means purposes not as mere givens, but purposes understood as people's ideas — their arguments and reasonings — about what sort of country they should be living in and the ideas of justice and human excellence they proclaim and live by or betray. Indeed, the way politics presents itself empirically to our senses is precisely in the form of arguments made by politicians, governments, citizens, parties and the like, regarding virtue or justice or the common good. Such rival opinions about what a country should do and what its common life should be are the empirical stuff of politics. What forms and influences such opinions, and what they influence in turn, is political in its essential quality. And we all know that such opinions — whether in the form of normative prescription or empirical description — are formidable causes of political behaviour, indeed, they are the *fulcra* by means of which the levers of power work.

I suspect that every political scientist, no matter how narrowly he limits his formal definition of politics to the question of power, in fact proceeds in the classroom on the basis of the understanding of politics suggested here. Let us take a classroom example: teaching of students that moulds their expectations of the presidency will consequently determine to some degree the kinds of candidates they will support. Times like the present offers examples of this. Presidents, speaking *ex cathedra* as it were, powerfully affect public opinion on those underlying moral and philosophical principles, by whose force 'opinion ultimately governs the world'. We teachers of political sciences speak from a different chair, but ours too is a 'bully pulpit' as we all know. Our teaching of political science inevitably speaks directly and closely to the purposes of power, to the 'normative' issues of justice and human excellence, to 'factual' questions of the nature and limits of the political. And by virtue of our inescapable impact upon opinion, our subject matter unlike that of, say, geometry or logic, draws us inexorably into the political realm, both as it brings us to the interested attention of the political world and as we influence our charges in political directions. No formalistic limitation of politics to manipulations of power will exorcize the reality: if we are in the business of professing politics, we are thereby in the business of influencing politics.

Perhaps at this point it will be illuminating, and prudent, to refer to a great political philosopher whose good standing with modern political scientists is matched only by that of Machiavelli — namely, Hobbes. He says that, in defending their political interests, men switch from 'custom' to 'reason' and back again, depending on which, at the moment, supports and flatters them. That is why the claim of scientific reasoning, he tells us, in matters like the causes, and original consitution of right, equity, and justice, is perpetually disputed, both by the Pen and the Sword: whereas the doctrine of Lines, and Figures [Hobbes's own method of reasoning], is not so; because men care not, in that subject what be truth, as a thing that crosses no man's ambition, profit, or lust in our subject area, the effort to teach the truth inevitably 'crosses . . . man's ambition, profit, or lust'. That is why, in a very special and constrained sense, and with inverted commas firmly in place, the teaching of political science may be considered a 'political act'.

But it is more accurate and less susceptible of mischief to say only that the classroom teaching of political science *partakes of the character of* political things. It remains now to explore that 'partaking' by examining some ways in which the political and the scientific are drawn together in the teaching enterprises, and how they are yet separate, and how this duality may be understood and lived with well.

Revisiting Weber

To conclude this paper we now have to turn to the question of how Weberianism 'comes to terms' with the polity. Since, as far as I can tell, it has said so little, we must search out its implicit strategy. This must be inferred from the functions or services or goods which Weberian political science claims to be able to perform or provide. As we will see these come down to two: the clarification of values may be either maximized or optimized.

Now these are the services that Weberianism offers to all comers alike. For example, Max Weber says that teachers should compare the various forms of democracy and then compare these with non-democratic forms so that 'the student may find the point from which in terms of *his ultimate values*, he can take a stand'. Any student; any ultimate values. The Weberian strategy seems to believe that this neutrality will purchase freedom for the student's scholarly and educational enterprises. Not implausible. If you promise equal service to all, will not everyone be nice and leave you alone? Teaching politics is a liberating exercise; unfortunately, this works only in a liberal democracy. Only easy-going liberal democrats will allow Weberians to compare kinds of regimes and let the student ultimately take his pick. Illiberal regimes — and not just modern totalitarian tyrannies, but respectable Puritan, Spartan, and medieval regimes, for example — would not allow any such freedom. The Weberian terms would be unacceptable to them and, on Weberian principles, political science could not be taught there. Is this not a fatal limitation? For if it is a fundamental fact about political life, as was argued above, that something like political science is and must everywhere be taught, then an approach to political science which limits its teaching to one epoch and to one kind of country, is an approach that cannot account for a fundamental aspect of its own science.

Moreover, Weberian political science can only be taught in liberal democracies so long as it has no serious effect, that is, so long as the majority of students after such instructions come out relatively unimpaired from the point of view of the liberal polity. Remember that Weber commands the teacher to present to the students the various kinds of government so as to allow them to choose among them whichever they ultimately value. If we take Weber seriously, this means that, as a result of instructions in Weberian political science, many students might actually opt against liberal democracy. But if this really happened on a significant scale, the liberal democracy would soon have to clamp down on the subverting instruction, and Weberian political science could not even be taught in a liberal democracy. And if it did not thus clamp down, the liberal democracy would soon be replaced by some illiberal system chosen by the now non-democratic students and once again Weberian political science could not be taught. The Weberian then is able to come to terms with the polity, but only a liberal polity and one in which he or she does not upset the applecart. This may do for a while and is sufficient for a parochial political science, but not for one that claims a universal scientific standing.

We must pursue a bit further this discussion of how Weberian political science fails to solve the problem of 'coming to terms' with the polity, both to settle this matter and at the same time to form a bridge to our final problem, namely, the good which the Weberian teacher of political science can claim justly to return to his students and to the polity.

Weberian political science, we must remember, necessarily 'serves all comers', that is, it presents its scientific findings in the same way to all students regardless of what their 'ultimate values' are or become in the process. But this means serving especially the ruling element in the polity, because that element is what typically prevails among the comers. This is why leftist critics have complained that Weberianism is a species of establishment's political science. By abjuring scientific jurisdiction over 'ultimate values',

Weberian political science leaves these unchallenged; that means to leave the prevailing ones, which is to say the status quo, unchallenged. But this is not the whole story. While it self-denyingly does not leave these values quite untouched, it undermines them — and all political values — by its radical distinction between fact and value and its denial of 'cognitive' status to the realm of values.

In the real world, all 'normative' theories typically claim to derive from reality and fact. Political scientists may postulate a radical distinction between fact and value, but 'real world actors' still believe that they derive their *oughts* from *ises*. They believe and claim to see in factual reality the pointers to the ways humans ought to live. Polities are in fact constituted by precisely such convictions; and holding such convictions in common is what makes them communities. Now Weberianism does not say that these convictions are false. It only says that science proves that no one can *know by reason* whether they are false or true 'values'. But mild as this is, it is corrosive of political life which — and this, I think, is a fact — lives by the conviction that its beliefs are grounded in reason.

A simple example. American political life, we might all agree, rests upon (or at least once rested upon) the conviction that certain truths are self-evident. The Weberian necessarily answers: to you they may be self-evident, but not as such. No moral or political values, such as those in the Declaration of Independence, can have objective evidentiary foundation. Now most of we Weberians may, like you, happen to prefer to believe in the Declaration's truths but we also have to say, 'our science compels us to tell you that they are only truths to you and us, that is, for people who share our "ultimate values". And they must, therefore, be treated by science as givens, varying from individual to individual, people to people, and age to age, but all incapable alike of cognitive foundation.'

But if it is a fact, indeed the premier political fact, that the vast majority of mankind believes its 'ultimate values' to have such a foundation, and if polities are constituted by just such a belief, then Weberian political science, far from serving all comers, is ultimately a nihilistic destruction of all political values — at least as they are held in the 'real world.'

With this, we have completed our discussion of the Weberian difficulty with the problem of coming to terms with the polity and have already begun to consider the just goods which Weberianism claims to supply. They are two. The first is simple. To the student it says: bring to us your muddled values and we will help you clarify them; we will teach you to treasure consistency and to think things through; we will help you to think your values through and make them consistent one with another. But as to your deepest values, your 'ultimate values', we say to you: do not try to think *them* through; it cannot be done. Precisely when teachers should lead their ablest student to the deepest questions, Weberianism would seem to assure them at the outset that they need not make the effort. It assures them that they need not disturb their deepest prejudices, only their inconsistent ones. This is a world of blind will; a person's 'value system' is a kind of weapon (or direction finder) that must be pointed while blindfolded, but with the guarantee of micrometic accuracy in every ancillary ballastic (or gyroscopic) detail. What sort of a 'good' is that? And in any case, why should one wish to perform it?

What of the second good promised by Weberian political science, namely helping the student to maximize or optimize the real world, by means of scientific factual knowledge, his or her clarified values? Let us examine this seriously. The performance of this good depends on whether the important (a value or a factual judgment?) real-world political facts would be accurately disclosed by a scrupulously value-abstracting political science. If it could be shown that important political facts are thought to be facts only on the basis of a *particular* value-orientation, they would truly *be* facts only on the basis of the true value-orientation. If this could be shown, then Weberian political science, since it abjures the possibility of a true value-orientation, would likewise be incapable of truly disclosing factual reality.

There may seem something perverse in all of this to those friends and fellow political scientists who are successors to Weber. I do not mean to be or appear so. Let me suggest briefly a way that will make my meaning clearer and less perverse-seeming. The difficulty may lie in the word *value*. It is only two centuries ago, as far as I can tell (which means largely by recourse to the Oxford English Dictionary), that the word came to be used in contradistinction to *fact*. This revealingly modern usage has a rhetorical effect. It almost requires that one thinks of facts and *then* separately, one values (or likes) them or not. That is why I have sometimes used the word *value* in this paper with a kind of demurral indicated by inverted commas. I do not accept that the question is whether I like or value the facts; it is rather the inherently 'evaluative' nature of important political facts. Compare the case of medicine. We do not ask a doctor 1) is that a cancer? and 2) do you like it? We ask him or her: is that healthy or diseased tissue, no matter whether you are crazy enough to like (or value) it or dislike it? We know that the doctor cannot see the fact of cancerous tissue save on the basis of a true understanding of the distinction between health and disease, no matter which he or she may prefer or value. What I am concerned with as a political scientist is very much more like health and disease than valuing or liking.

Some of the difficulty can be traced perhaps to the way the English language translates as *virtue* the ancient Greek *arete*. For us, virtue came to mean morality which became moral *preference* which became liking or *valuing*. But *arete*, I am told, meant something much more like health, or better still, excellence. Thus Plato and Aristotle spoke about the health or excellence of body as *arete*, and then also, using the same word, of the political excellences and the excellence of the heart and mind. They did not understand how the body could have its health or excellences, discoverable by appropriate scientific inquiry, and the heart and mind not have theirs, discoverable similarly, albeit with much more difficulty and perhaps uncertainty.

It might seem inescapable to speak of a fact/value distinction — facts separately first, values separately later. But can one likewise speak of a fact/health-excellence distinction — facts separately first, health-excellence separately later? What I am suggesting, less perversely it will now appear, I hope, is that political facts and political health or excellence are not radically disjoined; and that, indeed, important facts *are* such only in the light of a true grasp of what is healthy or excellent political tissue. This is the crucial issue. If one accepts what I have suggested, then the question of whether one should *value* healthy political tissue would not prove very troubling

I suggest further that the only worthy political science is one that undogmatically, without any pretence to having the answers, rediscovers the perennial questions about political health and excellence, and takes its best reasoned shot at them, always aware of how easy it is to err in such matters, and therefore, always awaiting the discovery of its own errors so that it may improve its questioning and answering.

Not to proceed in this way, but rather to teach our students that there is no 'cognitive' basis for questions and answers about political health and excellence, is to make them philistines armed with science, cut off by us from all the pain and beauty of truly political, which is to say human, inquiry. This means that we cannot adequately teach what is factual and true about the *political* without actually influencing what people do politically. Max Weber was himself so aware of the hiatus between the political and the scientific that he devoted two separate lectures, polarized as *politics as vocation* and *science as vocation*, to expatiate the total severing of the political and the scientific, with politics as value and science as fact. But the modern preoccupation with bridging the fact/value dichotomy is part of the effort of looking for the unity of knowing and doing the political. Once they are posed as separate, how will the teacher be able to bring the political and scientific into unity? This duality comes into play every time in the classroom. We could pursue this indefinitely. Teachers of political science in Africa must be alive to this duality.

Notes

1. E.C. Ladd and S.M. Lipset, 'The Politics of American Political Scientists', *Political Studies*, Vol. 4, Spring 1971, 135–44.
2. Sheldon Wolin, 'Political Science as a Vocation' *American Political Science Review*, Vol. LXIII, December 1969, p. 1082.
3. Christian Bay, 'Politics and Pseudo-politics; A Critical Evaluation of Some Behavioral Literature' in Charles A. McCoy and John Playford (eds.), *Apolitical Politics* (New York, Crowell 1967), p. 15.
4. See the full treatment of this issue in Christian Bay, 'Thoughts on the Purposes of Political Science Education', in George Graham Jr. and George W. Carey (eds.), *The Post-Behavioral Era* (New York, 1972), pp. 88–99.
5. Lewis Lipsitz, 'Vulture, Mantis and Seal: Proposals for Political Scientists' in Graham and Carey, op. cit., p. 186.

6. Marvin Surkin, 'Sense and Nonsense in Politics' in Marvin Surkin and Alvin Wolfe (eds.), *An End to Political Science* (New York, 1970), pp. 13–33.
7. Alvin Gouldner, *The Coming Crises in Western Sociology*. (London, Heinemann 1971).
8. Henry S. Kariel, *Saving Appearances* (Belmont, California, 1972).
9. Max Weber, *The Theory of Social and Economic Organization*, translated by A.M. Henderson and Talcott Parsons (New York; Oxford University Press, 1947), pp. 145–54.
10. Robert A. Dahl, *Modern Political Analysis*, second edition (Englewood Cliffs, New Jersey, 1963), p. 6.
11. David Easton defines politics as interactions which are 'predominantly oriented toward the authorititative allocation of values for a society.' See his, *A Framework for Political Analysis* (New Jersey, Prentice-Hall, Englewood Cliffs, 1965), p. 50.

2. Science Vs. Philosophy: The Need for A Relevant Political Science

Henry I. Ejembi

I am not concerned with contending the 'scientific' status of our study and teaching of politics in Africa. This is not because I think the issue is not a debatable one. Indeed, we often hear more voices than one raised on this issue. For myself, I accept that the study of politics in African universities *can* be done scientifically, and that it *should* be done scientifically. The issue I am going to raise is the extent to which we should carry our preoccupation with the 'science' of politics. Since it would be foolish not to admit that it would indeed be enlightening in many significant respects to observe political and social phenomena in our societies, to group them and posit tentative conclusions in respect of that which we have observed, and then attempt to test the veracity of our conclusions, it would similarly be foolish to throw science out of our study of politics. There is indeed 'scientific politics'; not the only one, but one that is and has been gaining currency in political science departments in African universities. And that should be fine. But, the question is, should we pursue the 'scientific' study of politics to the near-total neglect of the valuational foundations of our inquiry? I believe that it is on this foundation that political science knowledge can save or sink a political system. I believe furthermore that for political science to gainfully contribute to society it must be preceded by creative speculation about society, by the settling of 'the great issues' beforehand, or else it must be *vigorously* accompanied by this endeavour even while it blooms. This is the position I intend to argue in this contribution to the critical review of political science in Africa.

Political Science: What Is It?

The question, 'What is political science?' is immediately relevant. The different branches of inquiry may be divided into two major groups: the empirical and the non-empirical sciences. The former seek to explore, to describe, to explain, and to predict the occurrences in the world we live in. Hence statements must be checked against the facts of our experience, and they are acceptable only if they are properly supported by empirical evidence. Such evidence is obtained in many different ways: by systematic observation, by experimentation, by interviews or surveys, by psychological or clinical testing, by careful examination of documents, coins, inscriptions, and so on. This dependence on empirical proof distinguishes the empirical sciences from the non-empirical disciplines of logic and pure mathematics, whose propositions are proved without necessary reference to empirical findings.

The empirical sciences may in turn be divided into the natural sciences and the social sciences. The criterion for this division is much less clear than that which distinguishes empirical from non-empirical inquiry, and there is no general agreement on precisely where the dividing line is to be drawn. Usually, however, the natural sciences are understood to include physics, chemistry, biology, and their border areas; the social sciences are taken to comprise sociology, political science (to which Aristotle enthusiastically referred as 'the master science'), anthropology, economics, historiography, and other related disciplines. The terms 'science' and 'scientific' are therefore often used to refer to the entire domain of empirical science, with as many qualifications as there are claimants, such as 'political' science. The claim therefore is that political science is an empirical science, relying upon the scientific procedures of observation, formulation of hypothesis, and verification. The sub-qualifications to political science, such as 'behavioural', for example, attempt to strengthen the claim that the study of politics is a science, though others, such as 'traditional' political science, are more timid in approaching this claim. But the heart of the matter is this, that 'traditional' or 'behavioural' 'political science' attempts to repudiate the 'bad name' tagged to its past: that it 'used' to rely on 'just hunch' rather than on 'knowledge' and 'understanding'. In doing this, two important warnings are brushed aside: 1) that a 'factual science by its very nature pulls down what prescriptive science endeavoured to build up'[1] and 2) that, for example, 'If any man hath been so singular as to have studied the science of justice and equity, how can he teach it safely when it is against the interest of those who have power to hurt?'[2]

Political Science: What It Used To Be

The evolution of political science is said to have passed through four stages.[3] According to Wiseman, these stages ran as follows: up to about 1850, '*a priori* reasoning and the deductive method were emphasized'. That is stage one. Stage two, 'From then until about 1900 the historical and comparative method predominated'. Stage three 'began with the Progressive Era and laid great stress on observation, survey and measurement'. And finally, stage four, 'there were the beginnings of a psychological treatment of politics and an attempt to make political science more "scientific"'. These phases describe the phases of American political science, but then again, there is very little in political science as we know it today that does not originate from its practice by the Americans.

I feel safe in collapsing these four stages into two broad ones: the stage of speculative political inquiry, a stage which Charles Merriam (who earlier discerned the stages described by Wiseman) rather uncharitably held to be preoccupied with '*a priori* reasoning . . .' dovetailing into stage two above, and the stage of empiricism beginning with the 'great stress on observation, survey and measurement' and which has been continuously maturing into 'real science' ever since. I make these two broad categorizations not only for convenience but also in order to emphasize what to me is a highly significant difference between them. This difference is in the realm of the *purpose of the subject matter*. It is in order to bring this crucial difference into clear perspective that I posed the two questions 'political science: what is it?' and 'political science: what did it used to be?' . There are several possible ways of answering these questions. One is just to describe the entire range of the procedures characteristic of each of the two broad phases of political science I have just drawn, and do this without comment. Another way is to emphasize entirely their *methodologies*, exclusive of any other consideration in respect of their objectives. Yet a third way is to inquire into the purpose of the study itself, methodologies merely helping or otherwise hindering the achievement of such a purpose. In respect of this third way, methods are seen as tools rather than as the end of inquiry. It is in these terms that I have chosen to answer the two questions I have proposed: 'what was political science?' and 'what is political science today?' from the point of view of the objectives of political science at each of the two stages.

I have distinguished 'traditional' political science from 'empirical' political science. The aim of traditional political science was citizenship training through imbuing the citizen with the normative values that uphold society. The political scientist during the traditional period 'got along with faith', to borrow Charles Merriam's phrase. Faith in the irreversibility of 'the system', faith in the proposition that 'all men were created equal and remain equal before God and man', faith in the 'fact' that 'no man shall govern another without the latter's consent', and faith in 'the democratic way of life'. The traditional political scientist was concerned not only to understand life but also to point to a better life, to what life *should* be. He or she was happy with 'happy guesses' and 'felicitous strokes of inventive talent'. For such a political scientist, science was an art, its ways of thought being primarily intuitive and imaginative. Like an artist, one *created* politics and depicted the 'political man' in its dynamics. One wrote about the tangible and the intangible, the precise and the imprecise, the real and the possible. In a word, one pre-empted the issues within whose framework today's empirical political scientists carry out their inquiry with the air of factual finality. The empirical political scientist arrived on the scene of political inquiry after the 'Great Issues' had been settled, so that democracy, autocracy, totalitarianism, fascism, among others, are today no more than systems of rule in the context of which the empirical political analyst derives meaning.

The 'new political science' — that is to say, empirical political studies — began with a quandary, both in methods and in goals, both converging in the unsureness whether to build from the bottom with narrow-gauge propositions or to aim for an 'over-arching' theory of political life. Its practitioners are governed by the admirable morality, *nullius verba* — or 'the words of no man'. Yet we know that there is a direct relationship between what we believe and what we do. Behavioural political scientists, writes Peter Harris 'protest against what they call historical and legal conceptions such as the "state", "legislature", "executive", to name but three. They prefer to talk of "systems", "inputs", and "outputs", suggesting, as a helpful alternative, that there are political systems (particularly in Africa and Asia) which are not states, but are subject to demands, or pressures, or inputs, and which make rules in response to these pressures and demands.'[4] The 'empirical iconoclasts' all too readily succumbed to the dangers of 'reification' — the idea that human beings tend to regard institutions which they themselves have in the past created as something objective and inexorable, the project of 'objective' law, something similar to the phenomenon of gravitation, whereas they can in fact be altered by sufficient direction of will-power and energy. Behaviouralists (who in my view are not significantly different from the 'empiricists') tend to make the newly discovered element — science — the independent variable to which perceived reality becomes merely a dependent variable. Earlier visions of man in society become denounced as pedantic and 'uninformed' by 'learning'. Instead, we see a proliferation of 'research areas' — and the smaller the area, the happier the man seeking after scientific verification.

The Responsibility of Philosophers

In all this, what is the responsibility of philosophers? It seems to me that political 'scientists' — the empiricists — assume, in the words of Ankie Hoogvelt, that 'cultural (i.e. ideational) diffusion appears as a friendly merchant traveller, a timeless Marco Polo, innocently roaming the world, gently picking a few ideas in one place and harmlessly depositing them in another'.[5] Personally, I believe that many of the crises confronting African countries are in some measure — a significant measure — moral, intellectual, and institutional crises. When we witness in our societies fundamental challenges to 'the system'; when we watch government programmes on education, for example, subverted because 'the kind of education we offer our children introduce into them corrupting Western influences'; when we hear soft, underground pledges to correct the malaises that infect our societies by pushing larger and larger doses of religious morality into the people; when we hear of the 'need' to 'revive' our traditional ways of life as a countermeasure to pressing national problems — then it is time the philosophers woke up to the challenge of national duty. Because these are fundamental challenges to the ideational foundations of our politics. To the extent that African political 'scientists' demand technical expertise as, let us face it, a precondition for facing the moral and intellectual challenges of society, to that extent do they renegue on their responsibility as social critics. And those who claim to be political 'scientists', more often than not, renegue on this duty. To look at much of the professional publications of African political scientists is to explore the disparity between the times and the men who lived in them. It is to see a near-total neglect of the social and economic squalor of the masses of African people which, after all, permits their indiscriminate mobilization in support of false causes. It is to witness an almost conspiratorial silence on the salient questions facing most African countries, questions of moral bankruptcy, or ideological poverty, and of indiscipline among the enlightened publics which even the newspapers are aware of and to which they draw attention daily. It would appear, indeed, that every charlatan is aware of these issues, save the political 'scientist'.

It may be argued that to suggest that philosophers have the responsibility I talk about suggests either that they have some unique competence to deal with the problems we face or that others — for example, doctors and mathematicians — are somehow more free to put these problems aside. This is not the case. Philosophers need no specific competence, through 'professional' training as philosophers, to deal with contemporary social problems, or to carry on the critique and implementation of public policy. The point has been made already that it is absurd for doctors and mathematicians, for example, to feel that they may freely dismiss these problems on the ground that others have the professional competence, the technical expertise, and the moral responsibility to confont them. As a professional, one has only the duty of doing one's work with integrity. The point is precisely that the philosopher need not be and is indeed not cast in the 'professional' mould, whereas the dream of 'scientists' is, indeed, to achieve 'professional' status. And this is the bane of the field of political science and its practitioners!

Let us try to understand the reason why I say this is the bane of political science and of those who lay claim to its 'correct' practice. It requires but little argument to state — as many others have stated — that the demand for a scientific study of politics has sometimes emanated from dubious motives. 'These,' says Victor Wiseman, 'have been said to include the search for prestige and status; envy of economists, psychologists, and perhaps even sociologists; the commercial and foundation value of the scientific approach.'[6] As far as I know, there are no independent foundations for political research designs which are a lucrative source of funds, funds which may not always be used strictly for the purpose they were disbursed to researchers. To these restrictions have been added false scruples about what is 'academic', or a false sense of 'professional propriety', even 'political funk' or 'a curious passion for the mannerism of the non-committed'. Unintelligible jargon resulting in dignified obscurity makes it unlikely that its practitioner will ever have to tell the truth on any matter (note John P. Roche's remark that in the olden days when political scientists wished to be obscure they quoted Greek; 'now they break out into differential calculus!'). What is more, perhaps the most important role of the intellectual in any society where enlightenment has made any headway has been that of unmasking idiology, exposing the injustice and the repression that exists in society, and seeking the way to a new and higher form of social life that will extend the possibilities for a creative and contented life. We can expect, as indeed we are witnessing not only in Africa but also in other climes where the intellectual becomes transformed into a professional, that this role will be abandoned, as the intellectual becomes more engaged in constructing an ideology that justifies dominance on the ground of technical excellence. This danger is more real for the industrialized societies than for our 'village' countries; yet the danger is there for us and our countries as well. As we are noticing in America, for example, industrial society is beginning to show signs that it will be marked by the access to power of the intellectual elite, basing its claim to power on a supposedly 'value-free' science and technology of social management.

In times like this, the importance of the social critic becomes more crucial than ever before. This critic must be capable of analysing the content of the claimed 'expertise', its normative (even empirical) justification, and its social use. I can see no one else to do this, or one who can do it as well as, the moralistic political scientist. Also, we notice in America, for example, where political science has matured in method and procedure more than in any other country in the world, that the same analytical tools that seek to explore the nature of scientific theories in general, or the structure of some particular domain of knowledge, can themselves be turned against the technology of control and manipulation that goes under the name of 'behavioural science'. For this 'science' serves as the ideology of the new perpetrators of domination and ruthless suppression of social discontent. As the 'scientist' gets steeped in this act, a programme of concerted exposure would be a natural and valuable concern of the philosopher.

There is another problem related to the foregoing, a problem I mentioned only in passing earlier on. There is a tendency, as a field becomes truly professionalized, for its problems to be determined less by considerations of intrinsic interest and more by the availability of certain tools that have been developed as the subject matures. Of course, it must be admitted that social philosophy is not exempt from this tendency. Yet it is absolutely vital to find a way in teaching, even more than in research, to place the work that is feasible and productive at a certain moment against the background of the general societal concerns which make some questions, but not others, worth pursuing. It is easy to show how certain fields, such as political science, have been seriously distorted by a failure to maintain this perspective. I think that in the study of politics especially, a student would benefit greatly from the experience, rarely offered in any academic programme, of defending the significance of the field of work in which he or she is engaged and facing the challenge of a point of view and a critique that does not automatically accept the premises and limitations of scope that are to be found in the discipline. Perhaps I am putting this too abstractly, but I think the point is clear. I think that it indicates a defect of much of what is taught in political science departments in African universities. Being more flexible because of its lack of pedantic attachments to specific methodologies, social philosophy is, I believe, less subject to this defect.

It was Ruth First who observed that there is a great deal of talk about politics in Africa, side by side with the growing poverty of political thought. It is a fact that political 'science' is capable of turning up much-needed data about human behaviour in society, about human desires, and the motivations that generate these desires. But in the context of what belief system is the political scientist to give meaning to the array of available statistical data?

The Nigerian Example

Let us take an example to which I alluded earlier on. In Nigeria, one need not be a member of any conspiratorial circle in the country to know that almost everybody blames 'the system' for the ills Nigerian society suffers from. In many of the northern parts, for example, one frequently hears that the country is operating an illegitimate social system; one that is in keeping neither with the traditional social values nor with the moral promptings of creed. There are signs in that part of the country that an Iranian solution would be seen as preferable to the problems Nigeria is facing today. While political scientists are busy explaining educational imbalance in the country from the point of view of when the first schools were established to offer formal (if one may not say functional) education in the country, how much dedication went into this, and so on, little do they know that what is at stake, when the chips are down, is the philosophy of education in Nigeria. Little do they know that the issue being raised is not how many formal education houses will be necessary to bridge the gap, but rather whether 'Western education' is acceptable all over the country. Is the education gap between the North and South a function of inability or of desire? Is there an underlying *unwillingness* on the part of those who complain about the imbalance to correct it, and why? To my mind, these are the questions that need to be asked about this particular issue. And the answer must be found. Instead of this, there is the all too glib resort to condemnations, to protestations of all kinds and from all sides. And again philosophy is challenged here. Philosophy is challenged to call forth what *should* be the function of education in Nigeria, and what kind of education is likely to achieve or otherwise approximate this function. This is an issue with serious *normative* implications.

I referred to Ruth First's cryptic comment on the condition of political philosophy in Africa. That there is a great deal of talk about politics in Africa is truer in no other African country than in Nigeria. Everybody in Nigeria talks of 'the Nigerian problem', and there is no dearth of proferred solution. Take a look at the newspapers. 'Commissioner identifies the cause of social unrest'; 'Local Government Chairman spells out the ills of our society'; 'A university don explains the causes of indiscipline in our schools'; and so forth. It seems to me that the more people who 'identify' the 'causes' of social problems the less people understand them. The more the problems are, to borrow the journalists' pet word, 'ear-marked' for solution, the more compounded the problems themselves tend to become, and the more confounded the social physicians. If I am correct, then one must ask and answer the question: Why is it that the more people who know about the nation's problems, the less advantaged the country is to deal with those problems? The reason, in my opinion, is this, that every one of the 'solutions' we read in the newspapers every day represents a greater and greater proliferation of values in the social system, an atomization of normative approaches to the issues highlighted. Indeed, one might be permitted the small exaggeration that if you have one million Nigerians discussing an issue, you are likely to find a million 'philosophies'. I say 'philosophies' instead of 'viewpoints' because I want to underscore the rather fundamental effect of this trend, the effect upon the development of a national philosophy of life, and the effect upon the activities of empirical political researchers.

I believe that for national values to develop in any country, what is necessary is the courageous elimination of irrelevant thought. And a thought becomes irrelevant only if one dominant thought arises to assert itself over all others. When, for example, the Americans proclaimed their unflinching belief in the democratic way of life, in representative government and institutions, they were talking in the shadow of John Locke who had, in England, subdued any significant protestation to the contrary. A viable political thought can never be founded on a million *prevailing* thoughts about an acceptable political system. I personally believe that the crux of the problem of national cohesion and other related issues derives from the failure to develop a single, dominant philosophy of rule for the country. And again, philosophers are challenged to arms.

Then I talked of the effect on behavioural/empirical political scientists. I do not know exactly what the position is in other universities, but at the Ahmadu Bello University in Nigeria, the department of political science is definitely one of the popular departments, as attested by high student registrations. Yet (and I hope there is no offence in saying this) most of the students graduate from the department convinced of the virtues of no particular political system, from democracy to anarchy. Then I ask myself, what are we doing? That these students will find jobs there is no doubt; but that they will reinforce any particular Nigerian political arrangement is far from self-evident. They surely leave the university knowing many things about almost all forms of government, but I suspect that they believe in none in particular. And yet I personally believe that they should. I believe that they should be *consciously* – let us use the correct word – indoctrinated in a Nigerian system of government, especially in what normative foundations should underlie governing in Nigeria. Can the political 'scientist' do this?

I suspect not, since it is one of the virtues of 'science' to try to avoid 'subjectivism'. I think this is sad enough, and sadder still when one considers that even the students expect the teacher to give out only 'facts' and keep his 'opinion' out of his lectures. I have witnessed walkouts from lectures on this score. Consequently, one must want to know what 'facts' are. We might say that it is a 'fact' that one who takes what is not theirs, and does so surreptitiously, has committed theft. But surely, this would be the case only in societies that do not permit people to take what does not belong to them. In societies where it is perfectly all right to take whatever one wants, even without its owner's permission, one is not a thief, since there are no moral sanctions against doing so. Therefore, it would not be a 'fact' that someone who has taken what is not theirs has committed 'theft'.

The significance of this point I am raising is that to practise political 'science' in the absence of an all-pervading value-conception of politics is to attempt to investigate what will continue to remain disputable in the normative sense. This is why I have come to the conclusion that, without the prior settling of the 'Great Issues' without the 'good' and the 'bad' in the life of any nation having been settled beforehand, without philosophy having taken root, I doubt that political 'science' can make much meaningful contribution to political development in any country. This is because it is normative philosophizing that can distinguish between political 'facts' and 'non-facts' on a national scale in any country.

The Need for Value-Orientation in National Life

I am not, by the foregoing, denying the need for a factual knowledge of political and social phenomena in any African country. Indeed, and unless we want to further confound the political, social, and economic problems in African societies, there is a clear need to intensify the search for factual knowledge. The point I have tried to make is that we cannot practise meaningful political science in the absence of a pervasive value-orientation in our national lives. We cannot conceive of political science as a retreat from creative and imaginative philosophizing in respect of African social conditions. I do not know of any country in the world where social science has achieved the social function of knowledge in the absence of clear ideological and normative concomitants. Therefore, I think that those of us who are employed in political science departments have two choices, either of which involves embracing philosophy: 1) We can practise political science and accept that what we are doing reflects our normative judgments, judgments that may be at variance with African social conditions – which is what we have been doing; or 2) we can do political science while at the same time working seriously to establish normative criteria for interpreting the 'facts' we throw up. Western societies were fortunate to have settled their own 'Great Issues' before science began to make claims in political studies. In our own case, we are faced with doing political science *before* we have the normative criteria for evaluating our 'findings'. This is not to say that at the moment we have no such criteria. It is rather to question the content of these criteria; whether they provide us with any meaningful insight into the nature of the African societies and the social conditions within them. What I have argued is that it is philosophy that can provide this insight, and that, unless we accept the challenge implied in this, the political science we are teaching and researching is unlikely to contribute to the development of stable, just and cohesive societies.

Notes

1. Berthrand de Jouvenel, 'The Pure Theory of Politics', cited in H. Victor Wiseman, *Politics, The Master Science* (London, Routledge and Kegan Paul, 1969), p. 2.
2. Thomas Hobbes, *Behemoth* cited in Wiseman, op. cit., pp. 1-2.
3. See Wiseman, op. cit., pp. 13-19.
4. Peter Harris, *Foundations of Political Science* (London, Hutchinson, 1976), p. 48.
5. Ankie M.M. Hoogvelt, *The Sociology of Developing Societies* (London, Macmillan, 1976), p. 18.
6. Wiseman, op. cit., p. 45.

3. Teaching Political Science in African Universities: A Problem-Solving Approach

Eme O. Awa

There are two kinds of basic issues that I am going to discuss in this paper. One is the question of whether we should take a teleological or a so-called scientific (value-free) approach to the study and teaching of political science. The other is to suggest ways in which political science can be better taught in the universities in Africa than is the case at the present moment. The views I am going to express on the first question are to some extent an affirmation of my support for the position which L.A. Jinadu has already articulated.[1]

The Science-Value Problem

In raising the science-value problem on a broader plane, Scott Greer has narrated the following story:

> A parade of social scientists from the new nations (the countries called, depending upon your optimism, 'underdeveloped' or 'developing') crossed the podium. Social Scientists of all colors and nationalities spoke to one point: What can social science do for our nation? How can we achieve our goals? These men were mostly from socialist countries and some were from the communist bloc. Underlying their speeches was a common assumption: Social Science theory fails us when it does not focus upon our pressing problems.
>
> A distinguished American sociologist spoke last. His presentation was clear and, in the language of an introductory method class, he argued the absolute necessity for an unbiased social science. Social Science must be value-free; it cannot be tied to the chariot of any given ideology or national goal. If it is, it becomes not science but apologetics.[2]

What the eminent American was in effect asking us to do was to ignore the following which summarizes the objective conditions which we find in our societies.

Poverty Amidst Great Potential Wealth
Africa has enormous wealth, a lot of which is undeveloped, but most of the

people live under conditions of abject poverty. That is, most of the African people cannot afford three good meals per day or meet their other basic necessities such as good shelter and clothing. The incidence of malnutrition is very high in some parts of the continent, more so, in the words of a hospital matron who returned from a trip to India recently, than in some of the poorest areas of India.

In Nigeria, for example, up to 95% of the great wealth of the country is controlled by about .01% of the population. Many of the wealthy Nigerians made their money off the backs of the poor farmers through the marketing board device or by serving as *compradors* to the multinational corporations which really control the economy and dictate the manner and pace of the country's development.

Ignorance
Most of the African peoples are not educated and cannot read or write in any language. Little effort has been made by our leaders to mobilize the masses and to raise the level of political consciousness among them. As a consequence, there exist two worlds in most African countries: a tiny enlightened world of the educated elite, of the politically active, on the one hand, and on the other, a large dark world of the masses of people grounded in ignorance and inertia.

Disease and Squalor
As is well-known, the class of people in any society who are uneducated, unemployed or underemployed and poor, is usually the class which suffers most from diseases of various kinds. In Africa, debilitating diseases such as kwashiokor, malaria, diarrhoea, blindness etc. abound in the ranks of the masses of the people.

Waste
A high percentage of our human resources is wasted, in the sense that most people are not able to acquire elementary and secondary school education and their capacity to participate effectively in the political and economic process is thus severely limited. Further, in all African countries, only a small percentage of those who qualify for admission into institutions of higher learning are actually able to secure the benefits of higher education.

In much of Africa, much of the natural resources are also wasted. This waste is more pronounced in Nigeria where the burning of natural gas, deforestation, shifting methods of agricultural cultivation, loss of produce through poor storage, the failure to export the bulk of cocoa, rubber and petroleum are all too well known. All these constitute great waste of African resources which could be handled more reasonably or utilized in more meaningful ways.

Inept Attempts at Industrialization
Most, if not all, African countries have pursued the import substitution

strategy in industrial development. The basic idea was to trigger the spirit of creativity and self-reliance among the indigenous people and thereby gain economic independence, that is, reduce the dependence of countries on foreign goods. In the process, many of the newly established industries have tended to concentrate unduly on the production of sumptuous goods such as beer, soft drinks and cigarettes.[3] The enterprises have remained largely foreign because most of them cannot be carried on without foreign expertise, machinery and vital raw materials (for example, hops for beer; gypsum for cement; the Coca Cola formula is a closely guarded secret). We find ourselves tied more tightly than ever before to the apron strings of the multinational corporations. And it is not appreciated yet that by the undue concentration on the production of some of these goods, we are creating conditions in Africa for the development or growth of alcoholism and cancer on a greater scale than was ever the case with traditional indigenous consumption patterns.

Corruption and Gross Indiscipline

It appears as if both Charles Darwin and Herbert Spencer are alive today and propounding their ideas specifically in the interests of the African upper classes, particularly in Nigeria. For the bitter strife of competitive enterprise, in which one uses every trick in the game, as is the case in Nigeria, effectively mirrors the natural world as portrayed by Darwin. Those who infringe both statutory laws and regulations and moral laws, and bluster their way to the top, are assumed to be the fittest to survive and carry on. For his part, Spencer contended that natural economic processes must be allowed to take place without the hindrance of reformers.[4] It is all in the spirit of capitalist democracy, especially at its formative stages, for people to engage in corrupt practices and commit acts of gross indiscipline in order to get to the top. Deliberate inflation of contract costs, embezzlement of public funds, flagrant disregard for regulations designed to curb price inflation, all these characterize the behaviour of the African elite groups, and especially so in Nigeria.

Centre-Periphery Problems

We have already mentioned the centre-periphery problem in the broader context in which African countries play peripheral roles with respect to the multinational corporations. Serious problems also flow from the urban-rural relations within these countries. Beginning since the colonial days, the rural areas of the territories were treated as centres for the production of food and export produce for feeding the urban population and metropolitan industries as well as generating revenue for the colonial governments. These rural areas have continued largely to serve this role even since the independence of these countries.

It is in the light of this background that we must pose the question: *What can political science do for our nations*? I do not think that we are faced with a choice between the use of the empirical or the teleological approaches in handling our subjects. Political scientists everywhere are concerned to assure the emergence of the good state, defined in some specific way. For instance, for most Americans the good state is a capitalist democracy predicated on the doctrine of competitive politics in a two-party system. For Russians, the good state is a Marxist state predicated on the doctrine of controlled competition.

The starting point of the study of social phenomena is a critical analysis of the empirical data. By this is meant that our teaching must incorporate an analysis of the socio-political conditions which are found in our societies and in some of the major foreign nations, especially those we are apt to use as yard-sticks to measure our own progress. We cannot afford to stop at this point. We must go beyond this and state the goals which we consider reasonable for our own societies. We must bring in the purposive approach for two reasons. The first is that everywhere other scientists do engage in basic or applied research, the latter being designed to solve some specific problems. Thus, social workers want problems of social welfare to be solved, clinical psychologists and psychiatrists want to cure the sick; economists want to make the economy work. Secondly, if we look at the matter from the point of view of empirical political theory, we will remember that theory seeks to explain socio-political phenomena. If we can explain, then we can predict. If we have predict, then we can control and eradicate weaknesses, that is, solve the problems which press us.

The Goals of Society and How to Achieve Them

All this is really elementary. And I do not think that there are many African political scientists who are concerned to any great extent with the science-value debate. The major problem we confront is to decide on basic goals for our societies and the means by which such goals can be achieved.

It would seem to me that practically everybody will agree that the basic goals are to eliminate the constraints in which our societies function today: poverty, ignorance, disease, unemployment, inflation, dependence of our economies on foreigners and foreign institutions.

How can we achieve these goals? In a paper I read at the conference of the Nigerian Political Science Association in 1977 I expressed the view that we ought to make a distinction between political growth and political development. I argued that the great advance that has taken place in the American and other Western political systems may be labelled growth and not development since, in spite of this advance, poverty, unemployment, inflation and civil strife still exist in their societies. On the other hand, the advance made by the major socialist countries has to a great extent relatively eradicated from their societies the constraints of poverty, unemployment and inflation. And I maintained that any society in which all the people are liberated from the shackles of poverty, ignorance, squalor, and other forms of social and economic constraints, can be said to be developed.[5] It is, of course, true that these socialist states are still plagued to a greater or lesser extent by the problems arising from what may be termed inadequacies in the incentive system and in the character and scope of the fundamental liberties. If the political and economic structures in a socialist state were made a little looser than they are in the places where these difficulties have occurred, then it is probable that these types of problems would disappear.

In other words, the empirical evidence we have shows that political advance along the lines of capitalist democracy leads not to political development but to political growth, while advance along the lines of socialist democracy leads for all practical purposes to political development. I shall say a word about this reservation regarding socialist democracy later but here it is necessary to note that this is the point at which there is some disagreement among political scientists. We should point out that those Africans who advocate capitalist democracy do so mainly because, I presume, like their counterparts in the Western world, they are concerned only to retain the advantages which the present state of capitalist development in African countries has bestowed on them. But their view is short-sighted because, so long as most of our people remain poor and our countries remain economically peripheries of the West, so long will we, individually and collectively, play only second fiddle to the more advanced nations. In any case, we must remember that every human is a moral being and as such possesses an intrinsic worth which can only be fully displayed when debilitating societal constraints are removed.

I have hinted at reservations about socialism and I have two practical problems in mind. One relates to the question whether socialism demands that we socialize all economic activities. The other refers to the question of what fundamental liberties we must curb, and to what extent, in order to achieve socialism. My position on the first issue has been stated in some detail in a previous article[6] and it is only necessary for me to say here that certain types of enterprises, especially in agriculture, small partnerships and the sole-proprietor type of commercial industrial enterprises, may be run on a private or co-operative basis without injury to the cause of socialism. We can sustain the fundamental human liberties firstly by building an incentive system into areas like agriculture which cannot function with maximum efficiency without it. Secondly we can give full play to dissent and criticism of the political system and political processes.[7]

The basic point that I am making here is that we should be free to modify Marxist theory to suit our purposes. And it is helpful to remember that Lenin himself made some important modifications to Marxism and then the modified version became the basis for developing the Russian political system; the Chinese, who accused the Russians of revisionism, seem to have embarked now on a massive backtracking from Maoism; Yugoslav socialism is in some important structural senses different from the Russian and Chinese types, and so on. When we part company with the capitalist democracy, the West may accuse us of embracing communism and make it sound like a crime or a moral offence. When we seek to modify Marxism to suit our conditions, the Russians are likely to look down their noses at the attempt, ignoring the revisionism which they themselves have committed in the past. We must not be deterred by the views of foreigners. The task before us is to forge tools of analysis and social engineering that will enable us to liberate our people

Once we settle the question of the required degree of socialization of enterprises, we must attend to the question of the basic political structures whose operation will aid in ushering in the new society. It is, for instance, distressing to find people advocating socialism as well as a competitive party system based on the free market ideology. For if two parties, one socialist and the other capitalist, compete for political power, the economic structure will be determined by the party which wins the elections. If it is the capitalist party, then socilaism will not be installed, or retained where it is already in existence. Given the goal of socialism, our traditional decision structures and the empirical evidence of our attitude toward party opposition in the post-colonial period, we should be able to argue for a one-party structure which provides adequate room for competition and for the preservation of the people's right to criticize governments.[8] Thus a competitive party system need not be, as it is in the West, an ultimate value, which makes it possible for some segments of the society to appear to exercise choice among a set of apparent alternatives while they remain severely poor. We are obliged to do a lot more thinking about the type of parties, decision-making and judicial structures that must be evolved to serve our purpose.

What I have said so far may be summarized as follows: political scientists in Africa must engage in more profound and critical analysis of the objective conditions which prevail in our societies. When they do so, they will see clearly the social ills which are strangling our countries. They are obliged by the nature of their training to suggest remedies for these problems and they should do so. Only insofar as we get our perspectives right can we teach effectively.

How To Teach Political Science for the Here and Now

But it seems to me that to acquire the right perspective is not enough. In fact it is debatable whether one can acquire such a perspective merely by reading up on the existing literature. Nothing prepares one more solidly for teaching than a knowledge gained from research and writing. So I think we ought to devote more attention to research and writing on relevant topics.

We must sharpen the tools of research and analysis and produce our own writing in this area. The tools of research and analysis are forever undergoing changes. Western scholars, especially Americans, have made commendable contributions to this area of our knowledge. It seems to me, however, that by and large, the tools which people forge are related to the nature of the problems they want to solve and their value-orientations. Thus important books such as Charlesworth's *Contemporary Political Analysis* and Mayer's *Comparative Political Inquiry* do not, for instance, consider class theory as a method of political analysis or a suitable subject for inclusion in studies in empirical political theory. Some approaches or models such as systems theory and structural-functionalism, which possess little explanatory value, seem to be popular with many of our students mainly because we, the teachers, lay undue emphasis on them. I have seen what looks like original work being done by one or two African political scientists and I do hope that their contributions will become available in the near future. But many other people should develop an interest in the field so that in due course we may come to have tools essentially of our own design.

It seems to me that our research effort should increasingly embrace specific types of activities of immediate relevance. The activities suggested here are conceived in the context of Nigerian problems but may have relevance elsewhere in Africa: 1) basic research in connection with methodological questions and the foundations of political analysis; 2) fundamental questions such as ethnicity (its explanation, control and social uses), revenue allocation, unity in diversity, centre-periphery problems, the legislative process in presidential government, pressure groups, strategic issues in relation to Nigeria's African policy (e.g. can Nigeria exceed the existing limit of her African policy without making more progress in her military preparedness and acquiring greater mastery of the strategy of conflict, as well as evolving a more viable and efficacious political system?), voting behaviour, etc.; 3) problems of the moment such as the administration of hospitals, the post and telegraph department, the customs, the police, etc. — the objective being, among other things, to avoid the existing 'post mortem' approach in which the country waits until things have gone entirely wrong and then sets up commissions to probe and punish those who have already done irreparable damage in one way or the other.

What is being called for is action on our part which can help minimize the maladministration of the existing institutions so that they may not strangle us in the meantime. Such activities need not prevent us from devoting adequate attention to formulating ideas and structures angled more towards the system we consider more desirable. It is unlikely that we would do an adequate job in handling the latter unless we understand fully what is wrong with the existing institutions.

Further, it seems to me that political science, as a relatively new discipline in the social sciences in Africa, ought to be seriously concerned with the question of its reception and use by the general public. Of course, if we study important problems of the moment, such as we have listed above, we are likely to make an impact on the society. But nothing impresses the public, including the government, so much as the appearance of sophistication and professionalism in a discipline. We must take up this matter very seriously, first, in order to allay the fears of those who think that political scientists are politicians and secondly to provide a sufficiently reliable guide to the solution of some of our political problems. We ought to take the opportunity too to re-examine the whole question of structuring the departments of political science in our universities with a view to avoiding the unnecessary proliferation of structures and waste of effort through types of empire-building which do not enhance the service goals of the discipline.

I think that undergraduate courses are already comprehensive in most universities. But we may be able to deepen the insight of the students into social problems and stir their imaginations more firmly toward a search for a solution to these problems if we prescribe a set of books as required reading in respect of the bachelor's degree. That is, in order that we can ensure more definitely that the graduate in political science may be of the best use to the country from the points of view of learning and culture as well as of problem-solving, we must develop the 'Great Books' idea, making them read and master some set books. It may be easier to delineate the scope of the reading involved in terms of the kinds of disciplines than to name actual books: economics, psychology, philosophy, history, sociology are the related disciplines which we must explore for good basic books.

On the postgraduate level there seems to be a lot of need and scope for innovation. The area of public administration and some aspects of international relations, especially strategic studies, lend themselves to some degree of professionalization which I think ought to be explored carefully by all departments of political science in African universities.

As we know very well, the last ten years or so have witnessed a phenomenal growth in the population, institutions and enterprises in many African countries. The older towns and cities are virtually bursting at their seams with an increase in the number of urban dwellers; new urban centres have been created in many rural areas; the traditional public utilities are stretched almost beyond their capacities; many public enterprises have sprung up, some owned and spearheaded solely by governments and some as joint ventures between governments and private investors. All these pose staggering managerial problems for the nations and oblige us to take another look at the public administration courses which we give in our departments or institutes. Is there something that public managers should know? Or to put it differently, is there not some skill that they can acquire which will enhance their performance on the job?

Requirements of Public Administration and Management

Such questions have been raised in many countries and today there is some consensus that public management is a profession and requires that administrators should possess certain kinds of education, knowledge, skills and values as prerequisites to effective performance in their jobs. I provide here a matrix of the subjects, skills, values, etc. which the I.A.S.I.A. has suggested as suitable for the effective training of administrators and managers.[9] I divide these into 1) subject matter areas; 2) tools and skills; and 3) public interest values. The basic idea is that training should as far as possible cover such matters or at any rate enable one to acquire some competence in them.
1) Subject Matter Areas: i) Political values and processes; ii) Cultural and social patterns; iii) Economic system, incentives and controls; iv) Environmental factors and resources available; v) Governmental institutions, power

and relationships in society.

2) Tools and Skills: i) Quantitative decision methodology e.g. accounting, parametric and non-parametric statistics, linear programming and modelling; ii) Electronic data processing and information systems; iii) Work measurement; iv) Behavioural science and methodology — value analysis, sociometric surveys, etc.; v) Logical analysis and diagnosis; vi) Administrative planning and organizational design; vii) Policy formulation.

3) Public Interest Values: i) Utilization of science to foster public purposes; ii) Use of data and analysis to enlarge the scope of public choice; iii) Programmes which foster equality of opportunity and well-being; iv) Measures to increase citizen understanding of public policies and their impact.

But can people engaged in such studies consider themselves students of political science and will lecturers be able to maintain normal communication with political scientists? This type of programme cannot fit in readily simply as an area of specialization in postgraduate political science. The core subjects, of course, do fall within political science but what gives it that touch of professionalism is the range of subjects. Each university should consider whether the public administration programme should be run by an institute, a school or a separate graduate division, and structure some effective linkage between it and the department of political science. It would also appear that each department should seriously study the question of whether students should study for the Master of Science degree in Public Administration (M.Sc. Public Administration) or merely for the Masters degree in Public Administration (M.P.A.), the Ph.D. degree in any case being the ultimate level.

Finally, let me say that I have been sorely tempted to talk about the problem of pedagogical skills and have been deterred by lack of knowledge in the matter. I suppose that for the foreseeable future we shall carry on with the assumption that anyone who possesses high intelligence and has received a certain amount of training will, by and large, make a good teacher of political science.

I have already indicated some areas in which we can do essential research. One of the ways of promoting co-ordinated research on national levels is to establish in each country or, better still, on a continental basis a Centre for Advanced Studies in African Politics. Such a centre or centres could serve as catalysts for advanced study of African problems and as rewards for established reputations of African political scientists.

Notes

1. See L.A. Jinadu, 'Some Reflections on African Political Scientists and African Politics', *The West African Journal of Sociology and Political Science*, Vol. 3, January 1979.

2. Scott Greer, *The Logic of Social Inquiry* (Chicago, Aldine Publishing Co., 1969), p. 177.
3. For a discussion of the Nigerian case, see P.E. Manu, 'Import Substitution as a Strategy of Industrialisation: Its Relevance to Nigeria', unpublished paper, University of Nigeria, 1979.
4. See a brief analysis of Darwin's and Spencer's theories in R. Hofstadter, *The American Political Tradition*, pp. 167–8.
5. See my unpublished paper entitled 'Constitutions and Political Change' presented at the Fourth Annual Conference of the Nigerian Political Science Association, Durbar Hotel, Kaduna, April 1977.
6. See Eme O. Awa, 'The Place of Ideology in Nigerian Politics', *African Review: A Journal of African Politics, Development and International Affairs*, Vol. 4, No. 3, 1974.
7. For an elaboration of this view, see Eme O. Awa, op. cit.
8. See Eme O. Awa, op. cit. and 'Toward a New Party System', *Journal of Business and Social Studies*, University of Lagos, Vol. 3, No. 1, 1970.
9. I have been a member of the Working Group on Curricular Development of the International Association of Schools and Institutes in Administration (I.A.S.I.A.) and have drawn these ideas from the work of the Group.

4. The African Peasantry: Neglected by African Political Science

Ebitini Chikwendu

Nationalist intellectuals are concerned with the formulation of theories of genuine development. Even in pre-colonial Africa, the foremost nationalist, Edward Blyden, enjoined the Young Men's Literary Association of Sierra Leone, as educated Africans, to take up their responsibility to uphold the righteous development of racial personality: 'The duty of every man of every race is to contend for its individuality — to keep and develop it'. He emphasized that 'When you have done away with your [racial] personality, you have done away with yourselves. Your place has been assigned you in the universe as Africans, and there is no room for you as anything else.'[1] He was opposed to those who would agree to be absorbed in another dominant race 'in cringing self-surrender and ignoble self-suppression'.[2]

Blyden also saw that the black race needed regeneration from the throes of slavery through a process of training which should be from within, instead of a package presented from outside. For Blyden, a university in West Africa should have a clearly indigenous character, although inspiration could be sought from other Western civilizations, while the racism of the West should not be allowed to detract from the core of Africanity.

Another nationalist, Casely-Hayford, advocated a university in West Africa, the promotion of an African racial consciousness which would enable Africans to determine their political and cultural destinies. Any kind of knowledge, even proficiency in industrial and technical training, must be pursued within an environment which would reveal to the student the higher qualities of the student's nationality and race. Even after benefiting from all that is best in Western culture, the black race must remain true to racial instincts and inspiration, customs and institutions.[3] In calling for a national university for the Gold Coast, Casely-Hayford advocated the teaching of history in such a way as to prove that 'Africa has nothing to be ashamed of, of its place among the nations of the earth . . . this seat of learning to be the means of revising erroneous current ideas regarding the African; of raising him in self-respect; and of making him an efficient co-worker in the uplifting of man to nobler effort'.[4]

Education for Underdevelopment

Recommendations on the appropriate approaches to African university education were still being made in the waning years of the 1970s because the quality of our current education for the upliftment of our nations and race falls short of our developmental needs. Our education is directed towards the wrong set of goals; it is focused on the creation of urban-based institutions, oriented towards interaction with Western capitalist institutions.
To staff these institutions, a small but inefficient middle class of local agents are trained along capitalist, liberal–democratic ideological lines to uphold unachievable models of Western development. The Western model is unachievable because, while the West operates capital-intensive technology, with the underdeveloped world as the hapless dumping ground for their contaminated surpluses, we in Africa are faced with the reality of a capital-short, labour-intensive society with no recourse to captive European markets. In order to maintain this unequal relationship, education has remained relatively conservative and stagnant, geared to the needs and self-image of a restricted elite. Education has lost its dynamic innovative and change-oriented potential.[5] The recipients of such an education are incapable of bringing about far-reaching social and economic changes, because the broader strata of society are denied full participation in a common political system.

As the policy elite ignores the broad periphery of society, the only kind of development left open for them is a contradictory and distorted market-oriented economy, tied to the economic system of European metropolitan centres.[6] In the field of education, rudimentary technical skills have been imported without using education to change the existing social order and the system of values.

In Walter Rodney's brilliant exposé, he argues that one of the functions of education is to promote social change. Pre-colonial African education was relevant to Africans; it had close links with social life; and it was directly connected with the purposes of society. By contrast, colonial education did not grow out of the African environment, neither was it designed to promote the most rational use of material and social resources, it was not an educational system designed to give confidence and pride to young people as members of African societies.[7] Instead, colonial schooling 'was education for subordination, exploitation, the creation of mental confusion, and the development of under-development'.[8]

President Nyerere of Tanzania has been one of the few leaders to make a hard assessment of the educational system inherited from colonial powers, for which 20% of hard-earned national funds must be invested in Tanzania. His opinion is that our education should have a proportionate relevance to the society Africans are trying to create. According to Nyerere, in his first post-Arusha policy directive, titled 'Education for Self-Reliance', the purpose of education 'is to transmit from one generation to the next the accumulated wisdom and knowledge of the society and to prepare the young people for their future membership of the society and their active participation in its maintenance or development'.⁹

A look at the educational system practised under colonialism shows that the system was inadequate and inappropriate for a developing agrarian society. Since Tanzania, like the rest of Africa, has a predominantly rural economy, and since most people live and work in the rural areas, it is in the rural areas that life must be improved. 'It is therefore the villages which must be made into places where people live a good life; it is in the rural areas that people must be able to find their material well-being and their satisfactions.'¹⁰

Tanzanian colonial education was also considered to have divorced its participants from the society it was supposed to be preparing them for. Both secondary schools and the university are situated many miles from the homes of the students, so that by the end of university education the new graduates have spent the larger part of their lives separated from the masses of their nation. Although their parents may be poor, university students rarely fully share that poverty: 'He does not really know what it is like to live as a poor peasant . . ., many of the people in Tanzania have come to regard education as meaning that a man is too precious for the rough and hard life which the masses of our people still live.'¹¹ Rather than understand the predicament of the masses, university graduates also participate in the domination and exploitation of the rest of the Africans.

The most persistently exploited group of Africans are the peasants. They were exploited under colonialism and our independent national leaders still exploit them. Colonialists advanced the argument that African peasants did not pay sufficient tax and therefore African children could not be provided with educational facilities. Advanced by both the colonialists and their post-independence successors, this is a fundamental distortion of reality because it ignores the fact that peasant labour and production are the real sources of national wealth. Our new university graduates must appreciate this truth that will enable them to exercise social responsibility towards the peasantry, who make up the vast periphery of society.

The neglect of the peasantry and their agricultural occupation originates in the colonial value system which assigned a low value to manual activity and a high value to white-collar bureaucratic work. The colonial economy also offered highly lucrative compensation to those who had a purely literary education, as opposed to those with manual skills. Therefore Africans strongly opposed agricultural education which would have helped to raise agricultural production. Even where farm or rural schools actually operated, the quality was decidedly inferior to literary education, and the schools functioned as avenues for introducing unpopular agricultural innovations, such as terracing, in Tanganyika and Nyasa.¹²

In summary, the core of our argument on relevant education for a developing society is that in determining the curriculum and syllabus at any level of education, focus must be put on how that education would contribute to the improvement of the life of the majority, the rural peasantry.

Taking the Peasantry Seriously

A Course on 'Peasants in Politics'
It is for the purpose of developing a relevant education system geared to the understanding of the problems confronting the majority of African people living in the rural areas, with the aim of identifying possible solutions to such problems, that a course entitled 'Peasants in Politics' is suggested for adoption in the curricula of political science departments in African universities. Such a course would deal with the interaction of peasants and governments, with special emphasis on peasants' forms of autonomous political organizations. This particular view of political studies could focus on power and participation in a modernizing polity, highlighting the reality that, in spite of partial mobilization of the general mass of the populace, the poor are usually not permitted effective control over their economic and political destinies. The political elite make policy decisions that persistently ignore the welfare of the preponderant masses of the people, because no value is put on the contributions of the peasant classes to national well-being. We have not studied the potentialities within the peasantry, in spite of our predominantly peasant backgrounds.

Traditional Conceptions of the Peasant
Peasants the world over live in rural areas; they plant subsistence crops, although they sometimes need to sell some surplus for cash requirements. They are generally poor, illiterate, in poor health, and are usually despised by urban dwellers.[13] Peasants are said to retain conservative world views, old and traditional institutions and customs.

The peasantry, being a pre-industrial entity, is looked upon as a residual phenomenon in industrial society, and their role within the prevailing market and urban-centred economy is increasingly marginal. Through capital concentration, spread of education, political power and population growth, the urban society rapidly overtakes the countryside and becomes the main determinant of social and economic change.[14] The village, which is the kind of community in which the majority of peasants live, is now a mere subordinate segment of a changed world. The town determines the manner of societal change and development.

One such developmental trend is the over-concentration of industries in the urban centres to the neglect of agro-based industries. This is a distorted trend to development, for development must be focused on our peasantries at the initial stages so that they will be willing and able to feed the urban dwellers, most of whom belong to the bureaucratic class. Peasants must be encouraged to do this until agriculture has become mechanized and there is sufficient industrial activity in the nation to transform the peasantry into industrial producers. Instead, we find our peasantry being considered irrelevant to national development; there is no clear agricultural policy to make the peasants feel they are an indispensable category in the national development effort. The peasantry is left disillusioned because they are underemployed, and they see themselves occupying relatively low positions on various critical dimensions.

The disillusionment of the peasantry is also due to the fact that economically they are undergoing a transformation process over which they have no control. They possess very few of the resources that allow them to participate in political decisions that should benefit them, such as land reform legislation, welfare, employment, education, etc. To put it precisely, the peasants form a subordinate and exploited group in their relations with their urban counterparts.

Peasants in a Stratified Society
In any polity, there is a distinction between the elite and the mass. The elite are those who exercise power while the mass have power exercised over them. According to Lasswell and Kaplan, the power group is usually more highly organized than the subject group, therefore power groups usually have greater power in their hands.[15] The elite also establishes a hierarchy of power relationships between superiors and subordinates; it establishes an order which assigns a specific and recognized place to each of the conflicting groups. Yet in the final analysis, all members of society must accept the rationale for their place in the power hierarchy and have a stake in the manner of power distribution.[16] However, in many instances, some members of the mass seek a greater voice in the making of decisions and a larger share of the values generated by the system, values which are accessible only through the greater exercise of power. In short, access to societal values is dependent on the exercise of power. A conflict situation arises 'in the desire of rulers to preserve their power and in the demand of the ruled to be heard and considered'.[17]

In colonial and post-colonial societies, peasants find themselves at the bottom of stratified societies because their occupations have been accorded the least value and they have not been given any training to upgrade their positions in society. Most stratification theorists agree that stratification creates conflict over the distribution of economic rewards between the classes: 'social stratification systems function to encourage hostility, suspicion, and distrust among the various segments of a society and thus to limit the possibilities of extensive social integration.'[18]

According to Marx, the exploited victims of society, having developed a group solidarity engendered by suffering and the alienation of their labour, would organize politically to engage in a revolutionary struggle against their oppressors, and liberate themselves and society. In spite of the fact that Marx's sympathies did not lie with the European peasantries, due to the weakness of their organizing capabilities, Marx certainly provided a useful tool in the analysis of conflict within stratified societies. The history of the 20th Century shows that African and other peasantries in China, Cuba, Vietnam, Algeria, Angola, Mozambique, are capable of becoming conscious of their status of exploitation and powerlessness and can become highly receptive to political organization; they can participate in direct political action, aimed at controlling their own destinies and, it is hoped, realize developmental goals within their societies. Peasants need no longer be depicted as a stumbling block to historical progress, nor as an embarrassing residue. Scholars must accept the need to reappraise the peasants' political role in the developmental process. The key issues that need to be investigated, as I see them, are: 1) to what extent have governments of non-industrial nations made decisions that are not beneficial to their peasant citizens? 2) do peasants show a propensity to participatory politics or are they merely passive onlookers in the political arena? 3) are peasants aware of themselves as a group with common interests and aspirations? 4) are they capable of inter-acting and communicating among themselves as a group to realize their interests? 5) what conditions induce peasants to participate in revolution or acquiesce to central governmental directives in a co-operative manner?

In order to make an intelligent study of the issues raised by the peasantry, students in this field should be aware of the different types of peasantries that exist in Africa and the various manners of their politicization.

Politicization of African Peasantries

Peasants the world over have never formed a homogenous group although they share general characteristics of low economic status and exploitation by non-agricultural superstructure. The different forms of their evolution guide the student on the role peasants can play within different national contexts. It is possible to consider three main types of peasantries in Africa:

Type A: A hierarchy of feudal relations of personal superiority and responsibility and subordinate dependence links the local community with the wider polity, as exemplified in the imposition of an indigenous African ruling class on sedentary cultivators in Ankole and Buganda, in present-day Uganda, and the Fulani over the Hausa and numerous other Niger and Benue peoples of Nigeria. Social stratification originally based on ethnic divisions was intensified under colonialism, through a conscious exploitation of the peasantry. European colonialism found peasant production convenient for exploitation and even guaranteed the peasant tenant security of his few acres of land, so long as he continued the effective cultivation of cash crops. This type of peasantry, once their land tenure is secure, develops non-revolutionary propensities in their attitude towards the state. In fact such a peasantry usually withdraws from active politics, and lives up to the image of an inward-looking class incapable of nation-wide political action. Such a peasantry can be indirectly exploited indefinitely as long as they are not removed from their land, but rather the products of their land and labour are extorted from them by the colonial and feudal superstructure.

Type B: Racial colonialism virtually transformed large nations of African populations into an exploited peasantry, while European settlers expropriated the Africans' land and forced the Africans to operate both as tenant farmers and grossly exploited rural proletariats. This form of development is typified by Algeria, Kenya, Mozambique, Angola, Zimbabwe, and South Africa. Here the class distinctions are clearly delineated by the racial complexion of the issue and the brutality of the manner of exploitation. The response of the national peasantry in Mozambique and Angola was to develop a tradition of resistance, right from the earliest times of colonialism, which culminated in the peasant-based nation-wide revolution leading to victory and independence of these countries. But this manner of exploitation of the peasantry which led to revolution also led to the creation of a new super-structure for national development. The new system grants political power to the peasants.

Type C: Instances abound in Africa where colonialism forced African cultivators to participate in the market economy through the rapid growth of the export and import trade with the metropolitan power. This was done without necessarily alienating the land from the primary producers, either by an indigenous ruling class or by Europeans. In order to convert the self-contained African economy to an appendage of the world market system, traditional authorities were given the role of keeping law and order and periodically engaging in other activities such as road-making, education and agriculture to provide the required infrastructure for better exploitation of natural resources for the benefit of the metropolitan economy.

Under this system, the peasants became politicized as a result of the heavy tax burden required to maintain the administrative superstructure — the Native Administration system, which allowed chiefs to corruptly acquire wealth far in excess of the finances available to the peasantry. Here again peasants reacted violently, though sporadically, to colonialism, and their targets were usually chiefs' property because chiefs were the agents of the colonialism that was responsible for the misery of the peasants.

The Impact of Capitalism on the Peasantry

Modernity is usually identified with the world-wide diffusion of a particular cultural system, capitalism, which has characteristic features alien to the areas which it engulfs. The key tenets of the capitalist ideology are that land, labour, and wealth are valued as commodities for sale, not for use. Under capitalism the value of human beings also lies in the market value of their labour.

Peasant societies, as created and crystallized by capitalism, have become communities in disarray; they have not unlearned the traditional culture which accompanies subsistence economy, nor are they learning the new market culture which accompanies money, commerce, machinery and literacy. The advent of capitalism also dislocated past social equilibrium. By transforming people into primarily economic actors, it disregards past social commitments to their communal environments. Commercialization of land under colonialism usually barred the peasant from claiming unclaimed public land; it threatened access to pasture, forest, and ploughland. The most traumatic experiences were outright seizures of land by foreign colonialists, which drove the peasants to concentrate and over-exploit the insufficient remaining land, thus making the peasant economy non-productive. Dispossessed peasants also became proletarianized, forced to migrate to urban mining centres, before being fully equipped with technological skills and values. They become alienated from their society and their work. Such a stratum of society cannot be motivated to work to achieve developmental goals. African peasant societies have become incapable of progressing further into a 'machine-using society of built-in growth and new cultural achievement'.[19] Due to their persistent exploitation, African peasant societies have been left stagnant and under-developed; with the resultant poverty, ignorance and disease, these communities have lost their capacity for self-renovation.

The Impact of a Petroleum-Centred Economy on the Peasantry

An oil-rich nation, such as Nigeria, gets a false sense of wealth from petro-dollars. The availability of ready foreign exchange opens up great opportunities for rapid industrialization, but usually this is done without a firmly developed labour base. Peasants abandon their farms for industrial centres without having been inculcated with a technological culture. The industrial centres can only use these untrained persons at the lowest rungs of their enterprises, while for technical and sophisticated work, foreigners of all ranks are brought in to control the decision-points of the national industries. Within the petroleum economy, foreign experts orient their decisions to favour their own national interest.

The nation loses on two fronts: 1) The peasants have left the farms, thus forcing a predominantly rural nation to import food. This is a great embarrassment to the national image, for a nation which refuses to feed itself must accept drastic dietary changes imposed by the other nations which care to dispose of their surpluses on our behalf. Most of our urban peasants cannot afford such dietary changes; coupled with the high cost of domestic food, the nation is faced with malnutrition and other common ailments of poverty in an oil-rich economy. 2) Reliance on petro-dollars as the primary source of national funds is unhealthy for the stability of the national economy. Most monies must come from capitalist Euro-American nations who are quite capable of switching their sources of petroleum supplies, leaving our economy to stagger to a halt.

An oil-rich peasant nation should adopt a phase-by-phase plan on the disbursement of petro-dollars: 1) the peasant economy must first be stimulated for higher productivity; 2) agro-based industries should be introduced; 3) the surplus labour force can then be retrained for technological positions in indigenous industrial enterprises; 4) indigenous personnel should control national heavy industries.

Overall, the amount of petroleum exploited should be limited to the nation's capacity to make rational use of its resources at each phase.

Education for Development

In order for the peasantry of any nation to have a decisive impact on national politics, it must attract the sympathy of friendly intellectuals. However, in the specifically African experience, most of the intellectuals who challenged colonialism and the traditional exploiting rural notables turned out to be primarily interested in their own 'elitist and entrepreneurial aggrandisement under the guise of nationalism and refused to integrate themselves with the peasant masses, preferring instead to demobilize the latter with ethnic and racial sloganeering.'[20] This resulted in false decolonization, so that in most of independent Africa there is a clear break between the nationalist parties and the intellectuals, on the one hand, and the peasantries on the other.

The rising class of intellectuals must be taught to understand the reasons for the abject condition of their national peasantries; how capitalist market conditions have hampered the growth of peasant productivity and incomes, which have in turn hampered the expansion of the internal market. The existing political-economic framework of neo-colonialism undermines, rather than enhances, the potentialities of the economy. In the opinion of Arrighi and Saul, mere disengagement from international capitalism is not a sufficient condition for development. The elite themselves must change from being a 'labour aristocracy' receiving a colonial salary and thus creating a huge gap between the salary of the elite and sub-elites in bureaucratic employment and the mass of the peasants and wage workers. The labour aristocracy with its exceptionally high wages and salaries, consumes most of the surplus produced in the money economy, but their consumption is not related to the products of the traditional economy.[21] The labour aristocracy uses its considerable political power to continue to appropriate for itself all the amenities produced under the state-controlled modern sector of the economy.

University students must be made conscious of the implications of high salaries for long-term development. They must be taught that, instead of the surplus being consumed by the labour aristocracy, it could be used for productive investment, which 'must be directed toward the creation of development stimuli in the traditional sector'.[22] Students must be educated to realize that there still exists among the peasants of tropical Africa surplus land and surplus labour-time which, with the right incentives, can be induced to higher productivity. If peasant production were properly organized into larger units, such as co-operation, collectives, or communes, then the new level of production could also be rationally absorbed into the national economy.

Most African states have already missed the opportunity of a revolutionary change in their power base. With overt colonialism gone and military governments preventing participatory politics for thirteen years in Nigeria, for example, it becomes difficult to arouse the populace to topple the bourgeois superstructure which is functioning as the local agency for international capitalism. The next best approach is to educate the new intellectuals about the heavy costs of running stratified, under-developed, neo-colonialist, and neo-capitalist states. Our universities must educate the new intellectuals to understand clearly the correct processes required for sustained development and structural transformation. With respect to political science in particular, university-educated persons must pay particular heed not only to the economic potential of the peasantries but also to their capacity for political organization into an effective opposition against the forces that oppress them. They must be taught that peasants do not necessarily sit back and play the role of the ruled majority or the non-elite, nor should they be mere objects of manipulation by the elite. Peasants are actually capable of participating in decision-making; they can also be educated and mobilized to change the power base in their favour.

The new intellectuals also need to be taught techniques for peasant mobilization through institutions based on traditional practice, such as co-operatives, and how such co-operative practices should be fully analyzed to utilize their organizational and productive capabilities. A communications infrastructure should also be created to permit continuous dialogue between the new intellectuals and the mass of the peasantry.

In the final analysis, the aim of such an intellectual pursuit is to prepare young political science graduates to seek responsible and rational ways of alleviating the poverty, disease and illiteracy prevalent in predominantly peasant societies. These ills have persisted despite the expenditure of large funds by national and international agencies. The new intellectuals must be made to acquire a better understanding of their peasants; national elites should no longer divert funds to promote industrial and commercial growth as the main avenues to economic development. Our new intellectuals must realize that it is the present-day peasant who must be transformed into a modern technologically-orientated citizen.

Nation-building can be carried out successfully only by the full mobilization of all citizens towards the realization of rational goals. All the aspirations of a nation should be in the form of a clearly stated series of policy goals which must be seen to be beneficial to all in order to attract the willing participation of all citizens in plan fulfilment.

Notes

1. Cited in Henry S. Wilson (ed.), *Origins of West African Nationalism* (London, Macmillan, 1969), p. 250.
2. Ibid., p. 249.
3. See 'Casely-Hayford's Synthesis' in H.S. Wilson (ed.), op. cit., pp. 366-7.
4. Ibid., p. 377.
5. S.N. Eisenstadt, *Modernization: Protest and Change* (Englewood Cliffs, N.J., Prentice-Hall, 1966), p. 122.
6. Ibid., p. 111.
7. W. Rodney, *How Europe Underdeveloped Africa* (Washington, D.C., Howard U.P., 1974), pp. 239-40.
8. Ibid., p. 241.
9. J.K. Nyerere, *Freedom and Socialism* (London, Oxford University Press, 1968), p. 273.
10. Ibid., p. 273.

11. Ibid., pp. 276-7.
12. W. Rodney, op. cit., p. 270.
13. Charles Wagley 'The Peasant' in J.J. Johnson (ed.), *Continuity and Change in Latin America* (Stanford University Press, 1964), pp. 21, 23.
14. Teodor Shanin, 'The Peasantry as a Political Factor', *Sociological Review*, Vol. 14, March 1966, p. 13.
15. H.D. Lasswell and A. Kaplan, *Power and Society* (New Haven, Yale University Press, 1950), p. 201.
16. Ibid., p. 205.
17. Fred W. Riggs, 'Dialectics of Developmental Conflict' in Jackson and Stein (ed.), *Issues in Comparative Politics* (London, Macmillan, 1971), p. 97.
18. M.M. Tumin, 'Some Principles of Stratification: A Critical Analysis' in R. Bendix and S.M. Lipset (ed.), *Class, Status and Power* (New York, The Free Press, 1966), p. 58.
19. G. Dalton, 'The Development of Subsistence and Peasant Economies in Africa', North-Western University Program of African Studies, Reprint Series No. 6, p. 8.
20. J.S. Saul, 'African Peasantries and Revolutionary Change' in J. Spielbery and S. Whiteford (eds.), *Forging Nations: A Comparative View of Rural Ferment and Revolt* (Michigan State U.P., 1976), p. 105.
21. G. Arrighi and J.S. Saul, 'Socialism and Economic Development in Tropical Africa' in Arrighi and Saul (eds.), *Essays on the Political Economy of Africa* (New York, Monthly Review Press, 1973), pp. 19-21.
22. Ibid., p. 21.

5. Class Interests in the Teaching of Political Science in African Universities

Wang Metuge

The goal of this essay is two-fold. First, it argues that there is class struggle in African academia. This class struggle manifests itself in three related ways namely 1) through the ideological persuasions of the intellectuals, especially university lecturers; 2) through the types of courses (especially their content) taught in the universities; 3) through the scientific methodologies employed in understanding and explaining social problems. Second, it intends to show that political science as a discipline in Africa has so far been an instrument of class domination. This again has been made possible by the scientific methodologies we have employed in understanding and explaining African problems, and by the types and content of the courses we teach.

Academics as Class Strugglers

University lecturers are intellectual workers. They all sell their labour power, in the form of scientific knowledge, for salaries. To this extent they are members of the same class. Now, the question may be asked: how is it possible to talk about class struggle between and among members of the same class? After all, the argument can be made that class struggle exists only between different classes, and not between members of the same class. On the surface, this question is valid, and the argument correct.

But we would like to note that a person may objectively be a member of a class but subjectively belong to a different class by virtue of his or her aspirations and ideological consciousness and persuasion. We will return to this point later. Suffice it for now to say that a person may be conscious of his or her class position, and yet aspire to the virtues of a different class or work for the interest of another class.

We have stated that one of the ways class struggle in academia exhibits itself in African universities is through the ideological persuasion of the lecturers. In these terms, we can identify four categories of lecturers.

First, there are those who are conscious of their ideological position but conceal it. Instead, they accuse others of being ideological in their work and couch this accusation in terms that make it sound as if having any ideology is criminal in itself. But we know that what is criminal is not that one upholds an ideology. In Africa, however, what is definitely criminal is to adhere to and defend an ideology which maintains and perpetuates the domination and exploitation of the many by a minute few. This is even more so if the individual is a university teacher. The vast majority of the lecturers in our universities are of this type. A few among them are honest enough to admit what their ideological preferences are.

Second, there are those who, though they have a particular ideological inclination, are not conscious of it. This group of lecturers refer to themselves as academics, and hold high the banner of professionalism. They abhor what they see as value judgment and emphasize the value of objectivity in our scientific endeavours. It is difficult for them to see that objectivity is real only in subjectivity. They will emphasize that, as academics,[1] we should see things from all angles. But in reality, they know only one method of looking at things, and do not care to understand the limitations of their tool of analysis, because they already accept it as correct. This group of lecturers is also large in our universities.

Third, there is the group, small in number, but fast increasing, and very vocal, which in actuality has one ideological persuasion but outwardly professes to belong to a different ideological group entirely. It is only a very careful reading of what they write and a thorough analysis of what they say that can reveal to us which ideological group they actually belong to.

The fourth group, also very small in number, constitutes those intellectuals in our universities who are conscious of their ideological orientation, uphold it, and are not ashamed to proclaim it. They manifest their position not only by what they say but, more importantly, by the way they conduct their scientific endeavours.

So, African intellectuals can be divided between those who have an ideology and are conscious of it, but refuse to admit it to others; those who have an ideology but are not conscious of it; those who are conscious of their ideological persuasion, but profess publicly to be something else; and finally, those who are conscious of their ideological orientation, and honestly uphold it privately and publicly, especially so in their work.

But how can we tell that a particular lecturer has an ideological orientation? And if we can tell, how do we know which is his or her ideological persuasion? We can determine this in two related ways; 1) by the scientific methodology employed in understanding and explaining social phenomena and 2) by the kinds of theories constructed and used as guides for enquiry and for social action.

Bourgeois vs. Non-Bourgeois Methodologists

Let us briefly examine these two related phenomena. First, the question of methodology. In social sciences in Africa today, one can delineate two major methodological schools. On the one hand we have the bourgeois methodologists and, on the other, the non-bourgeois methodologists.[2] The bourgeois social scientists employ traditionalism, structural-functionalism and behaviouralism in their methods of analysis and interpretation of phenomena. These three methods of analysis have developed over the years in the order of their scientific refinement. Accordingly, structural-functionalism is a more powerful tool of analysis than traditionalism. In like manner, behaviouralism is seen as more powerful than structural-functionalism. This phenomenon is perhaps due to the assertion of positivism and empiricism in bourgeois social science. To achieve objectivity and precision, phenomena must be quantified.

In Africa, it is the economists, more than other social scientists, who have taken a lead in this direction. It is fashionable to find almost every article in, for example, the *Journal of the Economic Society of Nigeria* today filled with sophisticated linear equations. This is the only way, it would appear, that the papers can claim scientific credibility. And, as a matter of fact, econometricians and statisticians dominate most of our departments of economics today.

In countries like the U.S.A., where bourgeois political science can be said to be most advanced, the behaviouralists dominate most major political science departments.[3] New books and courses on politimetrics are written and introduced with increasing regularity. There is fast developing what can be called the mechanization of the science of politics.

This trend has not yet gathered momentum in African universities because most of the political scientists are either traditionalists or structural-functionalists. But it is safe to assume that, since in bourgeois political science behaviouralism is an improvement upon traditionalism and structural-functionalism, behaviouralism will increasingly assert itself in African political science, and will eventually dominate.

Each scientific methodology breeds its own theory, and the theory in turn determines the methodology to be employed. Theory and methodology build on and refine each other. It is not an accident, therefore, that modernization theory, social order and stability theory, institution-building theory, and achievement-motivation theory have all emerged from bourgeois political science.

The non-bourgeois social scientists employ dialectical materialism as a method of analysing and understanding phenomena. Out of this method has emerged the political economy method of analysis and class analysis. This methodology has generated such theories as dependency theory, the theory of unequal exchange and unequal development, and centre-periphery theory, to explain problems of development in Third World countries generally, and Africa in particular.[4]

Combat in the Theoretical Zone

We have stated that every methodology breeds its own theories and every theory breeds its own methodology. Perhaps this point can be made clearer if we briefly state the three powers of a theory. Put differently, the importance and/or relevance of a theory can be judged by examining the three elements of its power namely 1) the ability of the theory to identify the fundamental and non-fundamental problems and help our understanding of the nature of these problems. Such are the *explanatory and analytic* powers of a theory; 2) the ability of the theory to provide the correct solutions to problems, and its ability to guide us in our endeavour to change reality or to perpetuate it, depending on what our interest is. We call this its *prescriptive* power. And 3) the ability of the theory to project the future. This is its *predictive* power.

Accordingly, therefore, what we teach and how it is taught; what is emphasized and what is not emphasized; which problems are identified as salient and which are not; the kinds of questions raised, and the answers put forward — all these depend on the methodologies we employ in our scientific work and the theories we use. The theories we build, support and use are a function of our ideological orientation.

Perhaps the best way to explain this point is to look at the objective situation in Africa today. We may ask, what is the nature of African society today? What are the fundamental problems of our societies? What are the strategies and tactics to overcome them?

The objective situation in Africa today can be briefly stated as follows: 1) Africa is a class society. The vast majority of the people in Africa are producers of commodities either by selling their labour power in industry, commerce, plantations and the household in return for meagre wages, or by cultivating small family holdings. These people are doubly exploited and dominated.[5] A small percentage of Africans live by selling their brain power in universities, and the bureaucracy in return for high salaries, or by engaging in commercial and industrial activities, more often than not in partnership with foreign monopoly capital or as its agents.[6] This small group participates in exploiting and dominating the rest of the Africans.[7] 2) Most African societies are peripheral capitalist societies. In other words, they are neo-colonies. 3) While Africa is endowed with vast material and human resources, tapped and untapped, the vast majority of Africans are poor. Africa is therefore suffering from a crisis of mass poverty. How African intellectuals view this objective situation reveals their ideological persuasions.

In all class societies, politics is essentially a struggle between classes for control of resources and for the domination of one class over the others. The study and teaching of political science therefore invariably involves any one or all of the following: 1) an understanding of the nature of class domination and exploitation; 2) ways of perpetuating and consolidating class domination and exploitation; 3) ways of destroying class society and abolishing class domination and exploitation. It is in this context that we can best understand the nature of class struggle in academia in Africa today.

Earlier in this essay we mentioned four categories of university teachers of political science — we also stated that a person may be conscious of his or her class position and yet aspire to the virtues of a different class or work for the interest of another class. Our categorization of African political scientists and other university lecturers revealed that there are those who are conscious of their ideological persuasion but deny this fact, only to accuse others of being ideological. This group of lecturers employs bourgeois methodology in their research and teaching. They are not interested in changing the status quo, at best they will reform it. As intellectuals, they are not really professionals, because they are also willing to engage in private practice — build houses for rent, own a farm with hired labour, etc. — if this is not disallowed; and they will jump out of the university if they are offered a directorship in a company or appointed to high public office. In other words, although these intellectuals are lecturers, in actual fact by aspiration they are subjectively members of the bourgeois class. Their interest rests in maintaining the existing system and they employ their scientific knowledge to justify and perpetuate it. They are what Oyovbaire has called system legitimizers.[8] Their concern as lecturers is not how to change the existing order, but how to make it work.

Those who are not conscious of their ideology, even though they have one, are the professional lecturers. Some of them question some aspects of the existing order; others do not. In either case, they are not concerned about changing our present state of affairs. Their major concern is to rise within the profession, ultimately to become professors. They work hard, and do a lot of research. How much the research contributes to the general good of the society is secondary because, as professionals, their work must be 'value free'. The primary aim for doing research is to enhance their chances of rising up in the professional hierarchy. In extreme cases, they engage in what Temu calls academic fetishism.[9] Since their goal is to enhance their professional interest within the existing order, they will do nothing to that order that would jeopardize their primary interest. The end result is that, careerists that they are, their work legitimizes the system as it is. Because of the methodologies they use in their teaching and research, and because of the theories they construct and use in understanding phenomena, and because of their status quo predispositions, this group of lecturers, too, even though they are intellectual workers, can be said to have the mentality of the bourgeoisie.

The group that publicly professes one ideology but in actuality has a different ideological orientation can best be identified not only by the scientific tools of analysis they use, but also by the policy recommendations they make from the research they do. More often than not, these recommendations contradict the theoretical formulations in their research and the data at hand. Such contradictions are explained away by these intellectuals in this manner: 'our problems are caused by the nature of the existing system; we cannot change the system now, so we must be able to correct things as best we can within it.' At best these recommendations are reformist, at worst, cynically populist. These intellectuals claim to be socialists, but they know little or nothing about dialectics, because they have never read about it. Those of them who have read about it have not bothered to understand it. The few among them who have bothered to read and understand dialectical materialism do not employ it in their research because they are afraid of its powers as a theory and as a methodology. To be convinced of these powers will mean to deny their real interests. So they fall back on what they know best and what suits their interest most — bourgeois theory and bourgeois methodology.

The best among them reveal a moral indignation about some manifestations of the system — corruption, inefficiency, etc. The worst and more 'radical' among them condemn the system solely because this condemnation breeds popularity for them in some quarters. They all talk about the masses, their poverty, illiteracy and other problems of the underprivileged, and recommend better houses, higher wages, etc., for the masses. How these measures in themselves will save the masses from exploitation and domination is not important, or better still, cannot be ascertained, because these intellectuals are neither scientifically equipped to tackle this fundamental problem, nor are they interested in changing the system itself. This group can be further divided into two sub-categories. Some among them are academic professionals, others are bourgeois aspirants: they are all passengers in the academic field. In the main, they are intellectual opportunists.

The last group of intellectuals, namely, those who have an ideological persuasion, are conscious of it and do not hide it, is also the smallest in number. These are the dialectical materialists, both by scientific commitment and by philosophical disposition. They are interested in changing the existing order, not merely on moral grounds, but because this is consistent with the logic of progress. This is why Oyovbaire calls them the subversives.[10] In reality, they are revolutionary intellectuals. They are concerned with distinguishing appearances from realities; symptoms from disease, and forms from substance. This is why their major concern with the masses is not about their poverty, but about their exploitation and domination. They are accused by their bourgeois colleagues of being rhetorical and ideological, forgetting that bourgeois science gave rise to bourgeois ideology in the same way that dialectical materialism gave rise to the ideology of the proletariat, and that each ideology in turn serves its own science. The revolutionary intellectuals try to see things in a broad perspective, in terms of their inter-relations and totality.[11] They have mastered bourgeois science, because most of them were trained and educated in the bourgeois tradition, either in advanced capitalist countries or in Africa. But they have gone beyond that. They have also mastered and continue to master the science of dialectical materialism.

Such is the nature of class struggle and ideological divisions in academia in African universities today. It is the struggle between bourgeois intellectuals and revolutionary intellectuals. Which theories are built, used and supported, and which are not; what scientific methodologies are employed in social inquiry and which are not — all this depends on the ideological persuasion of the individual scholars in the social sciences. The bourgeois intellectuals are interested not in changing the reality of Africa today but in how to perpetuate it. And they employ scientific methodologies and utilize theories which muddle our understanding of the African reality. They are interested in perpetuating the neo-colonial character of African societies. In other words, they are interested in consolidating class domination and exploitation in Africa; and they employ their scientific energies to muddle our understanding of the very existence and nature of the dependent character of African societies. To achieve their goal, bourgeois African political scientists have turned political science into an instrument of class domination and exploitation.

The revolutionary intellectuals, on the other hand, are concerned about changing the dependent character of Africa, about abolishing class domination and exploitation in Africa. To this end, they employ scientific methodologies and utilize theories that clarify the nature of exploitation and domination in Africa, the nature of our dependence and its origins. The revolutionary African political scientist is concerned with how to turn political science into an instrument for the abolition of class domination and exploitation in Africa.

The intensity and nature of this class struggle and these ideological divisions among African social scientists vary from university to university, and from department to department. The direction they take within a particular department depends on three factors, namely, the predispositions of the heads of department in terms of whom they employ and whom they do not; what types of courses they encourage and discourage; the ideological orientation of staff and the tradition in the faculty and the university.

In conclusion, let us try to answer the question: what should be the concern of political science in Africa? The answer depends on what type of Africa we want. We cannot over-emphasize the nature and character of African countries today, namely that they are all neo-colonies; they are class societies and all of them, without exception, are suffering from a crisis of mass poverty.

If, therefore, our interests are to keep our countries as neo-colonies and to perpetuate the existing class exploitation and domination, then we should teach and encourage bourgeois political science. If, on the other hand, we want to change African countries from neo-colonies to independent and self-reliant nations, if we want to abolish class domination and exploitation in Africa, then we cannot teach bourgeois political science because its poverty in helping us to change reality has been amply demonstrated both theoretically and empirically.[12] To change the reality of Africa as it is today, we must employ the science of dialectical materialism in our teaching of political science. But whether we can do this or not depends on whether the bourgeois intellectuals persist in their ideological persuasions, whether or not they continue to dominate and control our political science departments. In short, it depends on the direction, and outcome, of the class struggle in academia, in our universities in general and in political science departments in particular.

Notes

1. See A.J. Temu, 'The Cult of Facts and Fetishism in Professional African History', presented at the Postgraduate Research Seminar, Department of History, Ahmadu Bello University, Zaria, 18 November 1978.
2. For an extensive discussion of the history of social thought see G.P. Frantsov, *Philosophy and Sociology* (Moscow, Progress Publishers, 1975), especially sections 1 and 2.
3. For a lucid analysis of the explosion of behaviouralism in the U.S.A., see Heinz Eulau, *The Behavioral Persuation in Politics* (New York, Random House, 1967).
4. See for example, Samir Amin, *Unequal Development: An Essay on the Social Formations of Peripheral Capitalism* (Harvester Press, 1976).
5. See Claude Ake, *Revolutionary Pressures in Africa*, (London, Zed Press, 1978).
6. Ibid.
7. For discussion on the relationship between the different classes in Africa, see my paper 'Democracy in Peripheral Capitalist Societies: The African Case' in S. Egite Oyovbaire (ed.), *Democracy in Nigeria: Past Present and Future*, Proceedings of the 5th Annual Conference of the Nigerian Political Science Association, Zaria.
8. S. Egite Oyovbaire, 'The Responsibility of Political Science in Nigeria', paper presented at the 6th Annual Conference of the Nigerian Political Science Association, University of Benin, 26-30 March 1979.
9. Temu, op. cit.
10. Oyovbaire, op. cit.
11. For a thorough discussion of the science of dialectics see Joseph Stalin, *Dialectical and Historical Materialism* (New York, International Publishers, 1972) and Mao Tse-Tung, *Four Essays on Philosophy* (Peking, Foreign Languages Press, 1966) and Frantsov, op. cit.
12. See for example, Y.R. Barongo, 'Understanding African Politics', unpublished manuscript, 1977; P.C.W. Gutkind and P. Wallerstein (eds.), *The Political Economy of Contemporary Africa* (London and California, Sage Publications, 1976).

6. Towards a Development Orientated Political Science Curriculum

Olatunde J.B. Ojo

For decades the curriculum, the teaching and the research in the discipline of political science in Tropical African universities have, like most other aspects of life, unquestioningly followed the Western pattern. The colonial tutelage and heritage may be factors in this phenomenon. Continuing dependence on the West for the planning and development of the discipline, defined as 'intellectual enterprises', and of the profession, defined in terms of 'the trained and expert scholars who participate in the discipline',[1] might be another factor. But in recent years the rumblings of a convulsion in the discipline and in the profession have been felt in many parts of Africa.[2] While still too inchoate to describe in detail, the essence of the convulsion seems to be, first, a deep dissatisfaction with the failure of the professionals to articulate and play 'worthy' roles as advisers, social critics, and social engineers in the gigantic task of development and modernization of Africa. Secondly, there is a dissatisfaction with political research and teaching, especially of the kind labelled 'bourgeois scholarship' which purportedly perpetuates the grip of the 'colonial' and Western ethnocentric and teleological moorings on the search for reliable understanding of African politics. Thirdly, there is a dissatisfaction with the scant attention being paid to assessing the adequacy of our undergraduate curriculum or the extent of bureaucratism in the universities in terms of the possibility of making political science (or any discipline) relevant and action-orientated for achieving societal goals. The initial impulses of this convulsion have begun to affect the organization and curriculum of the social sciences in general, and political science in particular, in our universities.

This paper assesses the salient features of the convulsion and relates them to the search at one institution, the University of Port Harcourt in Nigeria, for an answer as to how undergraduate curricula can be made effective and relevant not only in the developmental and modernization goals of society but also in the development and commitment of the discipline and profession of political science.

The New Orthodoxy

Several factors account for the disillusionment with the curriculum and the teaching of political science in African universities and with the role of the discipline and the profession in the African development process.

First, there is the widening gap between the developed and developing countries and the even wider gap emerging between the more fortunate developing countries and the less fortunate ones. There is also the increasing alienation of the elite from the masses, between the urban bourgeoisie and proletariat on the one hand, and the rural peasantry on the other, occasionally erupting in peasant revolts. Then there is the instability of politics and, particularly in Nigeria, the uncontrollable waves of armed robbery, occasioned by domestic socio-economic and legal inequalities, all of which tend to exacerbate social conflict and deepen fears about the future of the country, the continent and indeed the world. These are continuing conditions which political science has been unable to explain and ethically justify.

Second, there is the reality of continuing African economic dependence on the West, despite formal political independence, the exploitation and denuding of the continent in the interests of foreign multinational corporations and capitalist economies, and the alarming overt and covert Western intervention in the internal affairs of the African. In the face of a human situation such as this, the legitimacy of raising doubts about the adequacy and relevance of political science in the contemporary world of African penury and continuing underdevelopment is quite understandable.

Finally, there is the agonizing individual and corporate self-doubt over the inability of political science graduates and professional political scientists to offer solutions to immediate developmental problems. At the very best, political scientists have provided little more than what Houghton called 'footnoted rationalization and huckstering' for poorly conceived and dangerous policies and strategies.[3] At worst, they have proved irrelevant to 'practical problems of administration' and 'the practical challenges of urgent development needs of a state in a hurry', to borrow the words of Governor Esuene in describing Professor Essien-Udom's contributions to the administration of Nigeria's Cross River State.[4] No wonder then that politicians, bureaucrats and business leaders have had misgivings about employing political science graduates and often urge students 'to study more useful things than political science'.[5]

It is, then, the groping for an answer as to how and why African and Africanist political scientists have proved so ineffectual in tackling these issues that has led to the rumblings of the as-yet inchoate convulsion in the discipline and the profession. The agonizing questions being raised are not new in the history of the discipline nor are they peculiar to Africa. In the late 1950s Neal Houghton and David Easton[6] articulated similar questions with respect to political science and the American polity and such questions are more especially pressing in the wake of what has since become known as 'post-behavioural' political science. Basically the issues involved merely reflect the old, inconclusive debate on the merits of slow-moving basic research *versus* applied research, and of normative (value) theory *versus* empirical theory. Like their professional predecessors elsewhere who raised similar concerns, the African political scientists are calling for political scientists and philosophers to 'reconstruct our value frameworks' and 'test them by creatively contemplating new kinds of political systems that might better meet the needs of a developing society'. They are pleading for a new world view that will enable the discipline and the profession to 'prescribe and to act so as to improve political life according to humane criteria', instead of becoming robot apologists and intellectual legitimizers of moribund policies, or technicians and mechanics tinkering with society rather than changing it.[7]

Specifically, the African political scientists of this genre call for three things. Together, I call them the 'new orthodoxy'.[8] First is the urgent 'decolonization' of both the curriculum and the teaching of political science in order to make it more relevant to the developmental needs of Africa. Excessive reliance on Western 'colonial' political science, it is argued, has distracted us from the significant questions about the operation of the African political systems. Hitherto the discipline has paid exclusive attention to 'such superstructural and epiphenomenal aspects like party systems, ethnic conflict, public administration and foreign policy' in line with prevailing Western capitalist orthodoxies which serve the status quo and distract the political scientist from his or her role as social critic. One such capitalist orthodoxy, structural-functional analysis, is signally an anathema because, as Richard Sklar is quoted with approval, it is 'not normally associated with social criticism and poses little threat of exposure to those who control the institutions of national power'. The other Western capitalist orthodoxy, the 'assumption of pluralist politics with its need to build consensus for national integration' (the so-called 'melting pot' thesis) is rejected because of its tendency to overlook the conflictual nature of politics.[9] The task of the 'new' orthodoxy is to change the status quo and to help the discipline reach out to the real needs of Africa to be independent of capitalist exploiters and to be self-reliant.

The tenor of this call for decolonization of the curriculum and the teaching of political science in Africa is nothing short of a call for an African Political Science.

The second strand of the new orthodoxy is a concomitant of the first but much more far-reaching. It calls for an awareness of the value premises — and ideology — which can wrest African society from dependence and decay. It is argued that we have learnt more about the operations of non-African political systems than about our own. And what we have learnt of both is all within a value framework that accepts the ongoing practices as basically satisfactory, subject only to the need for incremental improvements. The discipline has been incapable of escaping a commitment to others' political and value systems with the result that we have been unable to ask the right questions for discovering the basic class political behaviour which makes Africa a perpetual capitalist satellite and depicting the perverse and derivative nature of the African modernization process.

The new orthodoxy enjoins us to 'embrace and urge socialism as the only viable ideology for Africa'[10] not simply because it is progressive, moral and humane but because it alone can lead to real independence, self-reliance and the avoidance of internal and external exploitation. And, having embraced this ideology, the discipline and the profession are duty-bound to let it permeate and colour the curriculum, teaching and research.

The third aspect of the new orthodoxy, which is regarded as 'a step towards the decolonization of the study of African politics', is the call on African political scientists 'to study their own societies more than they study others', not only because it is desirable from the nationalist point of view but also because it will 'counteract the ethnocentric and teleological bias in the studies of African politics conducted by non-Africans'.[11]

In this paper I shall argue that one can recognize and accept the need for change and explore the best ways of revamping our curriculum and making our discipline relevant to African needs without going so far as to embrace these new orthodoxies which may be self-defeating at best or downright dangerous at worst.

Dangers of the New Orthodoxy

We should be sceptical of any explicit or implicit line that there is an African political science, one that is *sui generis*, simply because it is decolonized. Emotionalism and morale-building rationalizations have their place in human affairs but they are not the stuff on which objective scholarship is well nurtured. I am not aware that there is, or can be, an African political science that differs in scope, content, methodology, etc., from, say, Western, Eastern or Asian political science. The discipline, like other sciences, seeks the universalist dimension of phenomena, in this case, human political behaviour. No doubt it has been plagued by a number of weaknesses but it is also an evolving discipline and it requires no profound wisdom to conceive that its evolution would profoundly affect the profession and political life across the globe. Only on the assumption that 'Western' political science has exhausted all possibilities, has said the last word about methodological and epistemological questions, research design and value premises, could one begin to wonder if the time had not come for a separate discipline called African Political Science. In fact, however, the discipline throughout its history has been persistently concerned with the reconceptualization of significant variables, with the continuing search for adequate units of analysis, with the exploration of alternative theories and models of the operation of various types of systems and with basic normative and methodological assumptions and presuppositions, as well as technical requirements.[12]

True, Western political scientists may have been more hesitant than others in questioning the favoured normative premises of the discipline and examining the extent to which these premises determine the selection of problems, especially African problems, and their ultimate interpretations. But, as Easton points out, this is a matter of the narrow vision of the discipline[13] which Africans, Asians and anybody else need not accept. In fact Western political scientists have themselves questioned this narrow vision and offered new vistas which African political scientists have adumbrated and now wish to expropriate as 'distinctive' African political science somewhat in the same way we claim such phenomena as witchcraft as 'distinctive' African science![14]

This leads to my discomfiture about the second aspect of the new orthodoxy — 'socialism as the only viable ideology for Africa'. The evils of capitalism are well known and so are the dangers of the continuing dependence of African economies on capitalist multinationals and their states. But the capitalists and multinationals are unlikely to be safely pushed around, certainly not by socialist slogans and name-calling, as Nkrumah's Ghana was to learn.[15] On the contrary they are likely to do a great deal of pushing of their own, especially where there is a dearth of African technicians both in number and quality to make total and immediate socialism an economic proposition.[16] This caution, however, need not prevent us from re-examining the whole shimmery neo-capitalist fabric of our political and social life. Indeed we are duty-bound to formulate and construct radically different speculative alternatives in order to enable us to understand the shortcomings of our societies and explore avenues of changing them.[17] But this is a far cry from concocting and selling socialist remedies as the only answer, however pleasing, desirable or logically deducible from Marxist analysis they may initially appear. Scholarship is one thing; indoctrination is another. Jinadu's scholarship is not in question. But I know of none of his many serious works, nor indeed any definitive study by anyone else, which inexorably points to socialism as the only ethical or the quickest solution to African developmental problems.

There are of course warnings from respectable intellectual sources including Jinadu that Africa stands condemned to a life of penury and violence if the capitalist mode of development and the cozy transnational relations between African and foreign elites persist; if economic independence is not immediately extracted and if socialism is not adopted. But these warnings are not without qualifications. It has been asserted, for instance, that Africa's great powers, the 'sub-imperial' states within the capitalist system — Nigeria, Ivory Coast, Egypt, Kenya, Zaire and Zambia — do possess, at least in association with their external capitalist associates, 'a capacity for bringing order if not development to the continent, especially if a *de facto* division into spheres of influence is arranged'.[18] Rene Dumont, who has spent a life-time studying the prospects of African development and whose *False Start in Africa* remains a classic, sees corruption and the widening gap between the political elite and the masses as obstacles to socialism. For him a fiscal system that does not kill the initiative of 'native capitalists' but encourages them to invest within the framework of a sound development plan, if combined with state capitalism where necessary and with elimination of 'the tradition of parasitic relatives' which stifles motivation for personal and family success and denudes savings, could equally do the trick.[19] And he cautions against copying Europe in the very 'areas where it is rarely exemplary and is in fact re-examining its premises', such as Western socialism. Instead he urges African states to choose the political and economic institutions most suitable to their needs, having regard to both indigenous and international experience and, once having adopted those institutions, to put in the hard work necessary to pull them out of under-development.[20] 'There is no magical solution, including socialism,' Dumont warns[21] for, as he puts it elsewhere, there are various socialisms or socialist transformations, none of which is necessarily meaningful or feasible for African development.[22]

What all these arguments tell us is that there may be more than one solution to African developmental problems and we do an injustice to ourselves, the discipline and our students if we prematurely close our minds to other possibilities.

It is of course possible that socialism is an ethical solution but political science, by the very limitation of its tools and the fact that it deals with the real world of fallible and perverse human beings, cannot prescribe authoritatively and with certainty ethical goals for society. Is the melting pot ideal any less ethical than socialism which, in conditions of total 'lack of elementary morality — work, honesty and dedication to the country — of a good percentage of political leaders', cannot be achieved at all,[23] or if achieved, can be enforced only at the expense of another ethical ideal, that of freedom and individuality? These issues must be addressed if we are to stem the tendency toward indoctrination in our universities by otherwise sound scholars and if the profession is not to attract, by default, those who would eschew scholarship and teaching — bourgeois or otherwise — for charlatanism, dilettantism and sloganism.

There is the additional danger that scholarship and teaching predicated solely upon change in the total system of the working of society are likely to appear unrealistic and irrelevant. Changes of this magnitude, as Dayal rightly observes in a somewhat different context, are beyond executives, politicians and other practitioners of statecraft and seldom offer solutions for the host of problems that they face in their immediate environment.[24] This is the meaning of Governor Esuene's unflattering 'toast' to Professor Essien-Udom referred to earlier; this is the meaning of the popular if erroneous view of political science as a 'radical and subversive discipline which teaches students how to overthrow governments' or how to create industrial unrest in the hitherto blissful company plants.

The third strand of the new orthodoxy — that African political scientists should concentrate on the study of African societies — represents a shift in our practices only if it means the study of African societies to the exclusion of all others. A casual inspection of political science curricula in Nigerian universities will reveal, at least in recent years, a disproportionate emphasis on Africa that borders on myopia, if not ethnocentrism. Similarly much of the research by African political scientists understandably deals primarily with Africa, giving rise to what Professor Ake calls 'ethnic replicative scholarship' that hardly moves 'the theory and/or the methodology of the discipline to new frontiers'.[25] Yet even this concentration of effort on the study of African politics by African political scientists has not proved a guarantee against ethnocentric and teleological biases. Jinadu has pointed to the accusations and counter-accusations of ethnic and cultural bias by two Nigerian political scientists from two ethnic groups studying Nigerian politics. He rightly concludes that we cannot escape these biases but we can temper them by 'studied detachment' and seeking the 'universalist dimension of political science'.[26] If the universalist dimension is the essence of the discipline, we would be cutting off our noses to spite our faces if we failed to devote a sizeable portion of our resources to the study of other societies in addition to our own.

Care must be taken to avoid the probable if unintended excesses of this new orthodoxy in the teaching and planning of relevant, development-orientated political science in African universities.

Essentials and Dilemmas of 'Relevant' Curricula

To be relevant, the structure and curriculum of political science, indeed of any discipline, must be geared towards identified national needs. In the Nigerian case, a recent Public Service Review Commission identified specific needs and changes in the public sector (which are applicable to the private sector as well and may have validity for other African countries). In its *Main Report*, the Commission identified the major constraint on Nigerian development as 'the lack of skilled and experienced men and women to carry out the tasks at hand'.[27] Throughout the seven volumes of the *Report*, as the Commission's Chairman Chief Udoji put it:

> Constant references were made to the need for equipping public officers with requisite skills that would enable them to function effectively in the achievement of development goals. The one theme that ran consistently through the Report is that if the development goals of the nation are to be achieved, there must be a profound change in the way public services are managed, in the way they undertake their tasks, and in their internal social attitudes and behaviour.[28]

Chief Udoji emphasized the need for a change in the system of management from those previously in use which 'were designed for running a stable, unchanging country' to those 'which can respond to the demands of a rapidly changing and dynamic society'.[29] And the Commission noted that 'training will be the most urgent consideration in accepting and implementing our Report'.[30]

In his analysis of the Report, Professor Harry Green clearly shows the importance the Commission attached to training in all branches and at all levels of the public service.³¹ The Report suggests that universities shift from Public Administration with its emphasis on management by administrative control, which was useful in the days of Nigerianization of administration, to a management education that is development and results-orientated. ³² But while the Commission recognized the role of the universities as 'indispensable', it frowned upon the fact that 'most of the present training is traditional classroom instruction and of a duration that discourages participation by valuable employees', thus by implication criticizing the academic-type instruction that undergraduate and post-graduate students receive.³³ It therefore suggests *inter alia* that training in institutions must be linked with training on the job and curricula must be redesigned to allow for sandwich courses.³⁴

This suggestion no doubt reflects the Commission's major concern with high-level managers, a view supported by the fact that the operational knowledge of modern mnagement techniques — Management by Objectives (MBO), Project Management and Planning, Programming and Budgeting (PPB) — — which it advocated, can only be acquired after full theoretical understanding of the concepts and actual experience in their application.³⁵

But our universities primarily train undergraduates and, if the role of universities is indispensable, then the Commission implies that our undergraduate curricula and the traditional classroom instructions need modifications. Can the universities undertake such modifications to accommodate on-the-job training, given the universities' predisposition to eschew the practical and the applied? Can the universities accommodate training that is less academic in the traditional sense and can they meet the implied need to 'integrate subject matter for learning rather than dividing along disciplinary lines for research purposes, a requirement that calls for different types of staff than is customarily employed'?³⁶ Professor Green raised these questions and came to the conclusion that academic institutions in Nigeria are ill-prepared for what the Commission had in mind.

In general Professor Green's conclusion may be valid. But to the extent that neither the Commission nor anybody else expects undergraduates to be trained for a specific job in a specific organization, public or private, universities can still play a vital role in combining some aspects of the type of training the Commission advocates with traditional academic pursuits. With respect to political science, we would expect at the minimum that the universities would produce candidates who understand the factors and forces at play in a given social situation and are able to apply their analytical and decision-making ability to that situation, candidates who can encourage new ways of looking at things without, as the Commission explicitly rejected, proposing 'to alter the basic organization of the Nigerian Government' or society.³⁷

A happy medium between traditional academic and modern practical curricula — I call these 'development-orientated curricula' — is nevertheless difficult to achieve. It raises, in a different form, dilemmas for the political science discipline similar to those raised by Professor Green for the universities as a whole. In the first place, political science on its own is unable to produce solutions to social problems not only because 'social problems do not come neatly packaged as economic, psychological, political and the like'[38] and therefore call upon the specialized skills of other social scientists, but also because basic knowledge in political science is limited and what little is known is not necessarily applicable to practical issues. Yet political science cannot be merged with, or considered part of, any other social science. It 'has its area of human experience to analyse, its own body of descriptive and factual data to gather, its own conceptual schemes to formulate and test for truth'.[39]

In the second place while, for most students, the Bachelor's degree will be their final qualification excepting in-service training, a few will undertake post-graduate studies. But a development-orientated undergraduate curriculum necessarily takes as its goal the need to produce responsible, politically conscious and skilled citizens. An unavoidable dilemma thus besets a curriculum which must produce this kind of citizen and, at the same time, serve the particular needs of graduates who must go on to higher degrees in the interest of further intellectual growth of humanity and must compare favourably with their counterparts across the globe in terms of their knowledge, competence and intellectual rigour to analyse critically and evaluate literature of the field. A concomitant dilemma is the question whether a political science curriculum could simultaneously combine the abstractly academic aspect of the discipline with the application of what is learnt, assuming the latter is applicable to practical situations.

These issues suggest that we ought to pursue an optimizing strategy which combines specialization in political science with an itegrated, interdisciplinary broad background in the social sciences, coupled ideally with attachment periods when the student learns about a particular social institution or organization and appreciates its problems. With the co-operation and assistance of the management of the organization or institution, a problem area would be defined for the student who researches into it and writes up his or her findings with specific solutions.

The University of Port Harcourt Experience

Perhaps out of concern for a curriculum that is development-orientated, the Vice-Chancellor of the University of Port Harcourt stimulated a lively discussion when he produced a working paper for the organization of academic programmes at the university. He had suggested that the university be organized in schools and one of them, the School of Social Sciences, should aim at training not so much economists, sociologists, political scientists, etc., but social scientists as such, though each student should be allowed some measure of specialization in a specific discipline as his or her interests required. It was generally believed that this kind of arrangement would lead to a curriculum, and the production of graduates, better suited to the developmental needs of society. A Committee on Integrated Social Sciences was set up to consider the principles and details of the proposal.

One of the questions that preoccupied the Committee was how to combine integration of the social sciences with specialization in a particular discipline while making the resulting curriculum development-orientated and its graduates at least at par intellectually with their counterparts elsewhere. One difficulty was to overcome vested interests. Ideally, the objective of the curriculum was best achieved by integrative, interdisciplinary courses taught in teams representing the major social science disciplines. But this would demand that each lecturer be willing to get into other disciplines and, more radically, to get out of their cocoon, speciality within disciplines and favoured approach to the study of that discipline. This, it was argued, was too much to expect of young academics still struggling to perfect their tools in their specialities. Even among the older academics, the argument continued, the ideal has been approximated only when, tired of their specialities or particular school of thought, the scholar moved into other areas and therefore became receptive to experimentation and innovation with other disciplines and other schools of thought.

What then can be done short of the impossible task (*harakiri* for staff already employed) of recruiting older academics who have experimented with, and enjoy, integrated or interdisciplinary social science? This was the question the committee faced and which set the practical limitation on what might be proposed. The result was a special programme designed to make demands on all available skills, thus allaying the fears of lecturers who might worry about having nothing to teach, or students who might fret about having no traditional departments or degree programmes in economics, sociology, etc.

The second question on working out the integrated programme was what precisely is it we are trying to integrate? A partial answer had been provided by the rejection of existing university guidelines which listed, as major disciplines, Economics, Business Administration, Political and Administrative Studies in the traditional sense offered in Nigerian universities. The Committee came to conceive of development-orientated political science as analogous, to borrow Herbert Garfinkel and James Tierney's simile, to a wheel with three spokes each representing a major discipline within the Social Sciences.[40] In our analogy the hub is the Social System (sociology) while the spokes represent economics, political science and geography. This idea of the wheel with its hub and three spokes constituted the framework for the integrated political science programme.

The Committee, after careful study, proposed an integrated four-year programme, the first two years of which are fully interdisciplinary with respect to each course offering and are common to all students of political science and indeed all students in the School of Social Sciences. The last two years are less rigid in the demands for integration with other social science disciplines and the interdisciplinary approach to each course offering. Thus there are two phases, each of two years to the programme. In the first year of the first phase the student takes six foundation courses designed 1) to provide a sound background in the disciplines which constitute the hub and spokes of the programme and 2) to combine the acquisition of skills in the disciplines with the synthesis of these skills. Of the six courses, the Social

System introduces students to the interrelationship of the social science disciplines, how social systems evolve, differentiate, cohere, or disintegrate. Elements of Political Economy introduces them to the basic principles of capitalist and socialist economics, to allocation and utilization of resources, the components and determinants of national income and to financial institutions and planning for development. Political Analysis introduces the basic concepts, approaches, problems of technique and methodology as well as comparison of political systems. The Human Environment, for its part, deals with plant and crop ecology, population and settlement and environmental constraints on development.

A crucial aspect of this first-year programme is the two-semester Foundations of Social Science course. It serves as an additional arena for integrating the various principles and skills that are being learnt in the other five interdisciplinary courses. For this reason the course emphasizes the philosophical foundations of social science, its nature and scope, quantitative methods and methodological problems.

To round off the first year, the students study the polity and economy of Nigeria and their relationship with global politics and economics. They also take a communication skills course in which they study a local language (other than their mother tongue) to enable them to converse intelligibly with people in the area where the university is located.

The second year of this first phase is more exciting. That year a central core of the curriculum which extends to the third year of the degree programme is introduced. It is the Community Service Programme. In lieu of formal attachments to institutions and organizations for the purpose of practical as well as intellectual solutions to some aspects of their problems, the Community Service Programme intends to achieve the same purpose by a different method. It involves both staff and students in providing demonstrable practical solutions to some of the problems of our society, seeking thereby to inculcate in them a consciousness of their responsibilities to society and the habit of finding gratification in service to others. Specific projects are practical in nature, require the application of some skills acquired in the academic courses and generally involve manual work. The School of Social Science, for instance, has been involved in the problem of sanitation in Port Harcourt by actually going into the streets to clean up garbage and talking with people about the problems of sanitation. This has enabled the students to experientially identify obstacles to urban sanitation and to combine learning with communication and contact with those who usually benefit least from the fruits of modernization – the peasantry and rural masses and, in our case in particular, the urban proletariat, the groups least able to command the resources of expertise for which political science stands, according to Easton.[41]

In addition to the Community Service Course there are two general studies courses, namely, Africa and the World and Science, Technology and Society along with six interdisciplinary social science courses in this second year of the programme. One of the six interdisciplinary courses, Political Economy of Under-development, critically evaluates theories of and strategies for eliminating under-development, among them theories of limiting factors, trade, vicious circles, quasi-stable equilibrium, as well as sociological and psychological explanations such as achievement motivation and culture patterns and the role of colonialism and foreign capital. Another course, Human Organization of Space, examines the influence of historical, social, economic and political factors on the spatial distribution of population, industrial and agricultural production, wealth and resource use and considers the significance of the interrelationship of these factors for national, regional and international development. The other four courses are traditional offerings in the Principles of Public Administration, Economic History, Politics of Developing Areas and African Traditional Social Institutions.

The second phase of the curriculum is less rigid. The student is allowed two electives which may be chosen from any convenient part of the University's curriculum. But in the third year students take another Community Service course. For the rest of this two-year phase of the programme students are required to complete twelve courses in political science. The twelve are so designed that they form in themselves an integrated core of the discipline, distributed to cover the major sub-fields. Among these are traditional courses in each of four principal specialized fields within the discipline: Political Theory and Political Analysis; Comparative Politics (East/West International Relations and Foreign Policy); Local Government and Urban Administration. The rest, distributed among Marxism and Development, Peasant Societies, Public Finance and Financial Management, Policy Analysis and Development Administration, are designed to impart knowledge and skills in dealing with problems of development.

It would have been ideal to have a Problems in Political Science course which itself integrates the knowledge and skills the student has acquired, somewhat in the manner suggested by Garfinkel and Tierney, that is, a series of lectures delineating each of the core theoretical and practical areas of the curriculum plus a series of tutorials (involving written assignments) devoted to a discussion of a set of books each representing a core area and chosen as provocative, theoretically sophisticated and illustrative of the problems and possibilities of scholarly work in the core area under consideration.[42] But in lieu of this a Research Project is called for which should deal with a practical problem and find a solution to it. There will also be a comprehensive examination, involving external examiners, the scope of which will extend beyond the materials used in the course to test what Harvey Mansfield would call the students' 'integration of knowledge, perception of relationships and cultivation of mental powers beyond memory'[43] and ability to apply what has been learnt to social problems.

There is unlikely to be agreement on what constitutes an adequate development-orientated undergraduate curriculum in political science, but there could be a high degree of consensus about the basic construction of such a curriculum. The Port Harcourt experiment does not claim to be definitive but it seems to have the ingredients of the basic construction. To that extent it represents a step towards a development-orientated political science curriculum and one that is devoid of indoctrination and thus avoids the potential excesses of the 'new orthodoxy'.

Notes

1. For the definitions, see David Easton, 'The New Revolution in Political Science', *The American Political Science Review*, Vol. IXIII, December 1969, p. 1059.
2. See, e.g. B.A. Williams, 'Political Science and the Study of Public Policy in West Africa', paper read at the Nigerian Political Science Association Conference, University of Ibadan, 26-28 January 1973; Adele Jinadu, 'Some Reflections on African Political Scientists and African Politics', *The West African Journal of Sociology and Political Science*, Vol. 3, January 1979. (References to Jinadu's work refer to the mimeograph copy of the paper that was used by the author — Editor.)
3. Neal Houghton, 'The Challenge to Political Scientists in Recent American Foreign Policy: Scholarship or Indoctrination', *The American Political Science Review*, Vol. III, No. 3, September 1958, p. 678.
4. *Daily Times* (Lagos), 12 February 1975, p. 1, cited in Adele Jinadu, op. cit., p. 12.
5. Jinadu, op. cit., p. 6.
6. Easton, op. cit., pp. 1051-61; Houghton, op. cit., pp. 678-88.
7. Easton, op. cit.
8. Adele Jinadu's work, already cited, articulates this new orthodoxy and much of the references in the rest of this section refer to that work.
9. Ibid., pp. 25-7.
10. Ibid., p. 13-14,16.
11. Ibid, p. 21.
12. Easton, op. cit., p. 1056.
13. Ibid., pp. 1057-8.
14. There is of course African pharmacology or medicine, just as there are African superstitions. And there may be an authentic African science but witchcraft is not only African. For an interesting view see Nwankwo Ezeabasili, *African Science: Myth or Reality* (New York, Vantage Press, 1977).
15. Willard Scott Thompson, *Ghana's Foreign Policy, 1957-1966* (Princeton University Press, 1969).
16. Rene Dumont, *False Start in Africa* (New York, Praeger, 2nd revised edition, 1969), p. 120.
17. Easton, op. cit., p. 1058.
18. Timothy M. Shaw and Malcolm J. Grieve, 'The Political Economy of Resources: Africa's Future in the Global Environment', *The Journal of Modern African Studies*, Vol. 16, No. 1, 1978, pp. 1-32, esp at p. 32.
19. Rene Dumont, op. cit., pp. 259-60.
20. Ibid., p. 247, 258.
21. Ibid.

22. Rene Dumont, *Socialisms and Development* (London, Andre Deutsch, 1973).
23. Dumont, *False Start*, op. cit., p. 242.
24. Ishwar Dayal, 'Promoting Management Research in a Developing Country', *Quarterly Journal of Administration*, Vol. X, No. 1. October 1975, p. 48.
25. Claude Ake, 'Guidelines on Recruitment and Promotions', Internal Memorandum, School of Social Science, University of Port Harcourt, n.d.
26. Jinadu, op. cit., p. 23.
27. Federal Republic of Nigeria, Public Service Review Commission, *Main Report* (Lagos, Federal Ministry of Information, 1974), p. 14.
28. J.D. Udoji, 'The Implications of the Public Service Review Commission's Report for Management Education and Training', *Quarterly Journal of Administration*, Vol. X, No. 1, October 1975, p. 5.
29. Ibid.
30. *Main Report*, op. cit., p. 12.
31. Harry A Green, 'Administrative Training: Some Implications of the Udoji Commission Report', *Quarterly Journal of Administration*, Vol. X, No. 1, October 1975, pp. 55–68.
32. *Main Report*, op. cit., pp. 2–24; Udoji, op. cit., p. 6.
33. *Main Report*, p. 21; Green, op. cit., p. 63.
34. Ibid.
35. Green, op. cit., p. 60; Udoji, op. cit., pp. 6–8.
36. Green, op. cit., pp. 63–7.
37. *Main Report*, op. cit., p. 8.
38. Easton, op. cit., p. 1056, 1060.
39. 'Political Science as a Discipline', *The American Political Science Review*, Vol. 56, June 1962, p. 417.
40. Herbert Garfinkel and James Tierney, 'A Coordinating Course in the Political Science Major, *The American Political Science Review*, Vol. 51, December 1957, p. 1180.
41. Easton, op. cit., pp. 1059–60.
42. Garfinkel and Tierney, op. cit.
43. Harvey Mansfield, 'The Major in Political Science', *The American Political Science Review*, Vol. 41, June 1947, p. 502 cited in Garfinkel and Tierney, op. cit., p. 1182.

Part Two
Scope and Approaches

7. Elections and Election Studies in Africa

Denis L. Cohen

Political scientists working in Africa have devoted a great deal of attention to describing and analysing the phenomenon of elections. Some have made a particular election the focus of their study, while others have sought to use electoral data to illuminate the nature of the political systems as a whole. Much use has been made of borrowed theory to understand African elections, less of borrowed methods, and there has been a significant degree of theoretical, though less of methodological, innovation in this field.

Interest in election studies has followed the general fashions in the discipline: from a concern in the 1950s with elections as instruments of popular representation; to a greater awareness of their institutional fragility in the 1960s; to a renewal of attention to the possible significance of elections in the 1970s. On the whole, however, a focus on political output structures, such as bureaucracies and military elites, and on underlying processes, such as political economy and political socialization, has largely displaced the study of input structures, including elections, from the central attention of the discipline in Africa.

The author has himself been involved in the study of elections in Uganda and Botswana; has devoted much time to the literature on the electoral history of Ghana; and finds himself increasingly drawn, despite conflicting theoretical concerns, to an interest in the electoral struggle which has been reborn recently in Nigeria. Given these concerns, what follows is a product of both scholarly and practical experience. It is an attempt to work out some of the ambiguities surrounding the study of African elections, prior to the formulation of a substantive research strategy.

This essay is divided into three sections. First, the literature in the field is briefly surveyed, so as to give the reader a clear picture of the scope of the study. Second, several different approaches and methods which have been used in the study of African elections are described and assessed. Third, some of the major theoretical issues which have been raised by African election studies are examined.

Furthermore, the essay looks at the history, methods, content, and future prospects of African election studies. In doing so, it focuses on the world of scholarship rather than on the real political world which scholarship hopes to illuminate. However, the significance of election studies is necessarily intertwined with the significance of elections as real political phenomena. To assess the former we must also direct our attention to the latter.[1]

Surveying the Field

Elections, like many other modern political structures, are a relatively new phenomenon in Africa. Just as in these other cases, however, there often existed pre-modern political processes which carried out functions similar to those of elections, and their study is a rich source of material which is too often viewed as the domain of the anthropologist, not the political scientist.

For example, Schapera and Kuper have described the nature of decision-making in Tswana traditional councils (*kgotlas*)[2] ; while the methods of selection of authority-holders in pre-colonial Ghana have been described by Busia and Apter[3] (for the Akan-speaking peoples), and Staniland[4] (for the Dagomba). Neither process may, strictly speaking, be elections, but both may throw light on the meaning of the voting act for many of the people of Botswana and Ghana.

While Apter's (now discredited)[5] theory of charismatic legitimation sought to bridge the gap between traditional and modern authority through the medium of Nkrumah's election victories of the 1950s in Ghana, few other political scientists have followed him in trying to find continuity between modern electoral behaviour and pre-modern political behaviour. Most have instead looked at elections as 'new' modern structural arrangements, albeit influenced by operating in a context of 'traditional' cultures; and have emphasized the discontinuity between them, often judging either culture or structure inappropriate.[6]

Within the context even of modern elections, however, there is a relatively lengthy record of African experience. The people of Senegal, Ghana and Liberia,[7] among others, have had long experiences with elections. The fact that such elections were generally conducted on the basis of a highly restricted franchise should not make them of less interest, since universal adult suffrage is a relatively new phenomenon everywhere. The manipulation of property, income, educational, geographical and racial variables to limit the franchise characterized early African elections and, of course, still do debase the elections of the Republic of South Africa. Much of the early literature on African elections emphasizes the issue of franchise limitation.[8] The widespread recent acceptance of universal adult suffrage in most of the world has led to a turning away from interest in this issue, except in the southern part of the continent.

In the period 1950-65, the period of rapid decolonization in Africa, election studies enjoyed a leading role in the literature, as the electoral procedure was generally used to determine, or at least to legitimate, the form, rate and direction of the decolonization process.

Major studies of this period which focus specifically on elections include the work of Denis Austin on Ghana; Ken Post on Nigeria. George Bennett

and Carl Rosberg on Kenya; F.B. Welbourn on Uganda; David Mulford on
Zambia; and Ruth Schacter Morgenthau on French-speaking West Africa.[9]
Others who made significant use of electoral data include Dudley, Sklar and
Whitaker on Nigeria; Kilson on Sierra Leone; Gailey on the Gambia; Johnson,
Levine, Weinstein and Zolberg on Francophone Africa; and Lemarchand,
Weiss and Young on Zaire.[10] If monographs and articles are included, the
depth of the literature becomes even more pronounced, as can be illustrated
by taking the example of a single country.

In Ghana, as well as Professor Apter's book, at least ten articles and papers
dealing with the elections of the 1950s can be mentioned,[11] and research on
other countries which were deeply involved in electoral activity would
probably produce a similar array of material.

In the post-colonial decades of the 1960s and 1970s the change in political practices seen in most African states produced a change in political
studies. The limitation on mass political participation which was at the core
of single-party state formation, military coups and increasing bureaucratic
power resulted in a decline in the frequency of elections, a lessening in their
political significance, and a fall in popular interest in what had become, in
most African states, less of a struggle for power and more of a theatrical
display.

The elites which had inherited power through the electoral processes of
decolonization often treated the obligation to maintain electoral procedures
with disdain. They postponed elections for the flimsiest of reasons. For
example, President Nkrumah in Ghana decided that the 1960 Constitutional
Referendum was an excuse for postponing parliamentary elections from 1961
to 1965,[12] a practice emulated by President Obote in Uganda in 1967.

In other cases, restrictions were placed on the participation of anti-government parties and leaders which effectively guaranteed the ability of the
rulers to maintain their control. So, in 1969, the Kenya Peoples Union of
Oginga Odinga, securing a *de facto* single-party state. In 1972 President
Kaunda's regime in Zambia did the same thing to the United Progressive
Party of its leading opponent, Simon Kapwepwe.

The fragility of electoral processes has been further exposed by cases in
which relatively free elections have been allowed to take place but, when the
results are displeasing to the authorities, are simply nullified by state power,
as in Lesotho in 1970, or by military coup, as in Sierra Leone in 1968, or by
manoeuvres designed to prolong the rule of a rejected regime, as in Mauritius
in 1976.[13]

The most effective instrument for limiting the participatory scope of
elections has been the single-party state. It has rendered elections in most
of Francophone Africa into charades characterized by plus 90% majorities
for the official slate of candidates.[14] In certain countries electoral structures
have been created which seek to preserve a degree of competition while
limiting out 'undesirable' competition from the electoral arena. These
innovative electoral techniques, pioneered by Tanzania in 1965, and followed
by Kenya in 1969, Uganda in 1970, Zambia in 1973, Senegal in 1978, and

the Ivory Coast in 1980, have produced an extensive literature analyzing their structures and consequences, providing what little life remained in the field of African election studies for some time.[15]

Even where certain African political systems have been able to maintain a viable set of electoral procedures through several elections, thus establishing some degree of stability for the electoral system, the political value of this attainment is questionable. Botswana and the Gambia are the two best examples of such stability, but the former owes its resilience more to a lack of challenge than to its own strength,[16] while the latter has not been able to gain sufficient legitimacy from its model electoral history to prevent a recent coup attempt by an unsuccessful former candidate, which could only be repressed with the help of neighbouring Senegalese troops, thus putting in question the maintenance of the political system as a whole.[17]

In the 1970s the sorry story portrayed above has been relived by two forces. In the first place, the existence of competitive single-party elections has called into being, as mentioned above, a good deal of interest in understanding this phenomenon. While some have argued against taking these elections too seriously,[18] others have devoted considerable attention to their role in recruiting the political elite, legitimizing the regime, and socializing the electorate.[19]

Second, in some African states there has been a revival in the use of periodic, competitive elections as a central feature of the political process. The tendency of African military regimes to create ruling single parties and stage electoral facades, as in Zaire, Togo, Benin and the Sudan, testifies only to their rulers' recognition of the international legitimation function of elections; the re-establishment of constitutions providing for competitive elections in post-military rule Ghana (first in 1969, again in 1979), Nigeria (1979), Uganda (1980), and temporarily in Upper Volta (1978-80), and Central African Republic (1980-81), as well as the introduction of multi party competition in Senegal (1976), illustrates continued faith, or at least interest, by some African elites in elections as a means of popular representation.

The creation of an open, competitive electoral system in newly-independent Zimbabwe in 1980 also points in this direction. The effort made by Ghana in 1969 to re-establish an electoral system was of keen interest to scholars,[20] and the more recent efforts there and elsewhere will soon be producing their own literature.

These two trends have led the author of a recent study of African elections to conclude that they have become, in the 1970s, more frequent, more open, and more meaningful.[21] This finding provides sufficient reason, therefore, for us to turn now to an examination of the methodological and theoretical concerns raised by African election studies.

An Array of Approaches

A number of different theoretical and methodological approaches can be discerned at work in the literature on African elections. While the same researcher may make use of several approaches, each has its own content and character. For the sake of convenience, it is possible to categorize them into four main approaches: the Nuffield approach, the case study approach, the sample survey approach, and the systems approach.

The Nuffield Approach
The first of these we may call the Nuffield approach, taking its name from Nuffield College, Oxford, which has been responsible for a long series of British election studies,[22] as well as for encouraging electoral research in Africa. This approach, while making use of aggregate data, focuses on the issues of the election, on the mechanics of the electoral campaign, on the organization of the political parties, and the political history of the constituencies, parties and candidates. It presumes a model of the election in the mould of traditional Western democratic theory as a linkage device between the interests and ideas of the electorate, the policy pronouncements and party identification of the candidates, and the policy outputs of the regime. It seeks to explain the election result through the political and historical context of the electoral event.

This approach tended to dominate earlier African election studies,[23] which were unable, for practical reasons, to make much use of quantitative data beyond the aggregate results, to survey voter attitudes, or to include much coverage of electoral behaviour outside the centre of the political system. As a result, the flaws of this method, in the African context, were an over-emphasis on the centre of the political system and corresponding neglect of the political periphery; an over-reliance on urban and elite-based data, more easily accessible to the researcher than rural, mass data; and a reification of the rhetoric of the political leadership, which often went unheard by the masses, with the platforms of the parties generally unknown even by their own leaders.

The Case Study Approach
The shortcomings mentioned above were soon recognized and a second approach adopted to try to correct them. It relies on intensive case studies of small areas – a single constituency, town or district – in order to obtain a clearer picture of mass reaction to and participation in the elections. This case study approach has inspired a number of articles and monographs,[24] as well as being combined together with other approaches in larger volumes.[25]

The case study approach, however, has its own problems. It can develop into a political anthropology in which the interest in and data about the ecology of the chosen area is so intense that the reader loses sight of the connection between this local arena and the greater political system. The study may give an exhaustive picture, for example, of the connection between traditional politics in the area and party political cleavages, leading one to see the electoral contest as a secondary struggle between rival claimant groups to a chieftaincy title. How the candidates choose their party identification, their issue orientation, and their involvement in central politics, often go unexplained.[26]

A second difficulty is in the resources required to give comprehensive coverage to an election using case studies. Finding scholars with the necessary knowledge and experience of each constituency in Nigeria, for example, and then financing their work, and finally aggregating their results into a synthesis or even a manageable collection, would seem a formidable task. The strategy usually chosen instead is to select a 'representative' sample of cases to be studied. However, the representativeness of the sample is always suspect, as criteria for selection are usually practical (e.g., is there somebody already working in the area who is willing to observe the election?), rather than some unbiased sampling technique.

In the study which was undertaken of the abortive 1971 Ugandan General Election, for example, we planned intensive case studies of only four of the eighteen Ugandan administrative districts then existing, one each being selected from the northern, southern, eastern and western parts of the country, as well as a case study of Kampala. We had hoped to locate corresponding scholars in the other districts to provide some participation in the study, at a lesser degree of commitment, but were, in the end, successful in getting promises to assist in only an additional four districts. Consequently, somewhat less than half of the country was to be covered, and even so this would have been a better coverage than that achieved by Cliffe's 1965 Tanzanian study, or by Austin and Luckham's study of the 1969 Ghana General Eelction.

A final problem with the case study approach is the difficulty in ensuring some degree of consistency in the work of the various participants. The result, without strong central co-ordination and editing, can be a clash of conflicting points of view, differing methods, and divergent conclusions, making comparison and synthesis difficult. All these tendencies can be seen in the collections mentioned above. In our Ugandan study we hoped to assure some comparability in case studies by providing a check-list of certain issues to be investigated by all the participants. Such a technique would seem to be essential, but is certainly no guarantee that some central focus will prevail.[27]

The Sample Survey Approach

The third major approach which has been used in African election studies is that of quantitative analysis using sample survey techniques. This method has been associated with election studies in the United States of America, and would seem to be ideally suited to the study of elections, which produce large amounts of aggregate data accessible to analysis in association with the individual data produced by surveys. The series of American studies using these techniques, many sponsored by the Survey Research Centre of the University of Michigan, indicate the increasing methodological sophistication and success of this approach.[28] In terms of verifiability, reliability and comparability (both diachronically and synchronically) quantitative analysis is preferable to the other approaches discussed above. The sample survey method also gives an invaluable tool for testing the quality and meaning of mass participation in elections.

The problems associated with the use of survey techniques in Africa are, however, extensive.[29] These would include: 1) the cost of organizing and administering a large-scale sample survey over a large area in a condition of infrastructural underdevelopment, as well as of processing the data gathered; 2) the scarcity of available personnel trained in such techniques; 3) lack of the data-processing equipment, computers, and telecommunications networks generally utilized in such studies; 4) lack of experience with and consequent distrust of being surveyed often evinced by the masses; 5) problems of questionnaire construction in multi-cultural and multi-lingual societies; 6) physical and cultural problems of gaining access to some areas, and some segments of the population; 7) problems of applying sampling techniques when basic demographic data is often unavailable or unreliable, and enumerations of the population with their physical location are difficult to acquire or construct; 8) the fact that many Africanist political scientists are less well grounded in these techniques than is the profession as a whole; 9) the political sensitivity of such research, in which questions the regime would rather leave unasked may be asked, of people the regime might rather leave silent. As a consequence, most African election studies use only aggregate data, and make rough judgments relating the electoral results to geographically concentrated social factors such as ethnicity.[30] Even this is made difficult by the fact that most African election results are reported in rather large units, such as constituencies, rather than in smaller units, such as polling areas.

Despite these problems, the rewards of such an approach could be great, as indicated even by the limited use to which it has been put.[31] The 1971 Uganda Study did provide for the inclusion of a nation-wide sample survey as part of the overall study, which would have accounted for over half of the costs of the study. Specialized personnel were recruited to conduct the survey, a questionnaire was drawn up and administered to a pilot sample, a nation-wide sample was drawn, and the whole project had received governmental approval, so some of the most important hurdles involved in the project had been surmounted. Unfortunately, the Amin coup of 1971, which blocked the approaching election, also brought the study to a premature end. Otherwise, results might have been produced which would have represented an important advance in the use of survey techniques in studying African elections. It is to be hoped that further attempts along these lines will be made in the future.

The System Approach
This final approach to be discussed here is based on a systems theory model of the political system. It seeks to analyse the election as a structure of the system which produces certain kinds of functional consequences for the system as a whole. While it may make use of quantitative, case study and

political history methods, it is distinguished by its primary concern for the impact of the election on the political system, rather than for the explanation of the electoral event itself. The most important functional consequences of elections which have been focused on in the literature are those of legitimation, political socialization and political recruitment.

The pioneering study adopting this approach was Lionel Cliffe's *One Party Democracy*. The whole book is built around the structural-functional categories of systems theory, and Cliffe's conclusions revolve around the impact of the election on political recruitment, interest articulation, political socialization, the role of Parliament, and the role of the ruling party.[32] John Saul has continued this line of approach in his work on the 1970 Tanzanian General Election, emphasizing especially the role of elections as a means of finding an acceptable compromise to the tension between the need for elite control and the need for popular participation in a political system.[33] Professor Bienen's study of Kenya has emphasized the importance of elections as a legitimizing force,[34] and the effect of elections on political attitudes has been noted by a number of students of African elections.[35]

The use of electoral data as a source of information about candidates, some of whom will be recruited into political offices, is also a useful research strategy which has been applied in a number of African studies, including those in Uganda, Tanzania, Kenya and Botswana.[36] The advantage here is that an election isolates a pool of political recruits and those eligible for recruitment, often provides, or at least makes more accessible, data on the social characteristics of such individuals, and thus makes possible the testing of hypotheses on the relationship between social background and political recruitment. Similar data can be collected about political role holders, e.g., parliamentarians, bureaucrats or military officers,[37] but electoral competition has the advantage of facilitating comparison between potential and successful recruits.

For example, Tanzania requires the provision of certain biographical data by all prospective candidates for parliamentary election. President Obote's Uganda had intended to follow a similar practice. This data represents a useful source of material for a study of political recruitment. Even when such data is not centrally gathered, the researcher can collect a great deal himself through questionnaire and interview methods, as this writer did for the 1974 and 1979 Botswana elections.

We can conclude this discussion of approaches to the study of African elections by noting that all the methods discussed here have their uses, and their problems. Some of the most successful studies have combined several techniques in studying the same phenomenon. The most useful area of future methodological advance would seem to be that of quantitative survey methods, which have been the least used. Finally, the issue of techniques to be used is subsidiary to, and must be dictated, to some extent, by that of the theoretical perspective of the study — the issue to which we now turn.

Theoretical Perspectives

Like many other political phenomena, elections can be analysed with a number of different purposes in mind. Many questions can be asked for which electoral data is used to provide answers. A social psychologist has a certain way of approaching an election, certain theoretical interests through which he sees the election. A political theorist is likely to have a second perspective; a practical politician (who, despite considering himself a *practical* man, sees reality through his own *theoretical* lens), a third. We discuss here three of the many theoretical issues which political scientists have raised in relation to elections in Africa. They are: 1) voter choice; 2) voter turn-out; 3) political participation.

Voter Choice

The fact that an election usually entails some degree of choice for the electorate — between candidates, parties, perhaps policies — immediately raises the issue of the factor, or factors, determining the choice made. This is the issue which comes first to most students of elections; why did A win and B lose. Seeking an answer to this question has motivated a great deal of methodological and theoretical attention. Little application has been made in Africa of the statistical methods developed elsewhere for relating the many causes producing a voter decision, for the reasons discussed in the earlier section dealing with quantitative methods.

Nevertheless, if with less precision, the question has been investigated in the African context. In general, researchers in Africa have followed the argument made by W.G. Runciman that quantitative methods need to be subordinated to a sense of political history in the analysis of elections.[38] Such a 'loose' theoretical framework has made possible a number of judgments explaining election outcomes in terms of leadership popularity (often known as charisma),[39] regime support,[40] ideological commitment,[41] or ethnic loyalties,[42] based on rather flimsy evidence, rough correlations and untested assumptions.

The most important theoretical principle underlying most African election studies has been a consensus that African voters tend to make their electoral choice as communities rather than as individuals. Taking the key community of orientation to be an ethnic one for the great majority of Africans, most observers have seen this group identity as determining the individual's choice; electoral contests as being a vying for ethnic community support; and electoral success as usually based on ethnic coalition building.

This primacy of the community over the individual is seen as far more important than party orientation, issue orientation, social class or ideology as a determinant of voting behaviour. Professor Austin, for example, despite his concern with these other issues, has done some of his most illuminating electoral analysis in looking at individual constituencies.[43] There he generally found that the support of the traditional authority holders was all-important in winning; that the manipulation of traditional loyalties and conflicts to secure voter support was the substance of the campaign, and that the election was perceived by most voters as a contest between rival kin-based communities. The case studies of four Ghanaian districts in the 1969 General Election found little change in this situation.[44] Examples can be given of similar analyses of elections in Uganda, Kenya, Botswana and Zaire.[45]

A scholar who has given a somewhat different version of the nature of community choice is Professor K.W.J. Post. Observing the 1959 Nigerian General Election, he agreed that voter choices were more often made by the community than by individuals. Rather than seeing this community consensus as formed on the basis of traditional ethnic relations, and through the medium of traditional leadership, however, Post argued that it was the 'new men', that had acquired some Western education and held 'modern' occupations, who acted as opinion leaders in shaping the community decision.[46] Relying on Lerner's concept of transitional men and Katz and Lazarsfeld's 'two-step flow of communication' theory, Post's analysis leaves much more scope for intra-community conflict and political fluidity than does Austin's, since the final choice is not determined by pre-existing cleavages and sentiments, but by competition between rival 'influentials'. Support for Post's point of view can also be found in studies of Uganda, Kenya, Botswana and Zaire.[47]

It is possible to combine the perspectives of Austin and Post by arguing that the former's analysis is more relevant to areas of less social change, and the latter's to areas of greater social change, where more transitional men are available, both for leadership and emulation. This is somewhat too easy a resolution to the problem, however.

There are other difficulties with both theories. For one thing, why is it that, in some areas, elections seem to have been determined by something other than pure ethnic arithmetic, e.g., the victory of the Convention Peoples Party (CPP) over the National Liberation Movement (NLM) and the Northern People's Party (NPP) in 1956 in a number of Ashanti and Northern constituencies in Ghana, despite the latter's greater ethnic appeal in those areas; or Tanganyika African National Union's (TANU) success in resisting the localistic opposition to it in pre-independence Tanzania; or even the continuing success of white and Asian candidates in winning elections in Tanzania, Zambia and, most recently, Kenya, long after black majority rule.

More important, the theory seems to see ethnic community as a well-defined, stable unit for whose support politicians compete. However, much evidence would indicate that ethnicity is a very malleable factor and that the definition of a community of identity is often shaped by the political struggle itself. For example, the 1959 Nigerian election result produced the picture of a highly united North behind the Northern Peoples Congress (NPC); but in the 1979 elections the old North was split with the Great Nigeria Peoples Party (GNPP) successful in Borno and Gongola states, the Peoples Redemption Party (PRP) in Kano and Kaduna, the Nigerian Peoples Party (NPP) in Plateau, and the National Party of Nigeria (NPN) in Sokoto, Niger, Kwara, Benue and Bauchi, and with all five parties gaining pockets of votes in a number of areas. In Borno State the division between GNPP and NPN parties can be seen in terms of a Kanuri/Hausa ethnic cleavage, but many other ethnic divisions exist in Borno. What factors affect how these groups divide, coalesce and ally with each other?

Finally, while the above objections can be answered by refining the theory of community choice, a more fundamental objection exists. How secure is the evidence for our judgment? Does it rest only on the fact that it fits the view of the world many African leaders, who promote themselves as ethnic leaders, would like to have accepted? In Kenya, for example, a great deal of extra-legal force was required to eliminate the KPU challenge to the ruling Kenya African National Union (KANU) in 1969. Force was especially used to silence Kikuyu opponents of the Kikuyu-dominated regime, like Bildad Kaggia (and later J.M. Kariuki). It would seem that the Kenyan leadership had little trust in the strength of its ethnic support when faced with the class-based appeal of the KPU.[48]

To take another example, Ugandan politics was certainly characterized by inter-ethnic community conflict in the 1950s and 1960s although some of these communities, as in the case of Kenya, were based more on colonial administrative boundaries than primordial sentiments. Traditional authority was also used very effectively to control the vote in, for example, Buganda.[49] Yet, by 1970 some observers believed they had detected a surprising interest in intra-UPC elections by the supposedly disaffected Baganda, an interest based firmly on the perception of individual material interest, not ethnic group identity.[50]

It can be argued that the tendency for African voting behaviour to be dominated heretofore by ethnic factors results from the fact that ethnic community has continued to be the most stable source of material benefit and security for most voters. Consequently they decide, as individuals, to support a common choice as the best means of protecting and advancing their individual material interests. In many places, such as Kenya or Nigeria, the ruling class has chosen to prolong this situation by allocating benefits and opportunities on an ethnic basis. Where, however, this has been less the case, as in Nkrumah's Ghana, Obote's Uganda or Nyerere's Tanzania, voters of the same ethnic community but different socioeconomic status have been able to perceive their interests differently and have voted accordingly.

It could be argued further that initial electoral decisions are made through community choice on issues of group loyalty and symbolic identification (especially as these initial elections often revolved around questions of the definition of the political system, particularly relevant to the mobilization of inter-ethnic community conflict). Very quickly, however, issues of material self-interest, touching the differential class standing of individual workers, small peasants, large landowners, businessmen, etc., come to the foreground, and individual voting increases.

Depending on the existing political alignments and ideologies, these interests may be: a) channelled into ethnically-based parties, increasing inter-community conflict and resulting in the abandonment of the electoral system for a more politically repressive system (as in Nigeria in 1966 or Zambia in 1972); or b) channelled into class-based parties, increasing class conflict and resulting in the abandonment of the electoral system for a more repressive regime (as in Ghana in 1960 or Kenya in 1969); or c) the new demands of dissatisfied individuals may not find a means of institutionalized expression on either ethnic or class basis, resulting in the persistence of the electoral system while the dissatisfied become alienated non-voters (as in Tanzania or Botswana). This hypothesis will be further amplified in the next two sections.

Voter Turn-out
A second issue of great interest relating to electoral behaviour is that of voter turn-out (i.e. the percentage of the population eligible to vote who actually do vote), both because level of turn-out can affect the electoral result, and because level of turn-out itself can often be regarded as an indirect measure of such things as political participation and system stability.

Turn-out at Selected African Elections*

Ghana	Nigeria	Kenya	Tanzania	Zambia	Botswana
1954	1959	1960	1965	1964	1965
59% (30%)	80% (32%)	84% (34%)	77% (49%)	94% (86%)	75%
1956	1964	1963	1970	1968	1969
50% (30%)	26%	85% (57%)	72%	82% (68%)	55%
1969	1979	1969	1975	1973	1974
63% (40%)	35%	47%	82%	43%	32%
1979		1974	1980	1978	1979
35%		n.a.	n.a.	67%	+50%
		1979			
		75% (63%)			

*Figures in brackets represent turn-out as a percentage of eligible population; the other figures are turn-out as a percentage of the registered electorate.[51]

Leaving aside elections in which no real choice is presented to the electorate, in which the electorate is legally limited to something much less than universal adult suffrage, or in which the level of regime support is incredibly high (+90%), data is presented above on the turn-out frequency in a selection of African elections.

These figures need to be interpreted within the context of each particular election. The Ghanaian results indicate that only half of eligible voters have been registered throughout the relevant period, as well as a general decline in turn-out of registered voters, temporarily arrested in 1969 at the election which followed three years of military rule, but resumed again in the 1979 elections, following eight years of military rule.

In Nigeria, a high turn-out of registered voters was secured in 1959, but only one-third of the eligible electorate was registered (women were legally barred from voting in the North). The 1964 figure is very suspect. The initial election was boycotted by United Progressive Grand Alliance (UPGA) supporters, especially in the Eastern Region, and supplementary elections were held there several months later. Charges of illegal interference with voting were rife. The 1979 elections were carried out in a much more peaceful climate. The lack of reliable census data makes calculation of turn-out as a percentage of the eligible impossible, but the turn-out as a percentage of registered voters was very low in an election following thirteen years of military rule.

The early Kenyan election results show a pattern of high turn-out of registered voters and low turn-out of the eligible electorate. In 1969 the percentage turn-out of registered voters fell dramatically, probably as a result of the banning of the only opposition party shortly before the election and the subsequent establishment of a single-party competitive system. While 1974 figures could not be obtained, the last election results (1979) indicate the highest degree of participation in Kenyan elections yet. The Tanzanian figures also show a high stable turn-out in a single-party competitive system.

Zambia's 1964 results show a very high level of both registration and voting, which fell significantly in 1973, again immediately following the banning of opposition and introduction of a single-party competitive system. Turn-out increased in the subsequent (1978) election, but not to the earlier rate, and was particularly low in areas of earlier opposition success.

Botswana's figures represent the only unbroken series of competitive, open elections, and show a consistently decreasing turn-out rate. This was reversed at the last (1979) election, which was marked by the expenditure of one million *pula* on a government-sponsored 'get-out-the-vote' campaign. This was a vastly greater amount of funds than was available to any of the opposition parties for their campaigns. Registration in Botswana is deemed to be so nearly universal that double-registration has been given as an excuse for the low turn-out rate.

The general tendencies emerging from the data would seem to be: 1) generally low turn-out, even if one takes into account only the registered electorate; and 2) generally declining turn-out. Partial exceptions might exist in the case of some single-party competitive systems, and of some elections held after the end of military regimes.

A number of different explanations can be offered for these phenomena. Broadly speaking, they can be divided into technical and political explanations. Technical explanations are related to causes such as inadequate census data; physical problems of reaching the electorate with information and making polling booths accessible to them; use of voluntary rather than automatic registration procedures; poor weather; etc.[52] Political explanations usually relate to the turn-out being an indication of satisfaction or dissatisfaction with the regime.

The political explanation is likely to be the more helpful in most cases, given that the declining trend in voter turn-out generally parallels an increasing trend in provision of physical infrastructure, and that, often, turn-out is higher in rural areas, though infrastructure is generally better in the urban areas.[53]

The difficulty with the political explanation, except in the case of explicit boycotts as in Uganda in 1961, Nigeria in 1964, or Rhodesia in 1972 and 1979, is that the same data can be explained in opposite ways depending on the interpretation of the context. In Botswana, for example, to some observers the declining turn-out in post-independence elections, coupled with the consistent majorities obtained by the ruling Botswana Democratic Party (BDP) indicates generalized satisfaction with the regime and its policies, as well as increasing implausibility of the opposition parties. To other observers, however, the same data seems to point toward growing dissatisfaction, hopelessness and apathy amongst voters presented with no meaningful choice by the election.[54]

Discussion of this issue needs to be conducted while keeping in mind the points made in our earlier discussion of voter choice. To the extent that the voter chooses to vote as a member of an ethnically-based community rather than as an individual conscious of high class interests, it is not surprising that voter turn-out is higher in rural areas where communities remain cohesive and lower in urban areas where voters have become more individuated. Nor is it surprising that extremely high turn-outs can be secured in certain areas and near boycotts in others.

It is the gradual decline in turn-out experienced by countries like Ghana, Zambia and Botswana that would seem to be better suited to a theory of individual voter choice, with a community consensus either in support of or opposed to the regime gradually eroding as individuals become dissatisfied or merely apathetic, as outlined in option C above.

Political Participation

The most vital theoretical issue relating to elections is not what motivates voters to turn out, or to vote as they do, but what is the meaning of their voting behaviour for their political and social systems as a whole. It is not just the frequency and direction of political participation but its quality that is at issue here.

This writer recalls attending a meeting in 1970 between a number of political scientists and the then (and once again) President of Uganda, Dr. Obote, to discuss the President's proposals for the construction of a new electoral system for the country. President Obote raised the issue of the reason for holding elections at all. The assembled political scientists suggested as reasons accountability, recruitment of leaders, representation of popular demands, and achieving international legitimacy, as well as raising objections to the likelihood of, or need for, achieving any of these. The President finally decided that the primary value of elections lay in educating, entertaining and giving the people a *feeling* of participation. As a professional politician he saw elections from the top down, as a means of controlling the people, not as a means through which they could control him.

However, the primary importance of the quality of political participation is, on the contrary, the normative purpose of elections, not their empirical functions. Their purpose is wrapped up in the concept of representation, the linking of the interests of the citizen with the policies of the state.[55] While it has been argued that the representative function may need to be subordinated to the legitimation function in 'developing', 'plural' or 'unintegrated' societies,[56] I would maintain that the continued significance of electoral systems, and the main reason for making them a focus of research, is intimately connected with their viability as representative institutions.

One of the earliest students of African elections contended:

> In varying ways and at varying speeds, all the British territories in Africa are committed to the development of democratic institutions. The final verdict on this policy must depend on how it works; whether the methods adopted do indeed lead to competent and honest government.[57]

Most of us would certainly agree that the verdict can now be given, in most cases, in the negative. Competent and honest government did not, by and large, result. The policy did not work. There is something touching about the rectitude of the concern expressed, however, especially when juxtaposed with the judgment of many latter-day political scientists. For example:

> It would be a mistake to dismiss the many elections Kenya has had because participation has narrowed and the elections have not been completely open and unrestricted by Government. Elections have been important although they led to a *renewal* of the kind of elite that remained in power. Turnover of individuals gives people the *feeling* that there is a response possible to poor, that is, ineffectual representation.[58] (emphasis added)

The same point is made from a different point of view in relation to Tanzania:

> in an unreconstructed Tanzania, one possible function of such an electoral system was an *anaesthetizing* one, for if Prewitt and Hyden are correct it was not merely 'government' but the privileged who were being freed from popular pressure.[59]

John Saul, the author of the last quotation, is sufficiently committed and astute to go beyond celebrating the system-legitimating function of elections and to devote his attention to the way Tanzanian elections subordinate the desire for participation to the necessity (from government's point of view) of control. Nevertheless, his analysis leads in the direction of shifting the focus of the political scientist's attention away from elections to other phenomena, in the case of Tanzania the activities of the ruling party.[60]

In doing this his conclusion is similar to others who have tended to deride the importance of elections in African politics, and does not help to explain the re-emergence of elections as critical phenomena in places like Ghana, Nigeria and even the Ivory Coast, as noted at the beginning of this essay.

Instead, it is possible to see this resilience of electoral institutions as a consequence of the continued need for structural arrangements through which the representative function can be carried out, and mass participation expressed; a need which can only be partially met by stage-managed elections, restricted elections, military/bureaucratic consultative committees, and charismatic leaders.

The hypothesis outlined earlier can be further developed to allow us to argue that it is the demand for material benefits generated by the modern forces of embourgeoisement and proletarianization, originally responsible for destabilizing the 'exported' electoral systems in the first place,[61] which, although temporarily contained by more authoritarian regimes, eventually build up and produce further change. This may, of course, be in the direction of further intensifying authoritarian controls, or of producing revolutionary change.

Elections may be used to disguise authoritarian control, as in Zaire or the Republic of South Africa. They may be used to signify the advent of revolutionary regimes (as in Angola or Mozambique). Or, they can just as easily be dispensed with by either type of regime. Their continued crucial role in African politics, however, depends, if the line of analysis developed here is productive, on the persistence in Africa of a third type of regime — one in which class forces are still developing, in which a stable resolution of their conflict is impossible, and in which demands for participation from the masses and for de-participation[62] from the ruling class alternate in strength.

In this situation elections serve as a means of regulating conflict while preventing zero-sum politics; of recruiting political leaders in a loosely competitive rather than wholly monopolistic market; of allowing an arena for the development, rather than the control, of political socialization patterns; and of achieving an instrumental legitimation of regime rules rather than a consummatory legitimation of regime values. To the extent that all these operations are effected, elections would appear to have a continued, constructive future in Africa.

Notes

1. The writer would like to thank Dr. Y.R. Barongo of Bayero University, Kano for his invitation to contribute to this volume, and Dr. D.E. Udofia of Maiduguri University for his helpful comments on the first draft, and Dr. L.A. Igboeli of Maiduguri University.

2. I. Schapera, *A Handbook of Tswana Law and Custom* (London, Frank Cass, 1970, o.v. 1938); and Adam Kuper, *Kalahari Village Politics* (Cambridge University Press, 1970).
3. K.A. Busia, *The Position of the Chief in the Modern Political System of Ashanti* (London, Macmillan, 1951); and David E. Apter, *Ghana in Transition* (rev. ed. New York, Atheneum, 1963), Chap. IV.
4. Martin Staniland, *The Lions of Dagbon: Political Change in Northern Ghana* (Cambridge University Press, 1975), pp. 18-24.
5. See, for example, D.L. Cohen, 'The Concept of Charisma and the Analysis of Leadership', *Political Studies*, Vol. XX, No. 3, September 1972, pp. 302-4.
6. The unsuitability of African culture to British-style elections is frequently pointed out in T.E. Smith, *Elections in Developing Countries* (Westport, Conn., Greenwood Publishers, 1976, o.v. 1960); while the irrelevance of Western electoral structures to African culture is remarked by J.K. Nyerere, *Freedom and Democracy* (Nairobi, East African Publishing House, 1967).
7. See, for example, H.O. Idowu, 'The Establishment of Electoral Institutions in Senegal, 1869-1880', *Journal of African History*, Vol. IV, No. 2, 1968, pp. 261-77; David Kimble, *A Political History of Ghana, 1850-1928* (London, Oxford University Press, 1963), pp. 451-6; and J. Gus Liebenow, *Liberia: The Evolution of Privilege* (Ithaca, Cornell University Press, 1969), pp. 59-64, 117-19.
8. Smith, op. cit., pp. 85-108, contains a thorough discussion of such measures in British colonies.
9. Denis Austin, *Politics in Ghana, 1946-1960* (London, Oxford University Press, 1964); K.W.J. Post, *The Nigerian Federal Election 1959* (London, Oxford University Press, 1963); George Bennett and Carl Rosberg, *The Kenyatta Election: Kenya, 1960-1961* (London, Oxford University Press, 1961); W.F.B. Welbourn, *Religion and Politics in Uganda, 1952-62* (Nairobi, East Africa Publishing House, 1965); David G. Mulford, *The Northern Rhodesian General Election, 1962* (Nairobi, Oxford University Press, 1964) and *Zambia: the Politics of Independence, 1957-1964* (London, Oxford University Press, 1967); Ruth Schachter Morgenthau, *Political Parties in French-Speaking West Africa* (London, Oxford University Press, 1964); W.J.M. Mackenzie and Kenneth E. Robinson (eds.), *Five Elections in Africa* (London, Oxford University Press, 1960).
10. B.J. Dudley, *Parties and Politics in Northern Nigeria* (London, Frank Cass, 1968); Richard L. Sklar, *Nigerian Political Parties* (Princeton University Press, 1963); C.S. Whitaker, Jr., *The Politics of Tradition* (Princeton University Press, 1970); Martin L. Kilson, *Political Change in a West African State* (Cambridge, Harvard University Press, 1966); Harry A. Gailey, *A History of the Gambia* (London, Routledge and Kegan Paul, 1964); Willard R. Johnson, *The Cameroon Federation: Political Integration in a Fragmentary Society* (Princeton University Press, 1970); Brian Weinstein, *Gabon: Nation-Building and Ethnicity on the Ogooue* (Cambridge: Massachusetts Institute of Technology Press, 1966); Aristide R. Zolberg, *One-Party Government in the Ivory Coast* (Princeton University Press, 1969); Rene Lemarchand, *Political*

Awakening in the Belgian Congo (Berkeley, University of California Press, 1964); Herbert Weiss, *Political Protest in the Congo* (Princeton University Press, 1967); Crawford Young, *Politics in the Congo* (Princeton University Press, 1965).

11. Denis Austin and William Tordoff, 'Voting in an African Town', *Political Studies*, Vol. VIII, No. 2, 1960, pp. 130–46; Denis Austin, 'Elections in an African Rural Area', *Africa*, Vol. XXIX, 1961, pp. 1–17; George Bennett, 'The Gold Coast General Election of 1954', *Parliamentary Affairs*, Vol. 7, No. 4, April 1954, pp. 430–9; W.B. Birmingham and G. Jahoda, 'A Pre-Election Survey in a Semi-Literate Society', *Public Opinion Quarterly*, Vol XIX, 1955, pp. 140–52; Marguerite Cartwright, 'The Ghana Elections of 1956', *United Asia*, Vol. IX, No. 1, February 1957, pp. 71–9; Heidi Erlich, 'Plunkitt Revisited: the Machine in Accra', paper presented to the 14th Annual Meeting of the American African Studies Association, 1971; Fred M. Hayward, 'Political Participation and its Role in Development: Some Observations Drawn from the African Context', *The Journal of Developing Areas*, Vol. 7, No. 4, July, 1973, pp. 591–612; J.H. Price, 'The Gold Coast General Election of 1951', West African Affairs Series, No. 4, Bureau of Current Affairs, Department of Extra-Mural Studies, University College of the Gold Coast, 1951; J.H. Price, 'The Muslim Vote in the Accra Constituencies, 1954', Proceedings of the 4th Annual Conference of the West African Institute of Social and Economic Research, Ibadan, 1956; A.C. Russell, P.H. Canham and M.J.E. Patterson, 'The Gold Coast General Election, 1951', *Journal of African Administration*, Vol. III, No. 2, April 1951, pp. 65–77.

12. For a discussion of the sham election which finally took place in 1965, in which all candidates nominated by the ruling party were declared unopposed, without even asking the voters to signify their assent, see John Kraus, 'Ghana's New "Corporate Parliament"', *Africa Report*, August 1965, pp. 6–11.

13. See W.J.A. Macartney, 'The Lesotho General Election of 1970', *Government and Opposition*, Vol. 8, No. 2, Spring 1973, pp. 473–94; Anton Bebler, *Military Rule in Africa* (New York, Praeger, 1973); and Ram Seegobin and Linsay Collen, 'Mauritius: Class Forces and Political Power', *Review of African Political Economy*, No. 8, January–April 1977, pp. 109–118.

14. Such elections have been held recently in, for example, Benin (1979), Cameroun (1980), Mali (1980), and Zaire (1977).

15. See, for example, Lionel Cliffe (ed.), *One Party Democracy: the 1965 Tanzania General Elections* (Nairobi, East African Publishing House, 1967); John Saul, et. al., *Socialism and Participation: Tanzania's 1970 National Elections* (Dar es Salaam, Tanzania Publishing House, 1974); Henry Bienen, *Kenya: The Politics of Participation and Control* (Princeton University Press, 1974); G. Hyden and C. Leys, 'Elections and Politics in a Single Party System', *British Journal of Political Science*, Vol. 2, No. 4, December 1972, pp. 389–420; A. Milton Obote, *Document No. 5 on the Move to the Left: Proposals for new methods of election of representatives of the people to parliament* (Kampala, Milton Obote Foundation, 1970); D.L. Cohen and J. Parson, 'The

Uganda People's Congress Branch and Constituency Elections of 1970', *Journal of Commonwealth Political Studies*, Vol. XI, No. 1, March 1973, pp. 46-66; Ian Scott, 'Middle Class Politics in Zambia', *African Affairs*, Vol. 77, No. 308, July 1978, pp. 321-34.
16. A point made, but not sufficiently developed, in John A. Wiseman, 'Multi-Partyism in Africa: The Case of Botswana', *African Affairs*, Vol. 76, No. 302, January 1977, p. 77.
17. *West Africa*, No. 3342, 17 August 1981, pp. 1865-7.
18. For example, Hyden and Leys, op. cit.
19. Naomi Chazan, 'African Voters at the Polls: A Re-examination of the Role of Elections in African Politics', *The Journal of Commonwealth and Comparative Political Studies*, Vol. XVII, No. 2, July 1979, pp. 136-58.
20. Denis Austin and Robin Luckham (eds.), *Politicians and Soldiers in Ghana* (London, Frank Cass, 1975).
21. Chazan, op. cit., p. 152.
22. Commencing with R.B. McCallum and A. Readman, *The British General Election of 1945* (London, Oxford University Press, 1947). The method is briefly discussed by its leading practitioner in David Butler and Donald Stokes, *Political Change in Britain* (Harmondsworth, Penguin, 1971, o.v. 1969), pp. 26-31.
23. Examples include the work of Austin, Bennett and Rosberg, Mackenzie and Robinson, Morgenthau, and Mulford, all cited above.
24. Examples include Austin, 'Elections in an African Rural Area', op. cit.; Austin and Tordoff, 'Voting in an African Town', op. cit.; and J.J. Okumu, 'The By-Election in Gem: An Assessment', *East African Journal*, Vol. VI, No. 6, June 1969, pp. 9-17.
25. Examples include Cliffe, op. cit.; Austin and Luckham, op. cit., and Saul, op. cit.
26. See, for example, Staniland, op. cit.
27. A similar approach of a collection of case studies was adopted in the study of Botswana's 1974 General Election organized by J. Parson. This time the device of a conference of all participating researchers after the election, at which some comparability could be achieved, was adopted. Again, however, the study proved abortive for practical reasons – this time lack of researcher commitment and financial support, rather than the intervention of a coup. See J. Parson, 'A Note on the 1974 General Election in Botswana and the U.B.L.S. Election Study', *Botswana Notes and Records*, Vol. 7, 1975, pp. 73-81.
28. See Paul S. Lazarsfeld, Bernard Berelson and Hazel Gaudet, *The People's Choice* (New York, Duell, Sloan and Pearce, 1944); Angus Campbell and Robert L. Kahn, *The People Elect A President* (Ann Arbor, Survey Research Center, Institute for Social Research, University of Michigan, 1952); Angus Campbell, Gerald Guerin and Warren E. Miller, *The Voter Decides* (Chicago, Row-Peterson, 1954); Bernard R. Berelson, Paul Lazarsfeld and William N. McPhee, *Voting* (University of Chicago Press, 1954); Angus Campbell, Philip E. Converse, Warren E. Miller and Donald E. Stokes, *The American Voter* (New York, John Wiley & Sons, 1960); Angus Stokes, *Elections and the Political Order* (New York, John Wiley & Sons, 1966); and Norman H. Nie, Sidney Verba and

John R. Petrocik, *The Changing American Voter* (Cambridge, Harvard University Press, 1976).
29. See William M. O'Barr, D.H. Spain and M.A. Tessler (eds.), *Survey Research in Africa: Its Application and Limits* (Evanston, Northwestern University Press, 1972), for an extensive discussion of many of the problems involved.
30. A recent example of this can be seen in Lionel Cliffe, Joshua Mpofu and Barry Munslow, 'Nationalist Politics in Zimbabwe: The 1980 Elections and Beyond', *Review of African Political Economy*, No. 18, April–May 1980, Table II, p. 59.
31. See, for example, Birmingham and Jahoda, op. cit.; Kenneth Prewitt and Goran Hyden, 'Voters Look at the Elections'; L. Cliffe (ed.), *One-Party Democracy*, op. cit., pp. 273–98; and the work of Hall and Lucas in Saul, op. cit.
32. Cliffe, op. cit.
33. J.S. Saul, 'The Nature of Tanzania's Political System: Issues Raised by the 1965 and 1970 Elections', *Journal of Commonwealth Political Studies*, Vol. 8, Nos. 2 and 3, July and November 1972, pp. 111–29 and 198–221.
34. H. Bienen, *Kenya: the Politics of Participation and Control* (Princeton University Press, 1974).
35. Fred Hayward, op. cit., p. 602, suggests, for example, that increased cynicism, rather than legitimation, has been the response by most Ghanaian voters to their electoral experience.
36. Examples include: Robert O. Byrd, 'Characteristics of Candidates for Election in a Country Approaching Independence: The Case of Uganda', *Midwest Journal of Political Science*, Vol. VII, No. 1, February 1963, pp. 1–27; Helge Kjekshus, *The Elected Elite: A Socio-Economic Profile of Candidates in Tanzania's Parliamentary Elections 1970* (Uppsala, Scandinavian Institute of African Studies, 1975); Alwyn R. Rouyer, 'Political Change and Political Representation in Kenya', *The Journal of Developing Areas*, Vol. 9, July 1975, pp. 539–62; and D.L. Cohen, 'The Botswana Political Elite: Evidence from the 1974 General Election', *Journal of Southern African Affairs*, Vol. IV, No. 3, July 1979, pp. 347–72.
37. For examples of each, see Raymond F. Hopkins, *Political Roles in a New State* (New Haven, Yale University Press, 1971); Robert M. Price, *Society and Bureaucracy in Contemporary Ghana* (Berkeley, University of California Press, 1975); and Robin Luckham, *The Nigerian Military* (Cambridge University Press, 1971).
38. W.G. Runciman, *Social Science and Political Theory*, (Cambridge University Press, 1965), pp. 87–8.
39. For an analysis of the widespread misuse of the concept of charisma see D.L. Cohen, 'Charisma and the Analysis of Leadership', op. cit.
40. Parson, op. cit., p. 76.
41. Lapido Adamolekun, *Sekou Toure's Guinea* (London, Methuen, 1976) passim, argues that a high level of ideological support as well as identification with the charismatic leadership of the President underpins the stability of the Guinean regime.
42. The current Vice-President of Nigeria, Alex Ekwueme, gives a fine

example of such ethnic analysis of election results in *West Africa*, No. 3342, 17 August 1981, p. 1863.

43. See Austin, 'Elections in an African Rural Area', op. cit.; Austin and Tordoff, 'Voting in an African Town', op. cit.; and Austin, *Politics in Ghana*, op. cit., for examples.

44. Austin and Luckham, op. cit. The argument is put most clearly in John Dunn's contribution, 'Politics in Asunafo', p. 208, in these words; 'Tribalism is undoubtedly a danger from the point of view of the state, but it may also represent the painful construction of a political community. Whilst it was simply a matter of sharing out the contents of the public coffers among the successor elites such a perspective might seem perverse. When it can be shown, however fitfully, at work in the processes of a democratic election campaign, it may be easier to understand the moral substance which, along with its immoral and dangerous characteristics, it does beyond question display. The Progress Party in Asunafo advanced an image of Ahafo as a moral community. They elected a man from Ahafo who had grappled with modernity but returned to live within Ahafo to stand for them in the national tourney in which community struggles against community for the goods and evils which the government distributes.'

45. D.L. Cohen and J. Parson, 'The UPC Branch and Constituency Elections of 1970:, op. cit., pp. 58–69; Clyde Sanger and John Nottingham, 'The Kenya General Eelction of 1963', *Journal of Modern African Studies*, Vol. 2, No. 1, 1964, pp. 16–18; W.J. Brytenbach, 'Party Politics and Traditionalism in Botswana', *Bulletin of the Africa Institute of South Africa*, No. 1, 1975, pp. 24–7 and Lemarchand, op. cit., pp. 192–7.

46. Post, op. cit., pp. 376–89.

47. See Joan Vincent, *African Elite: The Big Men of a Small Town* (New York, Columbia University Press, 1971); Colin Leys, *Underdevelopment in Kenya: The Political Economy of Neo-Colonialism* (London, Heinemann, 1975), pp. 212–15; D.L. Cohen, 'The Botswana Political Elite', op. cit., pp. 360–2; and J.S. LaFontaine, *City Politics: A Study of Leopoldville, 1962-63* (Cambridge University Press), pp. 202–9.

48. Bienen, op. cit., pp. 103–4.

49. Ian Hancock, 'Patriotism and Neo-Traditionalism in Buganda: The Kabaka Yekka ("The King Alone") Movement, 1961-1962', *The Journal of African History*, Vol. XI, No. 3, 1970.

50. Cohen and Parson, op. cit., pp. 54–6.

51. Data drawn from the following sources: *Ghana*: Austin, *Politics in Ghana*, op. cit., p. 238, p. 247; Austin and Luckham, op. cit., p. 128, p. 140; and *Keesings Contemporary Record*, 5 September 1980, p. 30444. *Nigeria:* Post, op. cit., p. 203, p. 350; *Keesings Contemporary Record*, 1965, p. 20578; and Federal Electoral Commission, 'Report on the General Eelction, 1979'(Lagos: FEDECO, 1979), p. 4. *Kenya*: Bienen, op. cit., p. 90; Bennett and Rosberg, op. cit., p. 62, p. 217; *African Research Bulletin*, Vol. 16, No. 11, 15 December 1979, p. 5470; and Colin Legum (ed.), *African 1974/5 Contemporary Record* (London, Rex Collings, 1976), B199. *Tanzania*: Cliffe, op. cit., p. 358; Bienen, op. cit., p. 95; Legum, *African Contemporary Record 1975/6*,

op. cit., B321–3. *Zambia*: Robert Molteno and Ian Scott, 'The 1968 General Election and the Political System', William Tordoff (ed.), *Politics in Zambia* (Manchester University Press, 1974), p. 162; Scott, op. cit., p. 333; and *Africa*, No. 90, February 1979, p. 20. *Botswana:* Parson, op. cit., p. 75; and *African Research Bulletin*, Vol. 16, No. 10, 15 November 1979, pp. 5436–7.
52. For examples of such explanations, see T.E. Smith, op. cit., Ch. 4, 'Registration of Electors', pp. 20–84; and K.W.J. Post, op. cit., pp. 350–8.
53. Bienen, op. cit., p. 95, and FEDECO Report, op. cit., passim.
54. Predictably, the more favourable interpretation is that put on the turn-out figures by the ruling BDP, while the opposition favour the latter view. See Cohen, 'The Botswana Political Elite', op. cit., pp. 364–5; and Jack Parson, 'Political Culture in Rural Botswana: A Survey Result', *Journal of Modern African Studies*, Vol. 15, No. 4, December 1977, pp. 639–50.
55. For a classic statement of representative theory, see J.S. Mill, *Representative Government* (Chicago, Britannia, 1952, o.v. 1861).
56. See A.J. Milnor, *Elections and Political Stability* (Boston, Little, Brown and Co., 1969), pp. 122–84.
57. Sir B. Keith-Lucas, 'Introduction' to T.E. Smith, op. cit., pp. ix–x.
58. Bienen, op. cit., p. 112.
59. Saul, 'The Nature of Tanzania's Political System', op. cit., p. 204.
60. Ibid., p. 216, 'The electoral system is an arbitrary and somewhat misleading point from which to launch such an enquiry as the present one.'
61. W.J.M. Mackenzie, 'The Export of Electoral Systems', *Political Studies*, Vol. II, No. 3, 1957, pp. 240–57, used this concept in a much earlier survey in this vein.
62. See Nelson Kasfir, *The Shrinking Political Arena* (Berkeley, University of California Press, 1976), pp. 3–27, for a discussion of the concept of de-participation, or declining rate of political participation, which he believes characterizes post-colonial African politics and which he argues can be constructively related to further political development. More recent evidence may indicate that his judgment has been premature.

8. Public Administration in Africa: Separate Area or Sub-Discipline?

J.B. Ojo

The choice of topic of this paper has been provoked by two major developments. Firstly, there has been a growing tendency in some African universities to duplicate academic departments, with political science set up side by side with public administration. In other universities, political science and public administration exist together in one department under a single headship. Under this arrangement, few courses of public administration are designed and incorporated into the political science curriculum, with greater emphasis being on political science courses. Whatever explanations may be given for separating public administration from, or combining it with, political science, there are some obvious implications for not only our conception of the content and scope of the programmes but also for our approach to and methods of teaching them.

Secondly, there is also an observed dissatisfaction on the part of the relevant section of the public in African countries with the performance of fresh graduates of public administration coming into the public service for the first time. By the 'relevant section of the public' I mean the older public administrators, policy-makers and all those who, for one reason or another, are associated with or engaged in public affairs. This observed dissatisfaction arises largely from displayed inability on the part of most newly recruited public administration graduates to come to terms with the realities of administration when they take up office. This is noted both in terms of relating theories to real problems and also in terms of familiarity with the socio-political environment of the public service. In some cases, government departments have to allocate funds to equip new recruits with extra training by way of postgraduate diplomas.

Both issues are related in the sense that if our universities were clear about the philosophy or goal of public administration as a course of study in terms of our societal needs and realities, then the politics of whether it should be a separate department or part of political science should not arise in the first place. Also, if we were clear about the philosophy or goal of the course in terms of the circumstances of any given society, the content, scope and our teaching methodology, then the course would have been so designed as to avert, or at least reduce, the present observed dissatisfaction with the performance of fresh public administration graduates.

The purpose of this paper, therefore, is to examine briefly whether there is any need to bother about whether or not public administration should be designed and taught as an integral part of political science in our curriculum development. The point is that, whatever stand one takes in the matter, it is bound to reflect on the way we go about teaching the course in terms of content, scope, methodology and even the philosophy. The next task, which of course follows from the first, is to look at the way we can design and teach the course in the light of the developmental needs of African countries. Some concluding observations will be made at the end in the form of suggestions.

Public Administration and Political Systems

The task here is to see what place public administration occupies within the political science curriculum in our universities, so as to know the right approach to its teaching in the light of our societal needs. But we must first of all be clear about what public administration itself is. Public administration has been defined in many different ways by various authors. Pfiffner and Presthus for example, regard public administration as concerned mainly with the means for implementing political values,[1] while Dimock and Dimock define it as the accomplishment of politically determined objectives.[2] Davis Jr. takes the same stand when he says that public administration can be best identified with the executive branch of government.[3] Although these three views regard public administration as having a close link with the political system, their emphasis appears to be more on looking at it as an instrument in the hands of political authorities for acieving already determined goals. Taking these definitions as they are, the study or teaching of public administration will always end up treating public administration merely as a tool. This is because the authors are silent about the actual process by which the said goals or policies are determined. But Nigro and Nigro on the other hand feel that public administration has an important role in the formulation of public policy, and is thus part of the political process itself.[4] This view does not see public administration as a mere tool. Rather it is a part of the political process and cannot be said to operate in a vacuum but well intertwined with fundamental problems of the entire society. It influences and is influenced by issues of a fundamental nature which affect its environment of operation. Those who share this view are, again, likely to have different approaches to the teaching of public administration.

Also, Waldo is of the view that public administration is a highly eclectic subject that draws its theories and approaches from many areas of human knowledge, including political science, decision-making, management science, economics and history.[5] This definition also has a broad view of the subject and does not seem to attach public administration to any one department. However, there are other scholars who feel that public administration should not be defined anyway. Mosher, for example, claims that it is more an area of interest than a discipline, and more of a focus than a separate science.[6] Similarly, Parker asserts that 'no science or art can be identified by this title [Public Administration], least of all any single skill or coherent intellectual discipline'.[7] These views seem to be rather simplistic. This author is of the view that public administration has attained some level of self-consciousness already, even in Africa, to make it a discipline or, at least, a sub-discipline of a related subject.

Whatever one may make of the conflicting views about public administration as a subject of study, one point, at least, is worthy of note. And that is, that most scholars seem to agree about its close relationship with the political system, either that it is simply concerned with administering policies that are made by political authorities or that it is itself a part of the political process for bringing policies into being that affect the general public. It would, therefore, seem a wholesome approach to expose students of public administration to the concept of the political system and the theories relating to how it operates. Most students come into the field of public administration with the assumptions that they will read more about political than non-political matters and find out how the policies and resources of the state are administered. This, of course, derives from the fact that the notion of public administration itself dates from the time when political systems began to institutionalize links between those who make policies and those who administer them. And, indeed, public administration has been, as a matter of tradition, studied as a sub-discipline of political science.

However, the question that arises at this stage is whether, in the present stage of development in African countries, the emphasis should be on producing graduates of public administration or on producing those with mixed orientation but greater leaning towards political science theories. Until we are clear about this issue our designed programmes will be unlikely to be the best that we can offer to meet the requirements of our developing societies.

The Blinkers of Policy Implementation

Like other Third World countries, our problem in Africa is that of development. Our guiding philosophy in curriculum development, as in the way we teach our programmes, must necessarily reflect this. However, we may look at some of the advantages and disadvantages or the relevance, in the light of our present needs, of designing and teaching public administration programmes with emphasis on political science knowledge.

Firstly, public administration, at whatever stage of development, does not operate in a vacuum. From simple societies to the most complex ones, it is totally unreal to think of public administration as existing simply to execute policy decisions of political leaders, unaffected by the private political or ideological convictions of the administrators themselves. Rather than existing simply to execute the policies of political leaders, we do know from observation that bureaucrats not only make policies themselves but also acquire political influence far greater than shows up on the organizational chart. This, in essence, is what Norton Long argues in his essay on 'Power and Administration'. Long is of the view that all administrative institutions are continually competing for political survival and over the resources of the society. He writes, 'The life blood of administration is power. Its attainment, maintenance, increase and loss are subjects the practitioner and student can ill afford to neglect.'[8]

Bureaucracies are, in fact, interest groups. They build and win support for themselves, as well as pressing governments for policies that they want. It is only reasonable, therefore, that the theoretical aspects of such political realities in the environment of public administration are not overlooked in our course designs. In this regard, it would appear advisable that theories relating to the concept of power and resource allocation be designated as background knowledge for students of public administration. This becomes more reasonable in Third World countries, where resources to be administered or shared are more scarce than they are in the developed countries. It is not only desirable that we design our course contents to include such theoretical backgrounds, but their relevance to the actual world of administration should be emphasized in our teaching method.

Another related point is the fact that public administration in developing countries operates in a more competitive environment than it does in the developed nations. This arises from the fact that, apart from the scarcity of the resources to be distributed to various developmental needs, the component ethnic groups are divided and in continual struggle for their own shares of national resources. In addition, national identity is in some countries virtually non-existent. These pose special problems to administrators in most Third World countries, especially in Africa where ethnic consciousness still rates very high at the expense of central political institutions. The need to reflect national character in most national institutions often leads to recruitment of the representatives of the competing ethnic groups into central bureaucracies. Consequently, merit criteria suffer in favour of the quota system. These are vital issues which students of public administration in an African country cannot afford to neglect. They are among the elements with which the political environment of public administration is made in Nigeria as in most African countries. But what we often find in a country like Nigeria among the fresh public administration graduates, and which the older and more experienced administrators do worry about, is that they come into the service with ideals unrelated to the practical realities of the society. They emphasize merit, the economy of resource allocation and such theoretical and idealistic criteria. If part of our goal is to produce administrative personnel who are really useful in nation-building, then part of our efforts should also be directed to making our students understand the realities of the society they are to build. This cannot be achieved through courses which treat institutions and organizational behaviours in isolation. We may even discover that a good background knowledge of the political history of the country may be useful to our students if they are to learn to be more patient and appreciate why resources are administered in the way they are.

Furthermore, intensive and full specialization in public administration at the expense of relevant political science theories could have certain dangers in a developing country. Developing nations often face one form of turmoil or another. In addition, most interest groups in these countries are as yet poorly established. Political parties are largely in a fluid form while trade unions are yet to be well organized. During such periods, the national bureaucracy may be the only valuable source of innovation and political initiative as well as the only source of political advice to political leaders. Obviously, such roles can only be well played by bureaucrats who are well informed in theoretical backgrounds of political, economic and social problems rather than those who are taught to see public administration as being merely concerned with implementing policies of political leaders.

Another related danger is that the more we bring up our students to see public administration as merely concerned with the study of how to implement policies, the more we tend to design our course contents to present institutions or organizations in purely technical terms. In the same vein, human beings in the organization may appear to students as ordinary materials. While basic concepts should be taught as part of the relevant content of public administration, students should be encouraged to understand that such concepts have some favourable environments. Men and women in the organization should be seen in psychological terms and not as machines. The tendency to teach our basic concepts in isolation rather than in context has in turn produced the tendency on the part of our fresh graduates to think in narrow terms. This author was among a group of fresh graduates to be interviewed for an administrative post in the federal civil service of Nigeria in 1975. In an answer to a question 'why is it that some British administrative experts fail when they apply British solutions to Nigerian problems?' one of the candidates said that the administrators fail because there are more competent executive officers in Britain than there are in Nigeria. Although this may be part of the answer, the panel had expected the candidate to discuss such fundamental issues as environmental differences of the two countries and how a solution that may solve a public problem in Britain may be invalidated by the social and political conditions of Nigeria.

On the other hand, the extent to which we need political science theories in our public administration programmes is determined not only by the goal of our programme as regards our immediate needs but also the time at our disposal to accomplish such programmes. If our immediate goal is development and what we need are public servants who are just good enough to execute programmes for that purpose, then our task should be to produce graduates who are also just sufficiently familiar with the basic administrative techniques to achieve that goal. And if the time at our disposal is not enough to design a course content for this goal without limiting attention to political science knowledge, our immediate national needs have to prevail. In fact, public servants in most developing countries today have virtually become the only 'experts' around in most problems of a technical nature. They are engaged in technical aspects of preparing budgets according to the priorities of the nation, job classification in the light of developmental needs and also in the development of national resources for the achievement of societal ends within the context of changing political situations.

Also with the introduction of electronic techniques into the administration of the modern states, the average public administrator requires some special form of orientation to be successful in his job. In addition, a good proportion of the problems facing most African states are of such a practical nature that much emphasis on theoretical training may not be the best approach. Quite often, we hear political leaders accusing university 'class-room theoreticians' of approaching practical problems with theoretical solutions which in many cases do not work. Our course designs and teaching emphasis, therefore should be able to reflect more of these special skills than theories.

However, we may, on proper investigation, discover that we perhaps need to be more specific in appreciating national needs. We may also discover that the students need more of basic and specialized administrative techniques to be more useful to national developmental goals than if they were to be exposed to more of theoretical training. No matter how we look at the issue, our students are yet to be sufficiently exposed to practical training in any of our universities. This we must set right both in our course designs and in our time-tables.

The Need for Practical Training

There is no doubt that public administration has been taught, at least traditionally, as an integral part of political science in most African universities. It is true that our public administration programmes must include some related polticial and other social science theories to make our teaching more rounded. It is also true that the amount of theoretical exposure to other social science subjects must be related to the immediate needs of the society. Our programmes, therefore, should be designed to take note of the special problems of our countries in terms of needs and environmental factors without, in any way, sacrificing basic international standards.

To succeed in designing a meaningful programme in public administration with relevant content and scope, the teacher, I think, cannot afford to work in isolation from the contributions of the experienced field officers who are actually administering the system. While provisions should be made to invite experienced administrative officers regularly to give lectures based upon their experiences on the job, periods should also be created to enable students to make field trips to government ministries and public corporations to see how most concepts actually operate. If a continuing co-operation of this nature is established, both in our curriculum development and teaching process, much of the initial dissatisfaction with the performance of our fresh graduates will be reduced. This co-operation is even more important in determining the 'right' philosophy for the total effort. No single institution, not even the universities, can claim the monopoly on knowing the best guiding philosophy for the society in terms of curriculum development.

There is no doubt that we have special problems in the Third World, since some existing theories and approaches that work in most advanced countries do not seem to be relevant to our situations. Whatever theories or approaches that we may have to apply must necessarily be related to the special problems and needs of African societies. The same must guide the content and scope of our curriculum.

This is no less relevant to the way we must teach our students in terms of what to emphasize in the classroom. And, let me say again, we must first of all be clear about our goals in terms of our environmental realities. When ths this is done, our teaching of public administration, either as a separate or as a sub-discipline of political science, will naturally attract the right content, scope and approach.

Notes

1. John M. Pfiffner and R. Presthus, *Public Administration* (New York, Ronald Press, 5th ed., 1967).
2. M.E. Dimock and G.O. Dimock, *Public Administration* (1969).
3. J.W. Davis Jr., *Introduction to Public Administration* (1974).
4. F.A. Nigro and L.G. Nigro, *Modern Public Administration* (1973).
5. D. Waldo and R.J. Stillman in *Public Administration: Concepts and Cases* (Houghton Mifflin Co., 1976), p. 4.
6. F.C. Mosher, 'Research in Public Administration', *Public Administration Review*, Vol. 16, Summer 1956, p. 177.
7. R.S. Parker, 'The end of Public Administration', *Public Administration* Vol 34, June 1965, p. 99.
8. Norton Long and F.J. Stillman in *Public Administration: Concepts and Cases* op. cit., p. 80.

9. Political Science and Political Economy

Bjorn Beckman

The Department of Political Science at Ahmadu Bello University in Nigeria offers an undergraduate course entitled 'State and Economy'. According to the course description, students are supposed to examine 'the role of government in the management of a modern economy with special reference to Nigeria and other African countries'. The course is also expected to deal with such issues as the relationship between government and private enterprise, foreign capital and aid, indigenization of the economy, self-reliance, planning and development administration.

I believe that the offering of such a course is a step towards improving the social relevance of the discipline. It represents, as I see it, one attempt to break out of the straitjacket of a 'pure science of politics' and to relate to issues of development which affect the material conditions of the people. Other courses in the department have a similar problem orientation, dealing with food policy, health services, rural development, imperialism and underdevelopment, to mention a few.

The attempt to tackle such substantive problems of social and economic development, however, raises issues about the relationship of political science to other disciplines and economics in particular. These are issues of professional identity and specialization as well as of theory and method.

It is argued in this essay that much of current professional specialization within the social sciences is obstructive to an understanding of substantive social problems and that there is consequently an urgent need to develop theories and methods which allow us to treat issues as social wholes. Meaningful specialization can only be achieved on the basis of such a unified approach. Political economy, as developed within the Marxist tradition, offers one basis for the reintegration of fragmented knowledge.

First, however, I will discuss attempts within Anglo-American political science to tackle 'development problems' in the framework of a 'new political economy'. This has little in common with either classical or Marxist political economy and it fails to transcend the self-imposed constraints of political science. I proceed to outline the classical, neo-classical and Marxist positions. In the past decade we have witnessed an upsurge of scholarship within the latter tradition. I look in particular at its impact on the social sciences in and about Africa. Political scientists can make useful contributions to the development of political economy provided they are prepared to pursue the roots of the politics outside the ideological fence of the 'political system'. The study of the state may still be the focus for meaningful specialization within a common political economic framework.

The Trap of Specialization

Weber described the transition to 'modernity' in terms of increasing specialization and differentiation of roles. The social sciences have had more than their fair share of this process. The unity of understanding provided by such ancient disciplines as philosophy and history has been fragmented. Anxious to further their exclusive professional identities, each new discipline has tended to set its focus as far apart from those of the others as possible. In doing so, they have tended to distance themselves from the real social issues at stake, or have subjected such issues to 'analytical perspectives' which fragment and obstruct understanding. The consequent mystification of political science for example, with its separation out of the 'political system', has resulted in the ideological separation of different types of social power, where only some are seen as legitimate objects of study within the discipline. The question of democracy is treated as if it has nothing to do with control over the means of production. The power and control exercised by capital over labour is considered to fall within the realm of economics, not political science. The economists, on the other hand, have tended to eliminate power altogether from their analysis.

Questions of rural development, food shortage, health, sanitation, unemployment and others, are social problems which simultaneously involve the social, economic and political organization of the people; hence the focus must be on the interplay, supportive or obstructive, of such forces. Relevant knowledge is therefore not likely to be obtained by *adding* together observations derived from separate disciplinary perspectives because the dynamics which bind them together cannot be understood additively. Similarly, 'interdisciplinary' work will also fail to produce much understanding, if it is not rooted in an effort to deal directly with the wider context which determines interaction. Even more seriously, the result is not merely a poorly connected, fragmented, social understanding, but distorted or false knowledge because of the tendency to establish explanatory models which are *internal* to the 'system', invented and jealously guarded by a particular academic discipline.

I do not believe that the realization of this theoretical trap of specialization means necessarily that the separate disciplines must be scrapped before useful changes can take place. Nor do I believe that political scientists must all master economics, sociology and other social science disciplines before they can do any useful work on substantive issues dealing with the material well-being of the people. The immediate need is rather for all social scientists, irrespective of discipline, to pay much more attention to such general social theory as will allow them, however specialized they may be, to relate their own piece to a dynamic whole. This greater common understanding of a wider social and historical context will no doubt in due course allow for a different type of specialization; one based on the issues involved rather than on disciplinary analytical perspectives.

The 'New Political Economy': Reformist Tendencies in Political Science

> The ever-increasing specialization of political scientists and economists has tended to reify what is after all nothing more than an artificial boundary between two categories of social scientists each concerned with only analytically different aspects of a single concrete whole, namely human society.[1]

This quote from a well-known political scientist and 'Africanist', James S. Coleman, is evidence that the concerns raised above are not by any means new and that they in fact have been given some attention by the professional establishment. Coleman's text has been widely used in support of attempts to establish a 'new political economy'.[2] As we shall see, the notion of 'political economy' involved has little in common with either classical political economy or the critical political economy developed within the Marxist tradition. More important, however, this 'new political economy' fails to overcome the artificial boundaries which it has identified. The analysis is still at the level of separate 'systems', with their separate theories. 'Political economy', as developed by Coleman and his followers, is perceived as a new specialism within political science, as political sociology or political psychology. Let us first look at what Coleman has to offer.

The role of Coleman's new political economist is either to study the 'political preconditions of economic development' or, alternatively, 'the political consequences of economic development'. In the first case, the emphasis is on the need for 'deliberate planning and for governments to play a major role as entrepreneurs', and above all, the need for skilled leadership and efficient political structures. 'The overpowering logic of the African situation makes effective public administration a precondition for economic development.' It is thus the presumed growth in government 'economic' responsibilities in a 'developmental situation' which necessitates the involvement of political science in economics and thus in 'political economy'.

Leaving aside the ideological basis of Coleman's vision of social progress and its agents, it is clear that this 'political economy' is concerned with identifying separable 'political' or 'administrative' dimensions of development problems which can be handled by political scientists in their specialist role. It is not addressed to the problem of understanding the causes of development problems and their solutions. 'Bureaucratic efficiency' can only be meaningfully analysed in relation to the substantive functions of the bureaucracy in the society. If for example, the bureaucracy in a neo-colonial society serves as the accomplice of foreign capital in the exploitation of resources and people, is it the task of the political scientist to improve its efficiency in this respect? No meaningful 'recommendations' can be offered without dealing with the issues at stake.

We also learn from Coleman that his brand of new political economists are concerned 'not only with how political variables and constraints affect economic development, but also how the latter, as an independent variable, affects political behaviour and institutions'. He illustrates this latter aspect with three issues: first, how levels of 'economic development' are connected with 'political competitiveness'; second, whether or not 'rapid economic growth leads to political instability'; and, third, how uneven economic development affects the problem of 'political integration'. Here again, this political economy reveals its primary commitment to the abstract notions of political science. Such 'system variables' as competition, stability and integration can have no meaning except in relation to the content and nature of the contradictions involved. Only with such an understanding can we answer questions such as: competition between whom, over what; stability for what purpose, in whose interests; integration on whose terms; and only then will we be able to transcend the ideological obscurantism promoted under the auspices of such concepts.

For a more elaborate variety of this 'new political economy' we may turn to Ilchman and Upholff's *The Political Economy of Change*, hailed as 'an important landmark in the development of an integrated social science'.[3] The point of departure is itself revealing. The authors start with a discussion of the dilemma of a hypothetical team of political scientists flying in to Lagos (presumably from the U.S.A.) to advise General Gowon, the former Nigerian military Head of State. The concern is with what these political scientists may have to offer. They envisage and work out in amazing abstract detail (with input-output tables and all) a new science for the rational and efficient management of 'political resources'. Their political economy is based on a market model of interaction and exchange borrowed from economics (the most 'rigorous' of the social sciences) and applied to politics. 'Political choices' concern maximizing 'productivity' in the use of the 'scarce political resources' available to a 'statesman'. These choices involve coping with or inducing social and economic change, how to remain in power now and in the future, and how to construct the 'political and administrative infrastructure'.

Ilchman's and Uphoff's use of models from economics does not alter the abstract 'politicist' perspective. It is basically manipulative and managerial. 'Social problems' are identified from the position of the 'statesman' who is affected by them and thus has to act. The relation of this 'statesman', or rather of those social forces which have placed him in the position of statesmanship, to the problems, that is, the extent to which they are part of them, is beyond the grasp of such perspective. The 'model' is consequently unable to identify the causes of problems. Without this, there is no basis for offering any other solutions than, possibly, improvements in the manipulative efficiency of the regime. Despite its mildly liberal-distributionist concerns, the implications are distinctly sinister.

Coleman, Uphoff and Ilchman represent the lineage of development studies within the 'new political economy'. It ties up closely with the move towards 'policy analysis' in the advanced capitalist countries themselves.[4] One line which has emerged within that tradition is the new and laudable concern of political scientists with public revenue and expenditure as important variables of the political system. An early and energetic exponent of this approach is W.C. Mitchell.[5] He argues that budget figures should be basic data in all political science textbooks and that political scientists should identify and measure 'the incidence of benefits which governments create and distribute'. He draws support for this 'distributive' perspective from authoritative formulations of the content of political science, such as Laswell's 'Who Gets What, When and How'. This concern with the 'output' of public policy is clearly an advance on political science exclusively preoccupied with the internal structures and abstract functions of political systems. Little is said, however, about the basis for measuring and evaluating such impact, or what conclusions can be drawn from observed 'incidences of benefits'. Mitchell distinguishes this brand of political economy from economics on the basis of the nature of goods and services handled. His political economy focuses on *'public'* goods and services while economics deals with non-public ones. The identification of 'political' with public in this context is revealing of the ideological perspective built into political science. Even on a narrowly 'empiricist' basis it ought to be obvious that such a distinction is artificial. The state everywhere influences, regulates and participates in 'private' production. Nonetheless the separation of a 'political' from an 'economic' system is upheld and 'political economy' becomes the study of material transactions (taxes, expenditure, etc.) handled by the public sector. Political economy becomes public sector economy.

Classical Political Economy and Marxism

These 'new political economists' have little in common either with classical political economy, or the Marxist tradition which developed out of and as a critique of the former. Classical political economy (Smith, Ricardo, Senior, Say and others), was essentially a science of the economy. Their way of defining the problems of the economy, however, had a broad social orientation, including questions about the social organization of production and the distribution of income. Their approach was often historical and philosophical. They concerned themselves with the origins of the 'principles' which they saw at work. We may quote Ricardo's preface to his *Principles of Political Economy and Taxation*:

The produce of the earth — all that is derived from its surface by the

> united application of labour, machinery, and capital, is divided among three classes of the community: namely, the proprietor of the land, the owner of the stock or capital necessary for its cultivation, and the labourers by whose industry it is cultivated. But in different stages of society, the proportions of the whole produce of the earth which will be allotted to each of these classes, under the names of rent, profit, and wages, will be essentially different; ...
>
> To determine the laws which regulate this distribution, is the principal problem in Political Economy.

In neo-classical economics, which in some places retained the label 'political economy', the classical theories of factor allocation and income distribution were 'refined' into pure theories of markets and pricing. The social forces at work were reduced to abstract sources of supply and demand. The current orthodoxy is summarized by Edward Nell:

> It is not a theory of a social system, still less of economic power or social class. Households and firms are considered only as market agents, never as parts of a social structure. Their 'initial endowments', wealth, skills and property, are taken as given. Moreover the object of the theory is to demonstrate the tendency towards equilibrium; class and sectoral conflict is therefore ruled out almost by assumption.[6]

Marx's response to the classics was the opposite. While deriving some of the concern with the historical division of income and its relation to the process of accumulation from the classics, he set out to identify the dynamics of historical change. Marx sought to explain the social origins of property relations and their changes over time. It grew into a general theory of social change based on the development of the forces of production (technology, skills, etc.), the social relations of production (ownership of the means of production, the labour process, appropriation of the produce of labour, etc.), the class relations and class contradictions embedded in such relations of production, and the way social consciousness, legal and state institutions, ideology and other aspects of the superstructure of society both reflect and serve to reinforce property and class relations as determined by the dominant mode of production. Marx sought to identify the 'laws' governing the transition from one mode of production to another, and more specifically, those relating to the internal dynamics of the capitalist mode of production.

The theory and method of Marx's political economy is often described as historical materialism or dialectical materialism. 'Historical', because its concern with historical causation and laws of historical development; 'materialist' as opposed to 'idealist', that is, a focus on objective determinants as rooted in the material conditions of a society, rather than on subjective motives, ideologies and great personalities (not to speak of supernatural forces) in explaining social change. 'Dialectical', finally, stands for the significance attributed to interaction of opposites in the dynamics of social development, for example, class contradictions and interactions between base and superstructure in a social formation.

Some aspects of Marx's political economy had an early impact on Western social science, particularly in sociology and in economic and social history. Historians concerned with understanding the origins of capitalism, as for example, the group associated with the French journal *Annales* and the 'Cambridge School', as well as schools of general social theory (such as the 'Frankfurt School',) drew directly or indirectly on the Marxist 'classics' (Engels, Kautsky, Hilferding, Lenin, Bukharin, Luxemburg, Preobrashensky and others). There was a marked decline, however, in Marxist scholarship outside the emerging socialist countries. Very few influential works were produced in the 1920s, 1930s and 1940s. Before the mid-1960s there was no sustained and broadly based attempt to develop Marxist social science in the West. Contributions by scholars like Joan Robinson, Maurice Dobb, Althusser, Bettelheim, Baran, Sweezy, Hobsbawm, were mainly isolated individuals operating within a hostile academic environment. Less apparent from the academic horizon, however, was the continuous development of Marxist analysis which took place within the socialist movements in their struggles to understand the nature of the class forces and institutions which they were up against.

The expansion and consolidation of the socialist countries in the post-war period and the rise of the anti-colonial and anti-imperialist movements in the Third World created favourable conditions for an unprecedented upsurge of Marxist-inspired political economy studies in the 1960s and 1970s. This academic movement sought to understand the dynamics of contemporary capitalism on the world scale and its implications for the political struggle in individual countries. Students' support for anti-imperialist struggles created a broad base for this revival of Marxist scholarship within Western universities.

Many of these radical studies were at first based on very limited reading of classical Marxism. Their 'class analysis' was improvised and eclectic. But this freewheeling 'radical political economy' has increasingly been brought under the influence of more serious theoretical and empirical scholarship, concerned wtih exploring and advancing Marxist theory and method and its application to contemporary issues. The rise of more rigorous theoretical work seems to have been particularly strong outside the Anglo-American academic sphere in West Germany, France, Italy and Japan, which may also explain the relatively late impact in areas under Anglo-American academic domination, like much of Africa. Japan, for example, has probably a larger number of 'established' Marxist economists in its universities than any other capitalist country.[7] In West Germany, Marxist political scientists have published much serious work on theory of the state, including works on the peripheral capitalist state, which only recently have been introduced and translated into English.[8]

In the Anglo-American sphere, political journals with an academic base, such as the *Monthly Review, The New Left Review* and *Economy and Society*, have created common points of reference for a scattered Marxist academic community. In recent years alternative Marxist journals have been established within the individual social sciences: for example *Antipode* (Geography), *Critique of Anthropology, History Workshop, Insurgent Sociologist, Review of Radical Political Economy*, to mention only a few. Unions of 'socialist economists' or 'radical political economists' have recruited their membership from all the social sciences. Individual institutions and departments and, perhaps exceptionally, whole social science faculties have developed a political economy profile.[9]

African Political Economy

A number of influential contributions in recent years have marked the growing impact of radical or Marxist political economy on studies in and about Africa. Samir Amin has been particularly important in developing and introducing theories of underdevelopment and imperialism in the African context. IDEP in Dakar, where Amin has been the director, has promoted conferences and publications with a political economy orientation. The Algiers-based association of 'Third-World Economists' has encouraged the co-operation of political economists with varying disciplinary backgrounds. Individual universities, as in the case of Dar-es-Salaam, have developed traditions of radical scholarship. In Nigeria, historians and sociologists seem to have been the first to respond to this world-wide political economy movement. In the case of historians, they have been less hampered by the dead weight of *ad hoc* theorizing and model building which has plagued the other social sciences.

Academic developments inside Africa have been able to draw on an increasing number of scholarly publications from outside the continent. Chris Allen's bibliographies, begun as 'Radical Africana', a mimeographed bulletin, was later incorporated as a supplement in the *Review of African Political Economy* (published in England). It lists current publications, not necessarily Marxist or 'radical', but which are considered relevant from such perspectives. It covers mainly English language writings but also some French. The *Review* itself is an attempt to create a forum for this broad tendency. Annotated bibliographies also by Chris Allen are included in two important recent readers, Peter Gutkind's and Immanuel Wallerstein's *The Political Economy of Contemporary Africa* and Peter Gutkind's and Peter Waterman's *African Social Studies: A Radical Reader*.[10] These bibliographies, together with the selections included in the two readers and in the *Review*, may serve as a useful introduction to the field of African political economy.

Political Economy and the State

Much of the strength and attraction of political economy (for those outside the circles already committed to a Marxist political practice) has come from its break with conventional social science. It has thus corresponded to a commonsense perception of the unity of social reality and to a more acceptable notion about the superior importance of 'material' considerations. Many political scientists have been willing to redefine themselves as political economists and to shed their old professional identity. Facing final-year students of political science in our universities, who have never studied, for example, the World Bank or the International Monetary Fund — two key institutions in the international political economy, wielding immense political power — one may easily despair about the sanity of the discipline. While reforming political science may not necessarily be a social obligation to which we may attribute high priority, I believe that there exists a wide scope for reform within the discipline in the direction of political economy, which may be considered useful also to colleagues who have not adopted a Marxist perspective. Students of political economy should in fact be in a position to make a significant contribution to the development of the discipline and its usefulness to others.

We have already witnessed how varieties of 'class analysis' and 'underdevelopment theory' have had a strong impact on the study of African politics in recent years. Richard Harris' reader *The Political Economy of Africa* is an example of such attempts to blend the history of political regimes with some elements of political economy. Colin Leys' *Underdevelopment in Kenya* is a widely read and acclaimed effort by a political scientist in this direction. Issa G. Shivji has forcefully applied class analysis to the study of Tanzanian politics.[11] Mahmood Mamdani has interpreted political developments in Uganda in terms of the shifting relations between various factions of the petty bourgeoisie.[12] The theoretical basis of these early studies may perhaps be somewhat shaky, as has been freely conceded in self-critical exercises.[13] Mamdani's work was influenced by the highly sophisticated theoretical writings of Nicos Poulantzas, who has made ambitious attempts to create a basis for a new Marxist science of politics.[14] Politics, although seen as determined 'in the last instance' by the economy, is given a high degree of autonomy in Poulantzas' deductive system. We still find it far from a study of politics firmly rooted in an understanding of the political economy.[15] I agree with Holloway and Picciotto that there is a need for studies which are capable of placing specific development at the political level firmly in relation to an analysis of the development of production and the principal contradictions embedded in the social relations of production.[16] This is, of course, what is often attempted by the new generation of Marxist-oriented students of politics. Little attention, however, is actually paid to developments at the level of production. This contrasts with the strong economic determinism usually postulated. Most crudely, 'neo-colonialism', for example, is taken to explain everything at the political level without any sustained effort to examine neo-colonialism itself and what it actually means at the level of the development of productive forces, social relations of production, class contradictions, and so on. Facile assumptions about contradictions between, for example, 'peasants and workers', on the one hand, and 'imperialism and its local lackeys', on the other offer little concrete guidance for a closer class analysis of the state and its policies. Class analysis requires a sound understanding of the economic basis of society and cannot be improvised on an *ad hoc* basis. For political scientists studying the politics of peripheral capitalist societies it is therefore crucial to focus on the dynamics of captialist accumulation on the world scale as it affects the development of the peripheral formation. Close study must be devoted to the dynamics of incorporation and penetration by international capital and its interaction with processes of accumulation and class formation at the local level.

The study of political science would certainly gain considerably in realism and relevance by focusing attention on *the roots of politics* at the levels of production, social relations and social organization of class forces. But political scientists may also contribute significantly to an understanding of *the impact of politics* on economic and social forces and the contradictions and struggles to which they give rise. At the level of theory, *both* concerns require an understanding of the dialectical relationship of determination and interaction which connect the economic and political levels of society. Marxist political economy may lend itself to crudely deterministic application; still it is the only theoretical framework, as far as I know, which seriously and consistently addresses itself to this fundamental aspect of social theory.

The concept of the *state* itself provides a natural focus for the political economy approach to the study of politics. Far from diffusing attention to issues outside the perceived frame of reference of our discipline, political economy may in fact help it to recover the central theoretical focus.

Notes

1. James S. Coleman, 'The Resurrection of Political Economy', *Mawazo*, 1967; reprinted in Norman T. Uphoff and Warren F. Ilchman (eds.), *The Political Economy of Development* (Berkeley, 1972).
2. Uphoff and Ilchman, op. cit., pp. 30ff.
3. Warren F. Ilchman and Norman T. Uphoff (eds.), *The Political Economy of Change* (Berkeley, 1969) and later editions. The quote is from Kenneth Boulding in the 1971 edition.
4. See, for example, R. Eyestone, *Political Economy: Politics and Policy Analysis* Rand McNally, 1972).
5. See, for example, his essay, 'The Shape of the Theory to Come — From Political Sociology, to Political Economy', *American Behavioral Scientist*, Vol. IX, No. 2, 1967. See also W.C. Mitchell, 'The New Political Economy', *Social Research*, Vol. 35, No. 1, 1968.
6. Edward Nell, 'Economics: The Revival of Political Economy' in Robin Blackburn (ed.), *Ideology in Social Science* (London, 1972).
7. According to a report from the Japanese delegate to the Annual Conference of Socialist Economists, Bradford 1977.
8. See John Holloway and Sol Picciotto (eds.), *State and Capital: A*

Marxist Debate (London, 1978) and W. Ziemann and M. Lanzendorfer, 'The State in Peripheral Societies', *The Socialist Register 1977*. See also D.A. Gold, C.Y.H. Lo and E. Olin Wright, 'Recent Developments in Marxist Theories of the Capitalist State', *Monthly Review*, Vol. 27, Nos. 5-6, 1975.
9. A case of the latter is the Roskilde University in Denmark.
10. Chris Allen, 'A Bibliographical Guide to the Study of the Political Economy of Africa' in Gutkind and Wallerstein (eds.), *The Political Economy of Contemporary Africa* (Beverley Hills and London, Sage Publications, 1976) and 'Radical Themes in African Social Studies: A Bibliographical Guide' in Gutkind and Waterman (eds.), *African Social Studies: A Radical Reader* (London, 1977).
11. Issa G. Shivji, *Class Struggles in Tanzania* (London, 1976).
12. Mahmood Mamdani, *Politics and Class Formation in Uganda* (London, Heineman, 1976). See also his 'Class Struggles in Uganda', *Review of African Political Economy*, Vol. 4, 1975, and critical comments by Saul, Leys and Williams on the issue of 'petty-bourgeois politics' in subsequent issues of the *Review*.
13. See, for example, Colin Leys, 'Underdevelopment and Dependency: Critical Notes', *Journal of Contemporary Asia*, Vol. 7, No. 1, 1977.
14. Nicos Poulantzas, *Political Power and Social Class* (London, 1972) and *Classes in Contemporary Capitalism* (London, 1975).
15. For a critique of Poulantzas on this account, see Holloway and Picciotto, 1978, op. cit., p. 3ff.
16. Ibid.

10. Primary Requirements for the Unity of Political Science and Economics

Eskor Toyo

As we conceive so we teach. This paper is not concerned with the problems of imparting political or economic knowledge. It is rather concerned with the question of an approach that can integrate political science and economics in simple and systematic ways.

Why Unity At All?

In recent years scholars in underdeveloped countries have been very much agitated by the inadequacy of European and American received ideas to the situation in their group of countries.[1] In itself, however, this would be a lesser problem, one of adaptation. Far more important is the inadequacy of these concepts and methods even for the problems of the Euro-American milieu in which they originated. Levinson has put the problem pointedly as follows:

> To be a teacher implies having something to teach and this something is what constitutes a discipline, whether one is a rabbi, a professor of physics, or a teacher of astrology ... What differentiates the physicist, however, from his two counterparts is his commitment not only to a discipline but also to a methodology.[2]

A science is as good as its approach, which includes its paradigm and its methodology, taking this in the strict sense of a way of arriving at conclusions. Kuhn's research has shown that detailed hypotheses and the development of empirical methods are ultimately founded on a conscious or unconscious exploitation of an articulated or unarticulated general orientation — which Kuhn calls a paradigm — and can yield knowledge only to the extent of the power of the paradigm.[3] It follows that where the paradigm is subjective, ahistorical or static, the conclusions are bound to be arbitrary, ahistorical or static, and a discipline that lacks an accepted paradigm is bound to be chaotic as a science.[4]

That non-Marxist social science is theoretically chaotic is widely admitted. In the case of economics, there has been great concern with the gross 'limitations of pure economics as opposed to empirical economics',[5] with the 'causal' empiricism which has seemed for a time to be a sufficient basis for economic analysis',[6] with the unsettled state of methodology in the discipline,[7] with the 'variety of conflicting views ... on the conduct of enquiry into man's economic behaviour',[8] with the need for economists to construct a synthesis out of existing heterogeneity,[9] and so on.[10] An objective reflection of this state of non-Marxist economics is the existence of various theoretical schools: Keynesian, neo-classical, neo-Ricardian and institutional.

In the case of political science, there is disagreement on 'precisely what matters it should be concerned with, with what ends in view, with the use of what means.'[11] The unsettled issues are 'a chronic and prolific source of discourse and dissension',[12] and 'as the discipline of political science continues to undergo efforts to define and redefine itself in rather immodest degrees, the reverberations touch every student of politics from the undergraduate taking his first course to the President of the American Political Science Association.'[13] This disaffection with the discipline, Levinson rightly observes, 'calls into question any naive hope that we can confine our worries only to our research while continuing to "teach" as usual.'[14]

What, then, should political scientists be doing? But, as Meehan rightly observes, this is the wrong question, for it 'leads to a search for knowledge that is uniquely "political". Methodologically speaking, the search is futile.'[15] Meehan puts his finger on a sore point. The issue *is* methodological, and it is necessary to find an approach which abandons the false search for the uniquely 'political'. This paper discusses certain false starts that are permanent obstacles even to the proper conceptualization of social science and which have either led to or perpetuated the sundering of the political and economic sciences. Abandoning these false take-offs is then a primary condition of unity. The thrust of this paper is therefore critical.

Fighting Subjectivism

The very first condition of unity is the acceptance that economics and political science are empirical sciences. The issue has long been debated, but we shall deal with it here because there are important observations to be made.

First, let it be observed that a subjective approach is bound to have a residue of theoretical arbitrariness because there is no single conception of 'human nature',[16] the category on which such an approach is usually based. Besides, the subjective approach, as the example of economics shows, leads to abstract suppositions divorced from reality if based on a model of a 'rational man', for the theorists's own 'rational' imaginary constructs are the only rational models of 'rational men'. We are led into theories divorced from actual observation of behaviour. Moreover, the means-end or optimization exercise, with which this kind of 'rationality' is preoccupied, is static. We are 'given' values — goods, profits, power or votes — which have to be appropriated. A social science that is insensitive to how values appear, disappear or cumulate through time as products of history, and with what consequences, is hardly worth being called a social science.

It is saddening that just as economics is struggling to throw off the subjective, particularist, non-empirical and static orientation of the neo-classical economists, many political scientists are now finding this approach attractive, probably because of its alleged 'rigour' and applicability to 'welfare maximizing' policy. Thus Moon writes: 'In political science we have few well-articulated research programmes rooted in clearly worked-out models of man. Indeed it might be argued that there is only one: the rational choice model of human behaviour.'[17] He then welcomes, like one hailing a deliverer, the introduction of this 'paradigm' into political analysis by Downs[18] and others.

First, the narrowness and sterility of this 'paradigm' or 'model' must be pointed out. In economics the Cournot approach to oligopoly theory which ended up in games theory — the small-group bargaining theory which is the formal essence of this 'model' — is being given up because of its known restrictiveness, conservatism[19] and sterility,[20] and the search is on for a more empirical approach to oligopoly theory.[21] Welfare economics, where the 'rational choice' model is used as an approach to policy recommendations, is one of the most sterile branches of economics. Its narrowness arises from the fact that it deals with a static situation where only slight incremental changes have to be considered;[22] its sterility arises from its abstract character, for instance, its simplistic representation of even the choice situation itself.

Secondly, it is an astonishing error to imagine that no articulate 'rational' model of man or of man as a chooser has ever been used in political science. The social contract theory of political power and obligation was based on the rational man and the model was intended as a guide to choices by the rational man. The *laissez-faire* doctrine was a political as well as an economic doctrine and had enormous consequences for research and for political decision-making. So far there has been no research programme 'rooted in a clearly worked out model of man' as well articulated as that of the 18th-Century economist-jurist-political scientist, Jeremy Bentham. His 'rational choice model of man was applied to all economic, legal and political issues,[23] and not confined to isolated questions such as parliamentary contest. Heinz Eulau also laments:

> Unlike economics equipped with a central instrument of analysis — the price system — which enables the economist to develop useful theorems explaining a few of the facts of economic life, political science has been unable to evolve a central model that could serve as a reasonably stable point of departure into political enquiry.[24]

First, the price system is not an instrument of analysis. Excluding concepts, the only instruments of analysis used by non-Marxist economists are formal logic, pure mathematics and statistics, which are also available to political science.

Secondly, precisely because the market orientation and its 'theorems', so much admired by Eulau, abandoned the world of reality and concentrated on 'a few of the facts' (leaving a host of important facts unattended to) a long line of revolts have resulted. They range from the German Historical school and the utopian socialists to the swinging victory of development theory which is today finding the market focus and its few theorems more and more restrictive and embarrassing.

One is reminded of Somit and Tanenhaus's observation that the profession of political science is paying 'a heavy price in time, effort, and controversy for their failure to attend more closely to their past ... The quest for "rigour" [is but] the latest manifestation of an aspiration as old as the profession itself.'[25]

A science which proposes to progress both in empirical knowledge and in rigour must be objective to begin with. It must be emphasized that rigour is not confined to symbolic logic or mathematics. An approach to qualitative analysis that comprehends the data, is fruitful of hypotheses and is logically coherent, will yield a much more valuable kind of scientific rigour than mathematical pedantry and sterility.

Detotalizing the Fact-Value Distinction

Both economics and political science, but especially the latter, have been plagued with the perennial confusion concerning the place of fact and value in science.[26] If a wholeheartedly objective approach is to emerge — and this is crucial to the possibility of a sound theoretical unity between the two disciplines — the fog around this matter must be cleared.

Those who are disturbed about the subjective in social science fall into three groups. First, there are those who want judgments as to 'what should be' to be accorded the status of scientific judgments, for a reason which is best seen from examples. 'There seems no way,' Bose asserts, 'of constructing a theory of exploitation under capitalism [whether of the Pigovian or the Marxian variety] which makes such exploitation *entirely* a question of "fact", i.e. of what "is" as against what "ought to be" or "could be".'[27] Further examples can be given. An elaboration of a theory of 'perfect' competition implies that imperfections are *undesirable*. In-depth analyses of 'power' are usually undertaken by libertarians critical of departures from 'liberty' or 'freedom' considered as *desirable*. The analysis of 'bureaucracy' presumes the inefficiency or unfreedom of at least certain types or degrees of centralized authority. The word 'underdevelopment' carries the implication that 'development' is *desirable*.

To urge from such examples, as Bose does, that we should grant the 'ought to be' variety of statements a scientific status[28] appears to us to rest on a confusion. First, as we shall argue at greater length below, we ought to distinguish the motives that inspire a piece of research from the facts thrown up by the research. In research terminology, some 'value-loaded' words may be used. Keynesian literature gives the impression that 'saving' — still more 'hoarding' — is anti-social and 'spending' a very creditable act, but this has nothing to do with whether the income portions called 'savings', 'spending' and 'hoarding' actually do exist or whether they play the roles in economic depression attributed to them by Keynes.

Secondly, as we have pointed out elsewhere,[29] it is a common mistake to think that there are only two kinds of judgment: 'what is' and 'what should be'. Actually there are three: 1) 'what is' or 'what was'; 2) 'what can be' or 'what could be'; 3) 'what should be'. The first corresponds to a description of facts, the second to an assessment of possibility, the third to injunction. They refer to *actuality, possibility* (potentiality), and *desirability* respectively. Bose has the merit of being the only other person known to us who recognizes a 'could be' category of judgment. However, the English phrase 'could be' is slightly different in meaning from 'can be': the latter could refer to the future. Further, the fact that he brackets 'could be' along with 'should be' shows that he is still thinking essentially in terms of two kinds of judgment.

There are, then, three kinds of judgment. Statements of actuality and potentiality, in our view, can be scientific. Statements of desirability cannot be scientific — at least within the ambit of a descriptive positive science. In economics, we are familiar with the 'can be' type of judgment. Comparative statics and dynamics aim not only at answering the question *what exists or has existed*? but also *what can exist*? Whether that which can exist should in fact be made to exist is an entirely different matter.

The second group who are concerned with value judgment in science are believers in ultimate values who frankly urge that description should serve prescription or policy recommendations,[30] maintaining that mere description is pointless and cannot ever be value-free.

This position could be accepted without implying that policy relevance should become a criterion for judging the factual truth content of the kinds of propositions that have to do with 'what is' or 'has been'. It is perfectly possible to build a 'policy science', such as 'scientific management' or the science of economic policy in socialist countries. These are actually applied sciences. Their role is to specify the conditions of success of policy experiments, a kind of experiment not yet recognized in scientific literature as such, because they differ from the more traditional laboratory or field experiments of the agricultural or statistical kind.[31] Clearly such applied sciences presuppose results achieved in descriptive theoretical science. Moreover, they also require a clear specification of values, goals, and norms[32] as guides to the setting up and objective assessment of the results of policy experiments.

The third set of writers who concern themselves with values in social science are those who assert the impossibility of any objective laws in the social realm, because social facts are too heterogenous, because human experience is historical and history obeys no law, or because humans are possessed with 'free will' and their behaviour is unpredictable.

These contentions will be answered in the next section. Here, however, it is necessary to comment on the matter of subjective bias. It will be agreed that the fact that a doctor prefers healthy people to sick ones and regards harmful parasites as unwanted does not mean that hatred for such parasites should be used for judging the truth content of medical research.

Subjective bias enters into scientific research by influencing a) the research interest; b) the angle from which reality is observed; c) the language used in reporting; d) the ends to which the results are put; e) the claims made for the results. With historical materialist criticism, however, it is quite possible to distinguish what is an objective contribution to knowledge from the value infusions due to one or other of the foregoing sources of 'bias'. This is precisely what Marx did in respect of Hegel, the classical political economists and the utopian socialists in all of whose work he found valuable objective scientific insights, although the disagreed profoundly with them over 'should be' questions.

Possibility of Objective Laws

Unless we accept, to begin with, that even if things may never be seen without some bias, objective laws do exist in the realm of society and unless we know how they exist, there is no hope of uniting political science and economics. After all, a paradigm is a 'bias'. Moreover, the natural sciences achieve greater and greater proximity to objective truth not by each practitioner trying to avoid bias but by a) reliance on combined effort; b) the method of approach to truth (orientation and empirical facts, theory construction, test of theory, rejection of hypotheses in the light of evidence); and c) the public character of science which permits free and open criticism of procedures and results, excluding all claims based on mere prejudice, authority or revelation.[33]

The answer to the negative position taken in consideration of heterogeneity is given by Malinvaud: "The less strict the relationships the more important it becomes to use rigorous methods in their determination."[34] It need only be pointed out that it is an error, as already observed, to interpret 'rigorous' to mean 'mathematical'. Qualitative analysis can be rigorous, as geology, archaeology and chemistry make clear. The only such rigorous method in social science is the historical materialist method.

The answer to the defeatism suggested by historical investigation is that all reality has a history. Today we know that not only living species and rocks but also stars have a history, and it is not true that events, processes, relations and systems that are products of history must be absolutely dissimilar, cannot be compared and obey no regularities whatsoever. The answer to 'free will' can be given in the words of Madge:

> The fact that we cannot, and never shall be able to, predict exactly when a particular leaf will fall off a tree or where it will land does not help us prove or disprove a theory that the leaf launches itself when it feels like it; but this does not prevent us from predicting that most

leaves will fall in autumn, or that the rate of defoliation will be higher in windy weather.[35]

In fact, as Madge notes, a law in natural science operates under a number of conditions which may not be present for any number of reasons. We have to be clear about what is true to the objective 'laws', namely, the regularities and tendencies discovered and discoverable by science, called 'scientific law'.

First, a scientific law is a conditional statement. It is an 'if . . . then' kind of statement. Water boils at 100 degrees centigrade, but it does so only if there prevails normal temperature and pressure.

Secondly, a scientific law, as an empirical proposition, must refer to existing things and situations. Therefore, it operates only where and when those things and conditions exist. There is no law relating to fish behaviour where we have no water and no fishes. Therefore, it is only as an 'if . . . then' abstract and hypothetical condition that a scientific law has universal validity. As a reference to factual existence, it is a respecter of time and place, because it is pegged on conditions that may or may not exist.

Thirdly, scientific laws are of different degrees of generality within the realm of data to which they refer. The idea that the validity of an empirical law must have the universal and ever-present scope of the law of gravity is an error. Laws relating to all matter are the most universal. In the economic realm, for instance, the law of diminishing returns is true of all economic systems; the laws of supply and demand are true of all forms of market economy; the law of class struggle is true wherever there are exploited and exploiting classes; the law of cyclical development is true of capitalism only; and there are certain laws referring only to the boom phase of trade cycles. Regularities of such varying generality exist in other realms. The varying generality of laws is a direct consequence of the fact that there are different levels of organization of matter (including human society as a part of nature).

This observation is important, for unless social science can discover, consistently characterize and root itself in the different levels of organization of social systems, there is no hope of its arriving at satisfactory order and objectivity. Precisely because the historical materialist approach does this, that is why it is the most comprehensive and yet the most coherent and objective approach.

Orientation on historical materialism explains why that which is most baffling to non-Marxists is quite clear and definite to Marxists, namely: how can laws in social science be both generalizations and yet be historically specific at the same time? These laws are general in so far as they relate to all social situations or conditions for which they are formulated; but such situations or conditions do not come into existence in all places and at all times. Let us recall that whilst laws relating to atoms are true of the whole of the material realm and, as far as the earth is concerned, are true of the whole period of earth history, the laws relating, for instance, to the structure, life, and behaviour of mammals come into existence only during the epoch of the earth when mammals have existed. From this we cannot conclude that laws relating to atoms are 'general' but those relating to mammals are not.

It is really not possible to be clear on the extent of generality and specificity of laws without looking at the matter historically and without referring the question to different levels of organization of matter in the course of evolution. The Marxist position with regard to social law was clearly formulated with reference to economics by Stalin. The laws of political economy, he observed, 'are impermanent . . . They, or at least the majority of them, operate for a definite historical period, after which they give place to new laws.'[36] Yet this does not mean that the laws are not objective, just as the fact that many animals came into and went out of existence in the earth's history — like the dinosaurs — does not mean that objective laws holding generally for their lives and behaviour did not exist while they existed.

Fourthly, laws are of different degrees of strictness. A law that, given the right conditions, water boils not specifically at 100°C, but between 50°C and 100°C or even when 50°C has been exceeded, would still be a law. As is now known to us, a law stated not 'deterministically' but 'probabilistically' is still a law. Even a qualitative statement, such as that candle wax will melt in a flame sooner than lead will, that in a market that approximates to perfect competition a single seller will not unilaterally raise his price, or that in a parliamentary contest opposing candidates will exaggerate both their own virtues and their opponents' demerits, is a law. A law is simply a rule that things tend to follow, including the limits they tend to obey or the patterns they tend to assume, under certain conditions, if left to themselves.

Let us end this section, then, by asserting that the pursuit of a social science concerns only those who are convinced that there are discoverable objective regularities in the social realm. Further, the question of integrating economics and political science cannot be answered unless there is clarity on how scientific laws exist, that is, what is true or not true of them as stated in this section. As a minimum, unity implies common convictions and a paradigm common to both fields.

Avoiding Dead Ends: Factors, Facts and Systems

Since a common paradigm is important, given the arguments of the last section, we must indicate clearly the sort of theoretical approach that cannot yield an adequate paradigm. First, a synoptic or factor approach is grossly inadequate. Secondly, a historical systems approach is bound to have limited integrating, explanatory and predictive value. Thirdly, a parochial, undialectical and basically ahistorical concept of 'development' only succeeds in introducing one new complicating 'factor', that of 'change'.

As Engels observed, empirical science had to start by collecting, comparing and classifying objects.[37] Then followed the experimental method which consisted of an effort, under controlled conditions, to establish how an isolated object behaved in response to a change in one isolated factor or variable. From this developed what may be called the synoptic or factor approach to explanation, which consists in separately trying to establish the influence of this or that factor.

Today the positivist orientation has given us elaborate fact-gathering methods in social science, as summarized by Lee and Francis[38] and Madge,[39] methods which are still developing. An empirical investigation, however, has to be based on a theory. The theories in non-Marxist social science suffer from the eclecticism of the factor approach reinforced by the influence of philosophical individualism in social theory.

The 'factor' approach has severe limitations in social science, because in society, most of the time two or more inseparable factors are causally operating at the same time. As Lenin urged:

> Everything depends on the concrete historical situation in which the particular cases are to be found. Facts examined without regard to their context, gathered together at random, disregarding related facts, are mere play or even worse.[40]

The way that has been followed in non-Marxist circles to get around the problem of 'particular cases' is the comparative method. This, however, has been limited to anthropology and political science. Economics, as practised by the dominant neo-classical school, had no comparative method, since all other economies were supposed to be 'irrational' and only an economy based on the market, on autonomous profit-making enterprises and on competition was rational. Before the emergence of capitalism, we had only economic prehistory, a 'living death'.

But in political science where comparisons were attempted, this exercise was 'dissociated from serious historical study' and became concerned only with foreign, local and, in the United States, state governments, and even this narrow concern was 'descriptive and formalistic' and was 'concerned with political action rather than political knowledge'.[41] Roy Macridis summarizes these exercises as 'essentially non-comparative, essentially parochial, essentially static, essentially monographic'.[42]

Serious methodological questions are raised by this failure of comparative analysis to rise beyond the ahistorical, descriptive, formalistic, parochial, and static and their lack of concern with scientific knowledge or theoretical issues. To confound the matter still more, such comparisons had to be limited to the purportedly 'uniquely political', since there was not even a parallel development of concern for comparison in economics.

A new comparative discipline, Comparative Economic Systems, has come into existence in Western universities since about 1960. But this is an isolated study related to 'sovietology' and preoccupied with a very selective institutional comparison between capitalist economies and socialist economies, especially the Soviet Union. This elite speciality, which has no effect whatsoever on the actual teaching of economics, runs very much along the lines of comparative politics which we have been examining.

Comparison, whilst it attempts to transcend particular cases in the effort to generalize, does not necessarily get us away from the narrowness of the factor approach. A number of factors can be synoptically compared in respect to two or more particulars, for instance, the constitutions or price systems in two or three states.

For analysts who were always subjective and who pivoted their social theories on 'human nature', the emergence of *gestalt* psychology was a jolting experience. It forced a departure from the factor approach. The result was the 'systems approach' which now dominates the field. To be sure, thinkers like Durkheim had emphasized that society was a system, while anthropologists had empirically discovered that functions were interrelated in a society in much the same way as in biological organisms, but the systems approach, otherwise called 'structural', really got under way with the spread of the *gestalt* concept. This was reinforced by the rise of nuclear physics, from which those who had always tried to pattern the social sciences on physics learnt that the atom itself, the 'ultimate' building block of the universe, was not an indivisible particle but a system with a structure of relations between parts. Again this discovery was a jolting one to the particularist factor approach.

Yet even a systemic approach can be static, ahistorical in the case of society, arbitrary and, therefore, chaotic. If we take economics, the 'economic system' even of capitalism is a different thing depending on whether it is viewed by a Keynesian, a Leontief sectoralist, a neo-Ricardian, a Joan Robinson 'post-Keynesian' or a neo-institutionalist such as Galbraith or Mantoux.

This means that no coherent bridge at all exists between the present 'system' and past or emerging systems such as feudalism or socialism. The non-Marxist economists have no serious theoretical concept of an economic system except in terms of an exchange mechanism, although up to now the larger part of human economic life has been lived outside the market system.

The only 'systems approach' that has been introduced into political science to bring some order out of chaos is the functionalist approach which has been elaborated in this field in various ways by Gabriel Almond. But, as Rasmussen observes, whilst Almond's terminology is utilized widely, 'many of the users, unlike Almond himself, do not grasp the thinking behind it'.[43] This situation leads Rasmussen to observe:

> It is almost as though many political scientists fear it would compromise their reputation to be seen in the company of someone else's concepts ... Even in the swinging 1960s and 1970s the worship of virginity dies hard ... More mystifying is the failure of many political scientists to employ the conceptual frameworks they themselves have devised or to heed their own injunctions concerning the process of research.[44]

The emergence of the so-called 'Third World' countries, and the challenge to capitalism from the rapidly developing socialist countries forced dynamics and 'development' on the attention of analysts to whom the capitalist world had been the only world — at any rate the only rational one — and for that matter the best of all possible worlds. Sociology had jettisoned an 'evolutionary' approach and had become enamoured of functionalism; economics had abandoned evolution after John Stuart Mill; for political science, evolution existed only in books on the history of political thought.

The result is that although there is an overwhelming attention to the phenomenon of development in economics and political science — it is called 'social change' in sociology — it is marked by the incoherence and half blindness of a man just waking from a long sleep.

In economics there does not even exist a definition of 'development' itself and there are a host of theories or models of development. In political science there are at least three conceptions of 'political development'. It means to some 'a process of organic change in the nature of political institutions . . . [implying] cumulative change and growth,'[45] to others 'the evolution of fundamentally new forms of political life at each successive stage of history,'[46] to a third group 'the evolution of any institutional arrangement in the political sphere which is an appropriate instrument for achieving the goals of that society'.[47]

As in economics, outside Marxist circles concern with 'development' has been, in Rostow's terms,[48] confined to 'modernization', conceived vaguely as the 'transition' from 'traditional' to industrial society.[49] This arbitrary framework, though popular, has already been confronted with several important criticisms within political science itself.[50] First, it is based on a presumption, namely, that the transition will be towards a developed capitalist society, so that the possibility of an alternative development is ignored. Secondly, the analysis is preoccupied with institutions and the role they play in 'political mobilization' and 'political penetration', the narrow question asked being how far 'transitional' institutions are approaching Western parliamentary forms. Ignored are important changes in the outcomes of the political system in terms of such values and rewards as security, welfare, justice and liberty. Thirdly, attention is concentrated one-sidedly on the determination of the political variable by social and economic forces whereas the reverse is often the case.[51]

It should be remarked that non-Marxist political scientists have merely transferred their customary myopia to another part of the world in their 'development' writings. They have been used to describing the United States, for instance, as a democracy in terms of one-man-one-vote institutional formalism, ignoring the vastly undemocratic nature of the U.S. political system in terms of the structure that determines the real allocation of values and power.[52] It is hardly surprising that the impingement of development in Third World countries on the allocation of values is ignored, even though Easton's definition of political science as the study of authoritative allocation of values is widely accepted.[53] Again we are reminded of Rasmussen's criticism.

Thus the shifts in economics and political science to comparative, systems and developmental orientations remain at best myopic, ahistorical, formalistic, parochial and arbitrary.

Economics and Politics: One Reality, One Science

However loud the call for a multi-disciplinary approach, unless there exists a unique theoretical system in which economic and political phenomena can be seen as aspects of the same reality, there is no way of attaining a genuine multi-dimensionality, namely, one that is scientifically simple.

From the point of view of political scientists, Waldo has put the problem as follows:

> Political scientists cannot deny the *importance* of non-political phenomena for the political, nor do they generally wish to deny the relevance of what other disciplines have to 'contribute' to understanding the political. Indeed, the idea of a total understanding of the social realm, the concept of a 'unified social science', has not simply intellectual respectability but much emotional appeal. How, then, to find the optimum balance, the proper, fruitful interrelation.[54]

Waldo goes on to observe that the 'sundering' of economics and political science has 'always been considered an error, leaving both of the separate disciplines without an adequate base, either for explanatory theory or public guidance, and resulting in a varied pattern of *ad hoc* co-operation, amateur improvising, and "border raids"'.[55]

However, the road to a solution cannot be found by thinking, as Waldo and others do, in terms of optimum balancing, for this continues the concept of two separate 'factors' which have to be mixed or 'joined'.[56] It is rather a question of identifying something less vague than 'society', 'social structure' or 'social institutions' of which economic and political phenomena are merely aspects and defining clearly how they are related as aspects of this single entity. This unique category, moreover, must develop through historical time, and we must identify clearly the roles of the economic and the political sides in this development. It is a paradigm, a theoretical and methodological approach with such a framework built into it, that we need.

The foregoing discussion enables us to see and summarize the conditions which the candidate approach must satisfy. This approach must be dynamic rather than static, that is, capable of taking care of cyclical, evolutionary, developmental, revolutionary, disintegrating and other processes. It must be both theoretical and descriptive rather than merely descriptive; must be capable of application to concrete reality rather than dwelling, like most contemporary economic theory, in the region of abstraction.[57] It must not be ahistorical but must base itself on the historical process. It must be comparative, structuralist, and functionalist all at once. It must be fact-oriented like empiricism and positivism, yet enable us to rise above the eclectic and synoptic — 'factor' — arbitrariness of mere empiricism and positivism by being dialectical. It must enable us to enunciate social laws in such ways as to recognize the historical character of these laws, namely, that they are brought into being by historical process and that their generality or specificity is historically determined. It must be both comprehensive and penetrating, enabling the most detailed empirical observations to be integrated with the most general social-historical theoretical insights. While making possible an objective science in terms of methodology, it must be a potent guide to seeing the unity of the objective and the subjective in social reality.

It is true that 'politics as power consists fundamentally of relationships of superordination and subordination, of dominance and submission,'[58] but such concepts of *unequal relations* are absent from economics. As if relations of superordination and subordination are not equally important in the economic realm, non-Marxist economics bases its allegedly 'rational' calculus on readings yielded by the faulty balance provided by the concept of 'interdependence'. There can be no unity if economics continues to ignore that which is most important for politics, namely, 'power'. The candidate approach must remove such a prohibitive anomaly.

This approach must make possible not only rational explanation, but also rational prediction, for anything can pass for 'rational explanation'. The approach must be capable of making 'what is' and 'what can be' judgments objectively, enabling us to specify clearly, correctly and with logical economy the historical-social conditions of validity of such judgments.

Finally, without being dialectical, it must be emphasized, the candidate simply cannot keep pace with the bewildering many-sidedness, the baffling unities in contradiction and contradictions in unity, and the seemingly intractable complexity of social reality.

Do we have to invent this approach or does anything like it already exist? The needed approach has been in existence for a hundred years. It is none other than the Marxist historical materialist approach when it is properly understood. However, because this approach was originated by communist revolutionaries, the bourgeois world has only been concerned with distorting, castigating or ignoring it. The upshot is a snake walk from one blind alley into another.

Awareness of the futility of all sorts of non-Marxist false starts, of the preposterous and shameless distortions which Marx's works have received at the hands of generations of ideologically blinded scholars, and of the dogmatic interpretations sometimes given to Marx's insights by some of his followers — such awareness has led to the 'Marxist revival' now sweeping through not only universities in capitalist countries but scholarly circles in socialist countries as well.

One fact no one can deny. For Marxists there is no problem of having to unite economics and political science; they see this as a false sundering anyway. With dialectics and historical materialism the general problem of unity is solved. The problem of unity exists for Marxists only in the less acute form of how to apply a generally correct approach or solution to a specific case,[59] which implies interpreting, adapting and developing the general approach or solution. The historical materialist approach is but a guide to study,[60] even if it is an exceedingly fruitful one.

Economic and political data are products of history, yet these data also exhibit systemic correlations or regularities, otherwise their scientific study would be impossible. If this is granted and we are dealing with sciences, then it must be emphasized that historical materialism alone resolves the conflicts between logic and history, deduction and induction, the general and the specific, the functional and the dynamic, the objective and the subjective, that arise in the study of social phenomena. The problem of how to unite these seemingly irreconcilable opposites perennially plagues positivistic and eclectic social science. With historical materialism we emerge from the eclectic woods and the subjective morass.[61] For instance, it becomes possible to formulate laws which are both general as laws and specific as history.

The sundering of economics and political science comes about through the dominance of the 'factor' approach. The false start thus inaugurated and perpetuated is not overcome by any joining, mixing or balancing exercise. It is overcome only by the use of social-historical dialectics, guided by the hypotheses of the materialist conception of history when the latter is understood in a way free from malicious distortions and exaggerations.[62] A Marxist analysis, after all, may also start with factors. The difference between Marxist and others here is that the Marxist does not stop there. The factors are thrown into structural, comparative, and historical dynamic perspectives. Thus is derived a sense of the concrete totality of the situation in which the factors operate. This totality defines their essential interrelations, their potentialities and their limits.

A Marxist will typically move from factor analysis to dialectical analysis. Dialectical analysis focuses on interrelations between processes rather than things or 'factors' as such, processes that are historically conditioned, historically united and historically concrete, to understand the problems of society. We need to unify the sciences of society under a dynamic paradigm of dialectical and historical materialism. Only by doing so can we reasonably hope to make a concerted attack on the theoretical and practical problems confronting our societies.

Notes

1. For an extensive comment on this, see Ikenna Nzimiro, *The Crisis in the Social Sciences: The Nigerian Situation*, Third World Forum, Occasional Paper No. 2, Apartado Postal 85-015, Mexico 20. The other is our paper, *'Mode of Production' as an Integrating Nucleus for Politics and Economics*.
2. Sanford Levinson, 'On "Teaching" Political "Science"' in Philip Green

and Sanford Levinson (eds.), *Power and Community: Dissenting Essays in Political Science* (New York, Vintage Books, Random House, 1970), p. 60.
3. Thomas S. Kuhn, *The Structure of Scientific Revolutions* (Chicago and London, University of Chicago Press, 1972).
4. Ibid., pp. 16-22.
5. See Richard Stone, 'Three Models of Economic Growth', in Ernest Nagel, Patrick Suppes and Alfred Tarski (eds.), *Logic, Methodology and Philosophy of Science* (Stanford University Press, 1962).
6. See T.C. Koopmans, *Three Essays on the State of Economic Science*, (New York – Toronto – London, McGraw-Hill Books Co., 1957), p. 150.
7. Ibid. See also N. Georgescu-Roegen, *Analytical Economics: Issue and Problems* (Cambridge, Massachusetts, Harvard University Press, 1966).
8. Karon S. Thompson, 'A Transactional Approach to Economic Science', *The American Journal of Economics and Sociology*, Vol. 30, No. 3, 1971, p. 329.
9. See K.E. Boulding, *A Reconstruction of Economics*, (New York, John Wiley and Sons Inc., 1965).
10. The crisis arising from heterogeneity and chaos in economic theory is examined in the present author's work, *Marx and Keynes: A Study in Macroeconomic Methodology* (Warsaw, Polish Scientific Publishers, 1977) (in Polish).
11. See Dwight Waldo, 'Political Science: Tradition, Discipline, Profession, Science, Enterprise', in Fred I. Greenstein and Nelson W. Polsby (eds.), *Political Science: Scope and Theory* (London–Amsterdam–Reading (Massachusetts)–Sydney, Addison-Wesley, 1975), p. 1.
12. Albert Somit and Joseph Tanenhaus, *The Development of American Political Thought* (Boston, Allyn and Bacon, 1967), p. 2.
13. George J. Graham and George W. Carey, 'Political Science – What Next?' in George J. Graham and George W. Carey (eds.), *The Post-Behavioral Era: Perspectives on Political Science* (New York, David McKay Co. Inc., 1972).
14. Levinson, op. cit., p. 61.
15. Eugene J. Meehan, 'What Should Political Scientists be Doing?' in Graham and Carey, op. cit., p. 54.
16. Many may not agree with Cantril's concept of 'human nature' which emphasizes man's primary need for food and shelter, as did Malinowski and Marx, for this may remind them of the materialist emphasis. See Hadley Cantril, *Human Nature and Political Systems* (New Brunswick, New Jersey, Rutgers University Press, 1961).
17. J. Donald Moon, 'The Logic of Political Enquiry: A Synthesis of Opposed Perspectives', in Greenstein and Polsby, op. cit.
18. Anthony Downs, *An Economic Theory of Democracy* (New York, Harper and Row, 1957).
19. See Alpha C. Chiang, *Fundamental Methods of Mathematical Economics* (New York and London, McGraw-Hill Book Co., 1972), pp. 770-1.
20. See Richard G. Lipsey, *An Introduction to Positive Economics* (London, Wiedenfeld and Nicolson, 1974), p. 271. 'So far the attack on monopoly behaviour through the development of general models has

produced disappointingly few results.'
21. Ibid., pp. 270-7.
22. See Moses Abrmovitz, *The Allocation of Economic Resources* (Stanford University Press, 1968), p. 171.
23. J. Bentham, *An Introduction to the Principles of Morals and Legislation* (New York, Hafner, 1948, originally published in 1780).
24. Heinz Eulau, 'Political Science' in Bert F. Hoxelitz (ed.), *A Reader's Guide to the Social Sciences* (New York, The Free Press, 1970), p. 132.
25. Somit and Tanenhaus, op. cit.
26. See, for instance, the interesting analysis of Weber's positions on the issue by David Beetham, *Weber and the Theory of Modern Politics*, (London, George Allen and Unwin, 1974), p. 1.
27. Arun Bose, *Marxian and Post-Marxian Political Economy* (Harmondsworth, Penguin, 1975), pp. 48-9,
28. Ibid.
29. Toyo, op. cit.
30. Charles S. Hyneman, *The Study of Politics: The Present State of American Political Science* (University of Illinois Press, 1959), p. 178.
31. Excellent books dealing with such sciences are Arie T. Levin, *The Policy Sciences: Methodologies and Cases* (New York–Oxford, Pergamon Press, 1975); Csikos-Nagy, *Socialist Economic Policy* (London, Longman Group Ltd., 1973); Robert J. Ihierauf and Robert C. Klekamp, *Decision Making Through Operative Research* (New York–London, John Wiley and Sons Inc., 1975).
32. Levin, op. cit., p. 11.
33. See Karl Popper, *The Open Society and Its Enemies*, Vol. 2 (London, Routledge and Kegan Paul, 1952), pp. 216-20.
34. E. Malinvaud, *Statistical Methods of Econometrics* (Amsterdam–London, North-Holland Publishing Co., 1970), p. 5.
35. John Madge, *The Tools of Social Science* (London, Longmans Green and Co., 1963), p. 22.
36. J. Stalin, *Remarks on Economic Questions Connected with the November 1951 Discussion on the Character of Economic Laws under Socialism*, reprinted in Alec Nove and D.M. Nuti (eds.), *Socialist Economics* (Harmondsworth, Penguin, 1976).
37. F. Engels, 'Socialism, Utopian and Scientific', in K. Marx and F. Engels *Selected Works*, Vol. 1 (Moscow, Progress Publishers, 1970), p. 610.
38. A good discussion of these methods as they could be applied to political science is to be found in David C. Lee and Wayne L. Francis, *Political Research* (New York, Basic Books Inc., 1974).
39. Madge, op. cit.
40. V.I. Lenin, *Collected Works*, Vol. 23.
41. Waldo, op. cit., p. 30.
42. Roy Macridis, *The Study of Comparative Politics* (Garden City, New York, Doubleday and Co., 1955), p. 12.
43. Jorgen Rasmussen, '"Once You've Made a Revolution, Everything's the Same": Comparative Politics' in Graham and Carey (eds.), *The Post-Behavioral Era*, op. cit., p. 74.
44. Ibid.
45. Robert J. Jackson and Michael B. Stein, 'The Issue of Political

Development' in Jackson and Stein (eds.), *Issues in Comparative Politics* (New York, St. Martins' Press and London, Macmillan, 1971), p. 20.
46. Ibid.
47. Ibid.
48. W.W. Rostow, *The Stages of Economic Growth* (Cambridge University Press, 1960).
49. Jackson and Stein, op. cit.
50. Ibid., p. 23.
51. These criticisms are discussed in Jackson and Stein, op. cit.
52. See, for instance, V.O. Key, *Politics, Parties and Pressure Groups* (New York, Thomas Y. Crowell Co., 1964).
53. See Waldo, op. cit., p. 1.
54. Ibid., p. 75.
55. Ibid.
56. Ibid. — Waldo actually uses this term further on in the passage just quoted.
57. See K.J.W. Alexander, 'Editorial Forward' to Arun Bose, *Marxian and Post-Marxian Political Economy* (Harmondsworth, Penguin Books, 1975), p. 9. 'A notable weakness of contemporary economics is the extent to which much of economic theory is developed "in a vacuum", and without any serious intention that it should ever be applied to any particular real economic problem.'
58. Key, op. cit., pp. 2–3.
59. That this exercise is not a walk-over is evident from the papers collected in John Holloway and Sol Piccotto (eds.), *State and Capital: A Marxist Debate* (London, Edward Arnold, 1978).
60. See F. Engels, 'Letter to C. Schmidt' published in K. Marx and F. Engels, *Selected Works*, Vol. 1(Moscow, Progress Publishers, 1975), p. 679. 'But our conception of history is above all a guide to study, not a lever for constitution after the manner of the Hegelian. All history must be studied afresh, the conditions of existence of the different formations of society must be examined individually before the attempt is made to deduce from them the political, civil law, aesthetic, philosophic, religious, etc. views corresponding to them.'
61. This approach, observes Wolfson, helped Marx to 'restrain himself from excessive flights of fancy'. Murray Wolfson, *A Reappraisal of Marxian Economics* (New York and London, Columbia University Press, 1966), pp. 31-2.
62. An exposition of how the 'materialist conception of history' is to be understood is presented in my papers 'Economics as an Aid to History' and "Mode of Production" as an Integrating Nucleus for Politics and Economics', University of Calabar, Nigeria.

11. Imperialism and the Politics of Area Studies

Okello Oculi

Divide and Travel

The 'Greater Tradition' of political science today contains within it the 'Little Tradition' known as 'Area Studies'. Paradoxically, in European and North American traditions it was Area Studies that initially was the Greater Tradition including under its intellectual thrust and research such things as data on racial features of peoples, their inclinations and customs, the relative fruitfulness of the women, diseases, warfare, dress, languages, formal political institutions and religion. The study of 'formal political institutions' was but a small part of a larger landscape. The intellectual stimulation that lay at the root of this larger scope of Area Studies ranged from the tourist anxieties of educated English and European gentlemen (who by 1500 had created demands for travellers' guides which usually 'included queries on foods, habits, clothing of different occupations and social ranks, religions and social rites, and local laws')[1] to a passion to understand the common modes of living of Man. This last passion was expressed in a moment of exasperation by Fison in 1874 as follows:

> In the bitterness of my soul I said Satan made a mistake in troubling Job with boils ... and showed only a superficial acquaintance with the stupidity of human nature — he should have set him to making ethnological enquiries.[2]

The most significant impulse behing Area Studies, however, was the political goals of governments. The earliest Memoranda which were issued as guides to Spanish colonial administrators in the Americas between 1577 and 1792 contained information on the indigenous populations ranging from demography to Aztec tactics of warfare. When the Royal Society of London was formed in 1660 it soon began to produce General Heads or enquiries on countries such as Turkey, Egypt, Guinea, the East Indies and Hungary which were then perceived as potential colonial possessions. Between 1807 and 1824 the West African Institution in London designed research manuals 'to guide the collection of demographic, economic, and sociopolitical data on West Africa prior to colonization'.[3] In African contemporary politics, the collection of data on other areas of the relevant geo-political environment had direct connections with military and commercial interests of the ruling classes. Under Idris Aloma (1571-1603), for example, the Bornu Kingdom not only maintained already known strong commercial ties with Tripoli and North Africa, but also extended it to Turkey, 'perhaps the leading world power of those times'.[4] The expansionist policies of Mohammad Ali up the Nile Valley into Sudan was fuelled by reports of Egyptian researchers sent to investigate the potential resources of regions beyond the known edges of the Nile Valley, in the 1820s. Under British, French, Belgian and Portuguese colonialism Area Studies undertaken by scholars ranging from District Commissioners to missionaries based on the spot, to visiting anthropologists or economists, served the same purposes of conquest, political control, and socio-economic architecture, that the Spanish officials had set in motion in the Americas in the late 1500s.

Predicting Socio-political Events

In recent times the one immediate political interest that dramatized the value of Area Studies was the American interest in the Second World War. Although America was a relative late-comer as a colonial ruler to the areas of the Orient beyond the Philippines, the War created 'unprecedented demand for trained interpreters, analysts, and ultimately, administrators to deal with the military conquests and then occupations of Germany, and especially Japan'.[5] Moreover the War had not only confirmed the failure of capitalist states to destroy the Russian Communist state, but had also expanded its political frontiers into Eastern Europe. In practical terms this meant that Western capital had its frontiers frozen and contracted on two fronts. Internally, the Soviet regime had, after the revolution of 1917, gone on to nationalize the property of mainly American, British, German, and French companies.[6] Several companies lost investments worth several millions of dollars and uncalculated potential frontiers of exploitation of the Russian market. Singer, for example, had a manufacturing plant and 1,000 outlets in Czarist Russia worth $100 million at 1914 prices. Externally, the expansion of Communist political regimes into Eastern Europe also promised the same fate for the capitalist firms in these areas. A strengthened Soviet Union also posed the danger of undermining Western colonial empires by encouraging anti-colonial revolutions and thereby expanding the frontiers of denial of mineral and other raw material resources to capitalism and their states. It therefore became urgent that a body of scholars should be developed who would have data on the enemies of the West during the Cold War.[7]

Concurrent with the Cold War was the drama of decolonization that created winds of anxiety for Western political analysts both in libraries and parliamentary chambers. Colonialism had failed to create a body of scholars from among the colonized peoples who would undertake 'accurate studies' and create 'accurate knowledge of the politics' of these areas for Western policy-makers. This made it urgent for the West to supply its own scholars to serve 'a manifest need to diagnose and adapt to likely political trends in the Third World'.[8] Colonially planned structures of social, economic and political management were now threatened with change in the hands of indigenous nationalist politicians and political parties that had aroused the masses in urban and agricultural sectors: sectors which colonialism had systematically refused to let participate in politics and decision-making. If these nationalist parties and politicians made linkages with revolutionary ideas from the Soviet Union or China, the economic threat to capitalist firms again became nakedly alarming in the eyes of the West.

It is little wonder therefore that both multinational companies and Western governments developed a direct interest in Area Studies after the 1940s. In 1947 the Lord Scarborough Commission recommended studies in Oriental and Slavonic studies, a view broadened in 1959 by Sir William Hayter's commission which stated that:

> British universities should focus more on contemporary problems in foreign areas and produce more area specialists on Asia, Russia, Eastern Europe, and Africa.[9]

In the United States the link between Area Studies and national interest was militarized by the enactment of the National Defence Education Act Title VI. This act offered scholarships to students who were willing to study languages of foreign peoples, and/or the politics, history, geology, etc. of these areas. Pye reports that under this programme, between 1958 and 1972 a total of 68.5 million dollars was spent on language and Area Studies and 35,500 bachelors degrees and 5,000 doctoral degrees were awarded in this area, by American universities.

The Ford Foundation and the Rockefeller Foundation supported the Area Studies openly. Between 1950 and 1973 the Ford Foundation gave universities and research organizations 278 million dollars for international studies, and gave over 2,000 fellowships. The fellowships were given to research proposals linked to studies of specific areas of the world. 67% of the fellowships went to those who wanted to study the Soviet Union, East Asia, Africa and Latin America. Western Europe, a friendly and presumably better known area, got the least number of fellowship support with only 7%.

Area Studies 'Get Tough'

Comparative Area Studies has been taken beyond the zone of data collection and analysis, for the purposes of predicting and anticipating the nature of socio-political events, to the zone of attempting to actively intervene in shaping the nature of events in the Third World. Two areas illustrate this. The first is suggested by commentators on the pattern of military coups that took place in Indonesia and Brazil. Both Indonesia and Brazil in the late 1950s and

Distribution of Awards for Political Science, 1952-72

Area Studied	%
U.S.S.R	25.51
East Asia	12.31
Africa	17.31
Latin America	11.39
South Asia	9.11
Southeast Asia	7.74
Near East	7.74
Western Europe	6.61

early 1960s showed a momentum towards political change that in the one case would have brought the Indonesian Communist Party into power and in the other would have brought about radical policies in the interests of rural peasants and plantation workers, organized in associations, and urban workers, the urban unemployed and underemployed masses in the cities of Brazil. The policies being advocated by the Indonesian Communist Party directly threatened the interests of rural feudal Muslim classes and of the urban *prijaji* ruling classes in the bureaucracy and commerce. These groups had family and economic connections with the top-ranking classes in the military. In Brazil the militant rural peasant associations and labourers were direct threats to the *latifundia* classes, while the increasingly militant urban labour unions were in direct opposition to the interests of the local industrial bourgeoisie, the middle classes and the profit margins of the multinational corporations. Stepan has shown that the middle-level and top-ranking officers in the Brazilian armed forces were drawn from the middle class and the rural aristocracy.[10] The anxieties of the ruling classes in both Indonesia and Brazil against the threat of Communism were shared by the United States officials. Moreover, it has been suggested that ever since the late 1950s American policy-makers had evolved a new policy towards the military in the Third World.

In the new policy orientation, U.S. officials brought increasingly large numbers of military officers from the Third World for training in American military academies. The central thrust of this training was to extend the perception of the scope of military defence so as to include the active engineering of economic, social and political institutions against the emergence of socialism or communism. The military officers were therefore trained in skills ranging from economic planning to managing public corporations — in anticipation of their future roles at the centre of political and economic institutions.[11] Recent official admissions have suggested that when Brazil's President Goulart assumed certain radical postures in 1964, the then American ambassador to Brazil actively encouraged the Brazilian military to carry out a coup. The same scenario has been suggested for Indonesia in the coup against Sukarno.[12] Furthermore both the military regimes that assumed power in Indonesia and Brazil formed their own political parties, and put their people into management positions in the economy, including the signficant directorships of *Petrobraz* and *Potomina*, the state-owned oil corporations of Brazil and Indonesia, respectively, whose policies were of direct interest to multinational oil companies.

Another example of intervention is what has been popularly known as the 'Green Revolution'. The Green Revolution stood for a cluster of policy items, including:

> 1) the scientific invention of seeds that would yield greater quantities of harvest than existing traditionally adapted ones; 2) the extensive distribution of these seeds to farmers; 3) the supply of tractors, insecticides, pesticides and irrigation infrastructure to farmers using these new seeds; 4) the creation of a new class of rich farmers in a formerly peasant agricultural structure, or the reinforcement of already existing feudal landownership structures; 5) the creation of new markets for American and European companies that sold tractors, insecticides, pesticides, irrigation pipes, sprayers, etc.; in agricultural systems of countries ranging from Mexico to India and Nigeria.[13]

What is significant about the Green Revolution is that it has involved intensive Area Studies of the agrarian and agricultural characteristics of several countries, their political and social class structures, and the recommendation or introduction of a specific 'policy package' that would either drastically change or perpetuate existing socio-economic and political structures in ways seen as desirable by American policy-advisers like Lester Brown.[14] The Rockefeller Foundation has assumed a leading role in promoting the scientific research in the development of seeds that would be high-yielding in ecologies ranging from tropical rain forests to arid zones. The research stations include those in Ibadan, Hyderabad, the Philippines, Mexico, Colombia, and the cereals and food crops involved include yams, rice, wheat, maize, millet and groundnuts. The link between this 'intellectual multinationalism' and economic imperialism was suggested by the President of the American Agricultural Economists thus:

> Five firms dominate the U.S. grain export industry, accounting for 85 per cent of total exports. Since 1971 Cargil and Continental each have had 25 per cent of the U.S. exports; Cook Industries, 15 per cent; the Bunge and Louis Dreyfuss Corporations, 10 per cent each . . . of the remaining 15 per cent of the market, 8 per cent is divided among 5 small export companies and the remaining 7 per cent among 4 producer-owner cooperatives.[15]

Anti-Imperialism and Area Studies

There has existed a strong tradition of 'expository radicalism by documentation' in African studies. W.E.B. Dubois and George Padmore used radical social science research and analysis to thrust into the intellectual arena the thesis that European colonialism had destroyed African civilizations and economic and social formations. Padmore sought to demonstrate that the expropriation of land from Africans in Kenya, Rhodesia and South Africa, the giving of these lands to White settlers, the use of forced labour all across Africa had shown that Britain was fundamentally *irresponsible* towards the African peoples and that Britain should therefore abandon her *illegal* colonial occupation of Africa.[16] If Dubois' and Padmore's works are less visible today, their thesis has been most articulately restated by yet another African scholar from the Diaspora: Walter Rodney. Even the title of his book *How Europe Underdeveloped Africa* has loud suggestions of the 'ancestors have come back to us', being a continuation of the theme that Dubois and Padmore had pioneered in African scholarship. Yet Rodney himself was a product of a new intellectual consciousness that was aroused by yet another African from the Caribbean, Franz Fanon. Through his studies of the Algerian revolution, both as a psychiatrist-doctor in daily contact with Algerian victims of French violence, colonial and anti-colonial users of violence, and as an analyst of changes taking place in Algerian society including the impact of the revolution on the Algerian women, Fanon came up with the proposition that colonial violence against colonized peoples (African, Arab, Asiatic) *underdevelops the personality* of its victims. This he describes as a process of degeneration and stultification which can be reversed only when the victim experiences the cathartic trauma of brutalizing his or her brutalizer.[17] Only a people who have gone through this experience will know the freedom of the moment and process of decolonization and will develop a political consciousness that will enable them to keep their new African or Arab leadership in vigilant check against betraying the revolution and the people after independence.

In terms of 'expository radicalism by documentation' Rodney is perhaps even closer to Frank than to Fanon. Frank hit the front pages of intellectual consciousness and prejudices through reports of studies he had done on the history of development in Brazil, Chile and Mexico. The central message of his reports was that Brazil and Chile had been already developing their industrial capacities prior to the invasion of American and European capital. Through underselling local industrialists or buying them out, through creating a market for coffee in Europe and North America (in the case of Brazil), and developing local Brazilian importing agents and businessmen who made money through import-trade, foreign capitalists succeeded in turning these latter groups against the local industrialists and their allies in government who favoured the policy of 'Brazilian market for Brazilians'. A civil war was fought over this policy debate and the economic nationalists lost. Thus began a process of the *development of underdevelopment* in Brazil — a process which rests on the constant export of profits from the country by the foreign companies.[18]

The importation of underdevelopment theory into studies of African politics has recently been manifested in the works of Leys, Shivji, and Mamdani on Kenya, Tanzania and Uganda, respectively. These works place at the centre of their analysis Nkrumah's concept of neo-colonialism as a factor in African political economy, and link it to Fanon's warning of the dangers of an incomplete path to decolonization through the active desire by the local elite to form economic partnerships with foreign capital. In so doing they reject frameworks of analysis which use concepts like 'modernization', 'national integration', and 'political development'. They see these concepts as racially tinged with the suggestion that Euro-American social systems are superior forms to which Africans should aspire. More importantly, these concepts seek to ignore the fact and process of domination and exploitation of African political economies by Euro-Americans. Within Africa, the concept of 'national integration' is suspect, for it downplays the emergence of classes, especially the growing gap between the bureaucratic and commercial bourgeoisie and the rural peasants and urban poor masses.[19] Finally, this bourgeoisie establishes links with foreign capital, and uses the state to accumulate wealth for itself.

There is a link between the 'intellectual multinationalism' that underlies Area Studies and the political purposes of the state or the individual researchers who undertake it. Western governments and their multinational corporations have seen Area Studies as a means of defending or advancing their national intersts and imperialism. To this end, their scholars have researched political events and processes in Asia, Africa, Latin America, the Soviet Union and China for the purposes of enabling policy-makers to predict events accurately and to intervene appropriately. As Dunn put it in 1960:

> the comparative analysis of the political systems of the developing countries . . . has assumed considerable importance in this period of falling empires and emerging nations. If we want to know what to expect from the new political entities, we need some means for describing. . . the factors and interests influencing political behaviour in concrete situations.[20]

African governments can join this tradition and finance research into Russian, North American, Latin American, Chinese, Asian, and European studies. Post-graduate students receiving scholarship support in overseas universities should be actively persuaded to link their receipt of funds to specified Area Studies. Likewise some undergraduate fellowships and post-graduate fellowships in African universities should be linked to specified Area specializations. Specific research funds for teaching and research staff should likewise be linked to Area Studies projects. African continental academies for Soviet, Asian, American and European studies should be set up by the Organization of African Unity. With regard to African aspects of foreign policies of African governments, studies of the politics of sister African countries should be seen within the overall goal of ultimately achieving African Unity Government.

Both liberal Western scholars and radical African scholars share a concern for linking Area Studies with questions about who is benefiting from 'development'. Quick, for example, in his study of rural development policy in Zambia describes the interests of the elites who influence policy in the form of policy recommendations undermining Kaunda's commitment to the welfare of the rural masses. He reflects a commitment to exposing the nature of these policies.[21] Schatzberg shows that the regional administrators in Zaire are more concerned with expropriating the rural peoples and pocketing funds sent from Kinshasha than with their development.[22] African governments concerned about the development of African peoples will increasingly need both African journalists and specialists who act not only as 'a supplier of raw materials, rather like a miner, chipping away at the cliff face of a South African mine, who is supposed to ship the unrefined ore off to the master goldsmiths living elsewhere',[23] but also as analysts, theorists and comparativists. These specialists would provide comparative data and propositions derived from experiences in other African countries for the benefit of policy-makers to use both domestically and in foreign policy-making. As an example, policy-makers in the area of agriculture have the experiences of *ujamaa* villages in Tanzania or state and individual elite plantations using as cheap labour peoples recently made landless after independence in Malawi. Then there is the example of the allocation of vast lands taken from African peasants in Senegal and in Haile Selaise's Ethiopia to be given to American companies to grow vegetables and fruits for export to Europe during the months of winter, and also used to grow alfalfa grass for export to Japan for feeding Japanese cattle. All of this at the expense of rural livelihood and food production.[24]

Notes

1. Don D. Fowler, 'Notes in Inquiries in Anthropology: A Bibliographical Essay' in Timothy H.H. Throresen (ed.), *Towards a Science of Man: Essays in the History of Anthropology* (The Hague, Mouton, 1975), p. 18.
2. Ibid., p. 15.
3. Ibid., pp. 19–20.
4. R.A. Adeleye, 'Hausaland and Bornu 1600–1800' in Ajayi and Crowder, *History of West Africa,* Vol. 1 (London, Longman), p. 498.
5. Lucian W. Pye, 'The Confrontation between Discipline and Area Studies', in Pye (ed.), *Political Science and Area Studies* (Bloomington, Indiana University Press, 1975), p. 5.
6. For a record of Western companies nationalized in the wake of

communist revolutions in Russia, Eastern Europe and China see J. Wilczynski, *The Multinationals and East-West Relations: Towards Transideological Collaboration* (London, Macmillan, 1976), p. 2.
7. Harry Eckstein, 'A Critique of Area Studies from a West European Perspective' in Pye, op. cit., p. 203.
8. Pye, op. cit., p. 13.
9. Quoted in Pye, op. cit., p. 12.
10. Alfred Stepan, *The Military in Politics, Changing Patterns in Brazil* (1971), (Yale University Press).
11. David Ransom, 'The Berkeley Mafia and the Indonesian Massacre', *Ramparts*, Vol. 9, No. 4, October, 1970.
12. *The New York Times Book Review*, 25 June 1978, p. 26. Richard R. Fagen writes: 'Lincoln Gordon, United States Ambassador to Brazil at the time of the military coup, an official deeply implicated in plotting against the Goulart Government.'
13. Keith Griffith, *The Political Economy of Agrarian Change: An Essay on the Green Revolution* (Cambridge, Mass., Harvard University Press, 1974).
14. Lester Brown, *Seeds of Change* (New York, Praeger, 1970).
15. Roger D. Hansen, *The U.S. and World Development: Agenda for Action* (New York, Praeger, 1976), p. 77.
16. G. Padmore, *How England Rules Africa* (London, 1950).
17. Franz Fanon, *The Wretched of the Earth* (Harmondsworth, Penguin, 1967).
18. Andre G. Frank, 'Economic Dependence, Class Structure, and Underdevelopment Policy' in James D. Cockcroft, Andre Gunder Frank and Dale L. Johnson, *Dependence and Underdevelopment* (New York, Doubleday, 1972).
19. Colin Leys, *Underdevelopment in Kenya* (Berkeley and Los Angeles, University of California Press, 1974).
20. Frederick S. Dunn in Gaberiel A. Almond and James S. Coleman, *The Politics of the Developing Areas* (Princeton, 1960), p. v.
21. Stephen A. Quick, *Bureaucracy and Rural Socialism: The Zambian Experience*, Ph.D. thesis, Stanford University, 1975.
22. Michael Schatzberg, 'Blockage Points in Zaire: The Flow of Budgets, Bureaucrats, and Beer', mimeo, November 1978.
23. Chalmers Johnson, 'Political Science and East Asian Area Studies' in Pye, op. cit., p. 81.
24. Frances Moore Lappe and Joseph Collins, *Food First, Beyond the Myth of Scarcity* (Boston, Houghton Mufflin, 1975).

12. Alternative Approaches to African Politics

Yolamu R. Barongo

What I intend to do in this essay[1] is to indicate how African politics is to be understood and explained. In spite of the numerous differences between African countries (which no doubt produce variations in the nature of local political interactions) such as territorial and population size, historical and contemporary experience, structure of social organization, level of social and economic development, resource endowment and the number and quality of political elites, there are nevertheless common patterns that characterize African politics that can be discerned, described and explained. I am interested in the salient features of this politics namely, the intense and often violent political competition, acute ethnic and elite conflicts, tendencies towards aggrandizement of power both at personal and institutional levels, the adoption by governments of different ideologies of development in the face of more or less similar problems of development and the dependent nature of the foreign policies of many African countries.

To say that there are similar patterns that characterize African politics implies the existence of certain basic common features which condition and shape the political process. The task therefore is to identify those characteristic features of African societies that constitute an infrastructure of politics to influence the emergence of those peculiar patterns of African politics which we are interested in explaining. However, before we proceed to identify the foundations of politics in Africa, a brief review of the current attempts at explaining African politics is necessary in order to show the point of departure of the approach proposed in this essay.

Mapping the Continent: Previous Accounts of African Politics

Since 1960, the year of African independence, many Western scholars professing expertise in the various branches of the science of society have been attracted to Africa to undertake studies of the problems confronting the emergent nations. Right from the beginning, the political scientists among them were confronted with a host of political phenomena, some of them interesting and fascinating, some disturbing, which could not properly be accounted for within the established theoretical models and methodological approaches used in the study of the politics of the older states. These scholars found out quite early that, unlike the familiar patterns of politics in the West, the trend of politics in the new states was towards what Western theoretical precepts considered to be undemocratic rule — the emergence of one-party systems, authoritarian civilian and military regimes and lack of effective political participation at the mass level. It was further discovered that political activity in the new states appeared to lack well-organized and institutionalized procedures for political competition. Hence the relationship between groups of elites and among communities was one of conflict that quite often resulted in violent changes in governments and forced regimes in power to adopt various methods of political repression. In an attempt to comprehend the seemingly complex political problems confronting the new states, a set of new theoretical perspectives was developed that purported to offer heuristic guides in approaching the study, understanding and explanation of African politics. By using these perspectives, certain predictions were made about possible developments and future trends. Two perspectives namely, the modernization and cultural pluralism models, became particularly popular among Western scholars involved in the study and analysis of African politics.

Modernization

The modernization perspective was employed to analyze and explain a wide range of problems confronting the new states.[2] This perspective set out to provide an overall framework by which certain dominant features of African politics could be understood and explained. It became fashionable to see and explain the existing political problems in the emergent nations (such as the recurrent political instabilities, tendencies towards centralization of power, the intense ethnic and elite competition for resources and political power and the various forms of political repression) in terms of the rapid rate of modernization in the new states. The central argument of the modernization perspective was that African societies were experiencing rapid and multi-dimensional changes. The rapidity and intensity of the changes tended to weaken the traditional institutions. In some cases modernization created an institutional vacuum by completely supplanting the outmoded traditional institutions without allowing the changing society enough time to adjust and create viable alternative institutions to accommodate the impetus and the forces of change. At the same time the values and normative fabrics of society were being quickly fragmented, making social relations increasingly fluid. One's role in such uncertain and unstable relationships becomes difficult to define and to be recognized and accepted by others. Accordingly, in the new states modernity was being introduced and rapidly taking ground in situations where there were no supportive institutions and cultural values. Modern institutions capable of constraining political behaviour and structuring political relations were nonexistent and in cases where they existed they had not taken root in the culture of the society. For political life this meant that in the new states there was no agreed set of rules and procedures capable of governing political interaction, resulting in the use of unconventional means to gain elective office and unconstitutional behaviour of people in power. The absence of acceptable rules and procedures in political competition puts instability of one form or another high up on the political agenda as rival groups, determined to unseat the incumbents from power, employ various methods including enlisting the assistance of persons in the armed forces of the country. In the face of this challenge the government resorts to the use of power to suppress opposition. Opposition parties are banned, their leaders are detained and imprisoned and the regime sets out to consolidate itself in power from which it can be dismissed only through a military coup. On the whole, the modernization perspective accredits the various forms of political turmoil facing African countries to the fragility of political institutions and the lack of tradition in political competition.

In addition to the problems occasioned by the rapid changes taking place in modernizing societies, the modernization perspective also takes into account, as one of its analytical and explanatory factors, the scarcity of the resources available to African countries and the importance of this factor in the political life of these countries.[3] In a situation of acute scarcity of resources, politics is not only organized around the competition for the control of these resources but also, because of this, the struggle for them is usually very intense. Whoever controls state power controls much else: patronage in the distribution of jobs and award of government contracts, and decisions in the allocation of factories, hospitals, schools and other amenities. In situations of this kind politicians compete for power with the aim of controlling the use of available resources. Losing to an opponent does not usually augur well for the professional politician — it might signal the beginning of the end of his career. If at one stage he does not find himself in prison he would most certainly find himself losing popularity since he would not be in a position to dispense patronage to his followers in order to maintain political support.

For the successful politician the story is quite different. Being in control of the resources means a bright political future. He can manipulate the use of the resources of the country to the advantage of his political supporters. This means therefore that politicians representing certain ethnic and sectional interests engage themselves in intensive political battles in order to control governmental institutions through which they can also control the management of the scarce resources. The manner in which the regime uses discriminatory devices in the allocation and utilization of these resources inevitably alienates some sections of society and intensifies ethnic and elite conflicts. In consequence, a situation is created which breeds tensions in inter-ethnic and inter-elite relationships. The existence of these tensions in the political system very often leads to political instability.

The modernization perspective locates the factors and forces responsible for the various problems within the modernizing societies themselves and suggests that, because of the rapid rate of social and economic change being experienced by African countries, political instability and other problems contingent on the process of modernization are inevitable.[4]

Cultural Pluralism

The other popular theoretical framework — cultural pluralism or its variant, the ethnic-conflict model — attempts to explain African politics in much the same way.[5] Like the modernization perspective, it focuses on the social structure and identifies the social-cultural forces that influence the political process the determine the structure of political relations in society. The model is analytically geared to the existence of groups vying for influence, control and domination. Analysts who apply this model to the study of African politics find that almost without exception, African societies are made up of many ethnic groups of varying sizes and influence. These groups are seen as culturally distinct from each other on the basis of language, social organization, values, beliefs and other cultural characteristics. In addition the various groups have different interests and aspirations and tend to use the resources available to them to assert their differences and power in relation to other groups. Before the advent of colonialism, the disparate ethnic groups existed and functioned as separate self-contained communities but when colonial powers forced them to co-exist under centralized political systems, the relation between them became one of competition for allocation of resources and other forms of colonial favours. On attainment of independence, the struggle and competition among the groups became very intense indeed. Larger groups attempted to ensure their dominance over others by controlling the key governmental institutions while the minority groups struggled for recognition and a fair deal in the distribution of the national resources. The ethnic-pluralism model emphasizes the ever continuing aggressiveness, rivalry and competition among the various cultural groups in the polity.[6]

In terms of this model, political life in African countries is organized around the desire by the various ethnic groups to further and protect their own interests. And these interests are culturally defined and have to do with what groups possess as distinct communities and what they can get from others in a competitive situation. Accordingly the political behaviour of the people in power is influenced by particularistic considerations. Leaders use state power to ensure the dominance of the group to which they belong and those groups which are excluded from political power for the time being engage in the struggle for power and the resources. This creates a tug-of-war political arena and the intensity of conflicts based on particularistic claims ultimately leads to situations of instability.[7]

By the very nature of its assumptions and premises, the ethnic pluralism model offers no viable framework for understanding, interpreting or explaining contemporary African politics. The model assumes that the various groups which constitute the polity exist as separate communities each with its own distinct cultural values, institutional patterns and political orientations. Nowhere in black Africa does one find such well defined and self-contained cultural units. In its original formulation and application, the model attempted with remarkable success to grapple with the realities of a colonial society in which race or colour played an important part in structuring social relations and distributing wealth, power and prestige among the different cultural groups in society.[8] In contemporary Africa, the model might conceivably be applied profitably to the racially and culturally heterogeneous white-dominated societies of southern Africa. But in a black African country where patterns of action and political alignments on the basis of ethnic identity are fluid, depending on the situation and the issues involved, an attempt to make the ethnic factor a major variable in the analysis and explanation of African politics is problematic and indeed misleading. At the very best, and depending on how it is handled, ethnicity may be used in conjunction with class analysis to explain why a regime adopts a particular policy that appears to favour a particular section of society.

It should be emphasized therefore that the existing Western-derived theoretical perspectives used by analysts of African politics, two of which have been reviewed here, do not provide useful frameworks for understanding of the dynamics of African politics. Like all Western developmentalist approaches to African problems, the modernization and the ethnic pluralism models suffer from being static and ahistorical. Since they limit explanations to why a particular phenomenon occurs in a particular society, scholars using these perspectives do not seek possible explanations beyond the confines of the immediate environment in which it occurs. These approaches lead the analyst to look for explanations only within the boundaries of the social structure of the society concerned, usually overlooking even the incremental changes in society and the problems they create. They are ahistorical because they do not take into account the historical experience of a society as a major variable in explaining contemporary patterns of behaviour. The perspectives are primarily concerned with the present and to them the present has no past: what matters is to look at the existing society and identify the forces that account for what is happening in it. They are non-explanatory because, being static and ahistorical, these perspectives are not able to help the analyst in identifying the essential variables that must be taken into account to understand and explain the nature, the content and the dynamics of African politics. In other words what the perspectives offer as explanatory factors are either false or are not crucial to the phenomenon to be explained.

As has already been indicated, in an attempt to explain why African politics takes the form it does, the modernization and ethnic pluralism models cannot be of much help. They offer no satisfactory account of political instability in African countries, merely saying that the problem exists because of the fragility of political institutions and the lack of institutionalized procedures for political competition or because of the acute shortage of resources. But this begs certain questions which cannot even be easily formulated if the analyst is using any of these perspectives: Why are the institutions fragile? Why is there a lack of institutionalized procedures? Why are the resources in African countries scarcer than in other parts of the world? The search for meaningful answers to these questions must necessarily go beyond the mere fact of saying that African countries are undergoing rapid socio-economic changes occasioned by the process of modernization.

The History of the Present: Political Foundations

To answer these questions and hence to really understand the nature and dynamics of contemporary African politics, one has to go back into history to see how African societies have developed over time since the advent of imperialism and colonialism and understand the condition of their present material base. This must be accompanied by an appraisal of their contemporary experiences, and in particular an attempt must be made to understand how those countries are struggling to exist in an international system dominated by the Western capitalist powers. Institutional fragility, violent political competition and the existence of unstable political relationships among groups and individuals cannot be said to be inherent in the nature of African societies. Nor is cultural heterogeneity a peculiar feature of these societies making African politics different from that of the United States of America, Canada or even of the United Kingdom, all of which are equally heterogeneous societies. There are certainly reasons why African politics differs from that of the developed countries. These reasons are related to the differences in the historical and contemporary experiences of African countries as compared to others. And it would seem to me that the main difference is this, that whereas politics in the developed countries is founded on sound economic bases and material abundance largely made possible by overseas exploitation, politics in African countries is based on poverty created by historical and contemporary exploitation of the continent by the developed capitalist countries. A full explanation of African politics cannot be attained without regard to the operation of the international capitalist system and its impact on African economies, accompanied by a thorough analysis of the functions which African countries fulfill within this system.

In a very real sense, the nature of political life in a particular society, the types of institutions that are created and sustained and the peculiar patterns of political processes that emerge are a function of the interplay among three main factors, namely, the condition of the economic base of society, the historical experiences of that society and the actors' perception, interpretation and response to environmental stimuli. The role of culture, that is to say, the values of the people, their beliefs and the dominant systems of ideas in shaping the political process and in dictating particular forms of political organization, is by no means being minimized. But these values, beliefs and ideas have their basis in and reflect very fundamentally on the nature of the economic base (or the dominant mode of production, to be precise) and the relations it creates among the people as well as in the historical experiences of the society. It is primarily the material environment that determines the formation of cleavages between social groups and classes with competing interests, thereby defining the character and structure of political interaction in a competitive-bargaining situation. Moreover, it is the material resources actually or potentially available to individuals and groups in the polity that determines their relative importance, influence and power.

The historical experience of a society, on the other hand, relates to the cumulative developments and changes that have taken place over time and an awareness on the part of citizens, especially among the principal actors, of the factors responsible for these developments and changes. The historical experience of a society is important in influencing political behaviour insofar as it provides a perspective within which a problem can be perceived and defined. It is the experience of the past that helps an individual, particularly one faced with a problem, to understand and interpret the present and to be able to predict with a reasonably high degree of certainty the possible outcomes of his or her actions. History gives meaning to present problems, it generates new ideas, creates norms and lays down traditions which sanction and constrain behaviour. The historical experience presents the decision-maker with a set of experimented courses of action from which he can choose when approaching a particular problem. In the final analysis, however, it is the actor's perception of the total environment, his or her interpretation of and response to this environment, that influence his or her behaviour. The forces generated by the material environment form the axis of political activity, history supplies information about the origins of present problems and individuals produce actions, the totality of which structure themselves in a political process born out of the peculiarities of a particular interactional situation.

If therefore we have to understand the dynamics of contemporary African politics and if we are to be able to explain it correctly, we must first of all identify the foundations of this politics. The trends which we observe as characterizing African politics have their basis undoubtedly in certain common problems confronting African countries and the forces which these problems generate. The problems and the forces they generate combine to produce an environment that induces the emergence of patterns and processes of politics peculiar to these countries. We identify these problems as relating to poverty, dependence and the colonial experience. How these problems manifest themselves in the political life of any one country depends mainly on how the actors, particularly the political elites, perceive and respond to them and the kind of institutions created in response to the problems. Thus, although the infrastructure of politics may be the same in all countries, the manner in which it affects the political process and the responses to the problem which this infrastructure creates, may vary depending on the perceptions and the behaviour of the actors involved. But the common infrastructural problems do influence the emergence of a politics of a special character as we now proceed to illustrate.[9]

The Politics of Poverty

A common characteristic of African countries is that they are materially poor. Their economies are highly dependent on a world economic system dominated by the developed capitalist countries and, being both a cause and a symptom of poverty and dependence, their societies are grossly underdeveloped. These factors have created an economic base in African societies which generate political problems of a kind never experienced in the relatively more developed countries. African countries are poor and underdeveloped not because they lack the resources necessary for development. On the contrary, they have abundant human and material resources. But these resources, rather than being utilized for the development of African societies, have historically been exploited to foster the development of other countries and continue right up to the present day to be used to contribute to the development of the already developed countries of the world.

The historical and contemporary origins of this dilemma have been well documented in several studies and do not therefore require recapitulation.[10] We should rather indicate here how the condition of poverty, dependence and underdevelopment affects African politics and in doing so underline at the same time the fact that, contrary to what Western observers of African politics believe to be the case, many of the political problems existing in African countries today have a predominantly *external* origin.

Our firm position is that the dominant characteristics of African politics — such as the intense ethnic and elite conflicts, the recurrent tendencies of instability, the trends towards centralization of power, the excessive use of power for political repression and the submissive character of the foreign policy of many governments — are explicable, to a great extent, in terms of the material poverty of African countries and the dependent nature of these countries on the operations and manipulations of the international capitalist system.

Poverty and Elites

The politics of poverty is such that it fosters the formation of groups and classes with conflicting material interests and tends to divide society into hostile camps of people quite often armed with strong (ideological) convictions of how society should best be organized for the purpose of overcoming or at least weakening the tenacity of the condition of poverty. These conflicts and interests may manifest themselves randomly at the level of the individual or may structure themselves through organized institutions such as political parties, workers trade unions and employers associations or informally through facades of ethnic and religious sentiments. In the political arena and at each level of political activity, there are individuals, usually members of the intellectual and political elite, whose beliefs, ideas, actions and behaviour represent the economic interests of a particular class or one group or the other.

In most African countries, the various conflicts that usually develop in situations of instability are of an elite or ethnic kind. But these conflicts are not merely the manifestations of elite, ethnic or cultural differences.[11] Rather, they are a reflection of the material interests of the various groups in society which, in the context of scarce resources, manifest themselves in sharp and intense political competition. It is interesting to note, in support of this assertion, that ethnic prejudices and antagonisms are most prevalent and most violently expressed in situations where employment or business is involved. It is in circumstances involving employment in the civil service, in industry, in the universities and in other places, that one may become suddenly conscious of one's ethnic tags and one's difference from competitors, depending on how one's employment needs and interests are satisfied or denied. In situations where economic interests coincide, where they are not in conflict or where they are not at stake, as is normally the case among the poorer sections of society, two individuals of different ethnic origin are able to live together in remarkable harmony and brotherhood. In fact such people do often share common attitudes to life which derive from their similar material circumstances.[12]

In order therefore to understand why there are ethnic conflicts and antagonisms in most African countries and why these conflicts develop sometimes into situations of violence and instability,[13] one has to understand the basis of these conflicts, which is essentially material. Employing the ethnic pluralism model to explain such conflicts does not really reveal the true character of the factors behind inter-ethnic conflicts. And in the context of the present economic situation in African countries, ethnicity is an important political force simply because the resources are far less adequate to satisfy the material needs of individuals and groups who compete for them and therefore in many cases have to be selectively allocated by those in authority.

In the same way elite competition, and the conflicts and disagreements which arise therefrom, cannot be fully understood without reference to the material base. It is widely recognized, but often without proper explanation, that in Africa instabilities of one form or another are elite phenomena. We should restate the fact here that elite behaviour in (African) politics is a reflection of competing economic interests in society.

There appears to be in any one African country two categories of political elites, one ideologically inclined, the other limited in outlook by parochial preoccupations. There is, on the one had, a group of elites which acts as the champion and spokesman of the interests of economically stratified and well-defined groups, for instance, those elites which represent the interests of either the underprivileged classes of peasants and workers or of those of the more economically fortunate but numerically smaller sections of society. On the other hand, there is a set of elites whose behaviour is influenced by the economic interests of parochial entities such as ethnic groups and geographical localities.[14] In order to satisfy these interests, political elites compete for the control of state power and when they gain this control they formulate and slant governmental economic policies in favour of the economic interests of the groups which they represent.[15]

The fact that political elites by definition represent certain economic interests in society, however hidden and unarticulated these interests may be, the fact that these elites seek power in order to control the use of scarce resources to cater for these interests, has certain effects on the nature of political trends in Africa. In the first place, political competition tends to be intense, unstructured and sometimes violent. In a desperate attempt to control state power and all that this implies, politicians may violate established procedures for competition and resort to various tactics which promise success over opponents. We should refuse to accept the suggestion made by the modernization theorists that, because politicians do not always follow the rules and procedures of political competition known to Western political practice, this necessarily means that in Africa such rules and procedures are non-existent or are not recognized by society. African countries have constitutions and electoral laws which stipulate in a clear manner the rules of the game. But *some* politicians may not be inclined to follow them in every detail because what is usually at stake — the power to control the use of scarce resources — means a great deal to either of the competing parties and which must therefore be acquired or retained by any means not particularly consonant with the limits of the general standards of morality.

Poverty and Power

Political competition and manoeuvres do not usually end when the election results come in. The party in power is continually faced with challenges from the elites outside the government. The party which loses a particular election may accept defeat but this will seldom stop its leaders from organizing, planning and taking certain actions to enable the opposition elites to wrest power from the incumbent party in the short or long run. This creates a situation of ever-continuing tensions among the political elites. Two tendencies have arisen out of this situation in African politics in recent years.

First, primarily as a response to the destabilizing activities of opposition groups, governments of almost all African countries have at one time or another adopted measures that have strengthened the power of the state. And this has been achieved in two ways. There has been, on the one hand, measures aimed at weakening the opposition by abolishing the semi-autonomous centres of power dominated or used by opposition groups to challenge the government at the centre.[16] On the other hand, steps have been taken by governments to silence the opposition legally by adopting various kinds of repressive laws. The experiences of Ghana, Kenya and Uganda, among others, fully illustrate this trend. These countries started off with independence constitutions which dispersed power among the regions and which also provided a framework for the existence and operation of multi-party politics. But a few years after independence, each of these countries had either amended its constitution or replaced it with a republican constitution, mainly for the purpose of abolishing the power of the regions in favour of centralized consolidation. At the same time, detention laws have been added to the statute books of many countries to enable the governments to deal firmly with individual opposition 'trouble-makers'. Under these laws governments are empowered to detain in prison or in other such 'safe' places, individuals considered to be a risk to the security of the state, sometimes for indefinite periods of time. A sampling of a few countries will reveal the extent to which governments have used this legal instrument as a means of containing elite conflicts.

The second tendency has been the general trend towards centralization of power under one-party systems and under one strong leader. With the possible exception of Tanzania and the countries which emerged into independence with a single mobilizing party, all countries which have adopted single-party systems have done so mainly as a result of elite conflicts as well as disagreements among them over national policy. The national policies which provoked such disagreements invariably entailed the question of development and the related ethical and ideological issue of which sections of society should benefit most from the scarce resources available to the nation. Consequently, in countries where one-party systems exist, a set of leaders sharing more or less similar ideological convictions and commitments have sought to consolidate and perpetuate themselves in power under a strong leader and to use the power to develop and utilize the national resources in a manner consistent with the economic needs and interests of the classes or sections of society which they represent.[17]

Dependency of African Countries

The problem of poverty contributes in another important way to the explanation of the nature and dynamics of African politics. Being dependent, African countries have from time to time fallen victims to the manipulations of the international capitalist system. The growth or stagnation of their economics is determined primarily by the fluctuations in the needs and interests of the dominant nations. In cases where the primary exports have continued to attract high prices in the world market, the domestic economies of African countries have tended to prosper, albeit superficially, making it possible for these countries to enjoy periods of relative stability. But where prices of commodities have fallen on the world market, due to a lack of effective demand from the dominant consumers, the African domestic economies have been severely affected, leaving the governments in serious trouble. As a result of insufficient or diminishing foreign exchange, the volume of imports decreases, investments in the productive sectors are halted, inflation sets in, unemployment rates rise and the producers of the primary export commodities become poorer and restless. All these externally generated problems react on the government by weakening its capacity to cater for the needs of the people and consequently eroding its legitimacy from the point of view of its subjects. As the experiences of Zambia and Zaire in the recent past can very well illustrate, the problems that arise in the domestic economy of a dependent country as a result of a fall in world prices of the principal exports tend to snowball into situations of domestic political instability.

On another plane, the dependency of African countries on metropolitan powers have tended to plot the patterns of their foreign policy orientation. To a very significant degree, the foreign policies and alignments of the poor countries in an international system dominated by the economically advanced powers is determined by their needs for development and the perception of the leaders in power of how best they can manipulate these powers for assistance in the development of their countries. Since the issue is largely that of development, some countries like Kenya and most of the Francophone states have chosen to adopt and maintain a foreign policy posture which keeps them in close political, economic and cultural contact with the former colonial powers and their allies. By doing so, they hope to ensure continual enjoyment of the paternalism of Western capitalist countries in the form of investments, financial and technical aid and preferential trade agreements. Others have insisted on a foreign policy of non-alignment ostensibly to safeguard their independence, but in terms of practical politics, in order to have friends on either side of the competing power blocs who can offer assistance in times of need. Either of these brands of foreign policy, however, makes African countries less assertive and a little timid in international political controversies. For the non-aligned countries, a slight slanting of policy that appears to favour a country in the Eastern bloc immediately provokes the hostility and intrigues of the capitalist powers, sometimes with disastrous consequences for the non-aligned country's domestic economy, as the experiences of Tanzania can very well illustrate.[18]

For many of the problems we have discussed here one finds colonialism to be either a major cause or an aggravating factor. For instance, ethnic pluralism is a social fact in the life histories of African societies. As a political factor, however, ethnic conflicts have their origins in the antagonistic relations of production and exchange introduced into African societies first by the mercantilist system, then consolidated by the introduction of the capitalist mode of production and finally consummated by the long reign of colonial rule. Moreover, colonialism intensified ethnic particularism and set ethnic groups against each other in many ways.[19] Socially, the colonial system of education fostered attitudes of inferiority and superiority among communities by embarking on programmes of unbalanced education. Thus we find that in virtually all African countries there are ethnic groups which claim superiority over their neighbours on the basis of educational statistics. The pre-emption of jobs in the civil service and other sectors of employment by members of one ethnic group is a clear testimony to the educational superiority of a particular group and a basis of conflict in inter-ethnic relations. Added to this, colonial administrations are notorious for their encouragement of uneven development of the colonial territories as part of their policy of divide and rule. Some regions or districts, usually coinciding with ethnic boundaries, were favoured by colonial development plans with the result that some ethnic groups enjoyed the highest income, and had within their territorial boundaries the best roads, the best health facilities, the best schools and the best of other social amenities. The differences in the standards of living of the various groups created a platform for conflict and competition whose legacies still pose considerable problems for the politics of the independent nations. The colonial administrative structure and subsequent political arrangements for electoral politics had the greatest impact on the intensity of ethnic localism. Local administrative units were established along ethnic lines and groups tended to be administered as if they were self-contained political entities. In most cases electoral constituencies were drawn to coincide with ethnic territorial boundaries. Accordingly, ethnic groups become the power bases of politicians. In order to get elected to office, politicians were invariably compelled to play on ethnic sentiments. This situation made it difficult for a national leader acceptable to all communities to emerge in post-independence politics. A leader was first and foremost seen as a representative of a particular group and his leadership position at the national level was cited as an instance of domination of an ethnic group to which he belonged. All these problems created by colonialism were to impose a certain character and particular style on post-independence politics, such as can be seen today.

Colonial Political Institutions

Another aspect of colonial legacy that has a bearing on the patterns of contemporary African politics is the nature of inherited institutions through which state power is exercised. As is well known, the institutions built by colonialism were coercive in character. In building these institutions, the colonial power was guided by the need to provide an institutional framework through which to achieve maximum control and exploitation of the colonial peoples. Although at independence the purpose and functions of these institutions became redundant, many of them were retained without modification and used by the independence governments to govern and administer a people whose needs and aspirations had changed. This necessarily bestowed authoritarian characteristics on nationalist governments. And it is noteworthy that the behaviour of many African leaders today is a replication of the colonial tendencies. Political repression in the form of detention, banning and deportation of opponents of the regime was a tactic employed by colonial powers to silence the rise of nationalism or to slow down its tempo. The same weapon is being used by African governments today as means of silencing opposition and containing conflicts.[20] And since colonial rule was essentially a one-party state in outlook, hardly tolerating opposition and seeking to perpetuate itself in power, the same characteristics are vividly replicated today in tendencies towards centralization and aggrandizement of power under single-party systems as well as in the kind of instruments adopted by government for political repression.

Politics Past and Present

It is in contexts such as these that we can see clearly the impact of the colonial past on contemporary politics as well as on the behaviour of leaders. African politics, like politics elsewhere, is influenced by environmental forces in which it exists and functions. But what gives this politics the characteristics it has assumed since independence is the objective condition of the material base of the countries. As we have noted, this base is characterized by a severe shortage of material resources, the result of a long history of imperialist exploitation and contemporary manipulations of the dependent nations by the international capitalist system. Added to this is a colonial history which, apart from creating forces of conflicts within African societies and establishing a tradition of political behaviour inconsistent with democratic practice, also bequeathed to the young nations institutions that were incapable of stabilizing the political process. It is through a thorough analysis of these factors that we can be in a position to understand and explain the nature and dynamics of contemporary African politics. Accordingly, therefore, in the study of African problems, the political economy approach, which employs class analysis as its major methodological guide, accompanied by an analysis of historical variables, is superior to the approaches formulated by 'n the so-called Africanists who invariably tend to view African politics through concepts developed in the static tradition of Western bourgeois scholarship.

Notes

1. This is a slightly modified version of an article published in the *Nigerian Journal of Political Science*. Vol. 2, No. 2, December 1980.
2. The modernization perspective is used by sociologists, economists and political scientists. Leading exponents of this perspective among political scientists include: David E. Apter, *The Politics of Modernization* (Chicago, University of Chicago Press, 1965); Rupert Emerson, *From Empire to Nation* (Cambridge, Mass., Howard University Press, 1960); Dankwart A Rustow, *A World of Nations: Problems of Political Modernization* (Washington, D.C., Brookings Institute, 1967); and Samuel P. Huntington, *Political Order in Changing Societies* (New Haven and London, Yale University Press, 1968).
3. This view is scattered in the various studies of the problems of modernization in Africa and elsewhere. For a representative study see the work on India by Myron Weiner, *The Politics of Scarcity* (University of Chicago Press, 1962) and Bert F. Hoselitz and Myron Weiner, 'Economic Development and Political Stability in India', *Dissent*, No. 8, Spring, 1961. For a general theoretical statement on the relationship between economic modernization and political stability see Mancur Olson Jr., 'Rapid Growth as a Destabilizing Force', *Journal of Economic History*, Vol. 23, December 1963.
4. See for instance, James O'Connell, 'The Inevitability of Instability', *Journal of Modern African Studies*, Vol. 5, September 1967.
5. A theoretical discussion of this model in the context of African Studies

is in Leo Kupper and M.G. Smith (eds.), *Pluralism in Africa* (Berkeley and Los Angeles, University of California Press, 1969), Part I. Studies of African problems that have used this framework include: Robert Melson and Howard Wolpe (eds.), *Nigeria: Modernization and the Politics of Communalism* (Michigan State University Press, 1971); K.W.J. Post and M. Vickers, *Structure and Conflict in Nigeria, 1960-1965* (London, Heinemann, 1973); Holger Bernt Hansen, *Ethnicity and Military Rule in Uganda*, Uppsala, Scandinavian Institute of African Studies, Research Report No. 43, 1977; and all papers in Kuper and Smith (eds.), op. cit. Other studies are scattered in various journals among which may be mentioned: H.D. Seibel, 'Some Aspects of Inter-ethnic Relations in Nigeria', *Nigerian Journal of Economic and Social Studies*, Vol. 9, No. 2, July 1967; A. R. Zolberg 'The Structure of Political Conflict in the New States of Tropical Africa', *American Political Science Review*, Vol. 63, 1968; Pierre L. Van den Berghe, 'Ethnicity: The African Experience', *International Social Science Journal*, Vol. 23, No. 4, 1971; and R. Lemarchand, 'Political Clientelism and Ethnicity in Tropical Africa', *American Political Science Review*, Vol. 66, 1972.

6. The notions of 'communalism', 'aggressive ethnicity', 'political assertiveness of (ethnic) groups', and 'competitive modernization' are inherent in many studies of Nigerian politics which base analysis on ethnic categories. See, for instance, Robert Melson and Howard Wolpe (eds.), op. cit., especially the first theoretical chapter by Melson and Wolpe, and Post and Vickers, op. cit. For a critique of these studies, see the reviews of the above two books by S. Egite Oyovbaire in *Journal of Modern African Studies*, Vol. 11, No. 4, December 1973, pp. 655-8 and Vol. 12, No. 2, June 1974, pp. 336-8 respectively.

7. See, for instance, D.G. Morrison and H.M. Stevenson, 'Cultural Pluralism, Modernization and Conflict: An Empirical Analysis of Sources of Political Instability in African Nations', *The Canadian Journal of Political Science*, Vol. 5, March 1972.

8. The cultural or ethnic pluralism model owes its inspiration to J.S. Furnivall's study of colonial India and Burma. See his *Colonial Policy and Practice* (Cambridge University Press, 1948).

9. It should be mentioned that no attempt has been made in this essay to undertake a detailed discussion of the problems of poverty, dependence and the colonial experience identified here as crucial factors which determine and influence the patterns of contemporary African politics. The illustrations that follow are merely intended to show the linkages between these factors and the prominent features of African politics and to draw attention to the need for concerted programmes of research in these directions.

10. See, among much else, Leonard Woolf, *Empire and Commerce in Africa* (London, n.d.); Walter Rodney, *How Europe Underdeveloped Africa* (Dar-es-Salaam, Tanzania Publishing House, 1972); Samir Amin, 'Underdevelopment in Black Africa: Origins and Contemporary Forms', *Journal of Modern African Studies*, Vol. 10, No. 4, 1972; E.A. Brett, *Colonialism and Underdevelopment in East Africa* (London, Heinemann, 1972); Colin Leys, *Underdevelopment in Kenya: The Political*

Economy of Neo-Colonialism (Berkeley, University of California Press, 1974); Immanuel Wallerstein, 'The Three Stages of African Involvement in the World Economy' in Peter C.W. Gutkind and Immanuel Wallerstein (eds.), *The Political Economy of Contemporary Africa* (London and Beverley Hills, Sage Publications, 1976); and Kwame Nkrumah, *Neo-Colonialism: The Last Stage of Imperialism* (London, Ibadan, Nairobi, Heinemann, 1965). For general works on the roots of poverty and underdevelopment in the Third World see, among others: Paul A. Baran, *The Political Economy of Growth* (New York, Monthly Review Press, 1957) and Tamas Szentes, *The Political Economy of Underdevelopment* (Budapest, Akademiai Kiado, 1971).

11. Many studies of the elites in Africa have tended to emphasize the cultural and linguistic differences as the bases of elite conflicts. One sociological study which rejects the earlier theories, and identifies the economic basis of elite conflicts is that conducted at the University of Ibadan, by Pierre L. Van den Berghe (with the assistance of others). *Power and Privilege at an African University* (London, Routledge and Kegan Paul, 1973) especially Chapters 8 and 9.

12. The values, attitudes and life-styles found to be shared by members of a particular class in more developed class societies testifies to this political-economic tendency.

13. This was the case in Nigeria during the greater part of civilian politics from 1960 to 1966 when preoccupation with ethnic claims among the top political elites tended to create forces of instability. The more violent episodes among ethnic groups related to conflicting economic interests occurred among the Hausa and the Ibo in Northern Nigeria in 1966 and in Burundi among the Hutu and Tutsi in 1972.

14. In the politics of the first republic, most of the political elites in Nigeria fitted under the latter category. It should be noted that economic interests of leaders may not always be explicitly stated in their pronouncements or policies. These interests may sometimes be camouflaged in policies or sentiments that appear national in outlook and appeal.

15. This is more vividly seen in countries where politics is organized around identifiable ideological lines as in Kenya and Tanzania, for example.

16. The alternative in some more larger and more complex countries like Nigeria has been to diffuse the power of rival sub-national units by dispersing it among smaller state units which tend to compete among themselves rather than the centre.

17. This is true in a capitalist-oriented society, like Kenya, as it is in a society dominated by socialist values, like Tanzania. Even in countries under dictatorships, such as Amin's Uganda, or Zaire and Malawi, there are classes of people who benefit materially from the regime and for whose interests the regime attempts to consolidate and perpetuate itself in power. It should be noted further that in economies dominated by metropolitan capital, among the classes and interests served by the regime include the international capitalist classes and the whole range of interests of metropolitan powers. It is in this sense that we speak of a regime as constituted by national elites who are members of a *comprador* class serving the interests of foreign capital in the domestic

economy. And it is this class which operates as a purveyor of imperialist exploitation and unwittingly acts as an important agent of the underdevelopment of its own country whose interests it purports to defend.
18. In 1965 when the United Republic of Tanzania decided to recognize the People's Democratic Republic of East Germany, the government of the Federal Republic of West Germany reacted angrily by withholding its aid offer to Tanzania, earmarked for certain projects in the country's Second Five Year Development Plan of 1964-69. The withdrawal of this aid meant that the National Plan could not be fully implemented. See Julius K. Nyerere, 'The Costs of Non-Alignment', *Africa Report*, October 1966. From this experience, Tanzania was forced to shift her foreign policy of non-alignment a little in favour of the socialist countries such as China, where Tanzania now gets the bulk of its foreign aid, such as was used in the building of the Tanzam Railway.
19. These are discussed in greater detail by Professor Claude Ake. See his 'Explanatory Notes on the Political Economy of Africa', *Journal of Modern African Studies*, Vol. 14, 1976, pp. 1-23.
20. When President A. Milton Obote of Uganda was faced with a situation of potential instability in 1966 arising out of protracted struggle for power among elites within his own government, he had to look back to colonial history to find ways and means of containing the situation. Accordingly, his Attorney-General advised him to use the provisions of a Deportation Law enacted by the colonial government some two decades before the independence of the country. However, legal technicalities in the application of the law to the situation at hand made it possible for the courts to overrule the government and to free the deportees. The government had to use different manoeuvres to keep the trouble-makers in custody. In order to avoid a similar situation in future, whereby courts could rule the actions of government as unlawful, parliament hurriedly passed a Detention Law which limited the power of the courts in similar cases.

Part Three
Theory and Methodology

13. Non-Ethnocentric Flaws in Competing Non-Marxist Paradigms of Development

Eskor Toyo

'Truth emerges more readily from error than from confusion'. Francis Bacon

This paper examines the chaotic world of competing paradigms in non-Marxist social science with regard to development theory. It tries to trace this situation to basic failings in metropolitan social science quite independent of ethnocentrism.

It is now generally agreed that the social science imported into Third World countries from centres of learning dominated by non-Marxist scholarship was to a greater or lesser extent ethnocentric. This ethnocentrism, however, was not always conscious. Where it was not, it was associated with certain other defects within metropolitan social science itself. We thus contest the presumption that the methodology and conceptual foundations of metropolitan social science are basically beyond reproach save in respect to its myopia in dealing with underdeveloped countries — the malicious eye, the evil intent or the absent-mindedness which it employs for Third World problems of development.

If we are right, then it follows that it is not sufficient to invent new concepts such as 'underdevelopment', 'dependence', 'peripheral capitalism', 'neo-colonialism', 'client status', 'non-capitalist development', 'modernization', 'human capital', etc. Some of these terms have not been adequately defined or defined at all, some of them are employed unsystematically, merely added to an eclectic 'tool kit' that may well be already overburdened, judging from the current disillusion with theory.

Particular criticisms of this or that concept in the received metropolitan kit have often been made as part of the criticism of some aspect of development theory and as a step to substitute one's own theory. Alternative errors, however, can be developed this way.[1] What is needed is a systematic criticism of the foundations of metropolitan social science and the systematic exposition and development of an alternative foundation for the theory of development or underdevelopment.

Our method of attack will be as follows: First, since there is little space or time or even need for polemics, this is kept to the barest minimum. We shall go directly into stating what we think wrong with non-Marxist foundations. Secondly, there will be an emphasis on economic development since it is now generally accepted that the economic has a certain primacy over other spheres in the development of society. Given my area of specialization in university teaching, this inclination towards economic development is inevitable.

'Bombard the Headquarters', Attack Presuppositions

Let us borrow a phrase from the 'Great Proletarian Cultural Revolution' in China. We need to substantiate our allegation that it is the central paradigms of non-Marxist development theory themselves that stand in need of change and to indicate the necessary manner of renovation. If a scientific approach is subjective in its base, for instance, it will naturally tend to become ethnocentric. A static approach may also fall into this trap. The ethnocentric implications of the Ricardian theory of comparative advantage in international trade is thus symptomatic of the static and ahistorical character of that theory itself.

The functionalist anthropology begun by Malinowski during the First World War served the needs of imperialism. It did so by abandoning the evolutionary perspective initiated by Darwin and Morgan and taken over by Marx and instead embarking on a description of the world as if history did not exist. In recoiling from the 'naive' evolutionism of men like Tylor, it threw away the baby with the bath water.

Even this shift from an evolutionary paradigm to a static-functionalist one began not from anthropology but from economics, after John Stuart Mill (1806-73). As from 1870-71 the economists abandoned a developmental and dynamic paradigm in favour of a static apologetics for capitalism in opposition to the European working-class movement.[2] This was long before Malinowski and others, from 1915, made a similar shift in order to provide the sort of knowledge of conquered pre-capitalist societies needed by colonial administrators. Once development was forgotten, one had to assume that any 'non-tribal' feature found in 'tribal' society must have migrated from a 'non-tribal' source.

Sociology was modelled on the functionalist paradigm for the study of the industrial society of Western Europe and shaped its concepts for not only a static but a microscopic study of that society. Economics became a static study of individual minimax behaviour, which was pronounced 'rational', as it affected or was affected by the functioning of the commodity and factor markets. When anthropologists applied what this economics claimed to know to what were once called 'backward' but are now called 'underdeveloped' countries, nothing *could* result but ethnocentrism and confusion. The ethnocentrism thus arose from the market fixation of an economic science designed for the surface market phenomena of a capitalist culture. The confusion arose from the inability to decide whether *homo economicus*, as defined in capitalist culture, is a reality at all in a non-capitalist culture, or to what extent. The matter has not been settled to this day.[3]

As for political scientists, they concentrated on studying the functioning of political institutions of the 'civilized' West and presumed that any country that became 'civilized' enough to join the international community would join the club having those institutions. Departure from the standards of this club was a sign of relative immaturity or inherent lack of political ability.

Such was the orientation with which metropolitan social science forged its concepts and methods. And it was those concepts and methods with which it suddenly had to confront the phenomenon of development or underdevelopment in the 1960s. In this situation it was the absence of ethnocentrism that would have been surprising.[4]

As soon as we start looking seriously at the fundamental assumptions of metropolitan social science as a means of cognition, we are bound to treat seriously the scientific endeavours of its principal critics, namely, Karl Marx and Frederick Engels. A valid all-round criticism of metropolitan social science already exists in the work of Marxists; the foundation for an authentic social science was laid by Marx. By an 'authentic social science', we mean one based on an approach that is objective, dynamic, historical, systems-oriented, can relate the macroscopic to the microscopic and the objective to the subjective, can take account of social contradictions and conflicts, can come to terms with the complexity of relations or forms that characterize society, and do all this with a theoretical approach that is self-consistent. No approach to the phenomenon of development or underdevelopment, for instance, can be adequate unless its foundation has all these properties inherent in it.

Unfortunately, what Marx stood for has overwhelmingly been distorted in the West, whether deliberately or otherwise. The situation is not improved by the sort of 'Marxology' promoted by some of Marx's admirers who behave as if Marxism consisted in canonizing everything Marx ever said rather than in using his immensely powerful scientific method or paradigm for penetrating all forms of actual reality.

The methodological underpinning of non-Marxist social science is positivism. The non-Marxist social scientists have been greatly influenced by Karl Popper's rejection of the search for essential laws behing appearances and symptoms, regarding all this as 'metaphysics'.[5] Positivism therefore tends to be one-sided, particularist, anti-theoretical and eclectic.[6] The chaos in non-Marxist social science can be traced to the dominance of positivism. But does science in fact develop the way Popper claims it does and is Marxist methodology what he claims it is? To this question we must turn briefly.

Going Astray with Positivism

The research of Kuhn has made the term 'paradigm' popular. According to Kuhn, a paradigm is 'the source of the methods, problem field and standards of solution accepted by any mature scientific community at any given time'.[7] Let us say at once that by 'problem field' is meant, to begin with, answers to such basic questions as the following: 1) Is social science to be a study of *social* phenomena, namely, phenomena resulting from interaction and thus associated with groups and collectivities of people, or is it to be a study of the behaviour of 'indivuals in society' where 'society' is conceived as a vague 'environment' or even the abstract creation of the analyst 'for convenience'? 2) Are we to understand society to be a *system* or are we to understand it to be simply a *set* of interacting individuals and small groups? 3) Is a 'social situation' a historical product, and in what way? 4) Is society a changing thing, and how does it change? 5) How are we to define a society to begin with?

Kuhn insisted that no science has gained full maturity if it is still plagued with competing paradigms. If we divide the population of social scientists into Marxists and non-Marxists, thus identifying fundamental scientific traditions rather than theoretical or methodological 'schools', we find the non-Marxist tradition always split into rival 'schools'. On the other hand, no matter what their theoretical and methodological quarrels on specific questions — quarrels which do exist but which are not absent from other mature sciences either — the Marxists are agreed on their paradigm. It follows that the non-Marxist tradition is still at a pre-scientific stage of development, a statement which, by the way, may be unintelligible to a static and particularist epistemology which cannot accept the notion of stages.

There has been something of a conspiracy of silence on an important aspect of Kuhn's discovery: the fact that science *develops* dialectically through normal growth, accumulating contradictions and global changes of gear or paraidgm revolutions the way Marx and Marxists have long held that science, and indeed all reality, develops. According to Kuhn, science does not simply grow by routine formulation and falsification by tests of particular and isolated hypotheses, as Karl Popper thinks it does. Says Kuhn: 'No process yet discovered by the historical study of scientific development at all resembles the methodological stereotype of falsification by direct comparison with nature.'[8] Yet for those non-Marxist social scientists who believe social science ought to be and can be objective, it is Popper's particularist positivist misunderstanding of the Marxist method as 'metaphysics' that has held sway. Thus before Keynes revived 'macroeconomics' in 1936, Marx's macroscopic approach was dismissed as metaphysics. 'Classes' and 'nations', it was held, were mere concepts and corresponded to no empirical data. Such views among people who regard only individual acts as 'facts' and ignore social relations or the social meanings and implications of individual acts are, as we shall see, still current.

It is only recently that European sociology has begun to rediscover the macro-sociology abandoned as 'metaphysics'. American sociology is still steeped in Popperian particularist small-group research with at most so-called 'middle-range' theories. Political science is only now rediscovering the 'metaphysics' of macropolitical systems as long understood by Marxists. It seems that the 'non-metaphysics' of empirical research on particular institutions, political parties and electoral arrangements seen in isolation from the total political order and — what should be even more deeply 'non-metaphysical' — from the total social order no longer suffices. If Popper is right, then *systems analysis*, the new vogue derived from cybernetics and functionalism and meant to correct positivism, on the one hand, and replace Marxism, on the other, is 'metaphysics' par excellence. It does not even have the merit of the Marxist way of passing from formal abstraction to concrete historical reality.

At any rate, as Maurice Cornforth argues against the Popperian presumptions, it is not true that such very general laws and principles as the laws of thermodynamics and the thesis of the materialist conception of history cannot be empirically tested or falsified. These laws forbid certain things from normally happening and thus these laws would be falsified as soon as what they forbid happens.[9] In the case of the materialist conception of history, what it forbids is that, for instance, ideas about kings or banks should be found in the primitive communal world where the level of production did not permit the social processes leading to the rise of monarchical or banking institutions.

Popper claimed to have delivered a 'devastating' attack on the Marxist tradition in social science. In retrospect, it turns out that what he did was to confirm in one part of his work the devastating attack already launched by Marx and Engels on subjective approaches in social science. At the same time, however, he did non-Marxist social research a disservice by distorting Marx's historical and dialectical methods and finding spurious arguments to sustain an ahistorical, static and eclectic positivism. This devastation has taken a heavy toll. Its results, as things stand, ought to be brought to focus. We have a bedlam of competing paradigms, a situation which permits all sorts of *ad hoc* postulates as well as the persistence, even resurgence, of the psychologism which Popper himself had helped to dethrone from its presumed primacy in the sphere of social investigation.

The rest of this paper will be concerned with this reign of anarchy. First, let us consider the rival answers to certain basic questions on how society itself, that which develops, is to be looked at.

Subjective or Objective?

Should our approach be subjective — putting consciousness or psychology forward — or objective — putting groups, relations and processes forward? It may seem that this matter has been settled in favour of objectivity, but that is not the case, as we shall soon see. At any rate what do we mean when we say 'objective' in the case of society? As far as Marxists are concerned, 'objective' means proceeding historically starting from the given state of production activity.

Is social science a study of individual behaviour or is it a study of the results of the interaction of individuals? The matter is not settled among non-Marxists. Some claim that groups are not real because only individuals have a physical presence and actually behave. 'Group action' is only 'a methodological or semantic convenience' and only individual action is 'an empirically demonstrable reality'.[10] Others hold that the group is just as real as the person, 'that both are abstract, analytical units, not concrete entities, and that the group is understandable and explicable solely in terms of distinctly social processes and factors, not by reference to individual psychology.'[11]

As far as Marxists are concerned, there is agreement on this matter. Reality or concreteness is defined at different removes. As far as society or social science is concerned, it does not make sense to say that the individual is real and concrete but not, say, the family, the factory or the trade union. For Marxists, the 'individual', in the social rather than the biological sense, is a social animal by definition and a product of social history. We cannot understand the social individual in isolation from the history of his or her society and his or her place in it.

It is now generally admitted that society is a system, but how are we to conceive of this system? Non-Marxists do not have one general approach. The empricists would see society as a collection of small groups, regarding anything larger as too vacuous for 'positive' science. The macrostructuralists see a total culture as a system of subsystems. But how do we define concretely the specific system of which we have subsystems and what kind of connections exists among the subsystems? For instance, functionalists adopt a bio-functional approach and see society as an organic system in which groups and collectivities perform certain functions. But since one function, for instance, conflict resolution, is performed differently in different systems, what is it that decides this difference? In short, if fishes and monkeys are vertebrates, how do we decide that 'these are fishes and those are monkeys'?

Again Marxists have a definite approach to the definition of specific social systems for disciplined comparison, for what is true of all vertebrates will be true of fishes and monkeys, but not all that is true of fishes will be true of monkeys.

There is now a general consensus that society is a changing reality. But what, for instance, is the difference between variation and growth? Few non-Marxists even think this question worth asking. And what is the difference between 'growth' and 'development'? There are many answers even among economists, as we shall see. The inability to make this distinction leads to many development illusions that end up in frustration.

As for Marxists, they are agreed that variation is different from growth, growth different from development, development different from cyclical motion, and that again different from formation, disintegration, etc. In short, they are aware *ab initio* of different forms of motion. They distinguish between general forms of motion or general processes as illustrated above and the specific forms of motions of specific social systems which they see as historically defined and which they connect with the peculiar contradictions of these systems. In short, the Marxists are the only group of social scientists who are definite, agreed, and disciplined concerning the categories and handling of 'change'.

There is no dispute today about the fact that society itself and social change are very complex. But how do we approach this complexity so as to avoid myopic views, subjectivity, blind alleys and contradictions? There is no need to detail the chaos of competing non-Marxist schools.

In economics alone, there are at least four non-Marxian schools: the neo-classical synthesists represented by Paul Samuelson,[12] the Left Keynesians represented by Joan Robinson,[13] the neo-Ricardians represented by Pierro Sraffa[14] and the neo-institutionalists represented by Gunnar Myrdal.[15]

As for the Marxists, that society and social change are very complex is the reason why they think that a good training in dialectics is indispensable to consistent and cumulative theoretical progress in its study.[16] The result of a simplistic positivistic approach to the study of social change can be quite ludicrous. Zuvekas claims, for instance, that the development of the concept of 'human capital' has been immensely useful in clearing up 'some of our misconceptions about the development process'.[17] He adds: 'We now recognize, for example, that there is more to growth (not to speak of development) than capital formation. Skilled workers are needed to operate and repair machinery and equipment, ...'[18] Yet all this is what the development economists could have learnt from Marx or even from Adam Smith. Truly, thousands of excellent brains are being employed simply to rediscover what Marxists have regarded as commonplaces for more than a century.[19]

It is even common ground among social scientists today that history is relevant to their various preoccupations. But among non-Marxist social scientists there is no agreement on how to take account of history. Do historical tendencies exist in the sense of regularities characterizing definite epochs and constituting laws within those epochs? Scholars such as Weber, Schumpeter, Rostow, Kuznets and Myrdal would answer 'yes', although Kuznets, for instance, differs from Rostow on how to conceptualize stages of development.[20] Judging from Schumpeter's work he is also at variance with Rostow.[21]

On the other hand, there are functionalists, empiricists and voluntarists to whom the 'relevance of history' means that one can cite isolated events or data from the past to illustrate whatever theory one is building or to justify whatever refutation one is interested in constructing. It is this anecdotal use of 'history' that tends to prevail. The consequence is that isolated past events or data are extracted out of historical context and used to support arguments that are untenable.

A good example of this is the way conclusions are drawn as to the better performance, for instance, of a capitalist economy as compared with a socialist economy by using housing data from the United States and the Soviet Union in 1975.[22] From a valid historical point of view, however, such data in the Soviet Union today should be compared with data from the United States around 1890 when the United States was at a stage of industrial development comparable to that of the Soviet Union today. Alternatively, the comparison should be between the Asian republics of the Soviet

Union and those countries of Asia, Africa and Latin America that shared a common stage of development with these republics in 1917. Their conditions in 1917 and, say, 1975 should be compared. As V.I. Lenin, the dialectician, historical materialist and statistician, observed, before we compare we should ask whether the objects are at all comparable. The Marxists, of course, have a united basic view about how history should come into social analysis. What they think of the matter will be touched upon as the need arises in this paper.

These various schools bring to their theories some training in the following logical disciplines: formal logic, mathematics and statistics. In all the social sciences today, 'method' tends to mean among non-Marxists only these formal methods — if one is trained in them — plus empirical fact-gathering methods such as interviewing.

Of course, non-Marxist social science today is not what it was before 1960. In the last twenty years there has been considerable advance. When one examines the directions of advance, however, one cannot fail to observe that the movements are towards positions long held by Marxists to be the authentic ones. The objective as distinct from the psychological approach to theorizing, the systems approach, the interactional focus, the return to a global or macroscopic view, the discovery that society is changing, the discovery of growth and of development, as well as specific 'new' concerns in specific sciences such as the sociological discovery of 'conflict' and 'alienation'; of such things as the man-hour numeraire, inventory cycles, the use of the industrial reserve army as a stabilizing device (Phillips curve phenomenon), the Marx-Ricardian problem of what determines the rate of profit (on which capitalist motion depends), tableau or sectoral analysis, duality, etc. in economics; of such things as political systems as distinct from constitutions and states by political scientists — all this lies in a direction towards Marx.

The progress, however, has been partial, halting, impetuous. There is a residue of fear and suspicion arising not from genuine scientific doubts but from ideology. There is no study, for instance, of capitalist or socialist development. Macroeconomics still means a more or less modified version of the economics of capitalist cycles and their regulation as propounded by Keynes. Imperialism is evaded as if it did not exist. In metropolitan economics, such terms as capitalism, imperialism or neo-colonialism are not regular theoretical categories.

The contradictions brought up in this section have remained in spite of the undoubted progress which we have acknowledged. Given this welter of basic conceptual and methodological contradictions, such a miracle as a single acceptable paradigm for the theory of development or underdevelopment simply cannot happen. Such suggestions as exist, for instance, suffer from the unwritten injunction to avoid giving support to Marxists as much as possible and not to come to grips with the realities one would rather wish away, such as imperialism.

But bourgeois social science wished away industrial cycles for a hundred years, from the rise of what Marx called 'vulgar economics' in the 1830s to the Great Depression in the 1930s. If it wishes away certain aspects of underdevelopment, preferring devious ways of dealing with the phenomenon itself, it is not simply ethnocentrism but capitalist prejudice that is at work We shall now turn to the paradigms proposed by development theorists.

Movement in Keynesiana

When non-Marxist social science turned from static functionalism to take notice of change, it passed through post-Keynesian, Rostovian and systemic stages. Then it began to retreat into a new psychologism. This and the next four sections will be concerned with this evolution. First the Keynesian stage.

The first step in dynamizing non-Marxist social science was taken by economists. After the Second World War, what was seen in capitalist ruling circles as the 'communist challenge' urged policy-makers in capitalist states to promote the growth of their economics. It was not long before models of economic growth began to proliferate.[23] These were so-called 'post-Keynesian' growth models. The question asked by these models was how the rate of investment could be so chosen that there would be a positive per capita growth rate, preferably enough to prevent the 'communist' states of Eastern Europe from catching up, and at the same time maintain the economy on an even keel — free from industrial fluctuations. The growth models that were offered, given their Keynesian parentage, looked at capital or investment as the only growth factor.

When the Keynesian paradigm was applied to underdeveloped countries between 1948 when India gained her independence and 1965, the emphasis was on capital.[24] There were only two capital sources for these countries: foreign capital imports and export earnings. Within the underdeveloped countries, emphasis was on the multiplier effects that capital imports and export earnings would have.

Given these earnings, an import-substitution strategy was recommended for an underdeveloped country that wanted to industrialize, although industrialization was not seen as necessary to growth. Thus even in 1975, Meier still feels bound to warn that 'economic development is not to be simply equated with industrialization'.[25] The only new thing here is the word 'simply' which accused policy-makers in underdeveloped countries of a naivety that hardly anyone is guilty of.

Partly because of the Keynesian origin of this approach and partly from a justifiable fear of inflationary spending and consequent balance-of-payments problems which would result in uneven investment, there was much concern with equilibrium growth. We are only concerned here with the paradigmatic character of these prescriptions. A number of things should be noted.

First, one was concerned with growth; development was not yet a category. Secondly, the source of growth was to be external. Growth was to depend primarily on foreign capital imports. The exports of the developing country were only a way of maintaining the external inflow of investment by ensuring repayment capacity and enhanced internal purchasing power for products of direct investment of foreign capital. Thirdly, there was only one growth-promoting factor, namely, capital. Fourthly, the growth was to be equilibrium growth.

What all this means is that the mechanical and ahistorical character of Keynesian dynamics and the capitalist prejudice about all history depending on the owner of capital was transferred to underdeveloped countries.

It was not long before the emperor was seen to be naked. We cannot describe this here. Suffice it to say that no dynamic theory of society that is ahistorical can cope with either the practical task of dynamics or with the 'communist challenge' in theory. Therefore, the American Central Intelligence Agency set W.W. Rostow, a man who showed much concern for the 'communist challenge' to the 'Western world' in developing countries,[26] to write a 'non-communist manifesto'.[27] Dynamics as seen by non-Marxists involves equilibrium, circular or cumulative motions.[28] Keynes' focus was the first and second. Rostow turned to the third. It should be noted carefully that *cumulative* and *historical* movements or foci are not the same. Rostow's was cumulative — not really historical, as we shall soon see.

In the Rostovian Stagecoach

Rostow rejected what he thought were Marx's stages of modern development: feudalism, capitalism, socialism and communism. He claimed that Marx's 'stages' were an illegitimate attempt to generalize from the case of Western Europe to all societies. Against Marx, he posited his own five stages of development which he claimed to be of more universal application. 'The sweep of modern history,' he claimed, 'could be conceptualized under five stages: traditional society, preconditions for take-off, take-off, drive to maturity, the age of high mass consumption.'[29] It is not insignificant that the book where Rostow first proposed his 'stages' was sub-titled a 'non-communist manifesto'. The work fulfills its ideological assignment of concealing from the oppressed the source of their suffering and the path to their self-liberation. In this respect Rostow is like the subjective marginalism in economic theory directed against Ricardo and Marx from about 1871.

Rostow's stage theory has been subjected to a spate of criticisms by many economists along a number of lines.[30] It is not our business to repeat these criticisms. Since, however, his work purports to correct Marx, a number of observations must be made in this regard.

First, Rostow did not understand Marx, for Marx's work does not constitute a 'stage theory' in Rostow's sense. As we shall see, it is rather a theory that says that social systems do not occur haphazardly but are related to developments in the productive forces and have a certain organizational unity and character arising from the form of division of labour.

According to Simon Kuznets, 'stage theory is most closely associated with unidirectional rather than cyclic view of history'.[31] If so, then Marx's theory is, again, not a stage theory, since it is not 'unidirectional'.[32] In order to attain 'an understanding of the historical evolution which produced modern social forms', it was not necessary for Marx to hold that there are 'eternal' and 'inevitable' features of human social organization[33] imposing from the beginning a predestined line of advance for all peoples or even for any people.

It should also be remarked that it is not true that if a stage theory is not cyclical, it must be unidirectional in the sense that every situation leaves open one and only one social solution. Present-day underdeveloped countries, for instance, can attempt a capitalist development or a socialist one and can do each in a limited number of ways. This matter is more fully discussed later.

Secondly, Rostow's concepts, as has often been remarked, are a 'mere impressionistic interpretation of a number of historical experiences rather than a rigorous scientific analysis',[34] and is itself based on the history of capitalist countries. At least Marx did indicate a principle for the demarcation of stages of development, namely, that each state is inaugurated by technological revolution which compels and necessitates a social transformation constituting the economy into a new 'mode of production' characterized by new 'relations of production' which condition the character of political and legal institutions and ideology. There is no such disciplined approach in Rostow.

Thirdly, what Rostow does really is to divide the rise of modern industrial society into 'growth stages' in which the character of the relations of production is hidden. It does not matter for Rostow whether the country at the stage of 'pre-condition for take-off' is a colonial India, a semi-colonial Egypt, a neo-colonial Nigeria or a liberated and socialist-oriented Cuba or Angola. Of course, to bourgeois economists the term 'economic' excludes socio-economic relations among people: only sectoral, technological and superficial market relations are considered. However, as Georgescu-Roegen has urged 'what characterizes an economic system is its institution not the technology it uses'.[35] Although the level of technology is an important condition making one economic system different from another, it does not decide the specificity of the economic system. Marx himself stated long ago, for instance: 'Machinery is no more an economic category than the ox which draws the plough. The application of machinery in the present day is one of the relations of our present economic system, but the way in which machinery is utilized is totally distinct from the machinery itself.'[36]

Such terms as 'traditional society', 'take-off', 'drive to maturity' and 'age of mass consumption' actually describe nothing. Anyone can build empty stages,[37] indeed Rostow did pretend to the same kind of generality as the neo-classical market-oriented empty boxes, the Walrasian general equilibrium system and Parsonian 'social system', but such stages cannot provide a paradigm guide to any theory that wishes to relate itself to reality. To borrow from Georgescu-Roegen once more, 'for an economic theory to be operational at all, that is, to be capable of serving as a guide for policy, it must concern itself with a specific type of economy, not with several types at the same time'.[38]

Fourthly, it is not correct to interpret Marx's 'stages' of primitive communism, Asiatic society and slavery, feudalism, and capitalism as more than a rough identification of examples of global progress in social formation. The very language used to list these stages even in the Preface to Marx's *Critique of Political Economy* shows this. Says the Preface: 'In broad outlines, Asiatic, ancient, feudal and modern bourgeois modes of production can be designated as progressive epochs in the economic foundation of society.'[39] Marx and Engels warned that this attempt at a rough sketch of the way humanity has altered applies especially to Western Europe. It did not necessarily apply to other parts of the world nor was it intended to mean that each people were predestined to pass through each of these phases.

Fifthly, what Rostow calls 'traditional society' is for Marxists several social systems that had their own distinctive characters and marked very important stages of human development.[40] Capitalism also is not one simple stage.

Lastly, let us come to Marx's main purpose. It was not to present an exact list of obligatory stages for all people but to contend that capitalism was only a specific and transient and not an eternal form of modern society even if modern society could only have started with it.[41] It is noteworthy that he predicted a deep crisis for capitalism and the emergence of non-capitalist forms which actually began after World War I.[42] The way in which he came to these predictions, or predicted the rise of a monopolistic phase in capitalism as a natural consequence of capitalist competition, is an interesting commentary on the potency of his and Engels' method for the study of social development. Anyone can divide development into any number of stages without any method. Science is interested only in theories that have a method behind them.

Rostow had proposed that economies grew through leading sectors. One of the effects of this was the popularity of the agricultural export sector as the 'leading sector' in underdeveloped countries. But economists in underdeveloped countries were soon reminded that Japan had developed not by agricultural exports but through silk exports. The changed situations in the world brought about by capitalist colonialism were ignored by Rostow's ahistorical procedure. If the theory of comparative advantage was battered by the infant industry argument, the theory of 'leading sector' could show how concentration on agricultural exports was the best development policy.

It is true, as Okwuosa observes, that Rostow holds that industrialization and modern economic growth can be viewed as depending on the end of the systematic and progressive application of modern science and technology. This insight he combines with his leading sector approach. Okwuosa, in our view, is right to regret that this emphasis on the role of technology — rather than 'capital' — as 'the ultimate determinant of economic growth' has been lost sight of 'in the wake of other criticisms of Rostow'.[43]

Yet we did not need Rostow to know the great causal importance of technology. Marx,, institutionalists such as Veblen and some economists of the 'historical school' such as Schumpeter had long emphasized the role of technology. Moreover, there are ways and ways of handling the role of technology. 'Technology' may be conceived wrongly as machines rather than correctly as human labour ability historically formed. It may then be conceived positivistically as a 'factor' whose use is independent of the social system.

Positivism leads to growth or development factor theory: it is either capital or technology or leading sector, or it may be the psychological factor that is emphasized. Isolating factors for analysis is not wrong, but the factors isolated must then be placed in a concrete historical and dialectical analysis. Abstraction without such a subsequent integration is a faulty method.

Rostow wrote his book on growth in 1960. As the decade 1960-70 wore on, the success of the socialist countries and the failures of the schemes prescribed for capitalist-oriented Third World countries, the experience that growth economists gained from actually counselling Third World countries and events in the Third World such as coups d'etat that aimed at changes in the government, in land tenure, etc. – all this led to a growing awareness that growth theory had ignored so-called institutional elements in society. From a growth focus, the non-Marxist paradigm moved to a development focus. Development theory had to develop a new way of seeing society. The result was 'systems theory'.

Systems That Cannot Systematize

Systems theory, however, is a throw back to functionalism. Like functionalism, systems theory has three problems. First, it is concerned with the adjustment and equilibrium of a functioning status quo. It is not suitable for the study of contradictions and the discontinuities that result from their resolution or transcendence.

Secondly, systems theory, as it derives, for instance, from Parsonian sociology, is equipped with the concept of subsystems. The subsystems are separate parts so that what emerges is not a qualitative totality but a symbiosis of subsystems. Systems theory, therefore, has no way of integrating the economic, the political, etc. aspects. This is why it finds the so-called milti-dimensional approach a problem. The economists, as Bernstein points out, hold 'non-economic' factors constant, so that their models assume the social and institutional conditions in the experience of the metropolitan country reflected in the model. The sociologists and political scientists in their paradigmatic models assume Western society as developed or modern 'while tending to ignore the problematic economic dimension of Third World "modernization"'.[44]

With this approach, a host of economists, such as B.F. Hoselitz, P.T. Bauer, Imra Adelamn, E.T. Morris, C. Zuvekas, and S.P. Schatz proceed by way of listing institutional factors that have to be changed in order to achieve economic development.[45] Not being dialecticians, these economists cannot see that it is not a question of first changing these factors. The change is part and parcel of the process of development which is itself interactional.

Thirdly, systems analysis is ahistorical. Zuvekas notes, for instance, that a main reason for the declining interest in development theory is 'the difficulty of finding and incorporating into our theories and models, institutional and non-economic phenomena common to more than 100 countries'.[45] The complaint about heterogeneity is always a reflection of the importance of the theoretical approach. There is no reason why one should insist on finding the political systems of 100 countries in common. Defining structures historically helps us to separate what is general from what is not — to build models that start from the abstract and move to the concrete.

Poor theory always has three results: disillusionment with theory, resort to naive and eclectic empirical work, and subjectivism.[46] All this has started to happen with development theory. A psychological 'model of man' approach has emerged. To this we now turn.

Back to Psychologism

Emerging around 1970, the new 'model of man' approach is based on some of the theories of modern psychology. This approach is elaborately presented and urged upon social scientists by John H. Kunkel. According to Kunkel, we have to distinguish 1) 'conceptions of man' or 'views of human nature'; 2) 'models of man' — a selective set of propositions concerning aspects of individuals that are necessary for subsequent theoretical and practical issues; and 3) 'personality' — a narrower concept than a 'model of man'.[47] One of the best known of the models of man, says Kunkel, is that of Malthus. His concern with population led Malthus to postulate that humans must eat and engage in sexual relations, and that they will not voluntarily limit their numbers. These three propositions, though not a complete description of humanity, served as the basis for the construction of Malthus' theory.[48] Kunkel then sets out to emulate Malthus.

There are two alternative psychological approaches to the construction of models of man, we are told. Some psychologists make postulates about the individual's internal state — motives, needs and personality — which play a major role in determining actions. This can be recognized as the psychoanalytic approach.[49]

On the other hand, some psychologists 'attempt to explain behaviour by assuming that human beings behave in certain ways because they have learned particular actions in a specific environment'.[50] Here, as Kunkel notes, 'emphasis is shifted from man's internal state to the values and norms of the sub-culture and society to which he belongs'.[51] This is the 'learning' or 'behavioural' model.

We are concerned with the motivation of the individual because, according to Kunkel, 'groups as such do not behave, and when the consequences of action, such as building a nation, are ascribed to groups, this ascription is a semantic convenience'.[52] He contends that 'most social phenomena become apparent only through the actions of men,' and that 'it is the individual and his behaviour which constitute the basic elements of the sociological subject matter'.[53] This provides a setting for a psycho-individualistic approach. Going over to development, Kunkel, quoting from Claude Levi-Strauss, asserts that the 'great dramas of societal transition occur through individuals' involvement in solving their personal problems and living their private lives'.[54]

The point of view of the 'model of man' approach, we think, is not simply that humans have certain needs and drives, such as the once-celebrated 'instincts', and that these determine what they do in society. This would be a 'human nature' approach. The answer to the 'human nature' approach is that given by the Lenskis and others. It is now clear that humans have certain general inborn abilities, drives and needs, but that the way these abilities are used or drives and needs satisfied can be varied by human beings'.[55] Consequently, these 'basic behavioural tendencies rooted in mankind's genetic heritage' can have different effects in society.[56]

The contention of the 'model of man' school is different. It is that human action is influenced by the personality that results from both the genetic inheritance *and* the process of socialization. The point of interest is how this personality is influenced by either.

The psychoanalytical approach comes to a conservative conclusion. 'Since the social context which is introduced into the [individual personality] system is usually that of childhood ... adult personality characteristics and the actions arising from them are often quite independent of the adult's social environment.'[57] Severe criticisms have been launched against this approach which its adherents have not been able to meet satisfactorily.[58] Meanwhile, reports Kunkel, researchers have turned increasingly to the behavioural approach and their predictions have so far been confirmed by observations. The conclusion reached by this approach is that

> man's internal state — consisting mainly of his learning history, culturally determined deprivations, and learned expectations of particular consequences for specific activities — is little more than an intervening variable. The major implication for development analysis, and especially for the formation of action programmes, is that *behaviour can be changed at any time*. By judiciously altering those aspects of the social environment which constitute rewarding or punishing consequences for specific activities, it is possible to alter these behavioural patterns and to initiate and accelerate social change.[59]

If conservatives can be convinced by this conclusion, all well and good, but Marx and the Marxists have urged again and again that 'the individual' differs from age to age, from culture to culture and from one subculture to another in the same culture. In fact, they have urged that the very concept of 'the individual' is a product of history.

We can agree with the conclusions of the 'model of man' approach without having to adopt psychologism of any kind as the foundation for social development analysis. After all, as Kunkel himself recognized 'much of what man is ... depends on the society of which he is an inextricable part'.[60] It is true, as he further urges, that 'one must understand the social system even as one must understand man to understand the social system'.[61] But the correct interpretation of 'man' in a statement of this kind is not an individual isolated from society. Humans are social animals by definition. It is true that biologically they are a certain primate, but, as the Lenskis, Marx and others argue, *the qualities that are most distinctively human emerge only as a result of our association with others.*[62] However much, moreover, knowledge of human biological nature may help the understanding of social nature, the tasks of social analysis begins where biological analysis ends. Social psychology is, of course, part of social science, but knowledge and use of social psychology does not warrant the presumption that we may start development analysis from psychological postulates. Still less does it warrant doing *social* analysis by basing ourselves on an *individualistic* paradigm, for that is an epistemological contradiction.

The final verdict on all psychologism is recorded by Kunkel himself: 'Since every psychological "school" has a tendency to produce its own model of man, much of the diversity of development analysis can be explained in terms of the different models which are employed.'[63] This view is confirmed by Lesourne.[64] And there are different psychological schools and models of man because of the positivism reigning in psychology, the tendency to reduce social to individual psychology, and the absence of any disciplined way of handling the relationship between being and consciousness in society.

Psycho-individualism as a paradigm basis for social science suffers from a very profound form of reductionism. This tendency has already had effects on existing development or underdevelopment theory. To this we turn.

As Modernists See It

The Rostovian 'leading sector' approach leads to seeing a colonial, or neo-colonial or non-industrial socialist-oriented economy simply as a dual economy consisting of a traditional sector and a modern sector. Our aim here is not to criticize all the ethnocentrism which goes into the conceptualization of the relationship between these two 'sectors' or their forms of integration with the world economy.

The point we wish to make here is that the problem of development is then seen simply as one of 'modernizing', that is Europeanizing or Americanizing the 'traditional' sector. This leads to 1) listing obstacles to the modernizing of the traditional sector; 2) blaming the human element in the traditional sector; and 3) presuming that the obstacles first have to be removed and the human element modified before development can take place.

Differences in economic development are no longer explained on racial grounds, but by reference to peasant conservatism, attachment to tribal customs such as the extended family and bride-price, and lack of an 'entrepreneurial' outlook, all of which are represented as obstacles to development. The current scapegoat is lack of entrepreneurship — as if entrepreneurship were not a phenomenon that itself develops out of the historical context. Thus it is held by some in Nigeria that the indigenous African businessman would become more effective socially, and hence in practice, if he would first become integrated into the 'social world' of the locally dominant expatriate business community.[65] In his own study of the evolution of private Nigerian indigenous entrepreneurship, Akeredolu-Ale was looking for 'factors which have prevented a virile national organization of indigenous entrepreneurs from emerging'.[66] He found some of these to be the 'secretiveness and relative lack of communication between entrepreneurs which arise from and in turn fosters mutual suspicion and distrust . . . .'[67] Yet the entrepreneur one is writing about is a small capitalist and is behaving very rationally as such, given his objective historical situation. 'Virile national organizations' of capitalists do not emerge before the stage has been prepared for their emergence by the development of the society itself.

Apart from development theory's tendency to become ethnocentric via psychologism, it also tends to become microscopic and blame individuals for situations not of their own making and for practices they continue out of objective necessity. It tends, like much of positivistic observation, to mistake effect for cause. Finally, it tends to wishful thinking, like much ahistorical analysis. The 'modernization' focus, however, has one thing to its merit. Since it is based on the conception that the traditional sector can at least change along Western lines, as seen by Rostow, it takes us back to evolution. Yet social development theory does not have to be Rostovian.

Out of frustration with the various false starts we have had to undergo, there is now struggling to emerge a social development school in sociology which, if not self-consciously Marxist yet has a close affinity. And so the stone that the original builders rejected is turning out to be the keystone. In lieu of a conclusion, let us now say a word about this.

Marxist Method: The Stone the Builders Rejected

Basing themselves on the thesis of the materialist conception of history, Gerhard and Jean Lenski have developed a theory of social development and used it to explain the rise and fall of social systems. They argue that social systems rise on the basis of subsistence economies — simple horticultural, advanced horticultural, simple agrarian, advanced agrarian, fishing, herding, maritime and industrial societies.[68] These are subsistence modes rather than socio-economic modes familiar in Marxist literature, yet the Marxist socio-economic modes presume the existence of the Lenski systems.

The Lenskis have brought to their work the latest archaeological, biological, psychological and social scientific knowledge. In our opinion, they have, like the archaeologist Gordon Childe before them, enriched the development theory of societies in general. Important for us is the method by which their theory is constructed, which is the Marxist historical method.

Yet we must not forget that for Marxists there is not only the development theory of societies in general, but there is also the development theory of specific social systems as well as the development theory of important stages of a specific system. These more specified theories, it must be added, interest the Marxists more.

Economists use the term 'pure competition' to refer to a situation in which there is complete freedom of entry into the market for would-be competitors. As the situation is today in non-Marxist development study, there are no methodological or theoretical limits to entry for theories competing in the academic and governmental markets for development expertise. The situation approximates to 'pure competition'. There is, however, only one correct approach to development theory. For ideological reasons, anti-Marxists may never subscribe to it. The correct approach to development theory must be thoroughly historical and dialectical and cannot be guilty of ethnocentrism. Ethnocentrism, as we have shown, is a sure sign of faulty theoretical roots.

Notes

1. This has happened, for instance, with the 'development of underdevelopment' thesis. See David Booth, 'Andre Gunder Frank: An Introduction and Appreciation' in Ivor Oxaal, Tony Barnett and David Booth (eds.), *Beyond the Sociology of Underdevelopment* (London, Routledge and Kegan Paul, 1975).
2. See Maurice Dobb, 'The Trend of Modern Economics' in *Political Economy and Capitalism* (London, Routledge and Kegan Paul, 1937, revised 1960) reprinted E.K. Hunt and G. Schwartz (eds.), *A Critique of Economic Theory* (Harmondsworth, Penguin Education). See also Ronald Meek, 'The Marginalist Revolution and its Aftermath' in E.K. Hunt and G. Schwartz (eds.), *Studies in the Labour Theory of Value* (London, Lawrence and Wishart, 1956).
3. The controversy raging around this issue is to be found in all the papers in the book *Economic Anthropology*, edited by Edward E. Clair Jr. and Harold K. Schneider (New York and London, Holt, Rinehart and Winston, 1968).
4. For a critique of some orientations in metropolitan social science and the crisis it has created in social science in Nigeria, see Ikenna Nzimiro, *The Crisis in the Social Sciences: The Nigerian Situation* (Third World Forum, 1977).
5. Karl Popper, *The Open Society and Its Enemies*, Vol. 2 (London, Routledge and Kegan Paul, 1952).
6. It was V.I. Lenin who carried out a searching critique of positivism in his *Materialism and Empirio-Criticism*.
7. Thomas Kuhn, *The Structure of Scientific Revolutions* (University of Chicago Press, 1970).

8. Ibid., p. 77.
9. Maurice Cornforth, *The Open Philosophy and the Open Society* (London, Lawrence and Wishart, 1977), pp. 28-33.
10. John H. Kunkel, *Society and Economic Growth: A Behavioural Perspective of Social Change* (London and New York, Oxford University Press, 1970), pp. 13-14.
11. Ibid.
12. See P.A. Samuelson, *Economics*, 4th ed. (New York, McGraw-Hill, 1964). It is in this book that Samuelson first attempted the so-called neo-classical synthesis — an attempt to marry the Keynesian approach to the neo-classical marginalist microeconomic approach.
13. The left Keynesian economists comprise J. Robinson, N. Kaldor, K. Kurihara, A. Hansen, etc. J. Robinson's major left-Keynesian work is her *The Accumulation of Capital* (London, Macmillan, 1956).
14. Sraffa has published works on David Ricardo. See especially his *The Production of Commodities by Means of Commodities* (Cambridge University Press, 1960) where he defends and develops Ricardo's theoretical insights.
15. An example of Myrdal's writings is *Asian Drama, an Enquiry into the Poverty of Nations* (New York, Pantheon, 1968).
16. Good expositions of the Marxist dialectical method are rare. Valuable are B.M. Boguslavsky, *ABC of Dialectical and Historical Materialism* (Moscow, Progress Publishers, 1978), and Cornforth, op. cit.
17. Clarence Zuvekas, *Economic Development* (London and Basingstoke, Macmillan, 1979), pp. 13-14.
18. Ibid.
19. Karl Marx, along with Frederick Engels, regarded revolutions in forces of production, i.e. innovation and organization, as the prime mover in social development. Many of their writings are collected in K. Marx and F. Engels, *Selected Works*, 3 vols., (Moscow, Progress Publishers, 1970-77).
20. Joseph Schumpeter's work, *Capitalism, Socialism and Democracy* (London, Allen and Unwin, 1952) definitely agrees with Marx that capitalism will disintegrate and be replaced by socialism although he differs in a way with Marx as to the cause, whereas Rostow's aim is to deny such an outcome or at least wish it away. Besides, Schumpeter's conception of capitalist dynamics has very much in common with that of Marx and both are quite at variance with Rostow's stage theory. For Rostow's work, see, for example, W.W. Rostow, *The Stages of Economic Growth* (Cambridge University Press, 1960). Simon Kuznets criticized Rostow's stage theory in his work, 'Notes on Stages of Economic Growth as a System Determinant' in Alexander Eckstein (ed.), *Comparison of Economic Systems* (Berkeley, 1971).
21. The Nigerian Constitution Drafting Committee, for instance, made such a comparison in its (1976) report. See *Report of the Constitution Drafting Committee* containing the Draft Constitution, Vol. 1, Federal Ministry of Information, Lagos, 1976, p. xiii.
22. We are referring to the growth models of Harrod, Domar, Samuelson, Hicks, Metzger, Goodwin, Phillips, Kaldor, Kurihara, etc., as well as the capital accumulation theory of Joan Robinson and the stagnation

theory of Alvin Hansen. Some of these theories are reviewed in Roy Allen, *Mathematical Economics* (London, Macmillan, 1956).

23. The Harrod-Domar model with its concept of 'capital-output' ratio was the popular model.
24. Gerald M. Meier, *Leading Issues in Economic Development*, 3rd ed., (New York, Oxford University Press, 1976), p. 6.
25. In his anxiety for the interests of the 'free world', Rostow said: 'if the underdeveloped areas fall under communist domination, or if they move to fixed hostility to the West, the economic and military strength of Western Europe and Japan will be diminished, the British Commonwealth as it is now organized will disintegrate, and the Atlantic world will become ... incapable of exercising effective influence outside a limited orbit', cited by Pierre Jalee, *Imperialism in the Seventies* (New York, Joseph Okpaku Publishing Co., 1972), p. 218.
26. Rostow's book, *Stages of Economic Growth* is given the subtitle, 'A Non-Communist Manifesto'.
27. See Henry Bernstein's introduction to Bernstein (ed.), *Underdevelopment and Development* (Harmondsworth, Penguin Books, 1978), p. 17.
28. Rostow, op. cit.
29. See, for instance, Simon Kuznets, 'Notes on Stages of Economic Growth as a System Determinant' in Alexander Eckstein (ed.), *Comparison of Economic Systems* (Berkeley, 1971) and Alexander Gerchenkron, *Economic Backwardness in Historical Perspective* (Cambridge, Mass., Howard University Press, 1962).
30. Kuznets, op. cit.
31. The term 'unidirectional' is capable of several meanings. Some use it to mean 'cumulative'. Others use it to mean 'not reversible'. Yet others use it to mean 'devoid of alternatives and predetermined'. Marx says that human beings seldom give up what they have won in terms of civilization, but he does not say that they *never* do so. He states in the *Manifesto* that the struggle of contending classes 'can lead either to a revolutionary reconstitution of society or to the common ruin of contending classes': he admits that degenerations can occur; it is dialectical and historical. The word 'unidirectional' is better avoided altogether, for it is not even as clear in meaning as 'cumulative' or 'irreversible. See the *Manifesto of the Communist Party* by K. Marx and F. Engels.
32. See the argument by Harry Braverman, *Labour and Monopoly Capital* (New York and London, Monthly Review Press, 1974), p. 17.
33. See, for instance, Daniel O. Offiong, *Imperialism and Dependency* (Enugu, Nigeria, Fourth Dimension Publishers, 1980), p. 43.
34. N. Georgescu-Ruegen, 'Economic Theory and Agrarian Economics', *Oxford Economic Papers*, Vol. 12, No. 1, February 1960.
35. K. Marx, *Letter to P.V. Annenkov*, 28 December 1846, In K. Marx and F. Engels, *Selected Works*, Vol. 1, op cit., p. 663.
36. One economist has actually suggested that Rostow's stages are 'empty'. See Albert Fishlow, 'Empty Economic Stages?', *Economic Journal*, Vol. 75, No. 297, 1965.
37. Georgescu-Roegen, op. cit.
38. K. Marx, *Preface to Critique of Political Economy* in K. Marx and F.

Engels, *Selected Works*, Vol. 1, op. cit., p. 182.
39. In his *The Origin of the Family, Private Property and the State*, republished in K. Marx and F. Engels, *Selected Works*, Vol. 1, op. cit., Engels shows the evolution of tribal society through various stages. He also shows the different varieties of form of 'gentile society' of the communal clan.
40. According to Marx, in each economic system, humans 'develop certain relations with one another and . . . the nature of these relations must necessarily change with the change and growth of the productive facilities.' See K. Marx, *Letter to Annenkov*, op. cit., p. 664.
41. The rise of fascism was one of the expressions of this crisis. As Ernest Mandel observes: 'The rise of fascism is the expression of a severe social crisis of late capitalism. . .' in Mandel, *Introduction to Trotsky: The Struggle Against Fascism in Germany* (London, 1975).
42. See Emmanuel Okwuosa, *New Directions for Economic Development* (London, Africa Books, 1976), p. 59.
43. Bernstein, op. cit., p. 18.
44. See Bert F. Hoselitz, *Sociological Aspects of Economic Growth* (Glencoe, Ill., The Free Press, 1960); P.T. Bauer, *Dissent on Development* (London, Weidenfeld and Nicolson, 1971); Imra Adelman and Cynthia Morris, *Society, Politics and Economic Development* (Baltimore, Johns Hopkins Press, 1967); Zuvekas, op. cit.; S. P. Schatz, 'Economic Environment and Private Enterprise in West Africa' in O. Teriba and M.O. Kayode (eds.), *Industrial Development in Nigeria* (Ibadan University Press, 1977). In fact, most books on economic development employ the synoptic factor approach.
45. Zuvekas, op. cit., p. 13.
46. A good example in economics is the way sterile neo-classical theory led to disillusionment with theory among a group of economists at Harvard led by Wesley Mitchel, and to an eclectic approach which, as Schumpeter and others have noted, was not really an escape from unrealistic theory as the avowed edlectics imagined, but was actually the use of unarticulated theory. For every research implies a theory. Cf. J.A. Schumpeter, *History of Economic Analysis* (London, George Allen and Unwin Ltd., 1963).
47. John H. Kunkel, op. cit., p. 17.
48. Ibid.
49. Ibid., pp. 18-25.
50. Ibid.
51. Ibid.
52. Ibid., p. 13.
53. Ibid., p. 12.
54. Ibid., p. 13.
55. Gerhard Lenski and Jean Lenski, *Human Societies* (New York and London, McGraw-Hill, 1974), pp. 26-34.
56. Ibid., p. 33.
57. See Kunkel, op. cit., p. 19.
58. For a summary of these criticisms, see Kunkel, op. cit., pp. 22-3.
59. Ibid., p. 24.
60. Ibid., p. 13.

61. Ibid.
62. Lenski and Lenski, op. cit., p. 30. The emphasis is by the Lenskis.
63. Kunkel, op. cit., pp. 16-17.
64. In a work based on the 'model of man' approach in economic analysis, J. Lesourne describes modern psychology, whose propositions are supposed to supply 'models of man', as 'a kind of monster with multiple faces, sending out tentacles in many directions with no apparent consistency'. See Jacques Lesourne, *A Theory of the Individual for Economic Analysis*, Vol. 1 (Amsterdam and New York, North-Holland, 1977), p. 75. Lesourne's is actually an elaboration of neo-classical utility theory.
65. According to Nwosu: 'Among the major constraints on industrial production in the country, mention must be made of the shortage of industrial manpower and the relative unattractiveness of value added production to indigenous businessmen. In Nigeria, trading and so-called contracting activities are regarded as the quickest means of increasing income. This retrogressive [sic] entrepreneurial attitude accounts for the preponderance of foreign entrepreneurs in the manufacturing sector of the Nigerian economy.' See E.J. Nwosu, 'Patterns of Agricultural and Industrial Production and Their Implications for the Development of Nigeria' in E.C. Amucheazi (ed.), *Readings in Social Sciences: Issues in National Development* (Enugu, Nigeria, Fourth Dimension Publishers, 1980), p. 141. We may ask whether commercial and contracting activities only *seem* more attractive to local entrepreneurs, given their capital power and their experience or whether as a matter of fact they are attractive. If the latter is the case as, indeed, it is, then it is a subjective illusion to think they can simply put on 'value added' consciousness like the coat of mail of some brave knight going into battle to salvage the neo-colonial economy. This entrepreneur is, after all, a *capitalist* with capitalist instincts for what is profitable, rather than what is socially desirable, and neither Nwosu nor any of those who write like him think the entrepreneur should be anything else.
66. E.O. Akeredolu-Ale, 'The Evolution of Private Indigenous Entrepreneurship in Nigeria: Some Understressed Factors' in Teriba and Kayode, op. cit.
67. Ibid., p. 62.
68. Lenski and Lenski, op. cit.

14. Dependency and Revolutionary Theory in the African Situation

Franz J.T. Lee

This short essay consists of the following parts, namely, a brief sketch of the genesis of the *dependencia* movement; an attempt to classify the various authors of the *dependencia* theories; the basic theses of the *dependencia* theories for 'developing' countries, especially Africa, considering oil and revolutionary struggle.

Fundamental Hypothesis

For a people in the process of social emancipation under peripheral capitalism a theory of underdevelopment can *eo ipso only be a theory of social revolution* attuned to the given historic situation and being an immediate product of the concrete liberation struggle.

Genesis of the 'Dependencia' Movement

In explanation of the *dependencia* theories we have to state from the outset that, although they have not always been expressly formulated as 'theories of underdevelopment' (that is to day, a manifestation of the international social system), the concept of 'underdevelopment' has been in existence for a long time as a term of scientific analysis especially in the works of Marxist scholars. The *dependencia* approach originated in the 'classical' Marxist analyses of imperialism in the 1910s and 1920s, especially in the works of Lenin and Luxemburg.[1] After 1930, owing to the split of international communism into two main camps, Stalinism and Trotskyism, official Marxist social theory was practically absent in public debates. Between 1928 and 1960, it became ossified into a dogma under the severe pressure of the Soviet ideological monopoly and bourgeois political theories.

During this period the 'official' Communist Parties of Latin America — which led a mainly clandestine existence — repeated the various dogmas and directives from Moscow, and thus followed the various zigzag manoeuvres of Soviet foreign policy. With few exceptions, no Marxists attempted independent scholarly analyses of the Latin American reality until the

1960s.[2]

After World War II, as the Cold War intensified, the problem of 'underdevelopment' more and more became a central theme in international political discussion. During that period North American authors like Nurkse, Rosenstein-Rodan, Hirschman and Rostow were expounding their 'theories of modernization'. They had a direct political influence on the formulation of economic growth strategies for Latin America on the sub-continent itself. In fact, this was a deliberate strategy of the United States, which operated through the United Nations, at that time heavily under its influence. Thus the United Nations' 'Economic Commission for Latin America' (CEPAL) was founded in Santiago de Chile, under the directorship of Raul Prebisch.[3] It began propagating these 'modernization' theories, with a Latin American aroma, across South America. CEPAL's economic growth ideology – *el desarrollismo* – even penetrated the social sciences of Latin American universities, especially influencing sociology and political science. In university circles, various professors and lecturers began either apologetically to defend this ideology, or to criticize it from Marxist and non-Marxist *Weltanschauungen*. Well-known Latin American exponents of the *desarrollismo* ideology were Gino Germani[4] and Roger Vekemans.[5] According to these theories of 'social change', Latin American countries were to be transformed into industrialized states along Western lines within the shortest possible time. Foreign capital, especially in the form of direct investments and loans, and 'economic aid' (which turned out to be mainly 'military aid' for the ruling classes) was to accomplish this 'economic miracle' within a decade or two. A *sine qua non* for this 'modernization' process was to be a virulent anti-communism.[6]

It is against this background that the emergence of the *dependencia* movement has to be seen. It came into existence as a double critique: 1) against the *desarrollismo*, and 2) against the dogmatic 'Marxist' interpretations of Latin American reality.

Critique of 'Desarrollismo'
In one way or another, all *dependencia* authors directed their critique against the *desarrollismo* ideology. The heaviest ideological attacks came from scholars like Auilar Monteverde, Caputo, Pizarro, Cardoso, Falleto, Cordova, Silva Michelene, Dos Santos, Frank, Furtado, Garcia, Gonzalez Casanova, Riberro, Sunkel and Vasconi.[7] This rigorous debate led *inter alia* to the 'rediscovery' of Marxist social theory in Latin America.

Critique of 'Dogmatic Marxism'
Between 1930 and 1960 the Communist Parties (CPs) of Latin America rigidly applied the model of consecutive stages of the various modes of production, elaborated by Marx and Engels during the mid-19th Century, as an 'eternal law' to contemporary Latin American social conditions. Everything in Latin America that was not 'developed' capitalism, that is 'modernized' in the sense of *desarrollismo*, must necessarily be 'feudalism'. The

political consequence of such dogmatic reasoning was that the CPs were expecting and preparing the 'bourgeois-democratic revolution' — the Latin American 'French Revolution' — which would precede the 'October Revolution'. In order to accomplish this, alliances between the 'progressive national bourgeoisie' and the 'revolutionary proletariat' had to be organized, in its historic battle against the 'feudal oligarchy'.[8] Prior to the *dependencia* debate, various small Trotskyist groups had attacked the official CPs because of this 'neo-Stalinist' conservative attitude. But they also understood imperialism as the cause of underdevelopment in the classical Marxist sense as mainly an *external* factor. Both these Marxist positions were criticized by authors like Cardoso, Dos Santos, Frank and Gonzalez Casanova.[9] The *dependencia* authors, especially the Marxist-oriented ones, claimed that imperialism was not *only* an external oppressive force but, due to its structural presence within 'underdeveloped' societies, it controlled them *directly*. Hence the operations of imperialism had to be analysed *internally* and, in the first place, be fought against nationally. With this new approach most *dependencia* authors transcended the classical Marxist theories of imperialism. However, neo-Marxists like Paul A. Baran,[10] had already seen this problem and the necessity of revising and reformulating the concept of imperialism to be applicable to the contemporary 'Third World' conditions.

These political discussions led to serious debates within CEPAL itself, especially among scholars within its research institute, ILPES. The controversies spread to the State University of Santiago de Chile, especially to its Centre of Socio-Economic Studies (CESO—, within the Faculty of Economics. The next centre of serious political discussion was the National University of Mexico, especially within the Institute of Economic Investigation (IIE). In the 1960s all over Latin America around the capitals, *dependencia* study groups came into existence. About 25 *dependencia* authors became known internationally — among them were not only Latin American scholars but also authors like A.G. Frank (North American) and Franz Hinkelammert (German).[11] Basically, the *dependencia* exponents could be divided into three groups, namely, the 'bourgeois nationalists', the Marxists and the 'unclassified' group.

The 'bourgeois-nationalist' tendency understood 'dependence' as a sum of *external* variables, which build the outer framework of the national developmental process. This led to the conclusion that the carriers of dominance and dependence were basically the *national states* and that social groups, economic sectors or institutions play a minor role. The essence of dependence is therefore an 'asymmetric interaction'. The propagators of this tendency were mainly Furtado, Sunkel, Helio Jaguaribe[12] and Anibal Pinto.[13]

For the Marxists, the dependence approach was that part within the theory of imperialism which was not yet fully formulated, and which would describe the effects of imperialism directly *within* the peripheral states of world capitalism. For these scholars, generally, 'there is no theory of dependence independent of the theory of imperialism'.[14] They saw their approach as a *new* element, as the perspective from the 'Third World', and they did not 'only want to extend the theory of imperialism, but to contribute scientifically to its new formulation'.[15] It was not national states but classes which were the carriers of dominance and dependence.[16] The propagators of this Marxist tendency were mainly Cardoso, Cordova, Dos Santos, Vasconi, Marini[17] and Quijano.[18]

Owing to the fact that there is no single dependence theory, and that the authors are not even in agreement with regard to their fundamental concept of *dependencia*, many scholars cannot be classified, because they uncritically borrow concepts from both Marxist and non-Marxist tendencies. Within this ideological confusion we find authors like Aguilar Monteverde, Fernando Carmona de la Pena [19] and Marcos Kaplan.[20] Some, like Darcy Ribeiro with his 'evolutionist theory of dependence',[21] have developed their own independent trends.

Thus, only a specific section of the *dependencia* movement is Marxist. All tendencies, however, have in common one thing, namely that they are directed against the *desarrollismo* ideology and the 'neo-Stalinism' of the CPs of Latin America.

Basic Theoretical Statements and Critiques

Relevant contributions in the field of description of underdevelopment came from two sources: from the Latin American *dependencia* authors and from French scholars. Among the latter are Samir Amin, Charles Bettelheim, Pierre Jalee and Christian Palloix.[22] They concentrated their research work on the open or veiled *transfer of value* from the 'Third World' to the metropolitan countries, on the *correlation* between the two sections of the international division of labour. They mainly did this from the viewpoint of the metropolitan countries, under economic considerations. As we have seen, the *dependencia* authors did the reverse, beginning from the 'Third World'.

'Dependencia' Theses

According to *dependencia* theories the situation of underdeveloped countries can only be understood when the decisive role of *external* factors is considered. The social structures of colonies, ex-colonies or neo-colonies are not the results of autonomous historic development, but they are determined by foreign hegemony and exploitation. Thus endogenous and exogenous factors stand in an indivisible explanatory context of 'structures of dependence' of Third World countries.

'Under-development' and 'development' are not two different stages, the one following the other, but they are historic synchronous processes, functionally determining each other. Consequently, they are two sides of the same developing world capitalist system. Accordingly, one can at best speak about 'development of under-development'.

Although under-development has external historic roots, its effects are however, felt *internally*. The forced deformations and insufficiencies are essential ingredients of all internal social structures of 'developing' countries. Abolishment of under-development internally thus has as a prerequisite the eradication of the exploitative control exercised from outside. This is the direct attack on *desarrollismo* or 'modernization' ideologies.

The *dependencia* approach was chiefly developed from and for Latin American social conditions. That it is also applicable to other 'Third World' countries is not stated explicitly or worked out scientifically by these authors.[23]

Concerning these fundamental theses, there exists somehow a consensus among the various authors, but beyond this general framework a chaos of opinions has developed around the *teoria de la dependencia*.

Critique of 'Dependencia' Theories

The main scientific error of most theories is their conceptual vagueness. They criticized *desarrollismo* and 'dogmatic Marxism' which had transplanted concepts of European or North American origin to Latin American conditions. New scientific concepts to counter these they did not develop. Thus the *dependencia* literature is often pure description and wide speculation on a high level of theoretical abstraction, lacking intersubjectivity. This is especially the case of the 'bourgeois-nationalist' tendency. The Marxist tendency, on the other hand, has the problem of modifying Marxist concepts, such as 'proletariat' and 'class', in order to apply them realistically to Third World social conditions.

The theoretical and conceptual inefficiency is demonstrated by the term *dependencia* itself. There exists no clear scientific concept for this historic process. The given explanations mostly end in tautological, partial descriptions or metaphoric deviations. Hence dependence could be any one of the following: a theory; a part of a theory; a concept within a theory; a variable or even a concrete situation.

The same applies to a concept like *dependencia estructural*. One who expects scientific specification will be surprised to learn that this concept at one time means 'imperialism on a world scale' and the next time it is a component of internal social structures of 'under-developed' countries. It seems that the popularity of the *dependencia* theory was largely due to its lack of conceptual precision.[24]

The above dilemma arises because certain pre-questions of scientific inquiry have remained unanswered: How did the capitalist mode of production unravel itself in specific 'Third World' countries? What qualitative differences exist between these two forms? What is the theoretical status of the national state organization of 'dependent' societies in relation to a class analysis on a continental and world scale? Also, what is the relation between the social base and social superstructure of these countries — in other words, between economics and politics? If these questions are not answered, any formulation of the concept *dependencia* must necessarily be only provisional.

Added to the theoretical deficiencies is the lack of scientific praxis. The *dependencia* debate did not liberate itself either from the 'Hispanic' tradition of scholastic formalism, nor from what Lenin called the 'infantile disorder' of contemporary 'left' movements. There were bitter Latin American intellectual disputes concerning purely semantic problems. The necessity of empirical work to back theoretical questions was disappointingly neglected. This situation led to the stagnation of the *dependencia* debate, especially towards the end of the 1970s. Many recent publications are simply repetitions of the previous ones. Furthermore *dependencia* became a public slogan, an emotional political concept. In metropolitan countries, especially among the 'left', it gained 'exotic' dimensions, entered political folklore, becoming a household word in 'anti-imperialist' social functions.

On the positive side, the *dependencia* debate certainly had a regenerating and revitalizing effect on contemporary Marxism, with regard to its usage as a revolutionary method of emancipation on a global scale, as revolutionary theory of the 'under-developed' internationally, and as revolutionary praxis. Thus the critique of *dependencia* theories is politically significant for Africa in the sturggle to eliminate the social structures of dependence. But Marxism has to be emancipated from its 'Prolet-Aryanism', its dogmatism and Eurocentrism (or US-centrism). Only then will it become international proletarianism.

Relevance of 'Dependencia' Theories to Africa

The deliberations and critique expressed above apply to similar situations and conditions in other Third World countries, particularly in Africa. Over the last few years many works have been published by African and non-African authors, analyzing various social structures of dependence and revolutionary pressures in specific countries or illustrating general patterns of dependence in Africa as a whole.[25] The following general observations concerning research work in the theoretical and praxical fields are worth underlining.

Theoretical Relevance
The political relevance of the *dependencia* approach for the formulation of a 'theory of under-development' for African social conditions will depend on its ability to give theoretical precision to the already attained general conceptual reflections concerning structures of dependence, and on its potentiality to transform these dialectically into concrete empirical work and emancipatory praxis.

Theoretically, the exact locality of a theory of dependence has to be fixed scientifically, especially its categories and concepts, in relation to Marxism, that is in line with political economy and historical and dialectical materialism. Only by making it a part of revolutionary theory will conceptual precision and logical consistency be achieved.[26] 'Dependence' or 'under-development' are in all probability not suitable scientific categories. The

Marxist concepts have to be reformulated and enriched, in the sense of the 'eternal' dialectical method, in order to be applicable to specific African historical conditions. The universality of the Marxist method must withstand the iron test of real revolutionary praxis.

This is necessary to comprehend the complex systems of poly-dimensional contradictions and antagonisms in African societies. *Dependencia* as a possible theoretical concept includes an infinite number of factors. Hence it cannot be 'proved' or be operationalized as such.[27] For example, a case study of social structures of neo-colonialism in Kenya can contribute valuable information concerning 'structures of dependence', without necessarily once using the concept 'dependence' in its present form, simply because it operates on the concrete empirical plane.

Until now, the area of empirical work and case studies was unlimited. However, in view of the above, for future emancipatory-relevant research work, more emphasis should be laid on detailed analyses of classes and social groups in the various African states — of course, using the method of scientific socialism, Marxism. What are social groups like 'national bourgeoisie', 'petit-bourgeois intelligentsia', 'nationalistic military groups' in the Ugandan context, for example? What exactly is an African 'urban proletariat' or a 'rural proletariat' in the Nigerian or South African context?[28] Are they qualitatively the same? What about the 'marginal' social groups? Do they have any revolutionary potential? Is there a 'lumpenproletariat' in African capitals?

The concept 'structural heterogeneity', formulated by Cordova in 1973, has great scientific value for African post-colonial social conditions. It pinpoints the problem of 'combined development' of various modes of production in Africa. This 'heterogeneity' vertically forms part of the analysis of African classes, and horizontally explains the regional dynamism, enabling us to explain more precisely 'under-development' and to develop a revolutionary theory as a practical instrument to abolish it.

Praxical Relevance

It could never be our scientific intention and historical role *only* to interpret African structures of 'dependence' in different ways. The point is: we have to abolish, to *change* them. Thus our aim can only be a dialectical unity of scientific theory and scientific praxis. Anything else will land on the garbage heap of history.

It is exactly in the dimension of revolutionary praxis that the *dependencia* approach shows an alarming deficit. Not even the Marxist exponents could precisely indicate how praxically 'dependence' and 'under-development' can be abolished nationally, continentally and internationally. In their revolutionary anticipatory strategies they had to revert to the 'classical' Marxist theories of imperialism and international class struggle. Again, simply because Marxist pre-questions have not been answered, the conceptual apparatus is not efficiently developed and there is no consensus with regard to the precise meaning of historical and dialectical materialism in the present

African context; many promising scientific efforts end in a cul de sac, stymied by the question of revolutionary praxis.

It is not sufficient to demand the abolition of neo-colonialism and the introduction of socialism, supported by any adjective except 'scientific'. It is necessary to know the exact historical background of the emancipatory movements, their social setting, their dynamism, latency and tendency. The perspective of socialist reconstruction after colonialism or neo-colonialism must be a scientific analysis in the above sense. Otherwise, we are faced with transformation problems, experienced at present, for example, in Angola, Mozambique, Tanzania and Zimbabwe. Here clearly one can see the results of the division of emancipatory labour: of revolutionary theory and revolutionary praxis.

In conclusion, the question of abolishing structures of dependence is quintessential; on it depends any scientific deliberations concerning *dependencia*. Without a revolutionary theory, there will be no social revolution in any African state. In fact, no African revolution will have a chance against world imperialism.

Oil and Class Struggle

Living in Venezuela and observing the growth in international stature of African oil-producing countries such as Nigeria encourages me to mention briefly the problem of oil and the class struggle on a global scale. In reality there is no 'oil crisis' or 'energy crisis', as far as the 'wretched of the earth' are concerned, on the contrary, there exists a crisis of world capitalism, which is here to stay for quite a while. Many Marxist and non-Marxist analyses have been published concerning the oil industry,[29] its impact nationally and internationally, but we will be concerned here *only* with the relevance of oil in the process of anti-imperialist struggle. The oil or energy crisis of world capitalism, still our contemporary major mode of production, is a precise measurement of the severity of the crises within the international economic system (which is basically still capitalistic) indicative of its internal contradictions. It is also a measuring-rod for the emancipatory success of 'labour' on a global scale. The vital relevance of oil for capitalist development is well-known; also for socialist construction, especially in 'Third World' countries. Thus the exploited in oil-producing countries gain emancipatory relevance within the national and international class struggle; they acquire a special historical revolutionary task. In a nutshell, 'the internationalism of class struggle in oil is the cutting edge of much broader solidarity'.[30]

This means that Marxist scholars have a scientific duty to study 'oil structures of dependence' and a revolutionary task to be part of the 'broader solidarity' to abolish them by placing oil-producing countries in the frontline of the 'internationalism of class struggle'.

Otherwise, in Africa, we will only be left with the choice of 'barbarism'.[31]

Certainly, if the contradictions between 'labour and capital' (Marx and Engels) or 'under-development and revolutionary pressures' (Claude Ake) are not abolished in an emancipatory way, then, as Engels had already predicted, the African bourgeoisie and proletariat, together with their counterparts elsewhere, will historically end up in barbarism, in the total annihilation of the species *homo sapiens*.

Notes

1. See Christian Palloix, 'Die Imperialismus theorie bei Lenin und Rosa Luxemburg' in *Neuere Beitrage zue Imperialismustheorie*, Vol. I (Munich, Trikont, 1973), pp. 58-96. Also V.I. Lenin, *Der Imperialismus als hochstes Stadium des Kapitalismus* (Berlin DDR, Dietz, 1970) and Rosa Luxemburg, *Die Akkumulation des Kapitals* (Frankfurt am Main, eva, 1966). For Lenin and Luxemburg, the 'backward' countries were only of interest in so far as they were influencing the relations of production and the process of capital formation in the metropolitan countries. They did not analyze the disastrous effect of the flow of capital and commodities within the 'backward' countries. They did, however, indicate the *external* dependence of these countries on the world market.
2. Exceptions are: the Peruvian, José Carlos Mariátegui — see his book: *Siete ensayos de interpretación de la realidad peruana* (Lima, Libreria Peruana, 1928, 1934); the Chilean, Francisco Encina, the Argentinian, Sergio Bagú and the Brazilian, Caio Prado Junior; also various Trotskyist authors.
3. See Raúl Prebisch, *El desarrollo económico de América Latina y sus principales problemas* (New York, United Nations, 1949).
4. An Argentinian sociologist, author of *Política y Sociedad en una Epoca de Transición* (Buenos Aires, Paidós, 1968).
5. Other Latin American authors, propagating this ideology, were: Aldo Solari, Jorge Graciarena, Torcuato Di Tella and Federico Gil.
6. This is very clearly expressed by the Argentinian representative, Rogelio Frigerio, in his book *Crecimiento económico y democracia* (Buenos Aires, Losada, 1963), p. 168.
7. See a) Alonso Aguilar Monteverde, 'El capitalismo del subdesarrollo: Un capitalismo sin capital y sin perspectivas' in *Problemas del desarrollo* (Mexico), No. 8, July-September 1971, pp. 17-74; b) Orlando Caputo and Roberto Pizarro, *Imperialismo, dependencia y relaciones económicas internacionales* (Santiago, CESO, Universidad de Chile, 1970); c) Fernando H. Cardoso and Enzo Falleto, *Dependencia y desarrollo en América Latina* (Mexico, Siglo XXI, 1968); d) Armando Córdova and Hector Silva Michelena, *Die Wirtschaftsstruktur Lateinamerikas* (Frankfurt am Main, Suhrkamp, 1973); e) Teotonio Dos Santos, *Socialismo o Fascismo, Dilema Latinoamericana* (Prensa Latinoamericana, 1969); f) Celso Furtado, 'Externe Abhängigkeit und ökonomische Theorie' in Dieter Senghass (ed.), *Imperialismus und strukturelle Gewalt*

(Frankfurt am Main, Suhrkamp, 1972), pp. 316-34; g) Antonio Garcia, *La Estructure Social y el Desarrollo Latinoamericano* in F.H. Cardoso and F. Weffort (eds.), *America Latina: Ensayos de interpretación sociológica-politica* (Santiago, Universitaria, 1970), pp. 45-81; h) Pablo Gonzáles Casanova, *Sociología de la explotación* (Mexico, Siglo XXI, 1969), pp. 12-23; i) Antonio Garcia, 'Industrialización y Dependencia en América Latina', *Trimestre Económico*, Vol. XXXVIII, No. 151, July-September 1971, pp. 731-54; j) Darcy Riberro, *Der zivilisatorische Prozess* (Frankfurt am Main, Suhrkamp, 1971); k) Osvaldo Sunkel, 'Política Nacional de Desarrollo y Dependencia Externa', *Revista Mexicana de Sociologia*, Vol. XXXI, No. 4, October-December 1969, pp. 795-816; l) Trilman Tonnies Evers and Peter von Wogau in *Das Argument*, Vols. 4-6, July 1973, pp. 404-54. I am very much indebted to these authors for this paper.

8. For example, for the position of the Venezuelan Communist Party see Carlos Lopez, 'Di Kommunistische Partei Venezuelas und die gegenwartige Lage in Lande' in *Probleme des Friedens und des Sozialismus*, No. 10 (74). October 1964. pp. 825-31.

9. See F.H. Cardoso, '"Teoria de la dependencia" – o análisis de situacionas concretas de dependencia?', *Revista latinoamericana de ciencia politica* Vol. 1, No. 3, 1970, pp. 402-14; Theotonio Dos Santos, 'El nuevo cáracter de la dependencia', *Matos Mar*, 1969, pp. 175-7; André Gunder Frank, *Latin America: Underdevelopment or Revolution* (New York, Monthly Review Press, 1969), p. 407; Pablo Gonzáles Casanova, op. cit., pp. 9f. and 35-51.

10. Paul A. Baran, *The Political Economy of Growth* (New York, Monthly Review Press, 1957). This book had a decisive influence on the *dependencia* discussion; it was criticized by many authors, especially the Marxist-orientated ones.

11. See Franz Hinkelammert, *El Subdesarrollo latinoamericano. Un caso de desarrollo capitalista* (Buenos Aires, Paidos, 1970).

12. See Helio Jaguaribe, 'Causas del Subdesarrollo Latinoamericana', *Matos*, March 1969, pp. 201-19.

13. See Anibal Pinto, 'Notas sobre Desarrollo, Subdesarrollo y Dependencia', *Trimestre Economico*, Vol. XXXIX, No. 154, April-June 1972, pp. 243-64.

14. See Candoso, op. cit., p. 409.

15. See Dos Santos, op. cit., p. 176.

16. See Octavio Inni, *Imperialismo y cultura de la violencia en América Latina* (Mexico, Siglo XXI, 1970), p. 12.

17. See Ruy Mauro Marini, *Subdesarrollo y revolución* (Mexico, Siglo XXI, 1969).

18. See Anibal D. Quijano, 'Dependencia, Cambio social y urbanizacion en latinoamerica', *Révista Mexicana de Sociologia*, Vol. XXX, No. 3, July-September 1968, pp. 525-70. *Cum grano salis* one could also include A.G. Frank in this category.

19. See Fernando Carmona de la Pena, *Dependencia y cambios estructurales* (Universidad Nacional Autonoma de Mexico, 1971).

20. See Marcos Kaplan, 'Estado, dependencia externa y desarrollo en América Latina', *Matos*, March 1969, pp. 158-200.

21. See Ribeiro, *Der zivilisatorische Prozess,* op. cit.
22. These authors are well known to scholars of social sciences and it is not necessary to cite their works here.
23. Only recently did scholars like John Saul, Samir Amin, Giovanni Arrighi, C. Mellassoux, C. Palloix, A. Rweyemanu, C. Leys, W. Rodney, C. Thomas, C. Ake and Y. Barongo, among others, attempt to verify this approach of structural underdevelopment in Africa or Asia. See especially Samir Amin, 'Underdevelopment and Dependence in Black Africa: Historical Origin' *Journal of Peace Research*, No. 2, 1972, pp. 105-19; G. Arrighi, *Sviluppo Economico e Sovrastrutture in Africa* (Turin, Gulio Einaudi Ed., 1969); W. Rodney, *How Europe Underdeveloped Africa* (Dar es Salaam, Tanzania Publishing House, 1972); G. Arrighi and J.S. Saul, *Essays on the Political Economy of Africa* (New York, Monthly Review Press, 1973); H. Green and A. Seidmann, *Unity of Poverty: The Economics of Pan-Africanism* (Harmondsworth, Penguin, 1968); Colin Leys, *Underdevelopment in Kenya* (London, Heinemann, 1975); C. Ake, *Revolutionary Pressures in Africa* (London, Zed Press, 1978); Y. Barongo, *Neocolonialism and African Politics* (New York, Vantage Press, 1980).
24. To give examples of all these concepts which lack precision would go beyond the framework of a short paper ... but any critical reader could locate them easily in the *dependencia* literature.
25. See footnote 23. Also Samir Amin, *The Arab Nation* (London, Zed Press, 1978), *Maghreb in the Modern World* (Harmondsworth, Penguin, 1971) and his *Neocolonialism in West Africa* (Harmondsworth, Penguin, 1974).
26. From Nkrumah's 'Neo-Colonialism' to Ake's 'Revolutionary Pressures' remarkable work has been done in this direction of conceptual and emancipatory clarity.
27. See Evers and von Wogau, op. cit., p. 447.
28. See Franz J.T. Lee, *Sudafrika am Vorabend der Revolution* (Frankfurt am Main, ISP-Verlag), pp. 146-58 and 170-202; Franz J.T. Lee et. al., *Nigeria gegen Biafra? Falsche Alternativen. Uber Verscharfung der Widersprüche im Neokolonialismus* (Berlin-West, Wagenbach, 1969), pp. 49-68.
29. Of great value to this section is Petter Nore and Terisa Turner (eds.), *Oil and Class Struggle* (London, Zed Press, 1980).
30. Ibid., p. 2.
31. See Ake, op. cit., pp. 106-7.

15. African Elite Theories and Nigerian Elite Consolidation: A Political Economy Analysis

William D. Graf

Barely a decade and a half after inter-elite conflict brought down Nigeria's First Republic, intra-elite collaboration has succeeded in transforming the subsequent political system from a conventional military regime into Africa's most fully articulated liberal democracy. In the process, the Nigerian dominant classes have evolved from a fractious, ethno-centred and self-seeking series of groupings into a relatively cohesive, autonomous and self-confident stratum capable of regulating its potentially internecine conflicts while pursuing its collective interests against the interests of other social strata. These developments, set against a background of ethno-nationalism, civil war, a burgeoning economy based on oil revenues, and intensive political centralization, make Nigeria Black Africa's most intricate socio-economic formation. This very complexity defies analysis within the paradigms of conventional elite theories and urgently calls out for a broader, more differentiated theoretical instrument with which to comprehend the objective and subjective role of elite formation and consolidation in a developing neo-colonial capitalist African state.

The large body of literature on Nigeria which has emerged as the country made the transition to civilian government and its economic strength increased has so far been largely descriptive and atheoretical — a mass of observations and facts in search of a theory. Such a theory, surely, would as a minimum have to account for Nigeria's evolving neo-colonial capitalist economic structure and the constellation of elite interests and forces within it,[1] rather than merely ranking or classifying various ruling groups in terms of external criteria. For this reason, a number of extant theories about African elites may be rejected out of hand as unfruitful, namely: 1) Western-centred structural-functionalist theories which effectively exclude notions of class antagonisms or class struggle and concentrate instead on concocting categories of status, rank and behaviour;[2] 2) pluralist theories or intra-elite competition, again Western-formulated, which start from an assumption of basic system consensus and relative group autonomy; 3) ethnic reductionist theories which see membership in tribe or ethnic group as the determining factor in African politics; as well as the closely related 4) cultural pluralism theories which tend to absolutize ethnic awareness and ethno-centred politics into a generalized and permanent determining factor; and 5) generally home-grown theories of African socialism (as associated with Senghor, Sekou Toure, Mboya or Nyerere) which deny even the existence of classes by asserting that class divisions have not been part of traditional African society and therefore need not exist in the present, if only African societies can organically link up with the past. [3]

It is evident, therefore, that this paper advocates a political economy approach to elite theory-building. Rather than presenting a pre-formulated theory and fitting Nigerian elite structure and behaviour neatly into it, however, the paper will critically examine these structures and processes in the light of some political economy partial theories and approaches and thereby suggest some elements of a more comprehensive but not yet formulated theory. Here one might bear in mind Gavin Williams' injunction that: 'The central problems facing Nigeria, like all other societies, are no respecters of the conventions and conveniences of academia,' and that one may go beyond a critique of a specific neo-colonial form in order to analyse neo-colonial capitalism as a system. [4]

Pre-Independence Elite Formation

Historically, Nigerian elites have been a 'faulted' bourgeoisie [5] in the sense that their social position, economic pre-eminence and even values and personalities were shaped by colonialism. In this of course the Nigerian elites' experience is by no means unique: throughout Africa colonialism has had profound and permanent effects on social and economic life. Frantz Fanon and Kwame Nkrumah, among others, have pointed this out. This is especially true of those African states which have persevered in the neo-colonial capitalist mode of production and whose elites have thus had no revolutionary, system-transforming raison d'etre.

The form of British administration was designated as indirect rule. In terms of its effects on subsequent class-formation, this meant the superimposition of a 'higher' or 'national' political authority — colonial government — upon the various indigenous emirates, kingdoms and tribal chieftancies. Indirect rule thus throve upon and derived its effectiveness from the perpetuation of inter-regional and inter-ethnic differences. For the emirs' and chiefs' authority rested, in this system, upon their capacity to maintain intact their ethnic-group cohesiveness, tribal customs and distinctiveness from adjacent groups. Indirect rule tended to reinforce the most conservative elements among traditional ruling systems whose horizons were not likely to transcend the limits of kinship group or tribe. Moreover, it distorted the traditional rulers' fundamental basis of authority. Among the Yoruba, for example, who had evolved a kind of limited constitutional monarchy, derived from a broad cultural heritage, which was subdivided into units based on family, lineage and clan, colonial rule enhanced the chiefs' powers and backed these with force. Whereas traditionally the Yoruba chiefs had had to 'earn' their right to govern through wisdom, fairness and efficiency (and could be de-stooled if they contravened these norms), they were now emplaced by colonial might and shielded against any popular pressure from their people. The predictable effects of this process were often corruption, irresponsible rule and outright authoritarianism. In the East of the country the dilemma of indirect rule was even more palpable: since the segmented Igbo family groups seldom had an institution of chieftancy, the colonial administrators had to create it. A whole new class of 'warrant chiefs' was thus invoked. Naturally such chiefs seldom enjoyed the legitimacy and popularity of more 'organic' rulers and depended for their continuing authority upon the coercive powers of the colonial administration.

These developments point to a first fundamental defect of early Nigerian elite formation: while indirect rule was begun in order to serve and promote the capitalist interests of the mother country, its continuation largely depended on the co-operation of local authorities whose power was rooted in pre-capitalist forms of social organization, so that both the capitalist structure of extraction and its administrative superstructure depended on the maintenance of traditional societies whose existence was daily undermined by the workings of colonial capitalism. Yet the system of indirect rule could not accommodate the social and economic changes precipitated by colonial capitalism; on the contrary, it merely continued to bolster by decree the waning power of the chiefs whose role increasingly became that of enforcer, backed by the colonial regime's law, administration and coercive power. The traditional rulers' objective function came to be that of agent of social discipline facilitating colonial plunder of their territory. The nature of that plunder naturally varied according to the specific interests of the colonizer, but included: establishment of mono-crop or mono-mineral enclaves, disarticulation of regional economies, neglect of social infrastructures, wage exploitation and, above all, export of surplus value.

As colonialism enlarged its scope, the British administrators, lacking European manpower reserves which would have been furnished, say, from a white settler population, were increasingly forced to train 'indigenes' for lower-level administrative positions or for rank-and-file soldiering and policing. Basic education was provided by the churches and missions who also occasionally arranged higher education abroad for those who showed special promise or could afford it. Meanwhile, the artificially induced desire for manufactured goods promoted trade and commerce, which was largely dependent upon overseas suppliers.

Contrary to theories which suggest the formation of entirely new classes of indigenous administrators and traders attendant upon these developments, it is apparent that the chiefs, emirs and *obas*, and their kin, as the mediating agency between the colonizers and the people, were best placed to capitalize on the opportunities afforded by colonial rule. Their sons and (sometimes) daughters were sent to mission schools or for education abroad. They or their kin staffed the administrative positions opened to indigenes. They engaged in plantation farming, mining and trading — albeit in a subordinate role — and in this way accumulated comparatively large amounts of capital and expertise.

Of course only a minority of traditional rulers and their kin actually entered the colonial capitalist economy in this fashion; and not only traditional rulers' kin achieved positions in the administration or in business. But these general patterns of early elite formation have continued through time and do help to explain the origins of Nigeria's 'faulted' bourgeoisie.

The major criteria of pre-independence elite formation therefore can be summarized as wealth, education and traditional authority. Embryonic Nigerian elites, despite their ethnic, political, religious and sectoral differences, had and still have, high incomes, Westernized life styles, advanced education, special privileges such as private schools and trips abroad, and enhanced life prospects; possession or enjoyment of these things is what distinguishes them from the 'masses'. They also share in common — given national economic dependency on foreign capital and know-how and the corresponding absence of internally generated sources of wealth and power — the fact that they must cohere around the state apparatus. For the state, under colonialism (and neo-colonialism) was the principal employer, by far the largest source of finance and therefore the vehicle for the most rapid accumulation of wealth, status and power. More will be said about this presently.

Thus the distance between the rulers of Nigeria and the masses was immense, even prior to independence. Yet it was this elite which guided the nation as a whole into the post-colonial era. Their goal in shedding the British administration was merely to replace it. Relatively well-placed in the bureaucracy or in control of local or regional power centres, and in possession of the skills and means (literacy, command of English, wealth, connections) needed to prevail, the Nigerian colonial elite realized well in advance that the top positions in the leading institutions would accrue to them with the departure of the colonial masters, and so negotiated independence by degrees, with the least possible disruption of colonial institutions. Independence thus amounted largely to a negotiated settlement — a gentlemen's agreement — between the colonial administration and the emergent Nigerian elites. This fact may account for the popular phrase about Nigeria having produced not political martyrs, but successors. Independence, then, entrenched the ruling structure produced under colonialism and further increased the already well-developed elite - mass distinction.

But the struggle to convince the colonial administration to hand over political power had necessitated some measure of involvement and participation of the masses, since they could provide the aura of legitimacy and popular support needed to persuade the colonizer to effect the transfer as soon as feasible. This popular support derived not only from a widespread desire for 'liberation' and 'self-rule'; it was also purchased with promises of a better way of life and more material abundance after the departure of the British — promises which could only be kept if the system of rewards was drastically modified. Any such modification would of course be inimical to the interests of the successor elites whose overriding concern was to preserve the post-colonial status quo, with themselves in its commanding positions, as intact as possible. In other words, the masses who had been mobilized and politicized on behalf of a universal goal — national independence — now had to be depoliticized rapidly in the service of particularist ends — elite domination

Ethnicity and Class Struggle

From the preceding discussion, two things may be inferred about the Nigerian bourgeoisie: 1) As an essentially non-productive successor elite removed from direct ownership of the means of production, it was compelled to look to the state apparatus as its primary source of elite formation and consolidation. 2) As a non-revolutionary class lacking a historical raison d'etre, it had to seek out and deploy ersatz ideologies in order to retain a mass following and to forestall social reform. Primary among these was the ideology of ethnicity or 'tribalism'. These two imperatives must be considered in their interrelationship: as a *dialectic of ethnicity and class struggle*.

Colonial statism, organized according to the principle of indirect rule, had consciously sought to prevent the formation of a national bourgeoisie. It created instead a series of regionalized and tribalized bourgeoisies who could be managed according to the strategy of divide and rule. Economic power, thus held diffused, could not coalesce into a political power capable of challenging the sole 'national elite', namely the colonial administration. Hence the Nigerian bourgeoisie was rendered incapable of fulfilling the historical role played by its European counterparts: the development of the forces of production.

Instead, Nigeria's post-independence elites of necessity gravitated toward the state in order to use it to achieve economic and social power. For unlike earlier European and North American elites, whose political pre-eminence generally mirrored their pre-existing wealth or social status and whose state was, in a real sense, their state, post-colonial Nigerian elites were merely the recipients of a socio-economic system and state structure created by and for the metropolitan power. In order to re-deploy it — rather than transform it — in their own interests, they had to seize control of the system's centre: government, civil service and the military. This solution became all the more compelling, since the peripheral socio-economic structure had underdeveloped those groups who might have constituted a counterweight to a statist elite: there are few organized working-class movements, few business associations, and still fewer defence agencies of rural interests.

The relations prevailing in neo-colonial capitalist African states such as Nigeria, in other words, may be seen in terms of an inversion of the Marxist concepts of base and superstructure. If in advanced capitalist countries political power derives in the main from economic structures and relationships, the equation in Nigeria is reversed: 'it is rather political power (which here also means administrative and military power) which creates the possibilities of enrichment and which provides the basis for the formation of an economically powerful class, which may in due course become an economically dominant one'. [6] Here the problems of conceptually coming to grips with post-colonial elite statism point to the need for more adequate theory. The forms, if not the fact, of exploitation, for example, in such systems are not identical to those prevailing in advanced capitalism. As Claude Ake suggests:

> In Africa much of the exploitation is done not by individual capitalists, but by the state acting as a powerful entrepreneur, establishing businesses, hiring wage labour, and ruthlessly extracting surplus value from its subjects. Many of those who exploit the proletariat do not themselves own the means of production; but they control the power of the state which is used to control the means of production and to carry out exploitation. [7]

Possession of political power thus represents the *conditio sine qua non* to the good life: status, security, honours, benefits and, above all, wealth. Since wealth was thus largely a function of government office, politics centred around competition for top positions and political activities were geared to gaining access to state power and the revenue allocation and patronage dispensation connected with it. Successful appropriation of state resources, achieved by the manipulation of marketing board surpluses, capitation taxes, export levies and a variety of other devices, could enrich the state elites, enhance their security of tenure — and lead them to seek power by all means available.

These contradictions of the post-independence state elites might have been mitigated, however, 1) had political independence been accompanied by economic independence, and 2) had the dominant classes been able to constitute themselves as a coherent and self-aware stratum. But the Nigerian bourgeoisie were unable or unwilling to overcome the inherent structural dependencies and defects of colonialism, so that 1) neo-colonial capitalist relations persisted, thus perpetuating the elites' dependence on foreign capital and forcing them to remain firmly within the orbit of the (peripheral) state, and 2) the successor elites, lacking a real, dynamic, mass-based and progressive function, turned to latent, regressive and colonial-induced tribalist appeals. [8]

Setting aside for a moment the implications of neo-colonialism, the resort to ethnicity itself introduced a series of contradictions into the political life of the First Republic which ultimately debilitated it and led to its collapse. In the segmented national society, the elites' power base was confined to regional or ethnic-group support because colonialism had prevented the emergence of national leaders and had encouraged tribalism in a number of ways. Yet Nigeria's survival and development as a viable nation-state depended on the evolution of efficient, integrative national institutions at the centre capable of sustaining stability and progress. Furthermore, access to the decisive powers of patronage and distribution could be gained only via the central institutions. In this situation, the emergence of 'national' leaders and parties was all but impossible, and the federal government became essentially a loose, potentially antagonistic coalition of particularist elites based upon mutual advantage.

If the process of elite formation was thus contingent upon the several elites' capacity to concur on essential programmes and development plans, the demands of their various constituencies for immediate tangible rewards — government contracts, new projects, better roads and other infrastructures, positions in the bureaucracy, scholarships, etc. — subjected them to a cross-pressure to divert government resources to the ethnic and kinship groups whose support was needed to stay in power. Such diversions, within the context of scarcity, had to be accomplished at the expense of other elites' constituencies. Elite coalitions at the centre therefore tended to be factious, divisive and highly competitive. Where ruling groups realize that the extension of their power and influence are de facto limited by the ethnic, linguistic or geographical composition of their reservoir of popular support, they will logically seek to maximize that support in order to further their bargaining basis within the national or regional coalition, with the ultimate goal of dominating it. In the absence of a well defined social-class consciousness, or even a charismatic leader with an appeal transcending region or ethnic group, ethnicity presents itself as the most effective, most readily available ideological appeal to mobilize and retain as many of one's constituents as possible. Of this phenomenon, Yolamu Barongo writes:

> What is usually regarded as 'tribalism' by Western writers is no more than a reflection of the underlying conflicts among groups over the allocation and possession of material resources. In competing for resources ethnic or 'tribal' identity and solidarity are merely used by the elite members of ethnic groups as a means of mobilizing groups for corporate action against other groups, usually for the purpose of achieving personal interests of the elites such as political power, jobs and other material rewards.[9]

The natural corollaries of these complementary processes of elite factionalism and ethnic politics are stalemate, immobilism and hence ossification of political life.

A basically insecure and unstable position is common to the elite groups who are dominant in such a system. Since their power base was segmented, and complete domination of society and economy therefore out of the question, exclusion from power on the basis of shifting coalitions or even military coups was an omnipresent spectre. This was especially so in the regionalized and decentralized constitutional structure of the First Republic. Exclusion, however, would have meant loss of all the hard-won advantages already mentioned. Thus, 'the major activity of the ruling groups . . .' may be seen as 'an attempt to redress the insecure position they find themselves in' [10] and the principal means by which they did this was the utilization of public resources to cement intra-elite cohesion. The elites may be roughly subdivided into politicians, the 'intendent' class of civil servants and administrators, and a commercial-national bourgeoisie of traders, contractors, land speculators, independent professionals, etc. Solidarity among these disparate groups developed on the one hand from their utility to one another and, on the other, from a common awareness that their self-enriching activities must be carried on to the detriment of the broad majority. Thus contracts were awarded to ruling-party supporters; contractors contributed to parties or individual politicians, civil servants were large shareholders in contracting companies; government-owned banks financed the ruling parties and granted loans to party stalwarts, public corporations became syndicates for patronage dispensation; policies such as Nigerianization of the civil service or indigenization of foreign-owned businesses brought promotions and wealth only to a tiny elite class; government projects were used to create opportunities for private investment; and virtually all transactions involved obligatory payments of 'dash' all round. Enrichment accrued to all members of the elite stratum, and the wealth thus generated — and invested in shares, real estates, consumer goods or squirreled away in banks at home or abroad — went a long way toward ameliorating the elites' chronic feelings of insecurity.

On the other hand, however, the elites could hardly afford to alienate themselves from their sources of mass ethno-regional support, whose life situation was so different from their own. The connection could be sustained partially through patronage (which was limited), partly through charisma and the personalization of politics (which did tend to be effective at the communal level), but primarily through calculated ethno-nationalist appeals:

> A symbiotic relationship develops between politicians, who wish to advance their own positions, and their 'people', who fear political domination and economic exploitation by a culturally distinct group allegedly organized for these ends. A politician thus gains a tribal power base by successfully manipulating the appropriate cultural symbols and by articulating and advancing his people's collective and individual aspirations (which he himself probably helped to arouse).[11]

Stable government and with it an effective spoils-distribution system and growing wealth and prosperity are evidently all in the long-term interests of the elite class. Yet their appeals to ethnic sentiments and resentments, by fragmenting and dividing society, prevented the realization of these aims. Instead of working toward national unity and integration, which their educational skills and power positions might have equipped them to do, the political elites became a major agency of divisiveness and fragmentation. Or to recall Professor Dudley's terms, they failed to respond to their foreseen role as 'conflict managers' and degenerated instead into 'conflict generators' or 'the chief proponents and purveyors of parochialism and particularistic values'[12] in Nigerian political life.

Ethnic politics, thus utilized by the political class to conceal other intrasocietal antagonisms, such as class struggle and maldistribution, contains its own dysfunctional dynamic. If class struggle — whose emergence the elites had to prevent at any cost — calls into question the legitimacy of the prevailing socio-economic system *within* the polity, then communal conflict is the more invidious, for it challenges the boundaries and continued existence of the nation-state itself. Secession and/or civil war are its logical ultimate outcomes.

These acute and unresolvable — within the neo-colonial capitalist framework — contradictions, as is well known, manifested themselves in the immobilism, punctuated by recurrent crises, which preceded military intervention in January 1966. Political immobilism by itself need not have precipitated such a drastic change, had it not reflected economic stagnation which the growth-dependent dominant classes could not tolerate. But growth — even, balanced growth — was hindered by the dependent character of the Nigerian bourgeoisie whose prosperity had lost all connection with their capacity to develop the forces of production and who were by now compelled to seek political office and/or foreign alliances to further their own interests. These interests, moreover, were inimical to continued national development, for the economic redistribution and nationalization of some of the means of production, which further development demanded, could not be realized by the system-immanent, technical-incremental change of which only the bourgeoisie were capable.

Economic and Political Centralization

Thus the military — itself a part of the neo-colonial capitalist elite (although harbouring as well a considerable pre-capitalist ethos) — intervened and forcibly removed the main contradictions of the Nigerian ruling classes. It suspended the political parties as the main instigators of elite conflict and reduced the old political class to a subordinate role. In its place it substituted a new ruling alliance between the more national, rational and technocratic elite groups: the army and the civil service. Over time these groups became increasingly allied with and penetrated by representatives of indigenous business and multinational corporations. [13] Centralist by organization and outlook, relatively unhampered by local/regional claims and pressures, guided at least partly by ideals of nationalism and national greatness, and standing to further their own careers considerably, the military – civil service coalition promptly set about 'correcting' Nigeria's factional, divisive and therefore dysfunctional system of elite interaction by means of far-reaching, comprehensive — but not revolutionary — programmes of consolidation and centralization.

To be sure, the military government first had to reproduce within itself and finally enact the major socio-economic, sectoral and ethnic tensions produced by intra-elite conflict after independence. Coup and counter-coup, riots, massacres and civil war were the outcomes of this process. Seen from

Timothy Shaw's 'radical perspective', the succession of more or less violent intra-military personnel shifts in 1966, 1975 and 1976 — and by extension recivilianization in 1979 — was however merely 'reflective of fractional shifts within the local bourgeoisie and constitute stages in the evolution of social forces in this particular part of the semi-periphery'.[14]

The 'fractional shift' in the intra-elite balance of power which military intervention precipitated represented a relative aggrandizement of the strength of the 'intendant classes' [15] (military, civil servants, administrators) at the expense of the more narrow political class of locally or regionally based politicians and their clientele of traders, contractors, land speculators and the like — the main propagators of tribalism and regionalism. This is not to suggest that the latter groups were excluded completely from the ruling circles. Only their relative power declined, so that they became junior partners in the elite coalition rather than co-determining principals. Many of the old politicians, for example, retained government posts as civilian commissioners or as members of consultative bodies such as Gowon's 'Leaders of Thought', or as co-opted members of State [16] cabinets. And certainly many sectors among the business bourgeoisie carried on as before. But the nature of the *comprador* classes did change somewhat: as the civil service's powers grew in proportion to state intervention in the economy, many middlemen, whose function had been to 'mediate' between foreign interests and local political leaders, were now made redundant, since 'a statist' *compradors* thus were able to exclude local middlemen and in effect replace some triangular relationships with bilateral ones.' [17]

These fractional shifts within the bourgeoisie represent, in retrospect, the beginning 'nationalization' [18] of the Nigerian elite in so far as the leading groups now looked increasingly to the system's centre for the realization of their interests and goals, rather than to local or regional sub-systems. This tendency was enhanced by the conclusion of the civil war which lent a renewed impetus to national unity and above all, during the 1970s by massive oil revenues which were appropriated and disbursed by the centre.

Thus the Nigerian economy, directed by a more nationally-orientated bourgeoisie and reflecting its interests, after 1970 entered into a period of qualitatively new development beyond its 'robber baron phase of regionalized, tribalized and centrifugal commercial capitalist competition'. [19] The state played and pays a special role in this scheme of things. Claude Ake's term 'statism', I.V. Sledzevsky's characterization of 'a special stage in the development of state capitalism' and Peter Waterman's 'period of peripheral capitalist industrialization', [20] are all attempts to define and comprehend this new era of growth.

The state's role in the Nigerian political economy ought not to be misinterpreted as some variety of state socialism, much less as evidence of a 'mixed economy'. [21] Rather, state economic intervention has been a conscious means of, first, generating continued economic growth and, second, appropriating the surplus value for the power elite. Since the former, growth, has absolute priority — because the latter, private appropriation, is its precondition — the state occasionally must impinge on the interests of this or that sector of the bourgeoisie. But this is only a manifestation of state capitalism's raison d'etre: the co-ordination and, if necessary, the overriding of particularist elite interests in the long-term collective interests of the elite class as a whole. In order to ensure this necessary growth, the state first assumes control over the most dynamic sectors of the economy (oil) then creates or extends the infrastructure of extraction (transport, communications) while simultaneously eroding independent state sources of revenue-raising (abolition of separate taxation, derivation,[22] and in particular marketing boards) and integrating all sectors and regions by means of a comprehensive process of national planning (Five Year Plans) combined with revenue allocation by the centre which helps to overcome excessive regional imbalances. The private appropriation of the surplus thus generated follows quasi-automatically from the passive technique of failing to change the existing class structure and system of resource distribution.

Active state involvement in the economy then further enhances the process of elite consolidation. The state's economic role becomes more intensive and extensive, entering into such key spheres as banking, insurance, imports, foreign exchange and basic production, and especially into those areas in which Nigerian entrepreneurs lack experience and/or financial backing. In particular, the state moves into the 'structure-forming' spheres of the economy, namely those — crucial — branches of industry with a high capital intensity and gradual capital circulation.[23] This concentration on basic industries demonstrates the foreseen role of state capitalism as a motor for economic development with the object of creating an independent industrial base characterized by extensive import substitution and sustained attempts at technology transfer.

This context of state capitalism — the conversion of publicly created profits into private hands, *as if* the state sector were privately owned — defines the function of the much-misinterpreted state policy of economic nationalism or 'indigenization.' Indigenization, or the state-decreed transfer of ownership of selected enterprises and industries from foreigners to Nigerians, as part of a state-capitalist strategy of further development, does not address the important *structural* problems of the Nigerian economy, such as regional imbalances in the distribution and utilization of human and natural resources, massive urban - rural and upper class - lower class income differentials, and discrepancies between the public and private sectors. Rather, it is 'an attempt to secure a certain position for growing elite or private enterpreneurs whilst at the same time preserving the dominant place for foreign capital elsewhere in the industrial sector'.[24] Thus indigenization policies have fostered an 'indigenous "capitalism" with a framework of continued dependence on foreign enterprise in many sectors'.[25]

The fact that the takeover of, or achievement of equity in, foreign enterprises has been accomplished by the state on behalf of private capital has meant that those elites closest to the state machinery who either own capital or have access to the — largely stated-owned — lending institutions are by far the greatest beneficiaries of indigenization.[26] But the transfer of ownership/ control to Nigerians has not increased productivity or economic performance; it has only led to the evolution of a kind of 'drone capitalism'[27] dependent still upon the state and foreign capital.

The social classes whose fortunes are so interwoven with this economic structure have been aptly called an 'auxilliary bourgeoisie'[28] existing in the bureaucratic, managerial and commercial sectors. The auxilliary bourgeoisie consists, first, of Nigerians who have bought shares in the large public companies (Schedule 2, 1972; Schedules 2 and 3, 1977). Upper-level civil servants in particular, with their better access to credit and information and their direct links with foreign companies, have become the 'core of the emergent share-owning class'.[29] Second, leading Nigerian executives of foreign-owned companies have also acquired large shareholdings in public companies — often through stock options and special bonuses — especially in the companies which employ them. They are joined by, third, a number of large-scale businessmen and relatively wealthy professional people — but seldom by military personnel who tend to prefer the 'quick-gain' sectors such as contracting.[30] A fourth auxilliary category derives from Nigerians employed in the smaller foreign private companies which were not made public corporations and hence not subject to direct government surveillance. The social antecedents of these share-owners is somewhat more heterogeneous and includes 'top civil servants, professionals, big businessmen, some military officers, traditional rulers' families, former politicians, state commissioners and employees and distributors of companies selling the shares'.[31] Thus Collins rightly sees as one of the major effects of indigenization 'a tightening nexus between government and foreign capital', which he describes in this way:

> On the one hand important sections of the bureaucratic and managerial bourgeoisie have been co-opted as shareholders, while on the other chosen members of the commercial bourgeoisie have secured a niche in the alien-dominated distributive network and therefore tied in, as satellites, through the latter's monopoly of supplies and credit. The state must now protect even more the interests of foreign capital in which the local bourgeoisie has a stake.[32]

It is thus evident that indigenization's primary social function is to improve the position of the national bourgeoisie. It is neither productive nor redistributive. As such it lends support to Gavin Williams' thesis that:

> The development of neo-colonial capitalism substituted imports of intermediate and producer goods for imports of consumer goods. This consolidates rather than undermines dependence on foreign suppliers, since production, as well as consumption, now depends on foreign experts.[33]

Economic centralization was paralleled by an interrelated process of political centralization. (It has already been demonstrated that any conventional base – superstructure analysis does not apply in the African context.) The creation of 12, then 19, states in place of the former 4 regions broke down the ethno-regional power blocs and, coupled with enhanced revenue control at the centre, ensured that each State would in effect become a client of the federal government, forced now to look to the centre for leadership, economic planning and overall development. At the same time the States' former independent legislative powers, as embodied in the old concurrent lists, were arrogated by the centre.

The proliferation of States set off a rapid growth in the civil service establishment as the total number of governments increased from 5 to 13 and finally to 20. Absolute numbers of civil servants, already swollen from the post-independence Nigerianization of the bureaucracy, expanded still further with the growth of the 'politically relevant' population, which increased the quantity of demands placed on the system, and with the extension of the civil service into remote and rural areas in line with the policy of development administration. The civil service machinery was made to reflect the principle of federal supremacy. A sustained effort was undertaken to recruit leading personnel into the federal service, which was now considered primary. Among other incentives, the federal bureaucrats were offered higher wages and better conditions of service. For the first time, Nigerians from all over the federation were attracted into the national civil service in large numbers: southern-based civil servants who saw the federal apparatus as the best avenue to enhanced career prospects, since it was expanding more than twelve times as rapidly as the State bodies, and 'progressive' northern bureaucrats who saw in federal penetration into the North a source of new opportunities for advancement as well as a means of undermining the power of encrusted traditional authorities and thus of accelerating the process of development. And a number of inter-governmental administrative institutions – e.g., the Nigerian Council for Science and Technology, the Medical Research Council, Agricultural Research Council, Natural Resources Research Council – were '... created ostensibly to provide avenues of Federal - State consultation and co-operation but actually to provide additional pressure points for integration and federal dominance'. [34]

The inflation of the state apparatus in this manner certainly suggests the applicability of the 'over-developed post-colonial state' theory. But it would be misleading to attribute this over-development to the colonial administration – even granted that the colonized country's administration is essentially an extension of the 'over-developed' metropolitan colonizer's political system – since colonialism, in its search for profit maximization, tends instead toward minimal administrative expenditure, as the policy of indirect rule clearly shows. [35] Rather, post-independence pressures and elite responses to them have led to the 'overinflated' Nigerian state.

However that may be, the inflating state and expanding economy objectively require a high degree of elite cohesion for a number of reasons:

First, the military's pre-eminent position is structurally undermined over time. Lacking any system-transforming 'mission', by nature unresponsive to popular opinions and demands, and internally cross-pressured as a result of its accession to political power, the military government – every military government from 1966 to 1979 – was under a strong compulsion to 'return to the barracks' after its immediate post-coup 'corrective' objectives had been accomplished. Once the Gowon regime had reasserted national unity through the successful conclusion of the civil war, the creation of a new system of federalism and the centralization of power, and had laid the groundwork for a more functional national capitalism, it lost its historical raison d'etre and had to face a rising opposition from within. For it had no effective conflict-resolving capacity, lacked the dynamism necessary for mass mobilization to promote further development and above all its existence set limits on the rising capitalist classes' opportunities for expansion and profit-realization.

Second, conflict within the military itself developed largely out of the 'dual constituency' of the military leadership, namely the interests and objectives of the 'politicized group of governors, cabinet members and others directly involved in government – never more than 100 officers at any one time – and the great majority of the ranks who remained on the outside the political system looking in. Cohesion was initially not a problem: fighting the war and providing more benefits and amenities to the military ensured solidarity. But during peacetime the 'political' officers became progressively alienated from their original military constituency as they were integrated into the ruling class and engaged in the latter's self-aggrandizing and often corrupt practices – 10 of the 12 State governors under the Gowon regime were eventually found guilty of gross misappropriation of funds – while the on-governing military both deplored the resultant decline in prestige of the army and frequently engaged in intense competition for lucrative political appointments. Thus, far from their popular image as a united moral force operating 'above politics', the Nigerian military was, in fact, rent by a number of internal political cleavages. The vehemence of intra-military conflict is underlined by Martin Dent who writes that 'of the 300 or so officers with regular commissions in January 1966, something like 60 have been killed by their brother officers in the course of carrying out coups or executed following unsuccessful coups'. [36]

Third, conflicts were also produced within the governing coalition of military officers and civil servants. As the bureaucrats moved into policy-making, rather than policy-executing, positions, they too had become 'poiliticized' and highly visible. As in the case of the military, the civil service also developed an internal contradiction between those who desired to maintain the politically neutral, efficient and rationalized organization, and those who sought an even greater voice in political decision-making and with it a greater share of government 'outputs'.. In the absence of popularly chosen political mediating agencies, the civil service, as it moved toward increasing political involvement, came into direct conflict with the military itself:

The increasing visibility of the civil service and the perception among elites and non-elites in Nigeria that the civil service was a political actor made the civil service more vulnerable to the housecleaning that a new military leadership undertook in 1975. The civil service was now part of the political fray and thus fairer game. As some civil servants feared, the political activity of civil servants weakened the civil service as an institution. Some high level servants who were closely linked with the Gowon regime were not tolerated by the Mohammed regime. Low level civil servants and high level ones too became convenient scapegoats for a military regime itself vulnerable to charges of corrupt practices. [37]

Fourth, antagonism within the ruling classes also developed as those groups who, although now constituting an integral part of the socio-economic elite, did not enjoy a corresponding share of political power. In particular the class of large entrepreneurs and indigenous managers of multinational corporations — also the beneficiaries of indigenization — sought to rectify this imbalance between economic and political power to compensate for the top civil servants' inside track in the indigenization sweepstakes and to gain access to other sources of state largesse. Moreover, as the post-war political economy expanded and adapted in the ways discussed above, it objectively required a broaded basis of participation and decentralization of resource allocation, as well as adaptable institutions to contain and resolve intra-elite conflicts. The Gowon regime, however, beholden as it was to a narrow-based clique of top military officials, civil servants and big businessmen, both Nigerian and foreign, could not realize such reforms, since doing so would have undermined the power base upon which it rested. The old political classes with their greater responsiveness toward popular regional and sectoral needs, increasingly appeared a desirable alternative to the remote military government. Pressures for the return to power of these groups could not be abated even by overt attempts to 'buy off' the bourgeoisie with indigenization measures or with massive raises in public (1974) and private (1975) sector employees' salaries and emoluments.

If to these inter-related contradictions — intra-military conflicts, intra-bureaucracy differences, civil service - military and civil service - business rivalries, and growing ossification of the conflict-resolving capacities of government — one adds factors of gross mismanagement (ports congestion, botched 1973 census, inflation, deficient infrastructures), corruption (cement scandal, events in Benue-Plateau State) and a general weariness of military rule among the population, then the reasons for the third military coup in 1975 and its subsequent course of recivilianization are apparent. The Mohammed/Obasanjo regime, a self-styled 'corrective' transitional government, set out to inject efficiency, honesty and therefore resiliency into Nigerian political life. Within the parameters of these objectives, the regime was remarkably successful. It was able to resolve, or at least allay, a number of intra-elite contradictions by setting a firm timetable for military withdrawal from politics, while at the same time increasing the army's pre-eminence within the ruling coalition. The latter goal was largely achieved by a thorough purge of the bureaucracy, by further reducing the State governments' powers in favour of heightened centralism, and by embarking on an anti-corruption, pro-discipline crusade throughout the nation.

Entirely committed to its self-image as a transitional regime, the Mohammed/Obasanjo government evolved into 'a kind of symbiosis between bourgeois constitutionalism and military – civilian martial powers'.[37] In this way it effectively paved the way for a greater rationalization of the elite structure. The army resolved most of its internal tensions while remaining one of the major ruling groups with its privileges intact; the civil service withdrew from its overtly political role; the national bourgeoisie obtained a substantial share of political power, and a new group of professional politicians, organically linked to the latter two groups, re-entered the elite coalition. As intended, the political apparatus has remained a conflict-enancting and -regulating agency whose aim '. . . is to rationalize the purchase of state favour and the conversion of public resources to private advantage, not to eliminate it'.[38]

In view of the pronounced system-immanent character of the military itself, it is understandable that the civilian successor regime should display marked affinities with it. For, as is well known, departing military governors will seldom transfer power to civilians whose outlooks, socio-economic antecedents and political *Weltanschauungen* are too dissimilar to their own, since they will be concerned about policy reversals, loss of perquisites or even possible trials, retributive acts, etc.[40] No doubt such concerns were multiplied by the appearance in Ghana and Liberia, during the terminal stage of military disengagement in Nigeria, of the rank-and-file putsches led by Jerry Rawlings and Samuel Doe. Thus the military aimed at shaping and influencing the transition to civilian rule at every important stage. For example, the February 1976 creation of seven new states, the 1975-76 local government reforms and the 1977 Electoral Decree all represented military pre-emption of decisions which, strictly speaking, ought to have been taken within the new civilian governmental process (meaning also within the terms of reference of the Constituent Assembly). Similarly, the head of state, convening the constitution-making body, virtually prescribed a presidential structure, a system of federalism, public accountability, a multi-party system and in general, a liberal-democratic constitutional order,[41] while proscribing the adoption of 'any particular philosophy or ideology' from the constitution.

Recivilianization as a Holding Operation

Thus recivilianization and elite consolidation are the two sides of a single process. The implementation of a liberal – democratic political structure complements the neo-colonial capitalist economic system, and helps to vitiate a number of long-standing contradictions which have been discussed above.

1) Liberal democracy allows a functional interaction between elite agglutination and still-operative intra-elite conflicts. On the one hand, Nigerian elites have a collective interest in maintaining the neo-colonial capitalist basic order and securing it against any challenge from below. In this sense, one may speak, with Richard Sklar, of a 'fusion of elites'. The diverse elites in Nigeria, he argues, whether from business, public or private administrations, politics, the professions or prominent traditional elites, do represent different kinds and sources of power.

> Yet they identify with one another more firmly and in more ways than they do with their respective institutional bases or organizational activities. They appear to unite and act in concert — consciously so — on the basis of their common interest in social control, and this may be identified as the wellspring of class formation.[42]

The notion of political and economic domination by the elite classes as a whole, as against the masses, has recently gained currency in Markovitz' and Sklar's [43] attempts to conceptualize African elites as, respectively, an 'organizational bourgeoisie' or a 'managerial bourgeoisie' transcending all previous intra-elite cleavages such as modern - traditional, national - *comprador*, local - nationwide, technocratic - political and so on. But on the other hand — since state power and resources are finite — intra-elite competition persists, e.g., between dependent finance and industrial capital, or between regional capitals, so that the centre government has been converted into an arena for *limited* conflict-resolution of this kind. The multi-party system, the multiplicity of states and the structure of federalism provide the necessary institutional sensitivity and responsiveness to these pressures.

2) Since the Second Republic thus perpetuates elite rule and seeks to forestall substantial social change, it requires decisive and occasionally authoritarian leadership. But a permanent check must be provided against the dysfunctional exercise of such power. The presidential system presents itself as the appropriate means of resolving this contradiction. Klaus Hutschenreuter rightly sees the Nigerian and Ghanaian presidential democracies:

> as an example of how, on the one side, large sectors of the ruling bourgeoisie recognize the necessity for a strong hand, a powerful leadership, but on the other side endeavour to counteract, by means of constitutional safeguards of a bourgeois-democratic nature, any possible abuse of power, any tendencies (frequently evident in the past) toward the championing of group or sectoral interests at the expense of the interests of the relatively broad, forming new class. Further, these recent constitutions demonstrate an attempt normatively to confine the exercise of state power to pro-capitalist principles, partially mitigated by national or social reformism.[44]

3) Considered in the light of 1) and 2) above, ethnicity becomes a more complicating and problematic ingredient in the politics of elite rule. The collapse of the First Republic demonstrated that unbridled tribalism threatens the structure and boundaries of the state itself. For this reason both military and civilian elites have consistently guarded against its re-emergence. General Obasanjo warned at the height of the recivilianization exercises: 'Political recruitment and subsequent political support which are based on tribal, religious and linguistic sentiments contributed largely to our past misfortune. They must not be allowed to spring up again'. [45] The appeal was echoed by the five 'licensed' political parties, the mass media and the university dons. A number of provisions aimed at overcoming ethnic politics were anchored in the 1979 constitution, e.g., requirements that political party support must be nation-wide, that ethnic discrimination in any form be outlawed, that the federal cabinet include at least one member from each state, and that the personnel composition of all public agencies, save the armed forces, reflect 'the federal character of Nigeria'. But despite all these measures, ethnicity could not be simply wished (or legislated) away. The persistence of the neo-colonial capitalist order with all its contradictions provides no real basis for the extirpation of ethnic sentiments which are, after all, its product. In the absence of a system-transforming raison d'etre, the agglutinating elites still depend, for their mass following and legitimacy, on an ethnic support bloc. The mass social bases of the new political parties reveals this. Besides, the persistence of ethnicity, albeit now more functionally channelled, continues to retard the growth of popular awareness and to hamper class formation from below across ethnic boundaries, a tendency entirely in the interests of the elites. The 19-state federal structure helps to suspend this contradiction by providing an outlet for socio-cultural ethnic pluralism while sustaining the political-economic centralism which benefits the now 'nationalized' bourgeoisie.

4) And finally, recivilianization also has managed to resolve — or at least put into abeyance — a series of persistent elite-related problems. The state's more effective mediating capacities, for example, have all but eliminated the zero-sum quality of Nigerian politics, inasmuch as all factions perceive that losing an election does not mean losing everything. Indeed, there is evidence that an official opposition is already forming and coming to terms with its status. Gradually too, the capitalist bourgeoisie appears to be prevailing over communal and feudal remnants, as can be seen in the 1976 Local Government reforms, government land policies (Land Use Decree, etc.), and the elimination of the House of Chiefs from the political scene.[46] And the new political system has provided a number of necessary points of system access for younger, aspiring elite members. The 19 State civil services, the expanded federal civil service, the still-overbloated military, the new party bureaucracies and the patronage posts linked to them, all ensure the co-optation of a new generation of trained Nigerians.

In ters of its central purposes — consolidation of the elite formation process, maintenance of the neo-colonial capitalist order, production of legitmacy for both of these — the Second Republic has so far been demonstrably successful. Rather than an overwhelming number of competing political parties, the system has produced a manageable five relatively stable, system-maintaining political formations which could well be further reduced by the end of the current electoral period. Although the elections did demonstrate that the parties are still largely dependent on an ethnically defined mass basis, the national electoral machinery and constitutional provisions prevented any reversion to the structural factionalism of the First Republic.

But, as this chapter has sought to demonstrate, the abiding contradictions in the ruling classes' situation have not been eliminated, only suspended. Their pre-eminence rests now as before on the subordination of the urban and agrarian masses and the perpetuation of the have/have-not dichotomy in society. These in turn depend on continued economic growth, a growth whic which hitherto has failed to develop the productive forces of the economy. Thus the Second Republic harbours a number of potentially corrosive 'antitheses': the possibility of class formation from below with further industrialization, the eventual depletion of oil reserves, a resurgence of dysfunctional ethnicity, or a reversion to system-destroying intra-elite conflict.

Notes

1. I have already made an initial attempt in this direction: 'Political Economy, Political Class and Political System in Recivilianized Nigeria', Boston University, Walter Rodney African Studies Seminar, Working Paper No. 47, 1981, which admittedly wants for reliable, hard empirical data on insome distribution and class composition.
2. On this, see Yolamu R. Barongo, 'The Study of Development and Political Change in Nigerian Society: The Need for a Dialectical Orientation' in William D. Graf (ed.), *Towards a Political Economy of Nigeria: Critical Essays* (Benin City and Cambridge U.K., 1982).
3. For a critique of all these, and other, theories, see Stephen Katz, *Marxism, Africa and Social Class: A Critique of Relevant Theories* (Montreal, 1980), ch. 1.
4. Gavin Williams, Introduction to G. Williams (ed.), *Nigeria: Economy and Society* (London, 1976), pp. 1-2.
5. I use the term 'faulted bourgeoisie' in much the same way as Ralf Dahrendorf, in a different context, talks about a 'faulted nation'. See his *Society and Democracy in Germany* (London, 1967), p. 64. Although one has reservations about applying the term 'bourgeoisie' in the contemporary African context — since for Marx it refers to the owners of the means of production whereas in Africa ownership is qualified by state and foreign control, as will be discussed presently — one accepts current usage which seems to equate bourgeoisie with 'non-traditional dominant class'.
6. Ralph Miliband, *Marxism and Politics* (London and Oxford, 1977), p. 109.

7. Claude Ake, 'Explanatory Notes on the Political Economy of Africa', *The Journal of Modern African Studies*, Vol. 14, No. 1, 1976, p. 3.
8. That tribalism originated under the colonial system of indirect rule and economic sectoralization is at least implicit in the discussion so far, and cannot be demonstrated in detail here. Robin Cohen posits a high degree of 'congruence between inter-class and inter-ethnic relationships' in his 'Class in Africa: Analytical Problems and Perspectives', *Socialist Register 1972*, p.244. Further, see Okwudiba Nnoli, *Ethnic Politics in Nigeria* (Enugu, 1978), esp. p.iii et seq. Conceptually useful is Archie Mafeje, 'The Ideology of Tribalism', *The Journal of Modern African Studies*, Vol. IX, No. 2, 1971, pp. 253-6.
9. Yolamu R. Barongo, 'Ethnic Pluralism [in Nigeria] and Democratic Stability: The Basis of Conflict and Consensus', paper presented to 5th annual conference of the Nigerian Political Science Association, April 1978, mimeo., p.9. A revised version of this paper appears in S.E. Oyovbaire (ed.), *Democracy in Nigeria: Interpretation Essays* (Benin City, Koda Publishers Ltd, forthcoming.)
10. Cohen op. cit., p.248.
11. Richard Sandbrook, *Proletarians and African Capitalism: The Case of Kenya 1960-72* (Cambridge, 1974), p. 11.
12. Billy J. Dudley, *Instability and Political Order: Politics and Nigeria in Crisis* (Ibadan, 1973), p. 35.
13. On this 'triangular elite alliance', see Gavin Williams and Terisa Turner, 'Nigeria' in John Dunn (ed.), *West African States: Failure and Promise* (Cambridge-New York-Melbourne, 1978), p. 153; and Terisa Turner, 'Commercial Capitalism and the 1975 Coup' in Keith Panter-Brick (ed.), *Soldier and Oil: The Political Transformation of Nigeria* (London, 1978), pp. 166-7.
14. Timothy Shaw, 'Nigeria's Political Economy: Capitalism, Constitutions and Contradictions', *ODI Review*, No. 2, 1980, p. 80.
15. A term coined by Cohen, *op. cit.*
16. For reasons of convenience 'State' refers to a component unit of federalism, while 'state' refers to the national political structure.
17. Terisa Turner, 'Multinational Corporations and the Instability of the Nigerian State', *Review of African Political Economy*, Vol. 5, 1976, p. 69.
18. I have considered this process at greater length elsewhere: 'The "Nationalization" of the Nigerian Political Class and the "Particularization" of the Second Republic', paper presented to 7th annual conference of the Nigerian Political Science Association, May 1980.
19. Peter Waterman, 'Capitalist Development, Labour Control Strategy and the Working Class Movement in Nigeria' and in Graf, op. cit.
20. See, respectively, Ake, op. cit. and I. V. Sledzevsky, 'Entwicklungsprobleme des Staatskapitalismus in Nigeria der siebziger Jahre', *asien-afrika-lateinamerika*, Vol. 2, No. 7, 1979, p. 277; and Waterman, op. cit.
21. As the constitution makers of the Second Republic would have it, when they suggest that the mixed economy ideology is the appropriate one for Nigeria as against 'foreign' doctrines of socialism.
22. Derivation is a principle applied to the formula of revenue allocation to the States' in the Federal Republic of Nigeria whereby the States'

percentage share of national revenue is determined in relation to the size of revenue derived or originating from that State.
23. Sledzevsky, op. cit., p. 273.
24. Paul Collins, 'The Policy of Indigenization: An Overall View', *Quarterly Journal of Administration*, Vol. IX, No. 2, January 1975, p. 144.
25. Paul Collins, 'Public Policy and the Development of Indigenous Capitalism: The Nigerian Experience', *Journal of Commonwealth and Comparative Politics*, Vol. XV, No. 2, July 1977, p. 127; further see his 'The Political Economy of Indigenization: The Case of the Nigerian Enterprises Promotion Decree', *The African Review*, No. 4, 1976, p. 493 et seq.
26. As suggested by E.O. Akeredolu-Ale, 'Some Thoughts on the Indigenization Process and the Quality of Nigerian Capitalism' in Nigerian Economic Society (ed.), *Nigeria's Indigenization Policy: Proceedings of the November 1974 Symposium*, Ibadan 1974, p. 69.
27. As coined in Nigerian Economic Society, op. cit., p. 68.
28. Collins, 'Public Policy', op. cit., p. 141.
29. Ibid.
30. Ibid., p. 143.
31. Ibid.
32. Ibid.
33. Gavin Williams, 'Nigeria: A Political Economy' in Williams, op. cit., p. 29.
34. Olatunde J.B. Ojo, 'Federal-State Relations 1967-1974', *Quarterly Journal of Administration*, Vol. X, January 1976, p. 116.
35. The 'overdeveloped state' theory is set out in Hamzi Alavi, 'The State in Postcolonial Societies: Pakistan and Bangladesh', *New Left Review*, Vol. 74, July-August 1972, pp. 59-81; and is qualified by W. Ziemann and M. Lanzendörfer, 'The State in Peripheral Societies', *Socialist Register 1977*, pp. 143-77.
36. Martin Dent, 'Corrective Government: Military Rule in Perspective' in Panter-Brick, op. cit., p. 131.
37. Henry Bienen with Martin Fitton, 'Soldiers, Politicians and Civil Servants' in Panter-Brick, op. cit., p. 52-3.
38. Klaus Hutschenreuter, 'Einige Grundzüge der Fortbildung der politischen Systeme sowie des Staats — und Verfassungsrechts in Landern Afrikas und Asiens mit kapitalistischer Entwicklung', *asien-afrika-lateinamerika*, Vol. 3, No. 8, 1980, p. 434.
39. P. Collins, G. Williams and T. Turner, 'Capitalism and the Coup' in Williams, op. cit., p. 191.
40. On this see the two articles by Claude Welch Jr., 'Praetorianism in Commonwealth West Africa', *Journal of Modern African Studies*, Vol. X, No. 2, July 1972, p. 213; and 'The Dilemma of Military Withdrawal from Politics: Some Considerations from Tropical Africa', *African Studies Review*, Vol. 17, April 1974, p. 231. See also, following Welch, L.O. Dare, 'The Dilemma of Military Disengagement: The Nigerian Case', *Nigerian Journal of Economic and Social Studies*, Vol. 16, No. 2, July 1974, p. 297 et seq.
41. This may be inferred from Murtala Mohammad's address to the Constitution Drafting Committee's opening session, 18 October 1975,

reproduced in *Report of the Constitution Drafting Committee Containing the Draft Constitution*, Lagos 1976, vol. I, pp. xli-xlii.
42. Richard L. Sklar, 'The Nature of Class Domination in Africa', *Journal of Modern African Studies,* Vol. 17, No. 4, 1979, pp. 537-8.
43. See Irving Leonard Markovitz, *Power and Class in Africa* (Engelwood Cliffs N.J., 1977), pp. 208-9; and Sklar, op. cit., p. 546.
44. Hutschenreuter, op. cit., pp. 439-40.
45. *West Africa*, 2 October 1978, p. 937.
46. On this see Uzodinma, 'Ideological Dependency and the Problem of Autonomy in Nigeria', *Journal of Asian and African Studies*, Vol. XIV, Nos. 1-2, p. 61.

16. Essence and Empiricism in African Politics

Otwin Marenin

What is 'essence' and what is 'appearance' in African politics? Does class or interest-group analysis describe and explain the various realities? These questions are unanswerable without an examination of the methods behind such claims to correct understanding. All claims to knowledge are arbitrary until the methods of enquiry and the justification for their validity are made explicit.

I shall focus on Marxist analyses of African politics, and specifically on their methodological assumptions and justifications. The fundamental problem is the empirical verification of the concept 'false consciousness', for without a solution to the question of how falsity or correctness can be determined empirically, all claims for the correctness of any Marxist analysis of social life remain abstract, philosophical, and metaphysical. False consciousness points to a posited relationship of data and theory — of what can be observed to what can be interpreted — in Marxist thought. Its alleged scientific nature needs to be determined, and this requires a careful study of the relation of data to theory: the assertion that Marxist analyses provide the best understanding of reality — more true than competing forms of thought — needs epistemological justification.

Marxist writers claim that 'objective' bourgeois social science is superficial and descriptive — that is, ahistorical, static, fragmented, and deceptive. In effect, the accusation is that Western scholars are the bearers of false consciousness, since their methods systematically misrepresent reality; they study 'appearances' and describe the mere forms of life, as opposed to its underlying and determinate structure, the 'essence' of reality.

How is this distinction arrived at? How do Marxist scholars ply their craft, and do they follow the tenets of their own argument? In what ways are the results of their labour distinguishable from other forms of analysis? Empirical studies that use a Marxist approach have to describe in order to explain the complexities of social life — how are these descriptions different from interest-group analyses? Is the distinction between explanation and description, between what Marxist scholars do compared to others, reducible to the claim of 'correct' or 'false' consciousness? Does this distinction amount to an empirical, a theoretical, or a philosophical claim? By what criteria do Marxists attribute 'superficiality' to the work of other writers? In short, what is the basis for the distinction? How is it applied? Can it be upheld empirically? We cannot begin to answer these questions without examining the concept of false consciousness.

An example will make the issues raised here more explicit. In an article on class development in Africa, Bernard Magubane criticizes bourgeois scholarship for its concern with details and description, leading to a general incapacity to understand the overall 'structural relations' necessitated by the world system.[1] Efforts to define and locate class in the consciousness of people must fail, he argues, since consciousness is not the determining factor. The ability to make and recognize significant, rather than irrelevant, distinctions and categories of social life — for example, that class rather than ethnic identity is important — is lost, and 'superficial empiricism substitutes for the study of the underlying non-empirical structural reality'. What scholars should do, instead, is to follow the Marxist method of successive approximations, moving step by step from the abstract to the concrete. The 'determination of fundamental classes in society is not a task of empirical observation, but one for theoretical investigation of the relations of production that are the foundation of society'. The existence of classes is given; recognizing them depends on correct theorizing, and not on techniques of observation. Bourgeois theorists, though, fail to realize this, and mistake the specific forms of social existence for absolutes, without spotting the mediating elements which tie specific forms of group consciousness to the 'modes of being or the conditions that determine it', thereby confusing 'the essence of society with its outward appearance'. Africans who think that their interests lie with ethnic groupings also suffer from false consciousness.[2]

How does Magubane know what is non-empirical reality? More precisely, since essence is observable only through correct theorizing, how does he distinguish correct from false theorizing? He states that he will 'adopt a Marxian framework of the analysis of social classes in colonial and post-colonial Africa'.[3] The 'objective is to develop a theoretical understanding of certain definite conditions which do not exist in a pure form or empirically', and this must begin with an analysis of the 'structural and specific nature of capitalist production', and 'the workings of imperialism and monopoly capitalism'.[4] Classes, then, are the 'personification of the central economic categories of a given system of production'.[5] 'To study the class structure of modern Africa requires the study of the determinate mode of production — the CCMP (the colonial capitalist mode of production).'[6] His answer, then, is that Marxist theory reveals the essence, and he feels no obligation to justify why this should be so.

Of course, it might be argued that Magubane could develop the justification were he so inclined, elaborating on his statement that 'In contrast to the study of the superficial aspects of social life, the concept of class focuses attention on the various planes, contradictions, possibilities of analysis of human exploitation, and the possibility of liberation'.[7] This may explain what class analysis will produce, but it does not explain how essential reality is indeed perceived. After all, we are limited to sense perceptions and recognitions of appearances. So, how is the correct theoretical understanding achieved? How is it justified? It must be more than a question of 'just accept this method and you will know correctly'. What then is Marx's method, and why is the notion of false consciousness so crucial? Clearly, Marxist scholars do use data. On what basis do they determine those facts which are only 'appearance' and those which reveal 'essence'?

Consciousness and Class Consciousness

Class consciousness is, in Bertell Ollman's phrase, 'the theoretical link in Marxism between determined conditions and determined response'. [8] A class is not a class until it becomes aware of its common interests counterposed to the common interest of other classes, and organized consciously and purposefully to promote its interests by attempting to overthrow the system of which it is part, if that system is against its interests. A failure to become correctly aware of this interest within the totality of social life is 'false consciousness'. When people subscribe to an 'ideology that is inconsistent with their material base and therefore unwittingly respond to the call for their own exploitation', they think wrongly and will not act. [9] False consciousness conceals: the 'real motive forces impelling [the individual] remain unknown to him'; [10] theories yield wrong guidelines and 'prevent man from adjusting himself at that historical stage' [11] and 'objective conditions themselves cannot reach their full maturity'. [12] False consciousness is a systematic misperception of reality and the inherent potential for change.

Consciousness separates essence from appearance, and without a notion of false consciousness the distinction would be impossible. In Lucien Goldman's words:

> human action can no longer be defined by its actual reality without reference to the potential reality which it seeks to bring into being. The concept of actual consciousness must be supplemented by that of *bezogenes Bewusstsein* — the distinction which Marx made between class in itself and class for itself and without which we shall never understand anything about historical and social life.[13]

The validity of Marxist thought thus rests on the validity of 'imputed' consciousness, the argument that consciousness can be categorized by its truth content.

This claim is not easily accepted. Peter Berger thinks that the very notion of such graduated levels is 'cognitive imperialism', and sees 'no philosophical and scientific method by which this variety can be arranged in a hierarchy from lower to higher'. [14] W. G. Runciman believes it to be 'an arbitrary decision pure and simple, an ineluctable discretion' which the social scientist has in selecting his concepts. [15] According to Richard Sanbrook and Jack Arn, the classification is done by the degree to which what is found agrees with the observer's personal 'conception of progressive ideas'.[16] Robin Cohen feels that the concept is part of a whole 'set of now largely sterile aphorisms'.[17] Immanuel Wallerstein argues that consciousness is not an essential factor anyway, and will automatically come into being when objective conditions are right: 'An objective class status is only a reality in so far as it becomes a subjective reality for some group or groups and if it "objectively" exists, it inevitably will be felt subjectively'.[18]

> By relating consciousness to the whole of society it becomes possible to infer the thoughts and feelings which men would have in a particular situation if they were able to assess both it and the interests arising from it .... Class consciousness consists in fact of the appropriate and rational reactions 'imputed' to a particular typical position in the process of production.[19]

The actual beliefs an observer might find through research are not thereby correct, and in general Lukacs would argue that what is found is normally false. The imputation of correct and false consciousness is not through observation, but presupposes a theory of world history — in the past, now, and in the future. Since the proletariat is the future world class, its interpretation, or rather the imputed consciousness appropriate for the world proletariat, represents the criterion against which other judgments are measured. In Martin Shaw's words, Marxism and true consciousness are 'the intellectual forms of the practical movement of a certain class'.[20]

Knowledge of the reality and potential of history, in turn, demands a way of knowing. False and true depends on the validity of the method by which history is correctly understood, and on the basis of which it is categorized. Lukacs, therefore, answers his question 'What is orthodox Marxism?', by saying that 'orthodoxy refers exclusively to method'.[21] In sum, 'false consciousness' creates a wrong understanding of the world and its requirements for action because the perspective adopted is not that of the imputed 'revolutionary' proletariat. The concept points to the paradigmatic gap between bourgeois and Marxist science, which is fundamentally about what methods are proper to inquiry; that is, to the distinction between scientific positivism and dialectical understanding.

Problematizing a Marxist Methodology

What is this method? As Shaw argues, one has to be 'clear on the nature of Marxist theory', for otherwise it will be 'impossible to adequately define relevant empirical and critical work'.[22] For Marx, creating knowledge is a process of production — not merely finding the reflection of essence or appearance in language — which aims to develop the correct 'objects of knowledge' in theorizing. Knowledge flows from the ability to link 'thought totalities' with 'concrete totalities' by means of models. According to Robert

Tristram, Marx's methodological project for the creation of knowledge implies 'both the development of abstract theory and the construction of models of concrete processes'. [23] A 'model' such as, for example, 'the capitalist mode of production', is a specific statement of the concrete objective totality of the world using abstract concepts of the thought totality. Knowledge is not reflection, but arises from the interaction of thought and reality leading to an opposed and 'mediated unity between *essendi* and *cognoscenti*'. [24] In Lukacs's terminology, the concrete is the specific manifestation of the universality of the world, and correct knowledge is the specific manifestation of proletarian consciousness.

Marxism is then first of all a method, an 'essential heuristic tool'. [25] Marx is 'not a vendor of ready made truths but a maker of tools'. [26] These have been hammered into a variety of forms, ranging from an emphasis on Hegelian dialectics to imitations of positivist science, albeit with a materialist conception of reality. [27] The Hegelian variant is represented in Lukacs, Herbert Marcuse, or Martin Shaw; [28] the 'right-wing' deviations may be found in 'Stalinist' models of the universal laws of the dialectic. [29] Consciousness is central to the former, but matters little to the materialists.

Since much Marxist writing on Africa, especially when utilizing the superficial/essential distinction, has been influenced by Lukacs – a debt not always acknowledged – I shall concentrate on what he holds to be the key concepts of dialectical thought, namely: totality, change, mediation, and practice. First of all, things and events must be understood in their historical relation, not as isolated facts having characteristics in and of themselves. Since all is unity in world history, 'parts and aspects of that unity cannot be understood without reference to the dialectically developing whole (and its internal contradictions)'. [30] A theory of history is a necessity for understanding social phenomena, and will 'provide the standards for an objective critique of given social institutions which would measure their function and their aims against the historical potentialities of human freedom'. [31] Only world history in its totality can function to deny or affirm the truth of theoretical statement. To paraphrase Marcuse, to understand a glass of water one must understand the whole history of the world.

Secondly, all thought categories must be seen as dynamic and changing, since reality is ever in flux, possessing no permanent character, but experiencing qualitative and quantitative changes. Thirdly, knowledge is grounded and mediated. Actuality is 'mere immediacy' of the world, [32] and is not truly understood until linked to the social conditions from which it springs, and which can provide the 'historical agency for change'. Perception which is not mediated, not filtered through the standpoint of the proletariat, is of necessity incorrect. 'The essential link between "knowledge" and "consciousness" in Marxism itself [is] the connection between Marxist theory and the standpoint of the proletariat . . . the only clear basis for its incisive, critical and scientific viewpoint.' [33] The creation of knowledge always occurs within a historically given context, and cannot therefore be created in the abstract, for 'no-one is in a position to speak for the "general" relationship between "knowledge" and "reality" '. [34]

Lastly, knowledge requires practice for its validation, for only practice breaks through the unreality of the existing world. Reality itself is false, already a counterfeit, and cannot be the source of knowledge. Only action can do this, and the very act of changing the world brings into being the possibilities of knowing correctly. Practice confirms and creates knowledge, and concretizes abstractness. Correct theory is verified by practice:

> The criteria of assessment are not those of 'analytical clarity', 'logical consistency' or 'empirical generality' viewed as abstract criteria, as the 'scientific' social theorists would have them, but these criteria are considered in relation to the tasks of organization and political action.[35]

The solution to a real problem — namely that faced by the proletariat in changing the world — is action. In the words of Lukacs, 'in the age of capitalism it is not possible for the total system to become directly visible in external phenomena'. [36] That possibility awaits the practical transformation of the capitalist system, although indicators for correct understanding can be found in current times by the imputation of proletarian consciousness.

The opposition of universality (explaining reality) and temporality (describing appearances) is solved in this dialectical movement from totality through mediation to praxis. The ahistorical separation of subject and object is transcended in the revolutionary act which creates, and thereby confirms, thought and action simultaneously. Hegelian dialectics cuts 'the Gordian knot' of alienation. Universality and temporality are one and separate at once. A fact is concrete, rather than superficial, as it reveals the universal in the particular, and in revealing transcends both. Consciousness is the agency for this process, for it mediates between totality and praxis. If false, totality is misunderstood and praxis misguided.

The argument for a dialectical approach implies a critique of different forms of thought which find their base and are mediated in non-proletarian existence. For Lukacs, there are '*a priori* limits or advantages conferred by affiliation with the bourgeoisie or the proletariat upon the mind's capacity to apprehend external reality'. [37] Bourgeois thought is necessarily abstracted from existence, being essentially contemplative and non-active; while proletarian thought, based on actual experience under capitalism, sees history necessarily in terms of change, since that is the proletariat's own status as an object of history, and leads necessarily to union of thought and action as the proletariat grasps for the role of subject in history. Bourgeois and proletarian thought are not distinguishable by their content, by the specific beliefs held, but by the inner logic of history which structures the form of perception and explanations available. A bourgeois and a proletarian will see the same colour red or observe a strike, but, for Lukacs, the former will necessarily perceive the colour and the action in a static and ahistorical way, as real in themselves, while the latter will perceive them as part of the historical process, as appearance foreshadowing change. Intellectual leadership, then, requires the development of a proletarian way of thought. This question has always posed one of the fundamental challenges to the validity of Marxist thinkers who normally are not proletarian by birth. Antonio Gramsci's solution is the development of organic intellectuals, [38] while Colin Leys argues for the conscious adoption of the perspective of working class. [39]

For Lukacs, reality is not portrayed by sense, but by the mind which, as it understands, reflects and imposes its own forms upon the raw material of experience:

> Asserting the possibility of privileged insight into the logic of history, Lukacs, by implication, affirmed that philosophical conclusions were independent of the findings available to empirical sociologists, economists and political theorists. [40]

The contrast is between what is imagined in thought and what is found through observation. Authentic objectivity depends on the mediation of reality through categories of thought, specifically proletarian consciousness as the correct theoretical tool which pries open the essence of world history. The future will validate, ultimately. What is observable is not the determining criterion for correct consciousness. The reverse holds true, since accepting the appearance of things as determining is a form of false consciousness.

Marxism's Claim to Uniqueness
The uniqueness of Marxist thought lies in its methodology, and little else; otherwise its claims to understanding reality would be judged by scientific methods that are common to other approaches, and might be found inaccurate. The singularity and integrity of Marxist thought can only be maintained if isolated from bourgeois scientific inquiry; Marxism must have its own distinct method. This is precisely the argument advanced by Lukacs for the resurrection of the Hegelian dialectic as Marxist orthodoxy; the claims of this mode of thought and validation cannot be judged by the canons of bourgeois science, but only in terms of the laws of dialectical action, the production of thought and reality. The 'real' is not what is immediately perceived by the senses — bourgeois scientists are wrong when they think it is — for that is 'mere immediacy', but can only be known through mediated inquiry through the dialectical interaction of thought and matter, culminating in praxis. The essential core of reality, its character as a movement of totality historically given, is apparent only in terms of the 'conceptual reproduction of reality' and prior 'knowledge of the concrete totality'. [41] Marxist methodology must be anti-bourgeois and, since bourgeois science had staked its claims to validity on the basis of appearance, must also be anti-empirical.

In general, bourgeois and Marxist scholars differ in the way that the connection is made between thought and reality. For the former, something is proved (true, even though temporarily) by the preponderance of the evidence, and found false by examples; while for the latter, reality furnished examples which concretize an accepted theoretical understanding. The difference is between finding a pattern in order to build a theory, and having a theory and finding it exemplified.

The distinction between 'superficial' and 'essential' is not about proper facts but proper ideas. The validity of the analysis is achieved through theory, and this comes first. In Marcuse's words, 'the concrete is the specific manifestation of the essential in history. The idea gives shape and meaning to what we observe'. [42] The observable is always the particular, and only theory in application reveals the concrete, the essential within the appearance. Nicos Poulantzas expresses it differently, but the point is the same. To remain at the empirical level is not enough. The epistemological terrain must be displaced, the ideological organization of facts must be criticized by the scientific concepts of Marxist theory. [43] Facts do not destroy other explanation, but ideological critiques do. A preoccupation with empiricism risks undermining one's own theoretical problematic. It follows from this argument that appearances — whether facts as observed, or motivations that people feel — do not determine. Profit, for example, is not so much a concept as 'an objective category that designates a part of realized surplus values'. [44] Data are important in terms of how well they describe the 'actualization of the objective role' played by events and concepts, and they are irrelevant otherwise.

What, in practice, are the implications of these prescriptions for a Marxist social scientist? To explain something, do we have to understand the whole of history? Clearly, this is not possible each and every time, and can only mean that the past — history in its totality — must be categorized and reduced to key assumptions and concepts which function as sign-posts to a road not travelled, but well-known. As Stanislav Ossowski points out, 'Marxist circles have developed an unusual technique for employing vague metaphors', [45] for using semantic conventions as if they were social facts; these are the shorthand symbols for an underlying totality in theory and reality. However, this reduction of history to semantic conventions cannot be tested by research into specific complexities, for this would require re-opening the model. 'Understanding' history, then, is a *pro forma* exercise.

Marxist Mysticism

The semantic conventions which characterize Marxist writing are most apparent in the discussion of method, and frequently take on an almost religious tone. A leap to understand occurs — as Soren Kierkegaard jumped into the abyss? [46] — facts are 'transcended', and they 'illuminate' theory. These words seem to point towards some ineluctable process whereby the real meaning of social life becomes transparent, and the doors of perception (to use Huxley's phrase) are thrown wide. There is little that seems controllable about this process — certainly nothing systematic and scientific — in the same way that the mystic could not manipulate his 'blinding light'. Such phrases are not guidelines for action to producers of knowledge.

Marxist reconstructions of reality bypass many of the concerns of bourgeois social science: the problems of 1) generalizing from unique events ('the model provides the necessary concepts'); 2) comparing different contexts ('the model has universal applicability'); 3) testing explanations and theories ('the model is theoretically valid, and cannot be proved or disproved by reality'); and 4) accuracy ('the model is a guide to practice, and produces the desired results'). In general, there is little concern with the fundamental problems of epistemology, the bases and ways of knowing correctly about reality. The question is not whether the class struggle exists, but how it manifests itself; not whether labour alone creates value, but how value is expropriated from labour.

It is difficult to get a hold on the actual method, of what should be done specifically as a Marxist social scientist. Ollman lays down five steps in the production of knowledge, discerning these in Marx's own practice — ontology, epistemology, inquiry, reconstruction, and exposition. [47] Explanation starts from the abstract, a consideration of the nature of the world, and works towards the concrete. In proper perspective, workers become the proletariat, and strikes become class action. The model illuminates specific facts. Still, this description remains at an abstract level, sketching the main areas in which decisions must be made, but not how to make them.

A clear exposition of Marxist methodology in the Hegelian vein is Mao Tse-tung's article 'On Practice', first published in 1937. [48] The acquisition of knowledge involves a three-stage process from 1) the perceptual stage of cognition, to 2) conception, judgment and inference, or rational knowledge, to 3) social practice. Perceptions reveal mere phenomena, the 'separate aspects and the external relations of things'. [49] As these sense impressions accumulate through social practise and experience;

> a sudden change (leap) takes place in the brain in the process of cognition, and concepts are formed. Concepts . . . grasp the essence, the totality and the internal relations of things. Between concepts and sense perceptions there is not only a quantitative but also a qualitative difference. Proceeding further, by means of judgement and inference, one is able to draw logical conclusions. [50]

How is this done? Mao Tse-tung explains:

> Fully to reflect a thing in its totality, to reflect its essence, to reflect its inherent laws, it is necessary through the exercise of thought to reconstruct the rich data of sense perception, discarding the dross and selecting the essential, eliminating the false and retaining the true, proceeding from the one to the other and from the outside to the inside, in order to form a system of concepts and theories — it is necessary to make a leap from perceptual to rational knowledge. [51]

The truth of this leap is tested 'by objective results in social practice'.[52] 'Knowledge is verified only when it achieves the anticipated result in the process of social practice (material production, class struggle, or scientific experiment).'[53] Practice means the appropriate revolutionary action at a given historical stage of objective development; practice works and shows truth, because it parallels — that is, reflects and affects — the development of the 'objective process itself'.[54] Knowledge, then, is an open-ended process, a struggle cycling to higher levels as theory and practice interact dialectically.

This argument raises a number of questions, specifically the notion of a leap to rational knowledge, and of practice as the validation of truth. How the distinction is to be made between false and true, between dross and essential data, and by what criteria, is not really clear — unless one presupposes a theoretical assumption, namely that of an objective process of development independent of knowledge. The essential and the dross are then simply data which fit or do not fit the theory. But if the theory exists, and must exist prior to sense perceptions, no leap is necessary. The criterion of practice is also problematic, since it cannot mean any knowledge which works when used, a crude form of pragmatism (imperialism 'works' in that sense), but must refer to a specific form of knowledge, namely that which reinforces the objective process itself. How is failure distinguished from success? Do revolutions which fail indicate the falseness of the knowledge which guided them? The answer is probably 'yes', or 'yes'/'no' as regards tactics, but 'no' in the sense of the objective process itself.

How is this objective process, which functions as the criterion of truth, known? Neither by the leap nor by the practice, since it is itself the standard by which the validity of both concepts and practice is determined. The 'objectivity', the essence of the historical process in its totality, must be known prior to sense perceptions, thought, or action, if it is to function as the standard for distinguishing form from appearance, vulgar pragmatism from revolutionary practice.

Problems with Class Analysis

Another difficulty as regards making the Marxist distinction between 'superficial' and 'essential' concerns the nature of class analysis itself — namely, the specification of the structure that exists at historic periods. Since the concepts are abstract and theoretical, how can their empirical counterparts be found? For example, as explained by Catherine Coquery-Vidrovitch, 'The notion of the mode of production should be understood to be a theoretical model. Concretely, societies do not produce in the schematic form.'[55] Yet the labels 'superficial' and 'essential' refer always to the specific condition.

It is not easy to identify the class structure at any given time. As Ossowski made clear, Marx himself found it difficult to decide how to describe contemporary class relations, and vacillated over a number of criteria.[56] It is clear from several studies that, once past the notion that there are classes, any categorization only provokes disagreement. This practical difficulty points to a more fundamental problem; ascribing 'class consciousness' is not simply a matter of attitudes and subjective feelings, but a question of the objective class structure. Yet models of what actually exists differ among Marxist writers. For Claude Ake, any model which employs more than two classes is a distortion:

> [It is] a serious theoretical inconsistency to move from the core ideas of the Marxian concept of class to posit that more than two classes can exist in one society at one time – and it is an inconsistency which will have the practical effect of drastically diminishing the analytic value of the concept of class. [57]

Poulantzas thinks that Ralph Miliband's work is basically descriptive, disageeing with his methods and results; [58] Ira Gerstein accuses Wallerstein of being ahistorical in his explanation of how the world system developed; [59] John Horton and Fari Filsoufi think that Lukacs suffers from infantile disorders. In short, there is disagreement about the actual class structure, and such errors lead to the wrong designation of what is superficial and essential in specific studies. [60] Ossowski concludes that the determination of class 'must ultimately be reached by intuitive judgments made in a given milieu about the importance of various criteria, or by considering practical consequences and the requirements of action'. [61] If this is correct, as the disputes cited above indicate, what guidelines, if any, exist for the exercise of intuition?

What is clear is that even if the value of class analysis is accepted this does not determine our findings, since these are likely to be determined by various assumptions concerning class structure. In this context, 'essential' means those descriptions which are congruent or based on a specific model of class relation, not just class analysis as a method. False consciousness for the social scientist is the failure to pre-construct the right class-structure model.

Finally, how seriously are we to take the assertion that there is a revolutionary unity in Marxist thought and action?, that one cannot be divorced from the other, without losing the correctness of both? For clearly, the majority of Marxists embody in their life-styles just as much disjunction as do bourgeois academics; yet they do not, therefore, disclaim the validity of their ideas, or see themselves as hypocritical, or as falsely conscious. This is not just a 'Why don't you practice what you preach?' critique, but points to the fact that the distinction between correct and false consciousness as ascertained by method is not upheld. Theory reflects an emerging reality – in the phraseology of Karl Korsh, 'scientific socialism is the theoretical expression of a revolutionary process' [62] yet academic Marxism, being neither created by nor active in the revolutionary process, comprises its claim to 'truth' by its own arguments.

There is, as well, the practical question of what is revolutionary in specific circumstances. It is not as if it were obvious what produces, and what hinders, revolutionary progress; if it were so, arguments among Marxists would have been avoided. Historically, revolutionary changes are known only retrospectively.

The question of method in Marxist thought seems unresolved; and it is the main argument of this article that many Marxist scholars have not felt obliged to defend, or even establish, their method. They have relied instead on the assertion that theory determines everything, and this despite the fact that Marxism is seen as fundamentally a method, a way of analysis and action, that leads to correct understanding.

Marxist Methodology in African Studies

Let us turn to specific studies of class in Africa. These are legion, and most simply apply a Marxist framework, and its implicit epistemological justification, without worrying about methodology or recognizing any debt to Hegel and Lukacs. The issues raised earlier about the empirical nature of Marxist analysis can be examined by looking at what has been written about method (albeit not much) and about class. Both concepts must deal with what it means to be conscious. What are the implications of how analysis in these two areas has been done for the coherence and validity of Marxist thought — is the dialectical methodology used and upheld? How well is the argument supported that the relevant consciousness in Africa is class, rather than ethnic or interest group?

Dubious Claims to Knowledge
Claude Ake, in recent writings, raises the question of the relationship of data to concepts. Marx's notion that consciousness is necessary for a class to exist, at least *für sich*, poses an

> empirical problem of deciding where classes exist and where class analysis may be usefully applied. At what point do we decide that politicization of the basic contradiction in production relations has occurred? ... once we ... remember that politicization can be masked and 'distorted' in all kinds of ways. For instance, class conflict may be disguised as ethnic or religious conflict, and political conflicts — even very serious ones — may not have a class base. [63]

His answer is that Marx, in using consciousness as an element in the formation of class, was not really defining class by consciousness, but merely 'describing class as it is during a crucial stage in its metamorphosis'. The relevance of this analysis for Africa is 'still unresolved', and trying to use it as a method is 'full of hazards'. Still, Ake opts for class analysis on the grounds that 'if we can make a case for the existence of a basic [that is, class] contradiction in the relations of production, we can make a case for class analysis also. For ... the contradiction ... is pregnant with the future.' [64] Obviously, this case can be made, and the role of ethnic sentiments necessarily becomes a cloak for, or hindrance to, the development of class action. Class relations exist objectively, that is in potentiality, though not as yet in the consciousness or the reality of people's actions.

Ake arrives at the knowledge of the existence of the basic contradiction from a global model of conflict and a dichotomous class structure. Still, he is not free of the influence of positivist science – of which his first book was a good example [65] – nor its ideological presumptions. 'Primordial solidaristic ties have shown a remarkable resiliency in the face of the onslaught of capitalism. Many workers remain peasants at heart.' [66] He follows Karl Popper by arguing that 'logic is not truth', and 'empirical evidence, which has been provided by history itself, has . . . compelled a theoretical rebuttal of the assumption that socialist revolution always comes in the wake of the advanced development of productive forces.' [67] Evidence disconfirms theory.

Yet, Ake is not entirely consistent in his use of evidence, and the reason why facts disprove some theories, or elements of theories, and not others, is not really spelled out. His attempt to explain the existence of a revolutionary situation in Africa shows this clearly:

> A revolutionary situation exists . . . because the objective conditions are such that the class struggle presents itself immediately as the struggle for state power . . . When I say that a revolutionary situation exists in Africa, I am talking about the character of the class struggle (its quality), not about its intensity (its quantity). Its intensity may well be quite limited. However that is beside the point: a revolutionary situation exists nevertheless, in as much as the class struggle focuses on state power.[68]

That is, even though there is no class struggle that can be observed, the situation is revolutionary because if a class struggle were to occur (Ake outlines two scenarios), it would be revolutionary. The nature of the revolutionary situation, the quality of the class struggle, its 'essence', exists – the theory linking class to state power – even though its appearance is not as yet concretely shown. In this case, facts do not disconfirm. His elaboration of scenarios comes close to interest-group analysis. Factions of the ruling class will appeal to allies, on the basis of tribe, region, and religion. The dynamics of the revolution, when it comes, will not be seen in a class struggle, but in factional disputes. The similarity to polyarchy is obvious, in the description of how groups will interact – though not in the outcome postulated.

Joel Samoff examines the nature of class and class conflict in Africa, and argues that a new paradigm is required, one which does away with the Weberian and Parsonian influences existing even within Marxist thought. 'Entirely different concepts, categories, definitions and even rules for scientific inquiry' are necessary. [69] Things cannot be defined in 'terms of themselves', as if they could exist identically in different situations, but must include the terms 'of [their] own existence' [70] – that is, the relations of things to their context are necessary parts of their existence and definitions. The same thing is not always the same, but depends on the context. How is this done? Since 'the phenomena that concern us are unseeable and ungraspable directly', we must 'proceed to study by inference ... We must observe the effects of class and class conflict on behaviour and then make inferences about the nature of class and class conflict'. [71] In this process, theory must change to fit inferences, and data must influence theory – the method is dialectical. 'Class is not a positive object [and] cannot be studied as one.' [72]

Concepts must be decomposed and differentiated to fit different levels of analysis; particular states, time horizons, and concepts appropriate at one level and true there, are not necessarily so elsewhere. Strategies of inquiry and analysis must fit the topic, and different topics require their own form of analysis. Class cannot be defined as an aggregate of individuals, but only as a collectivity which must be studied by inference, that is theoretically. Specific variables used during class analysis must be conceived of as 'non-parametric, discontinuous and non-linear', for these only can grasp the 'essence of the concept'. [73] Attempts to measure concepts, and to argue for relationships among them, using parametric, continuous, and linear data, on the assumption that variables exhibit and yield this kind of information, serve to distort the essential and structural relationships among variables. Normal science cannot reach essential reality as long as it is tied to empiricist assumptions, and fails to 'transcend the Euclidian space' of finite points, shortest distances, and the logic of the excluded middle. [74]

The limitations of normal science are overcome by a 'process of making approximations and drawing inferences, repeated in successive iteration' refined and amended and again matched against the data', and refined again until the 'best-fit', 'most encompassing' hypothesis stands 'tentatively confirmed'. [75]

How is this way of gaining knowledge distinct from the positivist science that Samoff criticizes? The method of reiterative approximations seems remarkably non-distant from normal science, so the difference must lie in the definitions and conceptualization of variables, or the nature of the data collected about them. Yet, neither the data themselves, not the inference process, are described in any detail. What he argues for, basically, is a more holistic and, at the same time, more specific historical approach, one which he finds correctly done by Mahmood Mamdani and Issa Shivji, even though their work contains 'errors, inconsistencies and oversimplifications'. [76] Yet, how the data Asmoff would use in the inference process would be anything else but those used by writers whom he criticizes – Patrick J. McGowan, Robert R. Kaufman, Richard Vengroff – is left unclear. The distinction between the old, moral-science paradigm, and that advocated by Samoff lies neither in the method nor in the data, but in the assumptions about the nature of the variables.

What does 'non-parametric, discontinuous, and non-linear' mean, when applied to a variable concept such as class? Parametric measurements assume certain distributions of variable values within the population from which the sample under study is drawn; continuity implies a transitively ordered directional sequence of measurements; linearity, including curvilinearity, suggests the existence of a statable and determinate relationship between two or more variables. Non-parametric descriptions and assumptions are common in normal science, and it seems that Samoff means more here than an argument about validity of various confidence measures, though what is not stated. Discontinuity seems to imply qualitative shifts in variables — they are not the same, though the label remains unchanged. Non-linearity argues that numerous statable relationships, all determinate, can be found among variables — the same set of data has different forms of associations, with sometimes positive and sometimes negative correlations, sometimes monotonic and at other times not.

Putting the three traits of variables in the new paradigm together, we get the argument that all variables, and the concepts which they represent, are fluid, non-stable, open-ended, and that all relationships among them are possible. A cause can have all effects and all effects can have the same cause. No proof or disproof is possible, because the nature of variables and their relations cannot be stated except contextually, and since all contexts are unique, a failure to find a hypothesized relationship is no disproof, nor can finding the relationship be proof. How data are used to correct, refine, and amend, except in fairly arbitrary ways, is again unclear. Concepts which are non-parametric and discontinuous, and have non-linear relationships to each other, are immune to data. Samoff's argument, though interesting in that it uses a terminology from the paradigm he wishes to discredit, remains undeveloped and rhetorical.

Richard Sklar, in two recent papers, directly addresses various problems of methodology, notably the fundamental identification of groups. [77] To him, class is an analytical construct not directly observable. Group theory, and interest or conflict pluralism, may be descriptively more accurate than class analysis, since 'class action is not, strictly speaking, a matter of empirical determination', and 'the alleged manifestations of class action are purely mental constructs'. In fact, 'the evidence . . . to support the ideas of class formation and consolidation may readily be used to support alternative approaches, principally 'group theory' or epistemological pluralism'. [78] Class analysis is preferable, though, on moral grounds, as it focuses on domination, injustice, and inequality as the cause for group solidarity, and is 'committed to the ideal of social equality'. Class analysis is, therefore, both 'logical and realistic despite [its] empirical shortcomings'. [79]

Adjusting theory to data, Sklar redefines the process of class formation as a 'fusion of elites', [80] and argues that classes should be conceptualized on the basis of domination and power, rather than relations to the means of production. [81] It is his feeling that, since 'Marxist theory cannot readily cope with the findings to the effect that non-economic factors are often more potent than economic factors as determinants of solidarity and political action, [82] it must modify or abandon some of its claims. He finds

Marxist thought drifting, especially in the writings of Poulantzas, 'toward a repudiation of the class basis of political power',[83] yet would, having to choose, rather retain the connection of class to power and sever that of class to economic structure. He argues, following Ossowski, for a determination of class on the basis of power, control, and domination; that is, not abandoning the economic determinants of class and power, but removing their determining status. Since class analysis was chosen as theoretically correct by moral criteria, the concept of class which maintains moral commitment becomes determining.

How does the observer, then, observe or infer class activity in specific situations? Sklar argues that any 'collective action' is class action, if the 'effect is to strengthen or weaken the means whereby the domination of a privileged stratum is maintained'.[84] Since all collective action, one might argue in return, has such a consequence, it is by definition class action. It is hard to conceive of any collective action in the economic, social, or political sphere which, even if only marginally, does not have these effects. How class analysis differs from group theory in its empirical description is thus unclear. In reality, collective action has effects, and there is no way to choose what to call the groups, and determine what exists, but by the moral preferences of the observer. Though honest, this argument remains unpersuasive — why class analysis is more true to reality than group theory remains doubtful, especially if class is defined on the basis of power and domination, since these are precisely the criteria used in pluralist analysis.

Mahamood Mamdani exemplifies the difficulties of doing empirical Marxist analysis.[85] His description of Uganda includes all sorts of taxonomies, shuffled and reshuffled at will to fit the argument; theory simply disappears. For example, the petty and the commercial bourgeoisie 'formed two separate classes at the level of the economy', but acted as one 'single class at the level of politics'. The determination of class by economic position is reversed, and politics overcomes class division. On the other hand, the petty bourgeoisie 'formed three separated sections at the level of the economy' and 'failed to emerge as a unified class on the plane of ideology and organization',[86] meaning that it did not act politically. By a quick count, close to 30 different classes — or sections, if adjective modifiers are included — populate the landscape, and they interact to form a tapestry of alliances and conflicts. When compared with other descriptions of politics and party struggles in Uganda, the difference lies in the Mamdani's labels, not the substance of his argument. The theory imposes few guidelines on the description. Wyatt MacGaffey is correct when he remarks that:

> 'contradictions' covers any kind of tension, conflict or mere discontinuity that can be seen retrospectively as having given rise to some event, and serves the same tautological purpose in this 'scientific' style of argument that 'function' used to serve in an earlier one.[87]

The explanatory power of the labels used is never really argued — it is assumed. Since the underlying theory is 'scientific' and 'correct', recasting recent history into new categories transforms description into explanation. Piers Beirne states this mode of analysis precisely: 'A general description of a phenomenon utilizing Marxist categories of knowledge becomes its explanation and therefore leads to a transformation of that phenomenon.' [88]

The contrasting tendency to *ad hoc* categorizations which follows from the absence of a clear methodology is exemplified in Ake's arguments that there are no essential differences among African states. [89] Tanzania and Malawi, Nigeria and Guinea, all labour under the same compulsion imposed by their peripheral status. All elites cling to power, crush the opposition under one-party or military rule, and carefully control participation; only formalistic adherence to diverse ideologies distinguishes them. With one theoretical sweep, all distinctions are relegated to the category 'superficial'. Ake's approach would lead to the conclusion that, for example, the USA and USSR are essentially similar. Though partially true — both are industrialized multi-nation states — this seems to ignore many important distinguishing traits.

A major focus of Marxist writings has been the working class in Africa, and the degree to which it is conscious 'for itself'. [90] These studies, regardless of their conclusions concerning the emergence of class consciousness, raise theoretical contentions. First, the difficulties in raising consciousness, which Ollman has spelled out quite adequately, [91] or the reconceptualization of levels of consciousness, [92] tend to be ignored, and simple dichotomies are used — such as, are they or are they not conscious? Multiplying levels or foci of consciousness would require more and more precise means of measuring what exists. Secondly, the sub-division of classes into fractions, sections, strata, cores, or peripheries requires the introduction of non-class criteria, since economic relations can only separate inter- — but not intra- — class distinctions. Political, ideological, and cultural criteria — for example, 'modern' versus 'traditional' petty bourgeoisie — are filtered through almost haphazardly, and a 'subjective fragmentation into several antagonistic groups' within specific classes is perceived. [93] Class analysis loses its firm theoretical anchors the more it attempts to reflect reality.

One way out of this problem of how to deal with the influx of superficial, superstructural criteria into the categorization schema, is to define them as essentially meaningless as regards theory. This is Wallerstein's solution — all forms of consciousness, whether expressed in ethnic, regional, or nationalistic identities, are concerned with class, since that is required by the nature of the world system. [94]

More common, though, is empirical work on the nature of consciousness, and this raises the question about the collection and use of data. What would be different if a Marxist analysis were done? — for example, survey research as Marx himself attempted. Would the questions asked be different? — not necessarily. Would the sampling methods vary? — unlikely. It seems that the difference would lie in the motive for the research — not the techniques employed — and this, in turn, is linked to a specific theoretical understanding of world history.

The differences in the kind of facts which are used are not all that great between bourgeois and Marxist scholars. Marxist writings are replete with statistics culled from state publications (controlled by the bourgeoisie), 'imperialist outfits' such as the ILO, or research data from bourgeois social scientists. These statistics are frequently taken as correct in themselves, but interpreted for different meanings; and this presents problems. Accepting the accuracy of the data, collected by positivist scientific norms, means accepting the validity of the method, for how else could the data be correct? They can be, and are, used within Marxist arguments to say something about the essence, not just the appearance of social life. Yet, doing this vitiates the Marxist critique of positivist science, for this is fundamentally based on the argument that bourgeois science systematically falsifies. On what bases are some of the data created through false methods selected as being essentially correct, and others rejected as false? Why, for example, are attitude data on ethnicity called 'false', unlike those on workers' consciousness? The lack of an explicit Marxist methodology has led to a movement toward *ad hoc* empiricism and unjustified use of 'invalid' data. The explanatory power of the Marxist approach suffers. The search for substitutes for explanation is found in the value assumptions of the model, in the periodization the mind can impose upon history, and in functionalist logic.

Progress or Regress?

The notion of progress is embedded in Marxist thought. Marx argued that 'the country that is more developed industrially only shows to the less developed the image of its own future', [95] in the sense that knowledge of the most advanced allows a correct interpretation of lower levels of progress. 'The pointers of animals in the lower species can only be understood if the higher species itself is already known. Thus the bourgeois economy provides the key to the economy of antiquity.' [96] Oculi has pointed out the enthnocentrism in Marx's writing well enough, [97] and Ali Mazrui never ceases to illustrate the inauthenticity of Marxist thought in the African context. [98] Geoffrey Kay's argument that the continent was not exploited enough — which follows logically from the notion of progress embedded in the periodization of history — can only provoke profound distaste among African writers, Marxists included. [99]

The notion of progress in Marxist thought poses a problem because this does involve the concept of higher and lower levels of achievement. Since the colonialists were able to impose their domination on African societies by virtue of their advanced technology and greater control of nature, it follows that European claims to superiority in superstructural elements, dependent as these are on the base, must be seen as valid within the Marxist mode of thought. Yet, these ideas clash fundamentally with notions of African development and history held by African intellectuals, as well as their feeling and knowledge that colonialism was responsible for the destruction of 'in the interests' of people to what they themselves believe. On what basis can one deny that those who identify themselves with a group other than a class, are not conscious of their own interests? Not on an empirical basis, since that is impossible, but on a theoretical basis. The question comes back to that of method, and justification for the method, and the models of thought which will separate what truly is 'in the interest' of groups, and what is merely presumed to be, and falsely so.

It has been my argument that the defence of false and true consciousness — a distinction that is fundamental for the validity of Marxist thought — has been insufficient, whether on the basis of method, or an intuitively correct understanding of history, or moral indignation. What seems to be a more valid starting point are the notions of interest and consciousness as applied to all groups and not just class models. This is Marx's position: interest and consciousness are the truly universal concepts, with all others serving to make clear the differences in how groups organize themselves. The current Marxist theory which bases itself on interest, rather than class or modes of production, as the fundamental concept has been elaborated by Jurgen Habermas. [112] It is interesting to note how little of the thinking of the Frankfurt school has penetrated Marxist writings on Africa, and it might be a rewarding exercise, beyond the scope of this article, to look into the process and reasons why the particular schools represented by Lukacs and Poulantzas, the Hegelians and the structuralists, have become dominant.

The notion of interest, if elaborated, could deal with a number of problems in Marxist analysis. The proliferation of sections of classes in empirical description, as argued earlier, introduces superstructural elements and inconsistencies into theory. A notion of interest as basic to group identification, rather than economic relations or power, would alleviate this terminological confusion. Also, to show that ethnicity or interest group competition may be about economic resources, is not the same as establishing the validity of class analysis; in the same way, showing that people have attitudes, does not deny, within Marxist thought, that economics are important. Interests can incorporate economic factors, and consciousness also, and avoids the simplifications of a reality reduced to class-related concepts. Lastly, interests and interest groups need not be related to a consensual or a conflict model. This depends on the nature of resource and interest constellations at specific times.

Interest group interactions provide a dynamic conception of history — they certainly help explain why change occurs — and interested consciousness mediates between objective conditions and subjective illusions. Interested action, tied to group identities, could be the basis for a theory which is empirical, dynamic and morally defensible, and might provide the synthesis of empirical and theoretical elements which now separate positivist and dialectical science.

The Need for a Proper Marxist Methodology

What we have, then, in the analysis and examples above, is a patchwork of ideas, frequently unelaborated; an abandonment of empiricism — mean a redefinition of science as thought activity — and an inability to justify why certain items of experience are selected as concrete indicators of universality, and others not. Specifically, the criterion of false consciousness which buttressess the assertion that the distinction betwen superficial and essential is possible, indeed necessary, depends on positing certain models which are taken to be the standard by which to judge the consciousness of methods and actions. The models, in turn, require the acceptance of numerous philosophical assumptions — reality as negation, privileged insight, the dialectical *Aufhebung* of object and subject. One cannot be sure whether these would be acceptable to the writers discussed, yet they are the epistemological foundation for the distinction between superficial and essential.

The argument made here is not a defence of positivist, bourgeois social science. All forms of thought face the fundamental problem of linking their ideas to the nature of the world, of establishing that what is patterned in thought is also true to reality. Marxist thought has justified itself as correct in terms of *a priori* theorizing or value priorities, but has not defended the truth content of its thinking by systematic, structured appeals to reality. We have challenged this claim to being scientific and explanatory as unproved. Correct theorizing of a materialist conception of the social (life), or correct value choices (a critique of domination), do not establish that the choice made is true to reality — only a specified connection of thought to reality, testable in some stated way, can do that. Bourgeois science has at least that characteristic — that it attempts to defend its choices of theory and value by structured appeals to reality.

So far, Marxist methodology remains at the level of form rather than essence, using the distinction made in Marxist thought. The production of knowledge is a thought process. Materialist conceptions are the content of the theory, but not the way in which thought is produced or tested. Marxist thought as science needs more than the statement 'just think as a Marxist' to be persuasive. Shivji's assertion that 'notwithstanding the lack of formal definitions, clear-minded Marxists have not found it difficult to apply the concepts' creatively,' simple is insufficient as methodology or its justification.[113]

Until an explicit methodology is developed, Marxist analysis tends to preach to the converted. It must, to be persuasive in communication, develop a more empiricist justification. It is difficult to convince people that what they observe is not really true, that what they think motivates them is false, that what they know through pragmatic application is irrelevant. This will take more than an act of theory. Also, a mere assertion of being right without justifying, without having 'superficial' empirical support, is for practical purposes counter-revolutionary, for it is so easy to discredit. Ossowski's admonition should be kept in mind: 'The principle "social existence determines consciousness" does not entitle us to draw simple conclusions because "social existence" is not a simple matter.' [114]

The construction of a more convincing Marxist methodology is overdue, and until done will render doubtful all claims to certainty. The content of Marxist theory must also be modified to allow for the contributions of human action and motivation as integrated parts of the totality of history. In some ways, the downgrading of sense data and accurate description is based on a misidentification of the superficial with superstructural. Yet, superstructural elements are not unimportant in real life or in theory, and the restructuring of Marxist models advocated here will require, and lead to, the systematic and determinable integration of 'superficial' factors into explanation, a true dialectical interaction, rather than assuming the priority of theory, and thereby of base. Marx said what needs to be done well enough: history does nothing. It is man, real living human beings, that does all; 'history' is not a person apart, using human beings as a means for its own particular aims; history is nothing but the activity of the human pursuit of aims. [115]

In reaction to the ideological excesses of bourgeois science, Marxist writers have thrown out much that is empirically accurate, or important to people; and this has been done on quite abstract theoretical grounds. A new synthesis still lies ahead, which loses neither the moral nor theoretical validity of Marxist insights, and accepts the consciousness of people as factual and theoretical givens. My contention has been that Marxism has protected itself against the onslaught of 'reality' by denying the validity of bourgeois scientific method. All the Marxist arguments that their way of understanding provides true knowledge and correct guides to action must be supported by an empirical methodology if they are to be persuasive.

Notes

1. Bernard Magubane, 'The Evolution of the Class Structure in Africa', in Peter C. W. Gutkind and Immanuel Wallerstein (eds.), *The Political Economy of Contemporary Africa* (Beverly Hills and London, 1976), p.16.
2. Ibid., pp. 171-2.
3. Ibid., p. 173.
4. Ibid., p. 178.
5. Ibid., p. 180.
6. Ibid., p. 193.
7. Ibid., p. 195.
8. See Bertell Ollman, 'Toward Consciousness, Next Time: Marx and the Working Class', *Politics and Society*, Vol. III, No. 1., Fall 1972, p. 2, and also J. Lopreato and L. E. Hazelrigg, *Class, Class Conflict and Mobility* (San Francisco, 1972), p. 116.
9. Archie Mafeje, 'The Ideology of "Tribalism" ', *The Journal of Modern African Studies*, Vol. IX, No. 2, August, 1971, p. 259.
10. Marx, quoted in Lewis S. Feuer (ed.), *Marx and Engels* (Garden City,

N.Y., 1959), p. 408.
11. Karl Mannheim, *Ideology and Utopia* (New York, 1936), p. 95.
12. Istvan Meszaros, 'Contingent and Necessary Class Consciousness'. in Mezaros (ed.), *Aspects of History and Class Consciousness* (London, 1971), p. 93.
13. Lucien Goldman, 'Reflections on History and Class Consciousness' in Meszaros, op. cit.
14. Peter Berger, *Pyramids of Sacrifice* (Garden City, N.Y., 1976), p. 128.
15. W. G. Runciman, 'Ideology and Social Science' in Robert Benewick, R. N. Berki, and Bhikhu Parekh (eds.), *Knowledge and Beliefs in Politics: The Problem of Ideology* (London, 1973), p. 32.
16. Richard Sandbrook and Jack Arn, *The Labouring Poor and Urban Class Formation: The Case of Greater Accra*, Centre for Developing Area Studies, McGill University, Montreal, 1977, Occasional Monograph Series No. 12, p. 38.
17. Robin Cohen, 'Marxism and Africa: Old, New and Projected', Working Paper No. 2., Centre for Developing Area Studies, McGill University, Montreal 1975, p. 9.
18. Immanuel Wallerstein, 'Class Formation in the Capitalist World System', *Politics and Society*, Vol. V, No. 3, 1975, p. 370.
19. George Lukacs, *History and Class Consciousness: Studies in Marxist Dialectics* (London, 1971), p. 51.
20. M. Shaw, *Marxism and Social Science* (London, 1975), p. 113.
21. Lukacs, op. cit., p. 1.
22. M. Shaw, 'New Empirical Marxism', *Sociology*, Vol. 10, September 1976, p. 523.
23. R. Tristram, 'Ontology and Theory: A Comment on Marx's Analysis of some of the Problems' *Sociological Review*, Vol. 23, November 1975, p. 771.
24. Ibid., p. 773.
25. Umberto Melotti, *Marx and the Third World* (New York, 1977), p. 5.
26. Martin Nicolaus, 'The Unknown Marx' in Robin Blackburn (ed.), *Ideology in Social Science* (London, 1972), p. 333. See also Isaac Balbus, 'Ruling Elite Theory Versus Marxist Class Analysis', *Monthly Review*, Vol. XVIII, No. 1, May 1971, pp. 36-46; Alaus Wolfe, 'New Directions in Marxist Theory of Politics', *Politics and Society*, Vol. IV, No. 2, Winter 1974, pp. 131-59; B. Ollman, 'Marxism and Political Science: Prolegomenon to a Debate on Marx's Method', *Politics and Society*, Vol. III, No. 4, Summer 1973, pp. 491-510.
27. John Horton and Fari Filsoufi, 'Left Wing Communism: An Infantile Disorder in Theory and Method', *The Insurgent Sociologist*, Vol. VII, No. 1, Winter 1977, pp. 5-17.
28. Lukacs, op. cit. Also H. Marcuse, Preface to Franz Neumann, *The Democratic and the Authoritarian State* edited by Marcuse (New York, 1964), and Marcuse, *Counterrevolution and Revolt* (Boston, 1972); and Shaw, op. cit.
29. Maurice Cornforth. *Historical Materialism* (New York, 1971), and *Materialism and the Dialectical Method* (New York, 1971).
30. Hamza Alavi, 'India and the Colonial Mode of Production' in R. Miliband and J. Saville (eds.), *The Socialist Register*, 1975, p. 181.

The explanatory power of the labels used is never really argued — it is assumed. Since the underlying theory is 'scientific' and 'correct', recasting recent history into new categories transforms description into explanation. Piers Beirne states this mode of analysis precisely: 'A general description of a phenomenon utilizing Marxist categories of knowledge becomes its explanation and therefore leads to a transformation of that phenomenon.'[88]

The contrasting tendency to *ad hoc* categorizations which follows from the absence of a clear methodology is exemplified in Ake's arguments that there are no essential differences among African states.[89] Tanzania and Malawi, Nigeria and Guinea, all labour under the same compulsion imposed by their peripheral status. All elites cling to power, crush the opposition under one-party or military rule, and carefully control participation; only formalistic adherence to diverse ideologies distinguishes them. With one theoretical sweep, all distinctions are relegated to the category 'superficial'. Ake's approach would lead to the conclusion that, for example, the USA and USSR are essentially similar. Though partially true — both are industrialized multi-nation states — this seems to ignore many important distinguishing traits.

A major focus of Marxist writings has been the working class in Africa, and the degree to which it is conscious 'for itself'.[90] These studies, regardless of their conclusions concerning the emergence of class consciousness, raise theoretical contentions. First, the difficulties in raising consciousness, which Ollman has spelled out quite adequately,[91] or the reconceptualization of levels of consciousness,[92] tend to be ignored, and simple dichotomies are used — such as, are they or are they not conscious? Multiplying levels or foci of consciousness would require more and more precise means of measuring what exists. Secondly, the sub-division of classes into fractions, sections, strata, cores, or peripheries requires the introduction of non-class criteria, since economic relations can only separate inter- — but not intra- — class distinctions. Political, ideological, and cultural criteria — for example, 'modern' versus 'traditional' petty bourgeoisie — are filtered through almost haphazardly, and a 'subjective fragmentation into several antagonistic groups' within specific classes is perceived.[93] Class analysis loses its firm theoretical anchors the more it attempts to reflect reality.

One way out of this problem of how to deal with the influx of superficial, superstructural criteria into the categorization schema, is to define them as essentially meaningless as regards theory. This is Wallerstein's solution — all forms of consciousness, whether expressed in ethnic, regional, or nationalistic identities, are concerned with class, since that is required by the nature of the world system.[94]

More common, though, is empirical work on the nature of consciousness, and this raises the question about the collection and use of data. What would be different if a Marxist analysis were done? — for example, survey research as Marx himself attempted. Would the questions asked be different? — not necessarily. Would the sampling methods vary? — unlikely. It seems that the difference would lie in the motive for the research — not the techniques employed — and this, in turn, is linked to a specific theoretical understanding of world history.

The differences in the kind of facts which are used are not all that great between bourgeois and Marxist scholars. Marxist writings are replete with statistics culled from state publications (controlled by the bourgeoisie), 'imperialist outfits' such as the ILO, or research data from bourgeois social scientists. These statistics are frequently taken as correct in themselves, but interpreted for different meanings; and this presents problems. Accepting the accuracy of the data, collected by positivist scientific norms, means accepting the validity of the method, for how else could the data be correct? They can be, and are, used within Marxist arguments to say something about the essence, not just the appearance of social life. Yet, doing this vitiates the Marxist critique of positivist science, for this is fundamentally based on the argument that bourgeois science systematically falsifies. On what bases are some of the data created through false methods selected as being essentially correct, and others rejected as false? Why, for example, are attitude data on ethnicity called 'false', unlike those on workers' consciousness? The lack of an explicit Marxist methodology has led to a movement toward *ad hoc* empiricism and unjustified use of 'invalid' data. The explanatory power of the Marxist approach suffers. The search for substitutes for explanation is found in the value assumptions of the model, in the periodization the mind can impose upon history, and in functionalist logic.

Progress or Regress?

The notion of progress is embedded in Marxist thought. Marx argued that 'the country that is more developed industrially only shows to the less developed the image of its own future', [95] in the sense that knowledge of the most advanced allows a correct interpretation of lower levels of progress. 'The pointers of animals in the lower species can only be understood if the higher species itself is already known. Thus the bourgeois economy provides the key to the economy of antiquity.' [96] Oculi has pointed out the enthnocentrism in Marx's writing well enough, [97] and Ali Mazrui never ceases to illustrate the inauthenticity of Marxist thought in the African context. [98] Geoffrey Kay's argument that the continent was not exploited enough — which follows logically from the notion of progress embedded in the periodization of history — can only provoke profound distaste among African writers, Marxists included. [99]

The notion of progress in Marxist thought poses a problem because this does involve the concept of higher and lower levels of achievement. Since the colonialists were able to impose their domination on African societies by virtue of their advanced technology and greater control of nature, it follows that European claims to superiority in superstructural elements, dependent as these are on the base, must be seen as valid within the Marxist mode of thought. Yet, these ideas clash fundamentally with notions of African development and history held by African intellectuals, as well as their feeling and knowledge that colonialism was responsible for the destruction of cultural, religious and political modes of action which were authentic and effective in themselves and which should be preferred to the distorting and alienating values and institutions imposed by the conquerors.

Progress as the 'trend of history' has led to these results in Marxist writings: one theoretical, the other apologetic. The theoretical outcome has been the denial of the historical and current role of Africa as an autonomous shaper of its destiny. On the one hand, there is the rediscovery of 'primitive' Africa under the guise of modes of production in analyses that read suspiciously like the worst apologies for colonial rule. Coquery-Vidrovitch concludes that the land-tenure system in Africa, and the tendency towards egalitarianism in traditional peasant societies, hindered progress 'precisely because it forbade the concentration of wealth and power and hence, a differentiation into social classes based on the social division of labour'.[100] The result was a state of stagnation awaiting the impetus of outside contact, through trade, to awaken these societies from their slumber and bring them into history. Magubane's description of the 'communal mode of production' stresses its non-dynamic aspects.[101] Woven through these analyses, as well, are the contrasts between modernity and tradition, and the movement from lower to higher forms of social development. On the other hand, in current history, the importance of Africa as a shaper of its own destiny is relegated to fantasy; as part of the global 'periphery' the continent is controlled and shaped by the 'centre', with little autonomous capacity for action.[102]

The second outcome of accepting the notion of progress is a defence of socialist regimes, regardless of their specific policies. The belief that the march forward is inevitable, despite temporary delays, has led to a preoccupation with the dominance of the vanguard elite which, since it knows the correct interpretation of history, should be entitled to suppress counter-revolutionary dissent. Yet, as Sklar has pointed out, political domination within a country is a necessary virtue for socialism, and liberal values are not a necessary weakness — indeed, liberty and equality in all spheres of life are both socialist values. His remark that 'these notions would surely be scorned as ethnocentric' if they were 'not propagated by avowed socialists' is right on the mark.[103]

Another, and more important consequence of the absence of methodology, has been the substitution of functional logic for explanation. There is an almost studied vagueness about the precise determinants of action, about those factors in history that cause activities, about the way that essential and superficial realities are linked. Explanations of the past, and predictions of the future, are made imprecise by qualifying phrases: 'in some way', 'not completely unexpected', 'the probability is quite high' ... that revolution will occur.[104] Wallerstein knows why class conflict exists, namely because a group's social activities are in 'some ultimate sense determined by their role in the world-economy'.[105] In some ways, 'ultimate' is the theoretical *deus ex machina* appearing to rescue predictions and explanations when data fail to support them.

There is, as well, what Theda Skocpol has called the 'teleological assertion' technique, namely 'that things at a certain time and place had to be a certain way in order to bring about later states of developments that accord (or seem to accord)' with what the model predicts. [106] It is the historic purpose of a group to act in certain ways. Example: 'Given the weakness and underdevelopment of the petit bourgeoisie ... the state must intervene directly with imperialism to "aid and emancipate" the domestic petty bourgeoisie.' [107] Or, 'it is the function of local power groups to assist the metropolis in the export of surplus created by local labour power'. [108] Or, the Murtala Mohammed coup was necessary in order to save the national bourgeoisie in Nigeria from its own contradictions. [109] Or, the African situation demands, indeed imposes, particular political systems and ideologies congruent with its objective character. [110]

Everything that happens serves the progress of history; and if it had been otherwise — a coup that fails? — that also would have served the same function. Nothing in particular can be predicted and explained, because everything that has happened, and will happen, serves the same historic purposes. This criticism is not against the notion of 'function' — which can serve a heuristic purpose — or even the accuracy of the description in the context of which the argument occurs, but against the 'becauses' built into the statements. Functionalism provides no causal explanation, and in this case the use of the term serves to affirm the model, regardless of what is observed. Using functionalist explanations makes the model immune; there is nothing that has happened, and could happen, which will not support the model.

The Concept of Interest

The argument about what is 'essential' and what is 'superficial' in African politics is neatly encapsulated in the following question: are classes or interest groups to be considered central to the social process? There has been a theoretical movement away from ethnic groups as the basic unit towards class analysis and interest group theory. [111] But interest groups, in Marxist analysis, are meaningless as agents of historical change. Studying them, as if they could reveal the structure and process of politics, is a form of false consciousness, as are the ideas of those who identify with interest groups rather than classes.

Which of these approaches is more correct? The answer depends on the notions of false consciousness and interest. Marxists would argue that people are mistaken when they believe that their fortunes lie with a group other than a class, while interest group theorists would give some credence to the ability of individuals to discern their own interests. The distinction hinges on the notion of false consciousness, since this entails the capacity to judge what actions, including group identities, are 'in the interests' of groups, and the capacity of Marxists to counterpose their specific conception of what is 'in the interests' of people to what they themselves believe. On what basis can one deny that those who identify themselves with a group other than a class, are not conscious of their own interests? Not on an empirical basis, since that is impossible, but on a theoretical basis. The question comes back to that of method, and justification for the method, and the models of thought which will separate what truly is 'in the interest' of groups, and what is merely presumed to be, and falsely so.

It has been my argument that the defence of false and true consciousness — a distinction that is fundamental for the validity of Marxist thought — has been insufficient, whether on the basis of method, or an intuitively correct understanding of history, or moral indignation. What seems to be a more valid starting point are the notions of interest and consciousness as applied to all groups and not just class models. This is Marx's position: interest and consciousness are the truly universal concepts, with all others serving to make clear the differences in how groups organize themselves. The current Marxist theory which bases itself on interest, rather than class or modes of production, as the fundamental concept has been elaborated by Jurgen Habermas. [112] It is interesting to note how little of the thinking of the Frankfurt school has penetrated Marxist writings on Africa, and it might be a rewarding exercise, beyond the scope of this article, to look into the process and reasons why the particular schools represented by Lukacs and Poulantzas, the Hegelians and the structuralists, have become dominant.

The notion of interest, if elaborated, could deal with a number of problems in Marxist analysis. The proliferation of sections of classes in empirical description, as argued earlier, introduces superstructural elements and inconsistencies into theory. A notion of interest as basic to group identification, rather than economic relations or power, would alleviate this terminological confusion. Also, to show that ethnicity or interest group competition may be about economic resources, is not the same as establishing the validity of class analysis; in the same way, showing that people have attitudes, does not deny, within Marxist thought, that economics are important. Interests can incorporate economic factors, and consciousness also, and avoids the simplifications of a reality reduced to class-related concepts. Lastly, interests and interest groups need not be related to a consensual or a conflict model. This depends on the nature of resource and interest constellations at specific times.

Interest group interactions provide a dynamic conception of history — they certainly help explain why change occurs — and interested consciousness mediates between objective conditions and subjective illusions. Interested action, tied to group identities, could be the basis for a theory which is empirical, dynamic and morally defensible, and might provide the synthesis of empirical and theoretical elements which now separate positivist and dialectical science.

The Need for a Proper Marxist Methodology

What we have, then, in the analysis and examples above, is a patchwork of ideas, frequently unelaborated; an abandonment of empiricism — mean a redefinition of science as thought activity — and an inability to justify why certain items of experience are selected as concrete indicators of universality, and others not. Specifically, the criterion of false consciousness which buttressess the assertion that the distinction between superficial and essential is possible, indeed necessary, depends on positing certain models which are taken to be the standard by which to judge the consciousness of methods and actions. The models, in turn, require the acceptance of numerous philosophical assumptions — reality as negation, privileged insight, the dialectical *Aufhebung* of object and subject. One cannot be sure whether these would be acceptable to the writers discussed, yet they are the epistemological foundation for the distinction between superficial and essential.

The argument made here is not a defence of positivist, bourgeois social science. All forms of thought face the fundamental problem of linking their ideas to the nature of the world, of establishing that what is patterned in thought is also true to reality. Marxist thought has justified itself as correct in terms of *a priori* theorizing or value priorities, but has not defended the truth content of its thinking by systematic, structured appeals to reality. We have challenged this claim to being scientific and explanatory as unproved. Correct theorizing of a materialist conception of the social (life), or correct value choices (a critique of domination), do not establish that the choice made is true to reality — only a specified connection of thought to reality, testable in some stated way, can do that. Bourgeois science has at least that characteristic — that it attempts to defend its choices of theory and value by structured appeals to reality.

So far, Marxist methodology remains at the level of form rather than essence, using the distinction made in Marxist thought. The production of knowledge is a thought process. Materialist conceptions are the content of the theory, but not the way in which thought is produced or tested. Marxist thought as science needs more than the statement 'just think as a Marxist' to be persuasive. Shivji's assertion that 'notwithstanding the lack of formal definitions, clear-minded Marxists have not found it difficult to apply the concepts' creatively,' simple is insufficient as methodology or its justification.[113]

Until an explicit methodology is developed, Marxist analysis tends to preach to the converted. It must, to be persuasive in communication, develop a more empiricist justification. It is difficult to convince people that what they observe is not really true, that what they think motivates them is false, that what they know through pragmatic application is irrelevant. This will take more than an act of theory. Also, a mere assertion of being right without justifying, without having 'superficial' empirical support, is for practical purposes counter-revolutionary, for it is so easy to discredit. Ossowski's admonition should be kept in mind: 'The principle "social existence determines consciousness" does not entitle us to draw simple conclusions because "social existence" is not a simple matter.' [114]

The construction of a more convincing Marxist methodology is overdue, and until done will render doubtful all claims to certainty. The content of Marxist theory must also be modified to allow for the contributions of human action and motivation as integrated parts of the totality of history. In some ways, the downgrading of sense data and accurate description is based on a misidentification of the superficial with superstructural. Yet, superstructural elements are not unimportant in real life or in theory, and the restructuring of Marxist models advocated here will require, and lead to, the systematic and determinable integration of 'superficial' factors into explanation, a true dialectical interaction, rather than assuming the priority of theory, and thereby of base. Marx said what needs to be done well enough: history does nothing. It is man, real living human beings, that does all; 'history' is not a person apart, using human beings as a means for its own particular aims; history is nothing but the activity of the human pursuit of aims. [115]

In reaction to the ideological excesses of bourgeois science, Marxist writers have thrown out much that is empirically accurate, or important to people; and this has been done on quite abstract theoretical grounds. A new synthesis still lies ahead, which loses neither the moral nor theoretical validity of Marxist insights, and accepts the consciousness of people as factual and theoretical givens. My contention has been that Marxism has protected itself against the onslaught of 'reality' by denying the validity of bourgeois scientific method. All the Marxist arguments that their way of understanding provides true knowledge and correct guides to action must be supported by an empirical methodology if they are to be persuasive.

Notes

1. Bernard Magubane, 'The Evolution of the Class Structure in Africa', in Peter C. W. Gutkind and Immanuel Wallerstein (eds.), *The Political Economy of Contemporary Africa* (Beverly Hills and London, 1976), p.16.
2. Ibid., pp. 171-2.
3. Ibid., p. 173.
4. Ibid., p. 178.
5. Ibid., p. 180.
6. Ibid., p. 193.
7. Ibid., p. 195.
8. See Bertell Ollman, 'Toward Consciousness, Next Time: Marx and the Working Class', *Politics and Society,* Vol. III, No. 1., Fall 1972, p. 2, and also J. Lopreato and L. E. Hazelrigg, *Class, Class Conflict and Mobility* (San Francisco, 1972), p. 116.
9. Archie Mafeje, 'The Ideology of "Tribalism" ', *The Journal of Modern African Studies*, Vol. IX, No. 2, August, 1971, p. 259.
10. Marx, quoted in Lewis S. Feuer (ed.), *Marx and Engels* (Garden City,

N.Y., 1959), p. 408.
11. Karl Mannheim, *Ideology and Utopia* (New York, 1936), p. 95.
12. Istvan Meszaros, 'Contingent and Necessary Class Consciousness'. in Mezaros (ed.), *Aspects of History and Class Consciousness* (London, 1971), p. 93.
13. Lucien Goldman, 'Reflections on History and Class Consciousness' in Meszaros, op. cit.
14. Peter Berger, *Pyramids of Sacrifice* (Garden City, N.Y., 1976), p. 128.
15. W. G. Runciman, 'Ideology and Social Science' in Robert Benewick, R. N. Berki, and Bhikhu Parekh (eds.), *Knowledge and Beliefs in Politics: The Problem of Ideology* (London, 1973), p. 32.
16. Richard Sandbrook and Jack Arn, *The Labouring Poor and Urban Class Formation: The Case of Greater Accra*, Centre for Developing Area Studies, McGill University, Montreal, 1977, Occasional Monograph Series No. 12, p. 38.
17. Robin Cohen, 'Marxism and Africa: Old, New and Projected', Working Paper No. 2., Centre for Developing Area Studies, McGill University, Montreal 1975, p. 9.
18. Immanuel Wallerstein, 'Class Formation in the Capitalist World System', *Politics and Society*, Vol. V, No. 3, 1975, p. 370.
19. George Lukacs, *History and Class Consciousness: Studies in Marxist Dialectics* (London, 1971), p. 51.
20. M. Shaw, *Marxism and Social Science* (London, 1975), p. 113.
21. Lukacs, op. cit., p. 1.
22. M. Shaw, 'New Empirical Marxism', *Sociology*, Vol. 10, September 1976, p. 523.
23. R. Tristram, 'Ontology and Theory: A Comment on Marx's Analysis of some of the Problems' *Sociological Review*, Vol. 23, November 1975, p. 771.
24. Ibid., p. 773.
25. Umberto Melotti, *Marx and the Third World* (New York, 1977), p. 5.
26. Martin Nicolaus, 'The Unknown Marx' in Robin Blackburn (ed.), *Ideology in Social Science* (London, 1972), p. 333. See also Isaac Balbus, 'Ruling Elite Theory Versus Marxist Class Analysis', *Monthly Review*, Vol. XVIII, No. 1, May 1971, pp. 36-46; Alaus Wolfe, 'New Directions in Marxist Theory of Politics', *Politics and Society*, Vol. IV, No. 2, Winter 1974, pp. 131-59; B. Ollman, 'Marxism and Political Science: Prolegomenon to a Debate on Marx's Method', *Politics and Society*, Vol. III, No. 4, Summer 1973, pp. 491-510.
27. John Horton and Fari Filsoufi, 'Left Wing Communism: An Infantile Disorder in Theory and Method', *The Insurgent Sociologist*, Vol. VII, No. 1, Winter 1977, pp. 5-17.
28. Lukacs, op. cit. Also H. Marcuse, Preface to Franz Neumann, *The Democratic and the Authoritarian State* edited by Marcuse (New York, 1964), and Marcuse, *Counterrevolution and Revolt* (Boston, 1972); and Shaw, op. cit.
29. Maurice Cornforth. *Historical Materialism* (New York, 1971), and *Materialism and the Dialectical Method* (New York, 1971).
30. Hamza Alavi, 'India and the Colonial Mode of Production' in R. Miliband and J. Saville (eds.), *The Socialist Register*, 1975, p. 181.

31. Marcuse, 1964, op. cit., p. viii.
32. Lukacs, op. cit., p. 12.
33. Shaw, op. cit., pp. 108-9.
34. Richard Ashcraft, 'Implications of Recent Marxist Scholarship for Political Theory', Western Political Science Association Convention, San Diego, 1973, p. 20.
35. Ibid., pp. 20-1.
36. Lukacs, op. cit., p. 74.
37. Fredric Jameson, *Marxism and Form* (Princeton, 1971), p. 182.
38. A. Gramsci, *The Modern Prince* (New York, 1957).
39. Colin Leys, 'Studying the Political Consciousness of Workers and Peasants in the Third World: The Problem of Theory and Practice', Working Paper No. 10, Centre for Developing Area Studies, McGill University, Montreal, 1975.
40. George Lichtheim, *George Lukacs* (New York, 1970), p. 71.
41. Lukacs, op. cit., p. 8.
42. Marcuse, 1972, op. cit., p. 103.
43. N. Poulantzas, 'The Problem of the Capitalist State', in Blackburn, op. cit., p. 241.
44. Ibid., p. 244.
45. Stanislav Ossowski, *Class Structure in the Social Consciousness* (New York, 1963), p. 8.
46. Soren Kierkegaard, *Fear and Trembling* (New York, 1954).
47. Ollman, 'Marxism and Political Science', op. cit.
48. Mao Tse-tung, *Five Essays on Philosophy* (Peking, 1977).
49. Ibid., p. 4.
50. Ibid., p. 5.
51. Ibid., pp. 12-13.
52. Ibid., p. 4.
53. Ibid., p. 3.
54. Ibid., p. 16.
55. Catherine Coquery-Vidrovitch, 'The Political Economy of the African Peasantry and Modes of Production' in Gutkind and Wallerstein, op. cit., p. 102.
56. Ossowski, op. cit., pp. 74-88.
57. Claude Ake, *Revolutionary Pressures in Africa* (London, Zed Press, 1978), p. 59.
58. Poulantzas, 'The Problem of the Capitalist State', op. cit. See also Ralph Miliband, *The State in Capitalist Society* (New York, 1969).
59. I. Gerstein, 'Theories of World Economy and Imperialism', *The Insurgent Sociologist*, Vol. VII, No. 2, Spring 1977, pp. 9-22.
60. Horton and Filsoufi, op. cit.
61. Ossowski, op. cit., p. 141.
62. Karl Korsh, cited in Martin Shaw, 'The Coming Crisis of Radical Sociology', in Blackburn, op. cit., p. 43.
63. Ake, op. cit., p. 61.
64. Ibid., pp. 61-2.
65. Claude Ake, *A Theory of Political Integration* (Homewood, Ill., 1967).
66. Ake, *Revolutionary Pressures*, op. cit., p. 63.
67. Ibid., pp. 97-8. Cf. Karl Popper, *The Logic of Scientific Discovery* (New York, 1955).

68. Ake, op. cit., p. 102.
69. Joel Samoff, 'Class, Class Conflict and the State: Notes on the Political Economy of Africa', African Studies Association, Houston, 1977, p. 9.
70. Ibid., p. 31, fn. 10.
71. Ibid., pp. 9-10.
72. Ibid., p. 11.
73. Ibid., p. 17.
74. Ibid., p. 18.
75. Ibid., pp. 21-2.
76. Ibid., p. 32, fn. 12.
77. Richard Sklar, 'Socialism at Bay: Class Domination in Africa', African Studies Association, Houston, 1977, and 'On the Concept of Power in Political Economy', essay prepared for a Festschrift in honour of F. D. Wormuth, Salt Lake City, September 1979.
78. Sklar, 'Socialism at Bay', op. cit., pp. 19-20.
79. Ibid., p. 16.
80. Ibid., p. 21.
81. Sklar, 'On the Concept of Power in Political Economy', op. cit.
82. Ibid., pp. 15-16.
83. Ibid., p. 28.
84. Sklar, 'Socialism at Bay', op. cit., pp. 25-6.
85. Mahmood Mamdani, 'Class Struggles in Uganda', African Association of Political Science, Lagos, 1976 and republished in *Politics and Class Formation in Uganda* (New York and London, 1976).
86. Mamdani, op. cit., pp. 11 and 14. In the published earlier version of this paper, the first phrase reads 'but acted as a single *force* at the level of politics' (my emphasis). Mamdani, 'Class Struggles in Uganda', *Review of African Political Economy*, Vol. 4, November 1975, p. 33.
87. W. MacGaffey, review of Mahmood Mamdani, *Politics and Class Formation in Uganda*, and of Issa Shivji, *Class Struggles in Tanzania*, in *African Studies Association Review of Books*, Vol. IV, 1978, p. 831. See also Gavin Williams, 'There is No Theory of Petty Bourgeois Politics', *Review of African Political Economy*, Vol. 6, May-August 1976, pp. 84-9.
88. Piers Beirne, 'Marxism and the Sociology of Law: Theory and Practice', *British Journal of Law and Society*, Vol. 2, Summer 1975, p. 80.
89. Claude Ake, 'The Congruence of Political Economies and Ideologies in Africa', in Gutkind and Wallerstein, op. cit., pp. 198-211, and 'Explanatory Notes on the Political Economy of Africa', *The Journal of Modern African Studies*, Vol. XIV, No. 1, March 1976, pp. 1-23.
90. Peter C. W. Gutkind, 'From the Energy of Despair to the Anger of Despair: The Transition from Social Circulation to Political Consciousness among the Urban Poor in Africa', *Canadian Journal of African Studies*, Vol. VII, No. 2, 1973, pp. 179-98, and 'The View from Below: Political Consciousness of the Urban Poor in Ibadan', *Cahiers d'etudes africaines*, Vol. XV, No. 1, 1975, pp. 5-35; Gavin Williams, 'Political Consciousness among the Ibadan Poor' in Emmanuel de Kadt and Williams (eds.), *Sociology and Development* (London, 1974); and Richard Sandbrook and Robin Cohen (eds.), *The*

Development of an African Working Class: Studies in Class Formation and Action (London, 1975).
91. A. Giddens, *The Class Structure of the Advanced Societies* (New York, 1975), pp. 111-13; and Cohen, op. cit.
92. Ollman, 'Toward Consciousness Next Time', op. cit; see also E. Bott, 'Concepts of Class' in R. Rose (ed.), *Studies in British Politics* (New York, 1968).
93. S. Osoba, 'The Deepening Crises of the Nigerian National Bourgeoisie', lecture at Ahmadu Bello University, Zaria, February 1978, p. 19.
94. Immanuel Wallerstein,'Social Conflict in Post-Independence Black Africa: The Concepts of Race and Status-group Reconsidered' in Ernest Q. Campbell (ed.), *Racial Tensions and National Identity* (Nashville, 1972), pp. 207-26.
95. Marx cited by S. M. Lipset, *Revolution and Counterrevolution* (Garden City, 1970 edn.), p. 199.
96. Marx cited by Ashcraft, op. cit., p. 21.
97. O. Oculi, 'On Marx's Attitude to Colonialism', *The African Review*, Vol. IV, No. 3, 1974, pp. 459-71, also Melotti, op. cit. pp. 54-8.
98. Ali A. Mazrui, *Political Values and the Educated Class* (Berkeley, 1978).
99. Geoffrey Kay, *Development and Underdevelopment* (London, 1975).
100. Coquery-Vidrovitch, op. cit., p. 104.
101. Magubane, op. cit.
102. Samir Amin, *Accumulation on a World Scale: A Critique of the Theory of Underdevelopment* (New York, 1974). There is an emerging argument against this notion, though; see Nicola Swainson, 'The Rise of a National Bourgeoisie in Kenya', *Review of African Political Economy*, Vol. 8, January-April 1977, pp. 39-55; Kipkorir A. A. Rana, 'Class Formation and Social Conflict: A Case Study of Kenya', *Ufahamu*, Vol. VII, No. 3, 1977, pp. 17-72; and Colin Leys, *Underdevelopment in Kenya: The Political Economy of Neo-colonialism, 1964-1971* (Berkeley, 1975).
103. Sklar,'Socialism at Bay', op. cit., p. 30.
104. E. N. Ekekwe, 'Toward the African Revolution: The Peasantry, the Proletariat and Bourgeoisie', Canadian Association of African Studies, Quebec, 1977.
105. Immanuel Wallerstein, 'Class and Class Conflict in Contemporary Africa', *Canadian Journal of African Studies*, Vol. VII, No. 3, 1973, p. 377.
106. Theda Skocpol, 'Wallersteins's World Capitalist System: A Theoretical and Historical Critique', *American Journal of Sociology*, Vol. 82, No. 5, March 1977, p. 1088.
107. Eboe Hutchful, 'The Military-Bureaucratic State in Ghana', African Association of Political Science, Rabat, 1977, p. 4.
108. Peter C. W. Gutkind and Immanuel Wallerstein, 'Introduction' to Gutkind and Wallerstein (eds.), *The Political Economy of Contemporary Africa* (Beverly Hills and London, 1976), p. 11.
109. Paul Collins, Terisa Turner and Gavin Williams, 'Capitalism and the Coup', in G. Williams (ed.), *Nigeria: Economy and Society* (London, 1976), pp. 185-92.
110. Ake, 'The Congruence of Political Economies and Ideologies', op. cit.

111. Abner Cohen, *Custom and Politics in Urban Africa: A Study of Hausa Migrants to Yoruba Towns* (Berkeley, 1969); Nelson Kasfir, *The Shrinking Political Arena: Participation and Ethnicity in African Politics, with A Case Study of Uganda* (Berkeley, 1976); and Crawford Young, *The Politics of Cultural Pluralism* (Madison, 1976).
112. Jurgen Habermas, *Theory and Practise* (Boston, 1973).
113. Shivji, op. cit., p. 4.
114. Ossowski, op. cit., p. 193.
115. Cited in Melotti, op. cit., p. 7.

17. The Tyranny of Borrowed Paradigms and the Responsibility of Political Science: The Nigerian Experience

S. Egite Oyovbaire

This essay proposes to examine two paradigms currently popular in the study of Nigerian government and politics and, in the context of these paradigms, to enquire about the proper responsibility of political science in Africa generally and in Nigeria in particular. As a distinct area of knowledge in institutions of higher learning, political science (or government) has been in Nigeria for about two decades. Before then there were individual persons inside and outside the country, Nigerians and non-Nigerians, who had, as students, teachers or men of public affairs, engaged themselves in the analysis and promotion of knowledge of contemporary Nigerian government and politics. Since it could be inferred that those who have been so preoccupied must be conscious of the responsibility of their enterprise, to enquire about that responsibility may seem like debating a non-issue.

The object of political science in Nigeria, as elsewhere, is primarily the state — its character, structures and values. It is highly doubtful whether any serious-minded student of Nigerian politics will contend that the Nigerian state is a non-issue of debate. As will be made clear later, the state, like much else in the Nigerian system, is under-developed in terms of its character, structures and values. A major proposition here is therefore that political science has a supreme responsibility to conceptualize properly its primary object of study, namely, the Nigerian state, and that this can be done properly in the framework of idealism and working politics. Of course, excessive idealism in the guise of radicalism, or excessively descriptive analysis of working politics in the name of stability and peace, contain the seeds of irrelevance and irresponsibility. The essential role of political science is to sensitize and socialize; it is not to legitimize or subvert. The latter role belongs to the realm of practical politics — to actors who may be politicians, regime experts or revolutionaries. While there is usually a supportive relationship between scholars and actors in the form of 'committed scholarship', or of actors and scholars taking their cues from each other, the distinctive role of one must not be confused with that of the other. The responsibility of political science in a university is not the legitimation or subversion of a particular social system, regime or set of rulers. Rather its responsibility is two-fold: the identification of the fundamental and enduring parameters of a social order, and the sensitization and socialization of its audience to the benefits and problems of achieving a *just* social order. In carrying out its responsibility, political science may unwittingly contribute to the subversion or legitimation of an existing regime, set of rulers or social order but this must be seen as incidental to rather than the mainstream of political science. I shall attempt in the following pages to explore and explain some of Nigeria's fundamental features within this matrix of political science responsibility.

The Tyranny of Received Ideas

Perhaps the best definition of politics and the tradition of its study is the old Aristotelian one: politics refers to the activities and behaviour of individuals and groups as these relate to the public realm. It is the pursuit of the public interest or, as Weber views it, the operation of organized power or the state. 'Of all the authoritative institutions in society,' Wolin observed, 'the political arrangement has been singled out as uniquely concerned with what is "common" to the whole community.' [1] But Aristotle's 'public interest', Weber's 'state', or Wolin's 'political arrangement' is not a homogenous and harmonious entity. It contains fundamental features of heterogeneity, conflicts and contradictions either within itself or between it and the private interest, the extra-society or the non-political arrangement. There are also essential features of co-operation within and between these spheres. Perhaps much more important is the fact that the public interest is a historical phenomenon in the sense that its character, structures and values in any one epoch are those formed by historical forces.

All the same, politics and its study are concerned with the management or promotion of public co-operation and conflict: with the desirable employment of organized power in the interest of more or less all members of a political order. It is the art of production and distribution of public values. The building of the structures (the capital goods, so to speak) by which production and distribution take place; the determination of mobilizable resources for production and distribution; the morality which underpins the production and allocation processes together with the socio-economic relations which derive from this; and a balanced understanding of the environment of production and distribution — all these are central to the activity and analysis of politics. In a social order like the Nigerian one which was created, fostered and 'under-developed' by colonial domination, these parameters call for a framework which combines idealism (the vision of a better or just social order) and working politics (how actors, clients, the people and spectators perceive and contribute towards the solution and problems of public management). The two dimensions of the framework capture adequately the forces which motivate people in politics.

In politics, people are moved by a combination of interests, ideas and sentiments. Thus, in studying the activities and behaviour of people, it will be inadequate to assign determinants outside their actual motivations. There are no meaningful historical laws stating that all political occurrences are only the works of sentiment or ideas or interests, But these are always present in one dosage or another. For example, the Nigerian social order is confronted with a multitude of problems impinging upon social life simultaneously: the resources, rather than being items of solution to social problems, are often tansformed into or allowed to become problems themselves. There is a scarcity of creative and relatively stable structures and processes for the ordering of *national* social life; a paucity of dominant, national political values which define useful and predictable relations between rulers and ruled, between levels of government, among individuals, principal political actors, and the diverse social aggregates. Even crises ostensibly at the level of the elite are easily transposed into the people's crises, thus threatening the existence of the political community. These are issues which must be analysed and explained in a framework of the people's experience and not in some metaphysical constructs.

National life in the Nigerian social order is undergoing a process — indeed a long process — of formation, including the formation of a 'ruling class' as distinct from simply a coterie of the ruling elite who have, through manipulating the administrative, political and educational systems, benefited enormously by accelerating the alignment of the domestic economy with international capitalism. At the same time, there is the formation of a peasantry or working class conscious of the mechanisms of their exploitation and impoverishment, and therefore intent on strategies to overthrow the existing social order, as distinct from simply the masses whose interest and life conditions have been neglected by successive regimes and rulers. The continued existence and flowering of the Nigerian social system cannot be taken for granted by political science. The *biafranization* of the system may now be a remote occurrence but certainly not a future impossibility. Similarly, it would be 'social science criminality' for political science to equate the existing social order with the true interest of the mass of citizens. It is the combination of both factors of the Nigerian social system that 'idealism and working politics' are intended to capture in a framework for analysis.

It is against this background that one can charge the existing political science paradigms in Nigeria with tyranny and insensitivity to the responsibility of the discipline in the country. These paradigms, which derive from the existing literature, [2] have for convenience been grouped here into two: the neo-liberal and the neo-Marxist/structuralist paradigms. The essence of one seems to exclude the essence of the other. While one attempts primarily to legitimize or at least not to question the existing social order, the other sees itself as the historic bearer of the cross of subversion of this order. Thus both paradigms derogate from what we earlier asserted as the proper responsibility of political science. A brief seminal exposition of these paradigms is in order.

The Neo-Liberal Paradigm

Like the departments of political science in Nigerian universities or elsewhere in Africa, this paradigm was a legacy of colonial rule, simply adopted and propagated by the heirs to the throne of academia in political science. In this connection, the pioneering study by James Coleman confessed to 'the conceptual ethnocentrism characteristic of contemporary political science', and the lack of conceptual preparation by the discipline 'to cope with the new institutional patterns and social relationship – partly modernist and partly traditionalist – which characterize much of emergent Africa'. [3] Although covering some breadth of political terrain, Coleman's study of the rise and activity of anti-colonial nationalism emphasized the determining role of three structures, namely, the Westernized elite, ethnicity/regionalism, and political parties/institutions of colonial government. According to Coleman, nationalism refers to 'the movement to create new political nationalities (that is, Nigeria, Western Region, Eastern Region, Northern Region) as self-governing units in the modern world'. [4] The study describes and analyses how 'the relevant features of the physical, cultural, and historical setting' were manipulated by the products of the 'Western impact' against elements of colonial domination.

The maintenance and stability of the 'new political nationalities' became the purpose of politics and the responsibility of political science. The varied, antagonistic and contradictory interests served by such maintenance and stability were taken as axiomatic, harmonious and good. They were not properly distinguished, let alone lifted into a central focus of analysis. Politics was an unregulated market which measured and equated the supply and demand of the 'new political nationalities' and their self-imposed representatives.

The struggle for power and its possession was harsh and blatant, and the minimal rules which existed – both constitutive and regulative – were flagrantly violated. Politics, to actors as well as scholars, became 'a system of rewards' or 'allocation' [5] by Westernized elites acting in the name of ethnicity and regionalism. The constraints to productive capacity and the ethnic or ideological basis of supply and demand were seen and interpreted as matters of a free play of the political market. These are the elements of the new liberalism. Political science concentrated on the activities or non-activities of the emergent elite, ethnicity and regionalism, and constitutional and political mechanisms. The conflicts and co-operation among these elements were mediated and managed by a neutral colonial referee in the period leading to independence.

Thus, following the groundwork of Coleman, the main works in that period were devoted to the role of the regional or ethnic elites in constitutional and administrative developments. [6] These developments, together with the operation of political parties, gave rise to a series of descriptive analyses of political caricatures namely, the social transformation of traditional structures and values, the institutions of liberal democracy that hardly existed and law and order. [7] It is these developments that led Post and Vickers into constructing the rather confusing and controversial framework of 'Nigeria as a conglomerate society', 'the structural frame', and 'the system of rewards', which is really no more than a sophistication and up-dating of Coleman's earlier descriptive analysis of how the new Nigerian social system was manipulated by a Westernized elite and their allies. [8] The major operative forces are identified as the existence of numerous separate groups of peoples with differing cultures and traditions, the absence of a dominant and nationalistic bourgeois class, and the manipulation of the process of development by the elite representatives (self-imposed by the character of social change in which access to power, status and wealth increasingly depended upon the acquisition of Western values and skills through formal schooling or urbanization). These operative forces were the subject of a large collection of essays on modernization and the politics of communalism by Melson and Wolpe. [9] While lacking a commitment to produce the capital commodities of politics, the content of the neo-liberal paradigm is contained in the 'dominant concern of the vast majority of participants with the receipt of the largest possible share of benefits in the shortest period of time', [10] as exemplified in the politics of revenue allocation, siting of industrial, commercial and welfare projects, census administration and appointments of personnel. [11]

There are two important points about the neo-liberal paradigm. First, there is a marked inclination to elect the different interests at stake in the development process in terms, largely if not wholly, of what Coleman calls the 'political nationalities', Melson and Wolpe's 'communalism' or O'Connell's 'competitive modernization' by the elites of communal groups. In this way there is a marked disinclination to distinguish clearly between the objective, class or antagonistic interests and conditions between the minority of rulers and the majority of the ruled. This anomaly stems from, and this is the second point, the poverty of the paradigm in terms of its unwillingness or incapacity to locate politics in its proper historical environment, namely the character and structure of the domestic economy and its alignment with international capitalism. An understanding of this environment reveals the vested interests of colonial and neo-colonial domination in the creation and functioning of the Nigerian social system. Therefore, to remain only or mainly at the analytical level of the structural frame (constitutive and regulative rules), the conglomerate society (relationships between the socio-cultural aggregates) or the system of rewards (the competition for office and its spoils) is to mystify the development of the Nigerian political process. Herein lies the tyranny of the neo-liberal paradigm. I think that it is the attempt to correct this form of political science in Nigeria that called forth the neo-Marxist/structuralist paradigm.

The Neo-Marxist/Structuralist Paradigm

One interesting thing about this paradigm in Nigeria is that its protagonists are largely not regular scholars of political science. Trained initially as historians, sociologists and economists, [12] they feel a sense of alienation from their narrow disciplinary walls and therefore seek to examine society as a holistic and objectifiable entity whose purpose and direction can be identified fully, at least academically. The articulation of this paradigm is still very much a matter for the seminar and conference room rather than in print. Only a couple of scholars initially trained in political science but who also find their conventional boundaries less helpful have actually written within this paradigm, and interestingly, they are non-Nigerians. [13] Perhaps this is more a matter of the youthful state of political science in Nigeria than anything else: indeed one's acquaintance with the graduate schools indicate that very soon Nigerians will take up this academic cudgel. However, on the African continental level, a creative literature devoted to this paradigm has grown in recent years, including Nigerian names. [14]

Like neo-liberalism, the neo-Marxist/structuralist paradigm is an adaptation, and application to the Nigerian conditions, of Marxist dissent within, and critique of, European society. And as a matter of fact, as a critique of the neo-liberal perspective, the neo-Marxist/structuralist paradigm is a form of cultural and intellectual import-substitution. Beginning as a critique of what is wrong in the operation of the Nigerian social system, [15] it has acquired the paradigmatic status of what needs to be done. According to Gavin Williams, 'we proceed from a critique of the limitations inherent in the perspectives from which most work proceeds' to a concern 'with the emancipation of people'. [16]

Nigerian politics, we are told, is an activity in the periphery of the world capitalist system. The history of how Nigeria was created and incorporated into that system which is therefore central to the understanding of the activity and behaviour of the Nigerian state. There is no distinction between the state as the political community, as a regime or system of laws, or as sets of rulers or authority patterns. The Nigerian state is just a solid mass of durable entity meaningful only as a network of social relations of production and distribution. Individuals are ranked according to their objective access to the means of production and distribution, and their behaviour patterns are thus said to reflect this. The state is the regular of all life and everything else is a dependent variable: conflict, co-operation, management, the family, community, culture, traditions, religions, interests, ideas, sentiments, industry, labour, agriculture, etc. — all of these are dependent upon the regulative capacity of the state.

But as a peripheral capitalist state it has proved 'incapable of regulating factional competition'. According to Gavin Williams,

> In Nigeria, the state has promoted the development of capitalism, foreign and domestic, by shifting resources from more competitive to

less competitive producers, from craft to factory production, from agriculture to industry, from rural to urban areas, from the poor to the rich, and from Nigerians to foreigners. It has hardly given free rein to the ability of people to produce goods. It has promoted the 'wealth of the nation', but only by the impoverishment of the people. [17]

Unlike the neo-liberal paradigm whose primary elements are given by the triangle of multiple ethnicity, constitutional and political structures, and competitive Westernized elite, the elements of the neo-Marxist/structuralist paradigm are a triangle of 'foreign and local businessmen and state officials'. [18] The latter triangle constitutes both the ruling and exploiting class: it is the Nigerian state and the factionalism within it that cause the instability and unsteadiness of the social system. The vast majority of the Nigerian peoples are not members of the state or at best they are members only in their collective sufferance and unsung struggles. This is the structuralism of the Marxist/structuralist paradigm: Nigeria is a society at the periphery of international capitalism in which the state is the apparatus of an externally fostered ruling class exploiting and oppressing the mass of its citizens. There is thus a relationship of naked power and negativity between oppressors and oppressed. The paradigm provides the solution:

> Only classes which are opposed to the triangular system can do so. Workers and peasants have so far demonstrated their capabilities to resist oppression. What is required is that they organize themselves to transform the system which exploits and oppresses them. [19]

While Turner's paradigmatic prescription is merely for the exploited and oppressed masses to organize themselves, Metuge [20] and Nnoli [21] drum the battle song for social and political scientists to 'commit class suicide', perhaps transform the universities or departments of political science into bridges of the revolutionary armed peoples of Nigeria, provide the vanguard for the seizure of state power by 'peasants and workers and to form their own dictatorship, a true rule by the majority', thereby liquidating the oppressors. [22]

The first important observation about the neo-Marxist/structuralist paradigm is that, unlike the neo-liberal one which has a tendency to reify existing structures of working politics, it veers excessively towards idealism. It is the scholar who is invited by this paradigm to see the masses, often not the Nigerian masses seeing themselves. As observed elsewhere:

> I have always felt that in explaining *African* politics we run between the extremes of yesterday's tribes and tomorrow's classes, and in the process refuse to explain and relate to the experiences of contemporary non-tribe and non-class Africa. In refusing to see the behaviour of rulers and ruled whose observable mode is confused by or encapsulated in primordial elements and poverty and therefore wanting to see

tomorrow's probable class confrontation and resultant classlessness, we are bound to mystify. [23]

Perhaps, as earlier indicated, this is another problem of import-substitution. Ali Mazrui puts it much more poignantly:

> Sometimes the furthest that academic reformers in economics and political science will go is to substitute Marxist approaches to political and economic analysis instead of the standard Western techniques. Yet Marxist approaches to the study of African societies, though often adding new perspectives, must nevertheless be regarded as a form of intellectual dependency when they are invoked by African scholars. Unless an African scholar dramatically transforms the nature of a Marxist analysis for the understanding of African societies, he has not moved much further along the path of cultural import-substitution. The cultural packages in economics and political science, more so than in history and literature, continue to bear the label 'made in the Western world'. [24]

The second observation is the tendency to deny actors, 'the people', and their manifest behaviour an iota of autonomy. Everything in the Nigerian social formation is peripheral and dependent on colonialism, neo-colonialism, imperialism and the manipulation of international capital. This tendency is the direct product of the neo-Marxist/structuralist's failure to acknowledge and distinguish clearly between the Nigerian state as a 'conglomerate political community' struggling to solidify its legal and geo-political boundaries to win maximum legitimacy, on the one hand, and the state as an 'oppressive regime or set of rulers', on the other. It is less than clear or convincing that both phenomena are the same, or even that one is necessarily related positively or negatively to the other. It seems to me naive and inadequate to so imagine. [25]

This assumption is itself dependent on the basis of the neo-Marxist/structuralist paradigm. As a Marxist verity, the 'eternal laws' of historical materialism or economic determinism must provide the essential foundation. According to Barongo:

> The purpose [of the essay] is not to dispute the validity that ethnic rivalry, competition, antagonism or suspicion have indeed threatened the viability of the [Nigerian] federation in the past but rather to restate the fact that these problems arise out of the antagonistic material interests of individuals and various groups which are generated by the existing dominant capitalist mode of production. [26]

The tyranny of neo-Marxism/structuralism stems from the above points: the tendency to mystify, to erect a uni-definition and purpose of the state and to rob political forces of any autonomy in obedience to historical materialism.

The preceding exposition of the borrowed paradigms raises the issue of their political functions: what are they geared to serve? Obviously, the neo-liberal paradigm, by its tendency to reify the existing structures and moral basis of politics and to leave the contradictions of ruler – ruled interests to political market forces, demonstrates its inclinations to legitimize the existing social order. In the same way, as a basis for solution to the problems of development of the Nigerian social system, and not merely as a useful methodology for identifying some of the problems of social change, the neo-Marxist/structuralist paradigm has the tendency to impose its view of basic contradictions and to subvert the system.

As previously indicated, these political functions of the existing paradigms detract from the proper responsibility of political science. Even in its present fairly conservative form, political science, although very popular in Nigerian universities, has often been regarded as subversive to Nigeria's development process by both military and civil politicians, regime experts and functionaries, economic planners and bureaucrats. It is a discipline conceived as having unsettling effect on rulers, regimes and the political community. [27] The story was told in 1978 of a Vice-Chancellor of one of Nigeria's universities who, in a written memorandum to the Mohammed Commission into the university crisis of April/May 1978, advocated the abolition of the Department of Political Science at Ahmadu Bello University because of its assumed role in sensitizing students to the bankrupt moral foundation of the country's social system. And almost a year later a semi-government propagandist demanded that 'all departments of political science, and all courses in which even tangential reference to politics is likely to be made should be scrapped. In addition, all books, monographs and articles on politics should be removed from all university libraries and burned.' [28] Even the government-backed National Universities Commission's circular banning all university staff from 'participation in politics in any manner whatsoever' [29] must be seen beyond the symbolic political participation of university staff; indeed it raised the fundamental issue of academic freedom with regard to the academic opinions of political scientists and even the contents of courses. The point in all this is that paradigms which elect regime legitimation or subversion as their *modus operandi* should see that the sword is double-edged. In the case of subversion, the environment of political science seems to indicate already that subverting the state in its widest terms and present conditions may in fact be subverting the entire political community. This latter point is dealt with more fully in the next section.

The Environment of Political Science in Nigeria

The primary object of political science, as indicated earlier, is the state: thus the environment of the latter is *ipso facto* that of the former. The origin of Nigeria, and indeed of any other African country, is probably the 'open sesame' to an analysis of its existence as a state. The first important point of interest is that, prior to colonial imposition, the present social system was simply a geographical mass. Politically, this formation comprises empires, kingdoms, chiefdoms and village republics of varying territorial sizes and organizations and with varying degrees of autonomy from and dependence upon each other. They were also related and exposed to the outside world in a similar manner. There were, however, unique features in the historical processes of the pre-colonial social orders in terms of their common economic and military activities, cultural, technological and ideological traits, political and social organizations. Marked differences also existed in these matters.

It was this simultaneous existence of fundamental similarities and differences that the British, for purely imperialistic motives, created and dominated as a colonial state. At the socio-political levels, British control and repression ensured that the pre-colonial arrangements were re-ordered around a strategy of mutual hostility to each other yet co-existing under British protection. Herein lies the origins of ethnicity in the process of modernization — of a dual, sometimes multiple consciousness around the inclusive colonial state yet fiercely exclusive in perception of and relationship to each other. [30] This pernicious manifestation in the Nigerian framework not only continued but has been accelerated by successive sets of events and rulers: namely, the uneven character of the modernization process, the character of the anti-colonial or independence movement, the character of the structural frame inherited at independence, the orientation of the dominant actors towards British socio-political organizational format and ethos, etc.

At the socio-economic level, the double strategy of domination and exploitation ensured that the domestic economy, following centuries of systematic incorporation into the world system of capitalism as an appendage, was depressed in terms of independent growth and development. Production, consumption and distribution patterns were oriented outwards, same for skills and techniques of organization. These developments have had marked consequences for the possibilities of industrial, agricultural and technological growth in Nigeria. The net effect on the political economy has been the emergence of a lopsided system of social relations between a tiny elite with access to wealth, power and status through the manipulation of state apparatus, on the one hand, and the majority who do not have this access; between this set of domestic powerfuls and their foreign superiors who ultimately control the existing and inherited means of production.

It is the juxtaposition of the socio-economic and socio-political levels of Nigeria and the fact that these were created essentially for non-Nigerian, even anti-Nigerian, purposes that has given free rein to a number of ugly features: various dimensions of inequality of access to resources and in the distribution of the national product; inequality of access to power, justice and equity; various types and degrees of hate, anger, and vice, ethnicity and chauvinism, the existence of more than two publics and hence public distrust, avarice, bigotry and arrogance; the problems of inauthentic nationalism, institutional fragility, economic under-development linked with low levels of technology, productivity, organizational skills and perverse values. Every one of these features criss-crosses the horizontal as well as the vertical formations of the country.

But the Nigerian social system is not a story of negativity and hopelessness as the protagonists of the under-development thesis sometimes unwittingly insist. There is an endowment of substantial human and natural resources which would certainly turn the table of 'under-development' if properly managed. This, in addition to its geographic and strategic size on the African continent, places Nigeria in an enviable position, and is vital to any appraisal of its foreign policies. Its recent acquisition of substantial wealth in the form of crude oil has added a further fillip to its table of credits.

The foregoing features of the Nigerian social system constitute the environment of Nigerian political science and they should be adequately reflected in its framework of analysis. These features can hardly be reduced to a framework of either competitive modernization of elite and ethnic champions or one of an emerging relationship of naked hostilities between two opposing classes. No doubt the country has both dimensions and they are indeed growing along its path of rapid social change. It is thus the responsibility of political science to induct and critically sensitize its audience to the strengths and weaknesses on a note of optimism rather than pessimism. This can be done in a paradigm of idealism and working politics without necessarily becoming the organ of regime and rulers' legitimation or subversion. By way of concluding this essay the contents of both sides of the paradigm will now be sketched.

Working Politics Plus Idealism

More than a decade ago, Richard Sklar advocated the utility of 'a radical approach' in Nigerian political science 'in terms of class action including the dynamics of class formation'. [31] Neither then nor in his earlier monumental work on Nigerian political parties [32], in which the approach was operationalized, did Sklar identify any confrontation between Marxist perceived classes. The usefulness of the approach without the pretentious tag of 'class analysis', lies in a clear identification of the problems and resources of 'nation building' being padded by the class action of an elite stratum. [33] Sklar's 'radical approach' is much closer to political science responsibility than the two borrowed paradigms discussed above. The idealism-cum-working politics framework is an attempt to add further flesh to Sklar's outline.

Working Politics
Politics is about human beings. The Nigerian, as the 'political creature' of British colonial domination, exploitation and incorporation, has been propelled, coerced and carrotted to prefer, profess and proffer a commitment to the legal and geo-political boundaries — even structures and values — of the colonial state. For much of the time ever since Lord Lugard's dual

mandate, this Nigerian has been provoked by a variety of manipulators to demonstrate the conditions of unease and tension – of accepting the Nigerian social system yet wanting intensely to destroy it and withdraw into pre-colonial boundaries which seem more comprehensible and empathetic. This academically interesting tension of the Nigerian has nothing whatsoever to do with any consciousness that the modern capitalistically incorporated Nigerian state has been a much more devilish exploiter of his labour, capital and skills than the colonial past. For one thing, it is a matter of theoretical history, as Karl Popper would put it, [34] whether the historical forces within and between the pre-colonial empires, kingdoms, chiefdoms, and shifting village republics, some of which extended beyond their present encapsulation, would have ended up in the same post-1900 political formation. For another, contemporary international treaties and domestic imperatives have combined, or maybe conspired, to leave the Nigerian's legal and geo-political boundaries a *fait accompli*.

Herein lies the compulsive imperative of contemporary nation-building in Nigerian politicians. Past, present and I dare say future, military as well as civilian – all employ the language, symbols, resources, and instruments of nation-building, the need for order and integration of communal entities.[35] They appear much more relevant to and realistic about the people or masses than the arm-chair theoreticians of 'bourgeois and proletarian countries' and of the domestic bourgeoisie and proletariat-cum-peasantization. [36] Often the impression is created by the neo-Marxist/structuralists that the problems of order and social integration have been resolved in Nigeria or somehow would resolve themselves in the very long run of a successful socialist revolution. But politics is as much about the short run as it is about the long run. Issues of the short run are the objects of working politics. Either scholars are engaged in the analysis and interpretation of these phenomena in terms of causes, effects and possible solutions, or they are concerned with seeing what they want to see, and thus to remove themselves, like Thomas Hobbes of the English civil war anecdote, from the sentiments and motivations of the people.

The importance of nation-building as a responsibility of political science is the fulfillment of the Nigerian national objective to manifest, against complex odds, the will of the state as a political community to survive and to enable it strengthen the bonds of domestic unity and of unity with the African continent and its people in the diaspora. Its relative success in this regard would certainly provide an increasing opportunity to curtail the excesses of hostile foreign manipulations. Political science must occupy itself with analysis and interpretation of policies and actions (or of their absence) which seek to strengthen the country, not simply as an *ad hoc* governmental activity and pastime of successive rulers in and out of regimental uniforms, but as fundamental survival and integrative aims.

Idealism

Working politics must not be allowed to occupy Nigerian political science for its own sake lest it acquires the methodology of structural-functionalism and the role of a megaphone calling for the perpetuation of life presidents, obnoxious regimes and a repressive and an unjust social order. I have earlier called attention to the non-Nigerian and anti-Nigerian objectives of the colonial state. While Sklar recommends 'causal, genetic or historical explanations' [37] in deference to some variety of Marxism, the dimension of idealism is concerned with justice and equity in the Nigerian social order. It focuses on the gamut of existing moral claims made by and for the entire human composition of the social system — the quality of the production and distribution of national goods and services and of the various interests involved in these processes. [38] Political science has the duty to clearly identify and focus on the primary conditions for the effectuation of improved quality of public, and even private, values. Its audience should be sensitized to the moral foundations and moral purpose of the social order in terms of costs as well as benefits, if any. For example, the rights and duties of citizens compel a commitment to the Nigerian state as a political community within which to demand equitable allocation of resources, of the national product, not only within the calculus of geo-politics but perhaps more enduringly in terms of socio-economic classes of rulers and ruled.

In this connection, perhaps Nigerian political science has been hurried too early into scientism. The great issues of social morality and political philosophy have been neglected: What is the state in Nigeria? What is social justice? What is national unity? Who are the Nigerian people? What do we really mean by government? Why must people pay tax? What is public revenue and why should it be allocated — to whom and in what manner? What is power, authority, legitimacy? Who and what government should people obey — chiefs, emirs, state rulers, federal rulers? Why should people obey government or what is political obligation? I suspect, perhaps arrogantly, that not all Nigerian professors of political science, heads of departments, directors of institutes or centres of public affairs, lecturers and researchers, let alone graduates and students of political science and my lowly self, can easily provide adequate and satisfactory answers or discourse to each of the above representative questions. But only if we try to answer them can political science be said to have a semblance of the vision of a just and equitable object of study.

Within one's limited exposure to the history of political ideas of other countries, I also suspect that most of these great philosophical issues have been accorded consummate debate and indeed incorporated into the constitutive and regulative rules of the industrially advanced modern countries of the world, irrespective of their ideological variety. It is, therefore, a paradox of immense philosophical concern that in the exploited, under-developed ex-colonial political systems of African countries, politics and its study, where it does not concentrate merely on the allocative and manipulative skills of the elite, is made to focus on some confrontation in battle between the exploited and the exploiters. The alternative framework of working politics and idealism is posited to redress the negative pervasiveness of the existing perspectives.

The Nigerian state is a modern state in the sense that, as of now, it transcends the pre-Lugardian social orders both in scale and intensity. It is not the proper responsibility of political science to visualize, let alone seek to unbound, the legal and geo-political boundaries of the modern order. And modernity, as Mazrui has observed, [39] is here to stay: the task is to decolonize it. The principal discipline for this task is political science. But to be able to do this, first of all political science must decolonize its own frameworks — must liberate itself from the tyrannies of intellectual import-substitution.

Notes

1. S. S. Wolin, *Politics and Vision* (London, George Allen, 1960), p. 2.
2. This is a selective commentary on the existing literature. Not all published works are included but even those that are left out of the selection do not use any new framework. It should also be added that this is not an attempt to argue that the value of the works cited in each paradigm is the same for all such works.
3. J. S. Coleman, *Nigeria: Background to Nationalism* (Berkeley, University of California Press, 1958), pp. 419-20.
4. Ibid., p. 4.
5. K. W. J. Post, and M. Vickers, *Structure and Conflict in Nigeria: 1960-65* (London, Heinemann, 1973).
6. See, for example, K. Ezera, *Constitutional Development in Nigeria* (Cambridge University Press, 1964); O. I. Odumosu, 'The Nigerian Power Elite, 1952-1965' in P. C. W. Gutkind and P. Watterman (eds.), *African Social Studies: A Radical Reader* (London, Heinemann, 1977); Justice L. Brett, *Constitutional Problems of Federalism* (Lagos, Times Press, 1961); E. O. Awa, *Federal Government in Nigeria* (Berkeley, University of California Press, 1964), R. O. Tilman and T. Cole (eds.), *The Nigerian Political Science* (Cambridge University Press, 1962).
7. See, among others, J. P. Makintosh, *Nigerian Government and Politics* (London, Oxford University Press, 1966); K. W. J. Post, *The Nigerian Federal Elections of 1959* (London, Oxford University Press, 1963); B. J. Dudley, *Parties and Politics in Northern Nigeria* (London, Frank Cass, 1968); C. S. Whitaker, *The Politics of Tradition: Continuity and Change in Northern Nigeria, 1964-1966* (Princeton University Press, 1970) and R. L. Sklar, *Nigerian Political Parties: Power in an Emergent African Nation* (Princeton University Press, 1963). There is a fundamental sense in which Sklar's work on Nigerian politics is superior to others, a point which is taken up later in this discussion.
8. Post and Vickers, op. cit.
9. R. Melson and H. Wolpe, (eds.), *Nigeria: Modernization and the Politics of Communalism* (East Lasing, Michigan State University Press, 1971).
10. Post and Vickers, op. cit., pp. 46-7.
11. See A. Adedeji, *Nigerian Federal Finance: Its Development, Problems and Prospects* (London, Hutchison, 1969); B. J. Dudley, 'Federalism

and the Balance of Power in Nigeria', *Journal of Commonwealth Political Studies*, Vol. 4 and Dudley op. cit. and Dudley, *Instability and Political Order: Politics and Crisis in Nigeria* (Ibadan University Press, 1973); Post and Vickers, op. cit., J. O'Connell 'The Political Class and Economic Growth', *Nigerian Journal of Economic and Social Studies*, Vol. 8, March 1966 and 'The Inevitability of Instability' *Journal of Modern African Studies*, 1967 and 'Authority and Community in Nigeria' in Melson and Wolpe, op. cit.

12. Names that readily come to mind in Nigerian academia include the 'Ibadan Group' (Ola Oni, Bade Onimode and Omafume Onoge, among others), Ikenna Nzimiro of Nsukka, Segun Osoba of Ife, Bala Usman of Ahmadu Bello University and Eskor Toyo of Calabar. Outside Nigeria, at least the names of Gavin Williams of Oxford and Peter Waterman of the Hague deserve mention.

13. See T. Turner 'Multinational Corporations and the Instability of the Nigerian State', *Review of African Political Economy*, No. 5 and her 'Commercial Capitalism and the 1975 Coup' in S. K. Panter-Brick (ed.), *Soldiers and Oil: The Political Transformation of Nigeria* (London, Frank Cass, 1978); Y. R. Barongo, 'Ethnic Pluralism and Democratic Stability in Nigeria: The Basis of Conflict and Consensus' in S. E. Oyovbaire (ed.), *Democracy in Nigeria: Interpretative Essays* (Benin City, Koda Publishers Ltd, forthcoming.)

14. See, among others, C. Ake, *Revolutionary Pressures in Africa London* (London, Zed Press, 1978) and his *A Political Economy of Africa* (London, Longman, 1981); O. Nnoli, 'The African Social Scientist and his Society: Theory and Practice', *Journal of the Nigerian Academy of Arts, Science and Technology*, No. 2; C. Leys, *Underdevelopment in Kenya: The Political Economy of Neocolonialism* (London, Heinmann, 1975); E. A. Brett, *Colonialism and Underdevelopment in East Africa* (London, Heinmann, 1972); S. Amin, *Unequal Development* (Hassocks, Sussex, Harvester Press, 1976); Gutkind and Waterman, op. cit. and P. C. W. Gutkind and I. Wallerstein (eds.), *The Political Economy of Contemporary Africa* (London and California, Sage, 1976) and the *Review of African Political Economy*.

15. See S. Osoba, 'Ideology and Planning for National Economic Planning' in M. Tuker and O. Olagunji (eds.), *Nigeria in Search of a Viable Polity* (Zaria, Institute of Administration, 1973) and his 'The Deepening Crisis of the Nigerian National Bourgeoisie', public lecture, Ahmadu Bello University, Zaria, 4 February 1978 later published in *The Review of African Political Economy*, No. 13.

16. G. Williams, *Nigeria: Economy and Society* (London, Rex Collings, 1976), pp. 1 and 4. See also S. Osoba, 'The Deepening Crisis of the Nigerian National Bourgeoisie', op. cit.

17. Ibid., p. 13.
18. Turner, op. cit., p. 64.
19. Ibid., p. 79.
20. W. Metuge, 'Democracy in Peripheral Capitalist Society: The African Case' in *Democracy in Nigeria: Past, Present and Future*, Proceedings of the Fifth Annual Conference of the Nigerian Political Science Association, 1978.
21. Nnoli, op. cit.

22. See also Ake, *Revolutionary Pressures*, op. cit.
23. S. E. Oyovbaire, 'Some Observations on Dr. Barongo's Paper: Understanding African Politics: The Political Economy Approach', Staff Seminar, Dept. of Political Science, Ahmadu Bello University, Zaria, 1 February 1978).
24. A. A. Mazrui, *Political Values and the Educated Class in Africa* (Berkeley, University of California Press, 1978), p. 306.
25. For those who may wish to contest this observation, the issue may simply be posed for them to resolve: why was it that the Agbekoya revolt of 1968-69, the July 1975 coup and the university students' crisis of 1978 possessed only elements of challenge to the system of laws and rulers while the events at the universities of Ibadan and Lagos in 1965-66, the 1966 coups, the Constituent Assembly debacle of 1978 on the Judicature clauses in the 1979 Constitution (the Sharia issue), and even the university students' crisis of 1979 over university admissions possessed elements of threat to the entire social order?
26. Barongo, op. cit.
27. Adele Jinadu has referred to instances in which political science has been perceived by African governments as threatening to their interests. See his 'Some Reflections on African Political Scientists and African Politics', *West African Journal of Sociology and Political Science*, No. 3, January, 1979.
28. See *Daily Times* (Lagos), 6 January 1979.
29. See the National Universities Commission's circular letter No. NUC/ES/255, dated 8 December 1978.
30. See P. P. Ekeh, 'Citizenship and Political Conflict: A Sociological Interpretation of the Nigerian Crisis' in J. Okpabu (ed.), *Nigeria: Dilemma of Nationhood* (New York, The Third Press, 1968) and his 'Colonialism and the Two Publics in Africa: A Theoretical Statement', *Comparative Studies in Society and History*, Vol. 17, No. 1, 1975.
31. R. L. Sklar, 'Political Science and National Integration: A Radical Approach', *Journal of Modern African Studies*, Vol. 5, 1967, pp. 1-11.
32. R. L. Sklar, *Nigerian Political Parties: Power in an Emerging African Nation* (Princeton: Princeton University Press, 1963).
33. Ibid., pp. 480-512.
34. K. Popper, *The Poverty of Historicism* (London, Routledge and Kegan Paul, 1957).
35. See J. O'Connell, 'Political Legitimacy in New States' and 'Reflections on the Nature of the State', public lectures, Ahmadu Bello University, 1969 and 1975 respectively.
36. C. Ake, *Revolutionary Pressures*, op. cit. It is interesting to note as an aside that Professor Ake has moved from a concern with nation-building to peasant- and worker-based socialist revolution. Compare this with his earlier work, *The Theory of Political Integration* (Homewood, Illinois, The Dorsey Press, 1967).
37. R. L. Sklar, 'Political Science and National Integration', op. cit., p. 5.
38. This is discussed in some more detail in my public lecture, 'Students and National Justice', Ahmadu Bello University, Zaria, 1 February 1978.
39. Mazrui, op. cit., p. 314.

Index

Africa
  Class Society, 51-54
  Mass Poverty, 28, 51-54
  Objective Socio-economic Conditions, 27-29, 51-54
African Dependence, 57, 148-150; see also Dependency
Ahmadu Bello University, 24, 101, 247
Ake, Claude, 194, 198, 221-223, 227
Allen, Chris, 108
Amin, Samir, 108, 181
Apter, David, 88
Area Studies, 129-136; see also Comparative Politics
  Imperialist Interest in, 135
Aristotle, 14, 18, 240

Baran, Paul, 180
Barongo, Yolamu, 195, 246
Bay, Christian, 7-8
Behavioural Political Science, 18,20, 22
Bennett,George, 73
Blyden, Edward, 37
Bourgeois Intellectuals, 53-54
Bourgeois Methodology
  Critique of, 39-53
Bourgeois Nationalists, 180
Bourgeois Social Science
  Critique of, 50-56, 211-217; see also Non-Marxist Social Science
Busia, K.A., 73

Capitalist Democracy, 31
Capitalist Exploitation, 143
Casely-Hayford, 37

Centre-Peripheral Relations, 29; see also Peripheral Capitalism
Class Analysis, 109-110, 212-233
  Conflict in Africa, 223-224
  Consciousness, 212-214
  Domination, 48-54
  Exploitation, 49-54
  False Consciousness, 211-214, 230-233
  Interests, 48-54, 145-147
Cold War, 130
Coleman, J.S., 103-105, 242-243
Colonial Education, 1, 39, 149
Colonial Political Institutions, 149
Comparative Politics, 120; see also Area Studies
Convention Peoples Party, 81
Corruption, 29, 53, 60
Cultural Pluralism, 141-143

Dialectical Materialism, 50-54, 106, 125, 160, 216; see also Historical Materialism
Dahl, Robert, 9
Darwin, Charles, 157
Dependencia Movement, 178-186
Dependency, 148-150; see also African Dependency
Dependency Theory, 178-186
Development Theory
  Critique of, 156-173
Dubois, W.E.B., 134
Dudley, Billy J., 196
Dumont, Rene, 60-61

Easton, David, 10
Education

Index

Purpose of, 38
Relevance of, 40
Elections in Africa, 72-87
Election Studies
  Approach to, 76-79
  Case Study, 76-77
  Nuffield, 76
  Sample Survey, 77-78
  Systems, 78-79
Elite Conflict, 145-148, 189-207
Ethnicity, Ethnic Conflict, 141-149, 193-197
Ethnocentricism
  Western, 156-173

Fact-Value Problem in Social Science 17-21, 27, 115-117
Fanon, Frantz, 134-135, 190
First, Ruth, 23
Ford Foundation, 131
Frank, A.G., 134, 179-180
Functionalism, 162-168

Goulder, Avin, 9
Gramsci, Antonio, 217
Green, Harry, 62-63
Greer, Scott, 27
Group Interest Theory, 230-231

Harris, Peter, 20
Hegelian Dialectics, 216-217
Historical Materialism, 106, 118, 124-125, 160; *see also* Dialectical Materialism
Hobbes, Thomas, 11
Hoogvelt, Ankie, 20

Import Substitution, 164
Indigenization of Economy, 199-200
Intellectual Liberation, 8

Kapwepwe, Simon, 74
Kariel, Henry, 9
Kenya African National Union, 83
Kenya Peoples Union, 74
Keynesian Economics, 164-165
Kilson, M.L., 74
Kuhn, Thomas, 112, 158-159
Kunkel, John H. 169-171
Kuper, Adam, 73

Lenski, Gerhard and Jean, 172-173
Leys, Colin, 135, 217
Liberal Democracy, 7
Liberation, 8-9
Lipsitz, Lewis, 8
Lukacs, George, 214-217, 221-222

Magubane, Bernard, 212, 219
Mamdani, Mahmood, 108, 135, 224-226
Management by Objectives (MBO), 63
Mao Tse-Tung, 219-220
Marcuse, Herbert, 215-218
Marx, Karl, 41, 101-110, 117, 157-173, 178-186
Marxism (general), 101-110, 156-173
  Modification of, 31
Marxist
  Methodology, 172-173, 211-233
  Theory, 31, 179
  Tradition, 101-105, 160
Marxists, 156-173, 178-186, 211-233
Mazrui, Ali A., 228, 246, 252
Merriam, Charles, 19
Metaphysics, 159
Metuge, Wang, 245
Modernization Theory
  Critique of, 139-141, 171-172
Morgenthau, R.S., 74
Mulford, David, 74
Multinational Corporations, 29, 131-135

Nation-building, 250
National Liberation Movement, 85
National Party of Nigeria, 81
Neo-Liberalism, 241-243
Neo-Marxists, 180, 241, 244-247
New Left, 8
Nigeria Peoples Party, 81
Nigerian Political Science Association, 3, 30
Nkrumah, Kwame, 73-74, 135, 190
Nnoli, O., 245
Non-Marxist Social Science
  Critique of, 112-123, 158-173
Northern Peoples Congress, 81
Northern Peoples Party, 81
Nyerere, J.K., 38-39, 82

Obote, President, 74, 82-85
Oculi, Okello, 228
Odinga, Oginga, 74
Oyovbaire, S.E., 53

Padmore, George, 134
Peasant, Peasantry
  Revolutionary Struggle, 41
  Studies, 39-46
  Types, 42-43
Peripheral Capitalism, 51; *see also*
  Centre-Peripheral Relations
Planning, Programming and Budgeting
  (PPB), 63
Plato, 14
Politics, definition of, 9-11, 240
Politics of Poverty, 145-148
Political Economy, 101-110
  Bourgeois Reformist, 103-105
  Classical, 105-108
  Studies of African, 108-110
Political Participation, 85-87
Political Philosophy, Philosophers,
  20-25
Political Science Curricula
  Critique of African, 56-62
  Development-oriented, 62ff
Popper, Karl, 158-160
Positivism, 158-160
Post, K.W.J., 73, 243
Poulantzas, Nicos, 109
Praxis, 8-9, 182, 184, 216
Project Management Technique, 63
Psychological Model of Development
  169-171
Public Administration, 34, 94-100
Public Service Review Commission
  (Nigeria), 62-63

Review of African Political Economy
  108
Revolutionary Intellectuals, 53-54
Revolutionary Theory, 178-186
Rockefeller Foundation, 131-133
Rodney, Walter, 38, 138
Rosberg, Carl, 73
Rostow, W.W., 162-171

Schapera, I., 73
Scientific Objectivity, 69, 160

Scientific Socialism, 31, 60-61; *see
  also* Marxism
Shivji, Issa, 109, 135, 224, 232
Single Party System, 74, 150
Sklar, Richard, 225-226, 229, 249
Socialist Democracy, 31
Stages of Development, 165-168
Surkin, Marvin, 8-9
Systems Theory, critique of, 168-169

Tanganyika African National Union,
  81

Udoji, J.D., Chief, 62
Uganda Peoples Congress, 82
Underdevelopment, *see* Dependency
United Progressive Party, 74
University of Benin, Nigeria, 3
University of Port Harcourt, Nigeria,
  57, 64-67

Values, 13-15; *see also* Scientific
  Objectivity
Value-orientation, 25
Virtue, 14

Weber, Max, 6, 9-15, 102, 240
Welbourne, F.B., 74
Whitaker, C.S., 74
Williams, Gavin, 244-245
Wiseman, Victor, 18, 21
Wolin, Sheldon, 7-8, 240

AFRICA TITLES FROM ZED PRESS
POLITICAL ECONOMY

DAN NABUDERE
Imperialism in East Africa
Vol I: Imperialism and Exploitation
Vol II: Imperialism and Integration
Hb

ELENGA M'BUYINGA
Pan Africanism or Neo-Colonialism?
The Bankruptcy of the OAU
Hb and Pb

BADE ONIMODE
Imperialism and Underdevelopment in Nigeria:
The Dialectics of Mass Poverty
Hb and Pb

MICHAEL WOLFERS AND JANE BERGEROL
Angola in the Frontline
Hb and Pb

MOHAMED BABU
African Socialism or Socialist Africa?
Hb and Pb

ANONYMOUS
Independent Kenya
Hb and Pb

YOLAMU BARONGO (EDITOR)
Political Science in Africa: A Radical Critique
Hb and Pb

OKWUDIBA NNOLI (EDITOR)
Path to Nigerian Development
Pb

EMILE VERCRUIJSSE
Transitional Modes of Production:
A Case Study from West Africa
Hb

NO SIZWE
One Azania, One Nation:
The National Question in South Africa
Hb and Pb

BEN TUROK
Development in Zambia: A Reader
Pb

J.F. RWEYEMAMU (EDITOR)
Industrialization and Income Distribution in Africa
Hb and Pb

CLAUDE AKE
Revolutionary Pressures in Africa
Hb and Pb

ANNE SEIDMAN AND NEVA MAKGETLA
Outposts of Monopoly Capitalism:
Southern Africa in the Changing Global Economy
Hb and Pb

CONTEMPORARY HISTORY/REVOLUTIONARY STRUGGLES

AQUINO DE BRAGANCA AND IMMANUEL WALLERSTEIN (EDITORS)
The African Liberation Reader: Documents of the National Liberation Movements
Vol I: The Anatomy of Colonialism
Vol II: The National Liberation Movements
Vol III: The Strategy of Liberation
Hb and Pb

EDWIN MADUNAGU
Problems of Socialism:
The Nigerian Challenge
Pb

MAI PALMBERG
The Struggle for Africa
Hb and Pb

CHRIS SEARLE
We're Building the New School!
Diary of a Teacher in Mozambique
Hb at Pb price

MAINA WA KINYATTI
Thunder from the Mountains:
Mau Mau Patriotic Songs
Hb

EDUARDO MONDLANE
The Struggle for Mozambique
Pb

BASIL DAVIDSON
No Fist is Big Enough to Hide the Sky:
The Liberation of Guinea Bissau and Cape Verde: Aspects of the African Revolution
Hb at Pb price

BARUCH HIRSON
Year of Fire, Year of Ash:
The Soweto Revolt — Roots of a Revolution?
Hb and Pb

SWAPO DEPARTMENT OF INFORMATION AND PUBLICITY
To Be Born a Nation:
The Liberation Struggle for Namibia
Pb

PEDER GOUWENIUS
Power to the People:
South Africa in Struggle: A Political History
Pb

HORST DRECHSLER
Let Us Die Fighting:
The Struggle of the Herero and Nama Against German Imperialism (1884-1915)
Hb and Pb

GILLIAN WALT AND ANGELA MELAMED (EDITORS)
Mozambique: Towards a People's Health Service
Pb

ANDRE ASTROW
Zimbabwe: A Revolution that Lost its Way?
Hb and Pb

RENE LEFORT
Ethiopia: An Heretical Revolution?
Hb and Pb

TONY AVIRGAN AND MARTHA HONEY
War in Uganda: The Legacy of Idi Amin
Hb and Pb

LABOUR STUDIES

DIANNE BOLTON
Nationalization: A Road to Socialism?
The Case of Tanzania
Pb

A.T. NZULA, I.I. POTEKHIN, A.Z. ZUSMANOVICH
Forced Labour in Colonial Africa
Hb and Pb

LITERATURE

FAARAX M.J. CAWL
Ignorance is the Enemy of Love
Pb

KINFE ABRAHAM
From Race to Class
Links and Parallels in African and Black American Protest Expression
Pb

OTHER TITLES

A. TEMU AND B. SWAI
Historians and Africanist History: A Critique
Hb and Pb

ROBERT ARCHER AND ANTOINE BOUILLON
The South African Game:
Sport and Racism
Hb and Pb

WOMEN

RAQIYA HAJI DUALEH ABDALLA
Sisters in Affliction:
Circumcision and Infibulation of Women in Africa
Hb and Pb

CHRISTINE OBBO
African Women:
Their Struggle for Economic Independence
Pb

MARIA ROSE CUTRUFELLI
Women of Africa:
Roots of Oppression
Hb and Pb

ASMA EL DAREER
Woman, Why do you Weep?
Circumcision and Its Consequences
Hb and Pb

MIRANDA DAVIES (EDITOR)
Third World — Second Sex:
Women's Struggles and National Liberation
Hb and Pb

You can order Zed titles direct from Zed Press, 57 Caledonian Road, London, N1 9DN, U.K.